THE
ROYAL AFRICAN
COMPANY

THE
ROYAL
AFRICAN
COMPANY

by

K. G. DAVIES

OCTAGON BOOKS

A DIVISION OF FARRAR, STRAUS AND GIROUX

New York   1975

First published 1957 by Longmans, Green and Co., Ltd.

Reprinted 1975
by special arrangement with Longman Group Limited

OCTAGON BOOKS
A Division of Farrar, Straus & Giroux, Inc.
19 Union Square West
New York, N. Y. 10003

This book has been reproduced from an original in the
Brown University Library

Library of Congress Cataloging in Publication Data

Davies, Kenneth Gordon.
The Royal African Company.

Reprint of the 1957 ed. published by Longmans, Green, London,
New York.

Includes bibliographical references and index.
1. Royal African Company of England. 2. Slave-trade—Africa.

HF486.R6D3   1975   382'.44'096   74-28201
ISBN 0-374-92074-5

Manufactured by Braun-Brumfield, Inc.
Ann Arbor, Michigan

Printed in the United States of America

PREFACE

THE student of the slave-trade needs to be familiar with the histories of his own country, West Africa and the West Indies. While the first and last may be intelligible or at least compassable, the second presents problems which have not yet been elucidated and some of which may never be fully solved. Despite the work of Claridge on the Gold Coast, Gray on Gambia and Burns on Nigeria, I have, even within the modest limits here set, sometimes experienced difficulties of a kind more commonly met by the historian of the ancient world. Until the main course of African history in the eighteenth century is better understood, it will always be risky to comment upon the causes and effects of particular events. At the present time specialized work of great interest is being carried out by both amateur and professional historians; when this has been concluded and communicated I confidently look forward to the modification of judgments here made.

I wish to make it clear (though to those who know them it will be apparent) that much more than is here set forth can be learned about African history from the sources I have used. The case for publication of some part of them is a strong one. My own interest throughout has been the Royal African Company, and my book is intended primarily as a contribution to English economic history. The fact that I have been concerned solely with the economic aspects of the slave-trade perhaps makes it necessary for me to state that I regard the trade as an abhorrent blot on the history of both purchasers and vendors.

A number of colleagues at the Public Record Office, the London School of Economics and the University of Oxford have helped me. My chief obligation is to Professor F. J. Fisher of L.S.E. He directed the early stages of the work and read four chapters of the first version; as a result of his criticisms and those of Dr. A. H. John, also of L.S.E., three of these chapters disappeared and the fourth has, I believe, been improved. Professor Richard Pares of All Souls College criticized part of the Introduction and made a number of valuable suggestions. My debt to Professor H. J. Habakkuk, also of All Souls, began to accumulate when I was an undergraduate and is now very large. During the years 1947–9 I received a Leverhulme Research Studentship of £50 a year; this was of critical importance as it enabled me to escape from some of the spare-time activities which would otherwise have fallen to me as a junior clerk in the public service. My wife helped with the arithmetic and some of the transcription in the first year or two, and throughout in other ways. I am grateful to the editor for permission to use some material which was first published in an article in *Economic History Review*.

All dates given are Old Style except that the year is taken to begin on 1 January. All quotations are intended to preserve the original spelling but not the original punctuation or use of capitals; contractions have been extended. I should like to draw attention to the inclusion in the index of the names of all Governors, Sub-Governors, Deputy Governors and members of the Court of Assistants of the Royal African Company holding office between 1672 and 1712, whether mentioned in the text or not.

K. G. DAVIES

CONTENTS

Chapter   *Page*

1 INTRODUCTION

    I The Europeans in Africa   1
    II The Organization of the Trade   16
    III The Company of Royal Adventurers   38

2 CAPITAL AND FINANCE

    I Credit and Investment   47
    II The Formation of the Company   57
    III The Shareholders   63
    IV The Growth of the Debt 1675–1692   74
    V The Stock 1691–1708   79
    VI The Progress of the Debt 1692–1708   87
    VII Insolvency and Reconstruction   90

3 MONOPOLY AND COMPETITION

    I The Charter   97
    II Before the Revolution   101
    III The Downfall of Monopoly   122
    IV The Separate Traders   135
    V Free Trade   151

4 THE COMPANY IN ENGLAND

    I Courts and Committees   153
    II Exports   165
    III Imports and Sales   179

5 SHIPPING

    I Voyages and Vessels   185
    II The Cost of Shipping   194
    III War and Shipping   205

Chapter   *Page*
6 THE COMPANY IN AFRICA

      I The Commercial Regions of West Africa   213
     II The Terms of Trade   232
    III Forts, Factories and Men   240
     IV International Relations   264
      V Native Relations   277

7 THE COMPANY IN THE WEST INDIES

      I Deliveries and Prices   291
     II The Planters' Debts   316
    III The Company and the *Asiento*   326
     IV The Final 'Profit'   335

8 CONCLUSION   344

APPENDIX
      I Exports   350
     II Imports   358
    III Deliveries and Prices of Slaves in West Indies 361
     IV The Price of Sugar   365
      V John Snow's Letter to the Royal African
          Company   367
     VI The Separate Traders   372
    VII The Records of the Company   374

INDEX   377

MAPS

                                                     Page
West Africa   8
Gold Coast about 1700   246

LIST OF ABBREVIATIONS

A.P.C.   *Acts of the Privy Council*

Cal. S.P. Col.   *Calendar of State Papers, Colonial*

Donnan   E. Donnan (Editor), *Documents Illustrative of the History of the Slave Trade to America.* (Washington, 1930–5)

Ec.H.R.   *Economic History Review*

P.R.O.   Public Record Office

Scott   W. R. Scott, *The Constitution and Finance of English, Scottish and Irish Joint-Stock Companies to 1720.* (Cambridge, 1911–12)

Stock   L. F. Stock, *Proceedings and Debates in the British Parliament Respecting North America.* (Washington, 1924–41)

T. 70   Public Record Office, Treasury Records (Expired Commissions), Records of African Companies

T.R.H.S.   *Transactions of Royal Historical Society*

I

INTRODUCTION

1. The Europeans in Africa

THE seventeenth century witnessed a 'scramble for Africa' very different from the imperialism of the nineteenth century. Between 1880 and 1914 the European powers sought for, or were prepared to accept, territorial annexation in Africa as a preliminary to economic exploitation, and a large part of the continent was brought directly under their rule. In the seventeenth century attention was concentrated mainly on one part of Africa, the West Coast, and the aim was trade rather than territory. Both movements, however, were marked by fierce international rivalry. Whereas in the nineteenth century all the greater and several of the smaller powers competed for African territory, so in the seventeenth century eight nations, Portugal, France, the United Provinces, England, Sweden, Denmark, Brandenburgh and Scotland, staked claims to a share in African trade. This commercial rivalry was not without some bearing on the outcome of the later imperial conflict. The Portuguese, for example, though dispossessed in the course of the seventeenth century of their trading posts on the Gold Coast, retained their interest in Angola and Portuguese Guinea; their influence in West Africa had thus, by 1700, assumed something of the shape it was to exhibit two centuries later. Similarly, England by the establishment of trading settlements and forts in the Gambia and Sierra Leone regions may be said to have laid in the seventeenth century the foundation of the empire which would later accrue to her. The territorial partition of Africa in the nineteenth century did not, however, invariably proceed on lines suggested in the earlier period. On

I

the whole discontinuity is more evident than continuity. The most powerful contender for African trade in the seventeenth century was the United Provinces, whose settlements on the West Coast were eventually to melt away. France, though she won and consolidated her position in the Senegal river, gave little indication before 1700 of the great future which lay before her as a colonial power in Africa. Germany, represented by Brandenburgh, was amongst the weakest of the competitors for African trade, and in fact abandoned the struggle early in the eighteenth century. Similarly the Scandinavian countries have left few traces in modern Africa of their early efforts to participate in African commerce. Italy and Belgium, amongst the most important nations in nineteenth- and twentieth-century Africa, played no part in the seventeenth century. To a large extent this discontinuity is explicable in terms of the domestic history of the countries concerned; but for a full understanding it is necessary to turn to the peculiar characteristics of European settlement in West Africa from the fifteenth century onwards.

Although the coast of West Africa was familiar to the Portuguese by the late fifteenth century and known to sailors of other nations a hundred years later, European settlement continued at the barest minimum until recent times. Whatever may have been the motives which stimulated Prince Henry the Navigator to organize voyages of discovery, West Africa rapidly assumed in European eyes an importance which was almost entirely commercial. This phenomenon requires some explanation. The interest displayed by Europeans in discovery and expansion was not everywhere the same. In French Canada and the Spanish empire in America, for example, missionary motives certainly played an important part. Nor can the scientific quest, the search for knowledge as an end in itself, be entirely dismissed. It is no doubt true that economic considerations were always paramount; but this is not the same as a purely commercial interest. The desire for land, for example, was a primary urge in the settlement of both North and South America: this was an economic motive, but not a commercial one. And, even where the aim was simply trade, settlement and cultivation might, in undeveloped regions, be an essential condition of commercial exploitation. Had West Africa been other than what it was, European colonies comparable to those of America and the West Indies might have arisen.

The intercourse of European and non-European people initiated by the Discoveries gave rise, not only in Africa but in all parts of the world, to problems which were dealt with in ways chiefly dictated by the particular circumstances of the territories concerned. The solutions found were empirical, rather than the outcome of deliberate or long-sighted policy. To this general rule there are certain qualifications. But even if, as in the case of the Spanish empire in America, reasonably clear notions existed about the form which colonial development was expected to take, theories and intentions had often to be modified to meet unforeseen contingencies. In the example of West Africa, preconceived European theories of empire, if such can indeed be said to exist, played little or no part, and it is above all to the geographical, economic and political characteristics of the region that we must look for an explanation of the way in which European interests were developed.

The most obvious factor influencing the form of European imperialism was the kind of native population encountered in each region. It might be civilized or backward, friendly or hostile, warlike or docile, governed or anarchical, rich or poor; or there might be no native population at all. If the land was deserted or only thinly populated, the Europeans, if they wished to draw much advantage from their discovery, had to undertake settlement. More commonly there was a native population, and sooner or later there arose the problem of the relations to be established between this population and the Europeans. Perhaps the crudest answer to this question was that adopted in the occupation of some of the islands of the Caribbean, namely expropriation and annihilation. The Caribs of the Outer Antilles were too poor to hold out any prospect of profitable trade, too fierce to accept the status of serfs, and too backward to resist conquest. Their elimination was a necessary preliminary to any kind of gainful exploitation and they had to go. A somewhat more humane version of the same policy is provided by the history of New England, where the indigenous population was sufficiently thin to be brushed aside. Another and more original solution to the problems attendant upon early European expansion was that afforded by the Spanish empire in South and Central America. Here the native populations were swiftly conquered and absorbed into dependencies of the Spanish Crown. With great speed a whole apparatus of central and local government was erected and extended over enormous areas. Limits were set, and not entirely ignored, to the exploitation of the Indians, who found themselves at once subjects of the King of Spain and objects of missionary zeal.

European development in West Africa followed neither of these courses. In the first place, commercial exploitation with the minimum of settlement proved to be a practicable proposition from the beginning. There was no need for Europeans to create trade by introducing new crops, as they had to do in the West Indies. West Africa was not rich, but a European demand existed or could be easily created for the commodities it produced. Even before the Portuguese appeared, Africa had begun to be influenced by this demand, albeit indirectly. From the cities of the Middle Niger across the desert to the North African seaports, gold, slaves, and other goods had found their way to Europe in medieval times.[1] Trade was there for the taking, and the Portuguese discoveries were probably intended in the first instance to deflect that trade from the Sahara to the sea. In the next three centuries various attempts were made by Europeans to diversify the African trade,[2] but the staples remained gold and slaves, with ivory as the principal subsidiary. Although in the eighteenth century the slave-trade reached proportions so great as to exercise an important influence on internal African history, there was no catastrophic change in the condition or status of the native population such as occurred in the West Indies or America. Gainful exploitation was achieved without either war or conquest.

That conquest and settlement on a scale comparable to the Spanish empire in America were never contemplated must be attributed also to geographical factors. Not until recent times have science and medicine found adequate answers to tropical

[1] E. W. Bovill, *Caravans of the Old Sahara*, 1933, Chs. xiii and xvi.
[2] Below, p. 221.

diseases. Deadly enough for men in the seventeenth century, equatorial Africa was no place for white women and few went there. Only a handful of white men made Africa their home; the majority were temporary residents who reckoned themselves fortunate to get out alive. Other geographical features are also relevant. Much of the interior of West Africa was thickly wooded, and in some places the forest formed an effective deterrent to European penetration. Inland discovery was not impossible, as several attempts at exploration amply prove. Especially in the north-west, where the great rivers of Gambia and Senegal gave the explorer a flying start, some remarkable journeys were made in the seventeenth century.[1] An incentive to exploration certainly existed, the same as that which inspired the Spanish *conquistadores* in America, namely precious metals. It was the hope of striking gold that encouraged Richard Jobson in his voyage up the Gambia in 1620, Cornelius Hodges' journeys at the end of the century, and the French explorations a little later. None of these expeditions, however, yielded the spectacular wealth that accrued to Cortes and Pizarro; and when the Middle Niger was finally explored by Mungo Park the motive was scientific curiosity more than anything else.

Neither the climate nor the geography of West Africa, however, seems sufficiently unlike those of certain parts of South America to explain the utterly different course taken by Europeans in those regions. Another consideration is the differing political situations confronting the white men. In their dealings with Mexico and Peru the Spaniards were aided by the extensive, if shadowy, overlordship of the Aztecs and Incas. They could pose at once as liberators from and successors to this suzerainty. Very different was the political appearance of West Africa at the time of the Portuguese discoveries and for long afterwards. Little indeed is known or ever likely to be known about tribal and national organization in early times, but the general picture appears to be one of acute fragmentation. In contrast to the African interior, where an extensive and powerful empire flourished in the lands of the Middle Niger in the fifteenth and sixteenth centuries, the coastal

[1] E. Heawood, *A History of Geographical Discovery in the Seventeenth and Eighteenth Centuries*, 1912.

regions acknowledged no overlord into whose shoes the European could step. No nation enjoyed more than a local or
temporary hegemony. In such circumstances European conquest would have been extremely difficult. The Spanish armies
in America had capital cities to seize and even emperors to
kill; an army in Africa would have been master of little more
than the land on which it was encamped.

All these factors must be taken together. Commercial interests suggested, climatic, geographical and political considerations confirmed, the form to be taken by European exploitation of West Africa from the fifteenth to the eighteenth
centuries. The Europeans came to trade not to settle. Even at
the end of the seventeenth century the total number of white
men of all nations living between the Senegal and Calabar
rivers could not have been more than a few thousand.[1] Most
of them lived in forts or trading posts; a small number, chiefly
Portuguese, lived in the country. At any time the native population by sheer weight of numbers could have taken all but the
strongest of the forts.[2] That they seldom did so is an indication
less of white strength, more of negro disunion, and more still of
the advantages which the Africans themselves (or some of
them) thought they derived from the presence of European
traders.

During their first hundred years in West Africa the Portuguese had three principal aims, to explore, to develop trade,
and to defend their discoveries and commerce against other
nations; by the end of the fifteenth century they had gone far
towards achieving these ends. The exploration of the coast had

[1] For the most thickly populated part, the Gold Coast, Tylleman estimated 368 Dutch, 208 English, 85 Danes and 85 Brandenburghers, less than
700 in all. (Sir M. Nathan, 'The Gold Coast at the End of the Seventeenth
Century under the Danes and Dutch', in *Journal of the African Society*, IV,
p. 3.) This total would have to be augmented by English and French settlements in Gambia, Senegal, Sierra Leone, Sherbro and Goree, and by the
English and Dutch at Whydah. The Portuguese defy enumeration, partly
because some of them lived 'in the country' and partly because inter-
marriage produced persons of mixed blood. However, even if accuracy is
impossible, the common impression is that the total European population
was small.

[2] As the Akwamu drove the Danes from Christiansborg in 1693. W. E. F.
Ward, *History of the Gold Coast*, 1948, pp. 87–8.

been virtually completed; trade in gold, ivory and pepper flourished; and the foundations of the slave-trade had been laid.[1] These discoveries and the visible signs of their commercial significance inevitably aroused the jealousy of other nations, and in the middle years of the fifteenth century Portugal had to meet strong competition, especially from Castile. This early challenge was successfully beaten off. The interests of Castile were diverted across the Atlantic and the designs of both English and French interlopers were frustrated or held in check. For half a century, from 1480 to 1530, the Portuguese enjoyed a virtual monopoly of the African trade.[2] Nevertheless their position was insecure. At first they may have thought in terms of a territorial empire or at least of a series of client kingdoms with the King of Portugal as feudal lord.[3] The island of São Thomé was settled and sugar-planting introduced. The general application of any such notions must, however, have been soon abandoned, though the Portuguese were always more disposed to settle in the country than their later rivals. Missionary work was never entirely abandoned, but its achievements were small; the forts which the Portugese built were too few to provide an effective defence against determined attack; and little progress was made towards securing influence over the native inhabitants.

By the beginning of the sixteenth century the main lines of European development in West Africa had been drawn. Instead of conquest, a rough *modus vivendi* between white and black had been reached; European influence extended little beyond the forts; and trade, chiefly in gold and slaves, was growing. During the next 250 years the actors in the drama often changed, Portuguese giving way to French, Dutch and English, but the scene itself remained substantially the same.

The sixteenth century in West Africa was marked by the challenge of, first, France, and then England, to the Portuguese monopoly. This competition, though profitable to the challengers and damaging to Portugal, was not mounted with sufficient

---

[1] J. W. Blake, *European Beginnings in West Africa, 1454–1578*, 1937.
[2] *Ibid.*, Ch. iv.
[3] John II took the title of Lord of Guinea in 1485; E. Donnan, *Documents Illustrative of the History of the Slave Trade to America*, I, p. 4.

energy and resource to produce a conclusive result. Portugal remained the strongest European power in Africa and in some directions, notably Angola, extended her interests.[1] Her overthrow and expulsion from the Gold Coast had to wait, as in the

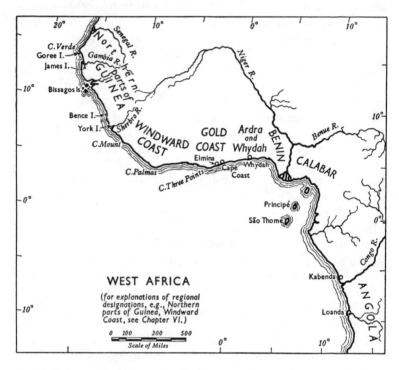

Far East, upon the coming to political and economic maturity of the Dutch. Early in the seventeenth century, the Dutch planted settlements on the Gold Coast and in north-west Africa on the island of Goree. In 1637 Portuguese power on the Gold Coast was broken by the capture of Elmina which henceforth was the capital fort and headquarters of the Dutch in West Africa. An attack on Angola, launched in 1641, ultimately failed, but by the middle of the seventeenth century the Dutch had won for themselves the position of the strongest European power in Africa. They had not, however, gained the

[1] Donnan, I, p. 6.

monopoly which the Portuguese had formerly enjoyed. Once the demolition of Portuguese power had been begun, other nations revived or developed an interest in African trade which the Dutch were unable to curb. The French had been the first to challenge Portugal in the sixteenth century, but their efforts had later fallen away and become intermittent. In the seventeenth century they were renewed with backing from Richelieu and Colbert. From 1664 the French have a continuous history in north-west Africa, particularly in the Senegal region, and it is probable that well before that date private French enterprise had secured a significant share in the trade. The English also profited from the work of the Dutch. Trade to the West Coast had been undertaken by Englishmen since the mid-sixteenth century but for many years appears to have been of an uncertain and fitful nature. No permanent forts are known to have been built in the sixteenth century, and it was not until after 1618 that the English interest in West Africa began to take a definite shape. The first known English exploration of the African interior went up the Gambia in 1620.[1] A factory was established at the mouth of the river, though it is unlikely that occupation was permanent; later a fort was acquired on James Island.[2] Further south, no permanent English settlement is known to have existed in Sierra Leone or in the vicinity of the Sherbro river, but English traders visited this region.[3] On the Gold Coast the chronology of English settlement is particularly obscure, partly through lack of evidence and partly because of the ephemeral nature of some of the lodges and forts erected.[4] The first important English settlement was at Kormantin, probably in 1631, and for some thirty years it remained the only English fort, though not the only settlement, on the Gold Coast.

By the third quarter of the seventeenth century, therefore,

---

[1] Richard Jobson, *The Golden Trade*, reprinted Teignmouth, 1904.

[2] J. M. Gray, *History of the Gambia*, 1940.

[3] J. W. Blake, 'The Farm of the Guinea Trade', in *Essays in British and Irish History*, ed. H. A. Cronne, T. W. Moody and D. B. Quinn, 1949, p. 89.

[4] A convenient summary of the history of the Gold Coast settlements will be found in W. E. F. Ward, *op. cit.*, pp. 363–7. This should not, however, be regarded as definitive.

three nations, the United Provinces, France and England, had secured interests in the trade of West Africa, while Portugal, though much weakened, was not yet negligible. The domination of a single nation had been ended and West Africa had taken on the international appearance it still possesses. These events, the successful if not decisive challenge of the French and English in the sixteenth century, the overthrow of the Portuguese in the seventeenth century, and the failure of the Dutch to hold their gains against renewed competition, are all important symptoms of the difficulty of upholding a monopoly of the African trade and have important bearing on the history of the Royal African Company. The possession of forts by the Portuguese and after them by the Dutch was not enough to guarantee a monopoly of the trade. Throughout the seventeenth century much the greater part of the coast remained innocent of European settlement. Only in the north, from the Senegal river down to the Sherbro, on the Gold Coast and a little further to the east, and in Angola, were there permanent posts; and everywhere except on the Gold Coast these settlements were few and far between. In the region of the Calabar rivers, for example, an important centre of the slave-trade, no permanent settlement was made by any nation in the seventeenth century. And even where forts were built their range of influence was limited. The African trade was highly esteemed, highly enough for a nation to covet a monopoly, but it was not valuable enough to warrant the construction of all the forts that would have been needed to uphold a monopoly. Naval power could extend the range of influence, and indeed was of far more value for both defensive and offensive purposes than fortifications. In the last resort hegemony in West Africa depended on the maritime strength which a nation was able to allocate to the region, and until the question of naval supremacy had been finally decided in England's favour in the eighteenth century the balance of forces in Africa was fairly even.

The overthrow of the Portuguese was a signal for the intensification of international rivalry, especially between 1641 and 1667. But out of this rivalry there emerged a tacit acknowledgement of the difficulty, if not impossibility, of excluding other nations. A policy of live-and-let-live, born of weakness and exhaustion not of principle, came to prevail and even to cut across the lines of international enmity in Europe.[1] What is true of the rivalry of nations is also true of the rivalry of different groups within nations. The governments of both England and the United Provinces, for example, committed their interests in the African trade to companies endowed with a monopoly against other nationals. Great exertions were made by both companies to enforce these monopolies, but to little effect. The Royal African Company, as we shall see, could no more defend its rights against English interlopers than the Dutch could defend their claims to the trade of the Gold Coast against the nations which followed in their wake.

If the weakness of the positions taken up by the greater European powers in West Africa bred in the end something like mutual toleration amongst them, it also provided the smaller nations with an opportunity to participate in the trade. While the activities of Dutch, French and English traders naturally deserve most attention it should not be forgotten that the West African coast afforded an outlet for the commercial ambitions of Scandinavia and Germany. A Danish West India Company was formed in 1625, which later effected settlements on the Gold Coast;[2] it was followed in 1647 by a Swedish African Company.[3] Both these enterprises owed a good deal to Dutch initiative and capital and must be regarded as to some extent a cover for the activities of Dutchmen dissatisfied with the official organization of their own African trade.[4] The German Duchy of Courland had interests in north-west Africa, especially in the Gambia, in the middle years of the seventeenth century; later the Great Elector of Brandenburgh formed a company which built a fort called Gros Friedrichsburg at the western end of the Gold Coast. None of these enterprises met with conspicuous success, but they are evidence of how the smaller nations could gain some footing on the coast and some share in the trade. Because the situation of the Europeans in

[1] G. Scelle, *La Traite Négrière aux Indes de Castille*, Paris, 1906, I, p. 480.
[2] V. Barbour, *Capitalism in Amsterdam in the Seventeenth Century*, Baltimore, 1950, p. 134.
[3] Donnan, I, p. 77.   [4] *Ibid.*, and Barbour, *op. cit.*, pp. 134–5.

West Africa was so fluid, the smaller countries were able here
to express their commercial aspirations. Neither Denmark nor
Sweden nor Brandenburgh had, at the time of their entry into
the African trade, any interest in the West Indies or America;
they had therefore no immediate need to obtain slave-labour.
They joined in the African trade chiefly because the weakness
and preoccupation of the greater powers singled out this region
as one where small countries could hope to expand.

The seventy or so years following the arrival of the Dutch
were a period of particular fluidity in West Africa. The number of nations actively participating in the trade increased
swiftly, and forts were built, abandoned and captured with
bewildering speed. This rivalry reached its climax when West
Africa became the theatre of two major wars, that between
Portuguese and Dutch in Angola from 1641 to 1648, and that
between English and Dutch from 1664 to 1667. The Dutch
attack on Angola was, it is true, part of a hemispherical contest, but it was also an essential corollary to the seizure of
Brazil.[1] Both the Dutch assault in 1641 and the Portuguese
counter-attack in 1648 were successful, evidence that in West
Africa the advantage lay with the attacker and that it was
easier to destroy than to preserve. In the second Anglo-Dutch
war of 1664–7, African rivalry was again a major cause of
hostilities.[2] English and Dutch were competitors in many parts
of the world and war between them was probably inevitable;
but it was in West Africa that the explosion occurred and in
Africa that an important part of the fighting took place. First
an English fleet under Holmes took Goree and most of the
Dutch settlements on the Gold Coast except Elmina. Immediately afterwards De Ruyter recovered these conquests and
destroyed every English settlement on the Gold Coast except
Cape Coast Castle.[3] A clear demonstration was thus given of
the impossibility of defending forts and trading posts against
naval forces from Europe. This lesson was well-learned and

[1] C. R. Boxer, *Salvador de Sá and the Struggle for Brazil and Angola*, 1952.

[2] D. Ogg, *England in the Reign of Charles II*, 1934, I, pp. 283–4; K. Feiling,
British Foreign Policy, 1660–1672, 1930, pp. 125 ff.

[3] For details see G. F. Zook, *Company of Royal Adventurers Trading to Africa*,
Lancaster, Pennsylvania, 1919, pp. 65–6.

henceforth the rivalry of the two nations in Africa stopped short of open war. Thirty years later the English and French, after a series of assaults and counter-assaults, began to grope towards similar conclusions.[1]

The rise in the temperature of international rivalry for the African trade in the middle years of the seventeenth century was chiefly connected with developments on the other side of the Atlantic. The purchase of slaves in West Africa had begun as soon as the Portuguese appeared on the coast in the fifteenth century and had been stimulated by the discovery of the New World. Spain herself took little direct part in the African trade and her union with Portugal in 1580 appeared to provide a perfect solution to the labour problems of the New World, one empire supplying the needs of the other. The revolt of Portugal in 1640 ended this marriage. Philip IV forbade all commerce with Portugal including the slave-trade, and Spain was left to make the best shift she could without her natural ally. Between 1640 and 1662 there was no organized labour supply to the Spanish colonies. Licences were granted only for casual consignments and there was a good deal of unauthorized trade, mainly by the Dutch.[2] This situation, though offensive to Madrid and fiscally unremunerative, appears to have satisfied the Spanish colonists. The less Madrid concerned itself with the slave-trade the better supplies became and the fewer the complaints from the colonies.[3] A trade in human beings was little suited to bureaucratic control; it needed above all flexibility and freedom. But this was an inference which neither Spain nor any other nation was yet prepared to draw.

The period of uncontrolled trade in the supply of negroes to the Spanish colonies which followed the revolt of Portugal stimulated the interest of other commercial nations in the African trade. So long as Portugal had remained under the Spanish Crown no other nation was likely to profit from the *Asiento*. Now the prospect was opened of selling negroes to Spain and, perhaps even more important, of thereby prising

---

[1] J. M. Gray, *op. cit.*, pp. 144 ff., gives an account of Anglo-French neutrality agreements during the Spanish Succession war.

[2] G. Scelle, *op. cit.*, I, pp. 481 *et seq.*   [3] *Ibid.*, I, p. 490.

open a door into the rest of the trade of Spanish America. These considerations certainly helped to shape the policies of England, the United Provinces and France. In 1662 the *Asiento* was revived and granted to two Genoese, Grillo and Lomelin, who could fulfil their obligations only by extensive sub-contracting.[1] Grillo's contract met with complete disaster, as did most of its successors, for the *Asiento* proved to be a chimera pursued in the hope of profits which were generally found to be illusory. Nevertheless its importance in promoting the quest for slaves and in exciting European interest in West Africa was real enough.

At almost the same moment that the revolt of Portugal was opening to the merchants of other nations the possibility of a share in the trade of the Spanish empire, another development was taking place across the Atlantic which was to exert an even greater influence upon European trade in Africa. This was the spread of sugar-cultivation to the English and French islands of the Caribbean. After Spain had occupied all or more than she could hope to defend and exploit there still remained, especially in the Outer Antilles, some room for late comers. Between 1620 and 1660 English, Dutch and French established themselves in numerous islands. The Dutch colonies of Curaçao and St. Eustatius were chiefly trading depots and not much concerned with cultivating the soil, but the English colonies of Barbados, the Leeward Islands and Jamaica, and the French islands of Martinique and Guadeloupe were agricultural settlements from the beginning. At first they grew a variety of crops, foodstuffs for subsistence, tobacco, indigo, ginger and rice, on small farms cultivated by the labour of the settler and his family, supplemented by indentured white servants from Europe.[2] About 1640 a dramatic transformation was set in train by the arrival of sugar-cane. Barbados was swiftly and completely conquered; thence sugar spread to the Leeward Islands, to Jamaica, and to Antigua. The speed of its advance may be measured as follows: little more than twenty years after its first introduction into the English colonies sugar

[1] Scelle, I, pp. 505 *et seq.*
[2] N. Deerr, *History of Sugar*, I, 1949, p. 160; S. L. Mims, *Colbert's West India Policy*, New Haven, 1912, Ch. i.

had overtaken tobacco and accounted for nearly a half (by value) of London's imports from the Plantations.[1]

The general effect of the cultivation of sugar in the English empire was to make colonies more desirable possessions. Within twenty-five years the edifice of the Old Colonial System had been erected; the Dutch excluded; and a policy of political centralization begun.[2] On the African trade in particular the effects were profound. From very soon after its introduction the cultivation of sugar was wedded to negro labour. England and France were thus given a direct incentive to engage in the African trade. Indeed, unless they were prepared to accept a position of complete subjection to the Dutch, they were bound to participate. In 1620 an English explorer in the upper waters of the Gambia river was offered slaves by an African merchant: his reply was that 'We were a people who did not deale in any such commodities, neither did wee buy or sell one another, or any that had our owne shapes.'[3] Despite Hawkins' raids in the previous century, that claim was probably broadly true; but the same boast could not have been made in 1650, much less in 1670. The development of the French sugar-colonies was somewhat slower than the English, but no less surely demanded increased French participation in the slave-trade. The Dutch too, though expelled from Brazil in 1654, were given a new interest in Africa by the spread of sugar-cultivation, for they could now hope to supply, illicitly, not only the Spanish and Portuguese, but the English and French colonies as well.

In 1672 when the English Royal African Company came into existence the rivalry of the European nations in West Africa can probably be said to have passed its zenith. Economic competition was still fierce and would always be so, and there was fighting in West Africa in the Franco-Dutch war of 1672–8 and again between 1689 and 1713. In the eighteenth century,

[1] Brit. Mus., Add. MSS. 38785 values London's imports of all commodities from the Plantations in 1662–3 at £484,641 2s. Of this brown sugar accounted for £175,500 and white sugar for £44,800. The value set on brown sugar, 27s. a 100 lb., does not seem excessive.

[2] C. M. Andrews, *British Committees, Commissions and Councils of Trade and Plantations, 1622–1675*, Baltimore, 1908.

[3] Richard Jobson, *op. cit.*, p. 112.

Africa was a sideshow in a number of wars. Not, however, until the nineteenth and twentieth centuries did it again furnish a major cause of a major war.

2. The Organization of the Trade

Given that the conquest of West Africa was impracticable or at least uneconomical, four solutions presented themselves to the problem of how the interests of European nations could best be regulated, controlled and developed. First, the trade might be organized as a department of state for the advantage of the government or ruling house. Secondly, the state might undertake, not the trade itself but the provision of the facilities which would enable members of the nation to trade. It could, for example, build forts, provide naval forces and fight wars, while leaving commerce to private individuals. Thirdly, the whole interest of the nation could be committed to a privileged corporation which would undertake both defence and trade. Or finally, a policy of complete *laissez-faire* might be adopted whereby the trade was open to unorganized merchants and defence matters left to take care of themselves.

Not all these solutions were equally practicable or well-supported. The participation of the state in trade was not, until the eighteenth century at earliest, theoretically objectionable. By this method, the risks attendant upon hazardous commercial operations would be carried on the broadest shoulders and investment in long-term projects such as exploration and defence made possible. On the other hand few monarchs were wealthy enough to undertake what might prove a heavy financial liability. To accept the burden of defence without the compensation of commercial profits was even less attractive to the impoverished governments of sixteenth- and seventeenth-century Europe. Yet by the seventeenth century the African trade had become too important a branch of commerce to be neglected. With the spread of sugar to the English and French colonies, the governments of both countries had perceived the critical importance of the West Indian Plantations in an imperial economy; the supply of labour to those colonies had become an essential feature of imperial strategy. If the state was not prepared to undertake this supply, current assumptions seemed to favour a strong corporation endowed with wide powers and privileges as the best alternative. Such a corporation would, if need arose, be susceptible to governmental direction; it would possess funds for long-term projects; it could negotiate and enforce agreements with native rulers; and it would not be discouraged by temporary setbacks. These arguments were thought to be confirmed by historical example. Both the Dutch and the English East India companies, in conditions superficially similar to those of West Africa, were strikingly successful; and in 1621 the Dutch had committed their interest in the African trade to a similar corporation. In questions of commercial organization most other countries in the seventeenth century were prepared to follow where the Dutch led, and indeed one of the most commonly employed arguments of English propagandists for the joint-stock corporation in the African trade was that it had been adopted by the Dutch. Between 1620 and the end of the century every nation concerned in the African trade experimented with companies. These corporations were very different from one another in many respects, but in each instance the outcome was substantially the same: failure. By 1700 the chartered company, though not yet eliminated from the African trade, was discredited and doomed, and the way open for private enterprise. Until the privileged corporation had worked out its own destruction, the notion that the trade could be handed over to private merchants was slow to gain support. The strategic importance of the slave-trade and considerations of defence appeared to rule it out. Private traders, it was thought, would cut one another's throats instead of outwitting rivals of other nations; they would be difficult for a government to manage; they would build no forts; they would make no agreements with native rulers and break those that were made for them; and at the first discouragement they would abandon the trade.

Such were the possible solutions to the problems of organization in the African trade. The solutions actually adopted were less clearly cut. They were often blends of two or even three of the methods described, as in the case of Portugal.

c

Portuguese exploration in Africa had been to a large extent the outcome of royal efforts and when profits began to flow in from the resultant trade it was natural that the Crown should look for a reward. In 1481 the Guinea trade was made a monopoly of the ruling house, oversight being vested in a government department.[1] This did not, however, mean that in the following centuries the Crown directly exploited the whole of Portuguese commerce with Africa. From time to time the trade of a particular region was farmed out to contractors or licences were granted to private merchants. Nevertheless both contractors and licensees traded within a framework of royal regulations, and royal officials were appointed to reside on the African coast. It is probable that amongst the Portuguese merchants engaged in the trade partnerships and small private companies were formed to exploit the grants purchased from the Crown, but the great chartered company was not a feature of Portuguese trade in Africa as it was of English, French and Dutch. In 1648 a Brazil company was founded, but its activities were confined to South America and its monopoly did not extend to the provision of slaves.[2] Not until the later years of the seventeenth century did a recognizable joint-stock organization emerge in the Portuguese African trade.[3]

In France, particularly in the last forty years of the seventeenth century, the chartered company was widely used as a method of organizing long-distance trade. Earlier, partnerships and small syndicates (*compagnies*) had predominated. Richelieu tried to weld them into a single and more effective body in 1626; his design had embraced the African trade. But the grandiose plan collapsed before it was properly working and the unchartered *compagnies* were left in possession of the field.[4] In 1633 a Rouen company was granted a monopoly of trade between Cape Verde and the Gambia, but little is known

[1] J. W. Blake, *op. cit.*, pp. 72 ff.

[2] C. R. Boxer, *op. cit.*, p. 290.

[3] Donnan, I, p. 107; C. de Lannoy and H. Vander Linden, *Histoire de l'Expansion Coloniale des Peuples Européens, Portugal et Espagne*, Brussels, 1907, p. 148.

[4] H. Hauser, *La Pensée et l'Action Économiques du Cardinal de Richelieu*, Paris, 1944, pp. 126 ff.

of its history.[1] In 1664 Colbert liquidated the surviving fragments of this and other companies and established the giant *Compagnie des Indes Occidentales*.[2] To this corporation was granted the trade of America, from Canada to the Amazon, including the Antilles and Newfoundland, together with the trade of Africa from Cape Verde to the Cape of Good Hope. Political, military and fiscal privileges were added. Despite these huge concessions, great difficulty was encountered in attracting private capital to the support of the venture. Special facilities were provided for foreign investors; in the hope that mercantile capital would be forthcoming the charter guaranteed that merchants would play a large part in the management of the company's affairs; and public officials were browbeaten into subscribing. In all the company raised about eight million livres, the greater part of which was eventually lost. But, notwithstanding the inducements, very little of this sum came from private investors. More than three million livres was contributed by the King personally and another two million came from public funds.[3] From the first the Crown had a controlling interest, and the company must be regarded as little different from a department of state. As a monopolistic trading enterprise, the *Compagnie des Indes Occidentales* had an effective life of only about three years. As early as 1666, licences were being granted to private traders on payment of a small fee;[4] thereafter the company sank under an accumulating burden of debt.

In 1672 a *Compagnie du Sénégal* was formed which bought for 75,000 livres the interest of its defunct predecessor in the northwest coast of Africa.[5] This was an important change, for it marked the end of the policy of yoking West Africa to French America in one giant monopoly. Theoretically such an arrangement had much to commend it. The Dutch, Danes and Scots, as well as the French, granted monopolies which extended to

[1] P. Chemin-Dupontès, *Les Compagnies de Colonisation en Afrique Occidentale sous Colbert*, Paris, 1903, Ch. i, Section iii.

[2] S. L. Mims, *op. cit.*, Chs. iii–vii; P. Bonnassieux, *Les Grandes Compagnies de Commerce*, Paris, 1892, pp. 369 ff.

[3] Mims, *op. cit.*, p. 178.   [4] *Ibid.*, p. 138.

[5] Chemin-Dupontès, *op. cit.*, pp. 89–90.

both sides of the Atlantic and were intended to embrace the marketing of colonial products as well as the supply of slaves. But in practice, and especially in the case of the *Compagnie des Indes Occidentales*, such monopolies reduced the West Indian planters to a state of helpless subservience that would have been barely tolerable under efficient direction and which under incompetent rule was insupportable. In 1672 the giant monopoly was abandoned and even the supply of slaves to French possessions in America was for a time left uncontrolled. For some years success attended the new arrangement. Goree and Arguim were captured in the Franco-Dutch war of 1672–8, and the *Compagnie du Sénégal* settled a number of factories. In 1679, however, the company contracted to provide 2000 negroes annually, receiving in return a bounty from the French government of thirteen livres a head for each slave delivered; at the same time its monopoly was extended to include the whole of the West African coast down to the Cape of Good Hope.[1] Within two years of the making of this contract the company was obliged by its debts to sell out to the *Nouvelle Compagnie du Sénégal*, handing over all its assets in return for 240,000 livres. The new company began with a capital of only 600,000 livres, much of which was consumed by debts inherited from its predecessor. Fresh debts were soon contracted and eventually crushed the company out of existence. A *Compagnie du Guinée*, formed in 1684, does not appear to have met with any greater success.[2] Thus failure succeeded to failure and the organizational history of French trade to Africa in this period is a melancholy record. These repeated failures may be ascribed partly to the lack of interest on the part of the private French investor. Sufficient funds could be obtained only by borrowing, in one way or another, from the Crown, with consequent loss of independence. The savings of French merchants went into the purchase of offices or into the *rentes* which, if they shored up French public finances, constricted the supply of capital to private enterprise.[3] Dependent on the state for

[1] Chemin-Dupontès, p. 102.

[2] Bonnassieux, *op. cit.*, pp. 225–33; Mims, *op. cit.*, Ch. xiii.

[3] H. Hauser, 'The Characteristic Features of French Economic History', in *Ec.H.R.*, IV (1933), pp. 262–3.

money, ships, subsidies and orders, the French companies lacked the flexibility that was needed in the African trade.

The persistence with which the privileged corporation continued to be regarded as the proper method of organizing the African trade was partly due to the Dutch example. The Dutch East India Company was indeed immensely successful, both from the public point of view and from the point of view of the investor. It is, however, open to doubt whether the history of the Dutch West India Company justified the adoption of a similar organization in the Western hemisphere. In the first place, this company was much less successful than its counterpart in the East and eventually went bankrupt; and secondly, while the Dutch provided a good enough model in the East, their interests in the West were different from those of France. France, by Colbert's time, had embarked on colonies of settlement; the Dutch concentrated for the most part upon trading posts. Conceivably (though even this is not certain) a vast monopolistic corporation might have been able successfully to organize purely commercial interests in the West; but to combine those interests with the organization of settlement, as Colbert tried to do in the *Compagnie des Indes Occidentales*, was beyond the capacity of any seventeenth-century company.

After an abortive beginning in 1607, the Dutch West India Company was finally established in 1621 and granted for a period of twenty-four years a monopoly of trade with America, the West Indies, and West Africa from the Tropic of Cancer to the Cape of Good Hope. The event coincided (not accidentally) with the renewal of war between the United Provinces and Spain, and from the first plunder was a main objective.[1] Many successes were won in the next thirty years. The Portuguese were ousted from the Gold Coast and harried elsewhere in Africa; the most productive parts of Brazil were seized and held for a time; and many valuable cargoes were captured. The company's record was magnificent, but it was war not trade. When peace came the company languished, incurring debts which could be liquidated only by a thorough reorganization

[1] G. Edmundson, 'The Dutch Power in Brazil', in *English Historical Review*, XI (1896); P. Geyl, *The Netherlands Divided*, 1936 (English Translation), pp. 189 ff.

in 1674.[1] Thereafter, what is generally known as the Second West India Company continued to exist for many years, but its work was much less spectacular, its privileges restricted and its profits modest.

The Dutch West India Company exhibits several points of contrast with those of other nations. In the first place, there was an element of formal public control, less noticeable than in France but more marked than in England. Supreme authority was vested in a Council of Nineteen, one of whom, the chairman, was appointed by the States General. Part of the capital was contributed from public funds, and the United Provinces also undertook to supply soldiers and war-material, though these were to be paid for by the company.[2] In England governmental control over trading companies was certainly exercised, but it was less formal and more haphazard. English monarchs from Elizabeth I to James II invested money in joint-stock enterprises, but generally the amounts were so small that even if they were withdrawn the company did not necessarily collapse.[3] In both the French and the Dutch West India Companies the contributions from public funds were an essential part of the capital.

The charter of 1621 granted to the Dutch West India Company a monopoly of trade on both sides of the Atlantic, thus providing the model for Colbert's *Compagnie des Indes Occidentales*. So comprehensive a concession had much to commend it for a company the chief purpose of which was to wage hemispherical war. But if stringently enforced such a monopoly could scarcely have been conducive to colonial settlement. The colonist would have been delivered entirely into the hands of a body controlling both the supply of his necessary purchases and the price at which his crop would be sold, a body over

[1] Bonnassieux, *op. cit.*, pp. 72–7; C. de Lannoy and H. Vander Linden, *Histoire de l'Expansion Coloniale des Peuples Européens: Néerlande et Danemark*, Brussels, 1911, p. 241.

[2] Edmundson, *op. cit.*, p. 235; E. F. Heckscher, *Mercantilism*, 1935 (English Translation), I, pp. 366–7.

[3] To this generalization there are certain exceptions. Half of the capital of the New River Company (1611) belonged to the Crown. In 1661 Charles II invested £9000 in the Royal Fishery Company. Other companies, however, managed without royal contributions or with small ones.

which his own influence would be so remote and tenuous as to be negligible. In the Dutch example, the evil effects of monopoly were mitigated partly because settlement was not the chief object of the Dutch in the West, and also, and more significantly, because the West India Company did not in practice engross the whole of the trade of the regions granted to it. A good deal of liberty was in fact allowed to private merchants to trade on their own account. The trade of Brazil, for example, was opened to all in 1635 on payment of a small duty. In 1638 it was restricted to Netherlanders who were shareholders of the company but left open to inhabitants of Brazil whether shareholders or not. Similarly before 1640 trade between New Netherlands and the United Provinces was open to shareholders; after 1640 it was free to all Dutchmen. Free trade at Curaçao in the West Indies, which previously had been permitted in practice, was formally recognized in 1675. Only in West Africa was the Dutch West India Company able to preserve even the outward form of a monopoly, and here interlopers deprived it of an important part of the trade. In 1730 the company's privileges, previously extending over the greater part of West Africa, were restricted to the Gold Coast, and in 1734 they were abolished altogether. The company retained a monopoly of the import of negroes only into Guiana; otherwise the slave-trade was open to all Dutchmen.[1] The history of the company is thus marked by the surrender of one privilege after another, and it is probably true to say that for the greater part of its life it functioned, except in West Africa, chiefly as an administrative body, drawing its income from war and taxes as much as or more than from commerce, and in return preserving Dutch interests and providing the framework within which private enterprise could do much as it liked.

Finally, the West India Company like the earlier East India Company embodied an important concession to Dutch provincialism. It was divided into five chambers, each of which raised a proportion of the capital and enjoyed a corresponding control over the enterprise. Unity of action was preserved through the Council of Nineteen, and in practice by the dominating position of the Amsterdam chamber to which the charter

[1] Lannoy and Vander Linden, *Néerlande et Danemark*, pp. 283–300.

allocated four of the nine shares into which, for the purpose of regional organization, the company was divided.[1] The provinces and outports were in this way given, nominally at least, a reserved interest in the corporate trade and profits of the company. No such arrangements are found in the English East India Company or in the various English companies engaged in the African trade. Thus while the provincial chambers of the Dutch companies were enthusiastic upholders of the monopolies,[2] the provincial merchants of England were generally opponents of monopolies the sole beneficiary of which was London.

The evolution of the English joint-stock company has been traced by both legal and economic historians.[3] At the time of the formation of the Royal African Company in 1672, the two principal features of the joint stock were incorporation and the association of capital; each of these features had a long independent history behind it, the novelty of the joint-stock company being to fuse them into an instrument of great economic possibilities. The notion of incorporation stretched back to the gilds, the boroughs and the ecclesiastical foundations of the Middle Ages. The privileges of an incorporated body, perpetual succession, a common seal, the rights to hold property and to sue and be sued, were recognized and defined long before the joint-stock company made its appearance in English economic life. The concept and practice of incorporation, indeed, owed little to economic needs; they were the product rather of political exigencies and charitable instincts. A concept and a practice, however, which had been devised for other purposes proved adaptable to economic ends of various kinds and, increasingly as the Middle Ages drew to a close, associations of craftsmen emerged, many of them formally incorporated by charter. Their aims were manifold and seldom

---

[1] V. Barbour, *op. cit.*, p. 80, quotes an estimate that about 1667 Amsterdam's share of the total capital was more than one-half.

[2] Lannoy and Vander Linden, *op. cit.*, pp. 284–6.

[3] W. R. Scott, *The Constitution and Finance of English, Scottish and Irish Joint-Stock Companies to 1720*; C. T. Carr, *Select Charters of Trading Companies* (Selden Society, Vol. 28), 1913; Sir W. S. Holdsworth, *History of English Law* (2nd edition), VIII, pp. 192–222; C. A. Cooke, *Corporation, Trust and Company*, 1950.

purely economic. They sought, for example, to regulate standards of workmanship and conditions of employment; some were more concerned to control entry into a trade or craft, laying down elaborate rules of apprenticeship. But non-economic features were also present. As has often been pointed out, some of the social and even religious elements in the medieval gild can be found in the joint-stock company of the seventeenth century and help to confirm the descent of the one from the other.[1]

Generally these incorporations of craftsmen served, or were made to look as if they served, some public purpose, and when the gild spread from industry and local trade into the field of overseas commerce the public aspect was given greater prominence. Gild-organization in English foreign trade is found at an early date in the companies of Staplers and Merchant Adventurers; in the sixteenth century with the broadening of English commercial interests the number of companies greatly increased. In the reign of Elizabeth I these organizations, later given the name of 'regulated' companies, captured the greater part of English trade. The 'regulated' company was not, of course, a form of ownership, any more than is a modern chamber of trade. It was an association of individual merchants, formed primarily for self-protection. Within its ranks can be found the three forms of ownership known in the sixteenth and seventeenth centuries, the sole trader, the partnership, and even the joint stock.[2] Plausibly these associations could be represented as conducive to public or at least to royal advantage. They were, first, authorities which could enforce governmental directions and which the Crown could make responsible for the behaviour of merchants at home and abroad. Since mercantile disputes were a fertile source of international friction, this was an important consideration. Moreover, some of the companies, notably the Merchant Adventurers, rendered valuable financial services to the Crown by

[1] Scott, I, p. 152.

[2] G. Unwin, *Industrial Organization in the Sixteenth and Seventeenth Centuries*, 1904, pp. 151–2. The example of a joint stock formed inside a regulated company is the Morea Joint Stock; for a list of shareholders see P.R.O., S.P. 105/162.

making or guaranteeing loans. Consequently the attitude of government towards such bodies was generally one of favour and encouragement. The strictly economic arguments for the 'regulated' company, however, were not always so convincing, and it cannot be doubted that the advantages accruing to the public and the Crown were overshadowed by the benefits which members of such organizations (or some of them) secured for themselves. Some of the commercial functions which they performed were for the general good. They secured extra-territorial rights in foreign countries, obtained concessions from foreign rulers and organized convoys for defence against pirates and enemies. But at certain times and under certain circumstances they made and enforced restrictive regulations which hampered the trade of non-members and even the trade of members themselves. A 'regulated' company consisted, in principle, of the English merchants trading to a particular region: but once such a company had been incorporated it obtained powers to control entry into its own ranks. The temptation to use these powers to restrict entry either by charging high entrance fees or by excluding altogether certain classes of person proved irresistible.[1] Almost all 'regulated' companies, for example, excluded retail traders from membership, not merely in fulfilment of abstract social ideas, but because shopkeepers could earn profits in their shops and, if permitted to engage in foreign trade, could undercut mere merchants. At the same time the rules imposed upon members often proved irksome. Inevitably companies tended to come under the control of the greater merchants and their regulations were not infrequently detrimental to the interests of smaller men: the outports in particular complained of being sacrificed to London.

The trend towards monopolistic and restrictive practices exhibited by the regulated companies generated an ill-will, part of which was inherited by the joint-stock company. This unpopularity was much increased as a result of the patents and monopolies granted by the Crown in the early seventeenth century.[2] The Monopolies Act of 1624 prevented the Crown

[1] G. Unwin, *Studies in Economic History*, 1927, pp. 168–86.
[2] W. H. Price, *English Patents of Monopoly*, 1906.

from bestowing monopolies upon private persons and forced Charles I to erect numerous corporations to which he could sell or lease monopolistic privileges, chiefly in the field of domestic industry and trade. Few of these creations met genuine economic needs, though most of them were made to look as if they served some laudable purpose; in fact they were the products of royal poverty and recklessness coupled with the greed of courtiers. Through them commercial and industrial corporations became more closely identified with unpopular monopolies and a public opinion hostile to both was fostered.

Partnership, like the corporation, had its roots in the Middle Ages; and just as it was through the 'regulated' company that the joint stock inherited the notion and practice of incorporation so it was from the partnership that the joint ownership of capital was derived. In the later Middle Ages a partnership was an association of two or more individuals who pooled part of their resources to achieve what might be a definite and limited objective, such as for example a single voyage.[1] The idea of permanent associations of capital (or indeed of long-term investment in anything other than land) appears to have spread only slowly, and it is probable that the terminable joint stocks of, for instance, the early East India Company were an echo of the short-term partnership. When facilities for disinvestment appeared in the form of a rudimentary market for shares, joint stocks could become permanent.

Owing so much to the 'regulated' company on the one hand and to the partnership on the other, it is not surprising that the joint-stock company retained so many of the characteristics of both; for a long time the distinction between them was blurred. The attitude of the law to these various forms of commercial organization, and especially to the joint-stock company, was uncertain, and until the law had been defined there was much variation in practice.[2] To begin with, the charters which incorporated the 'regulated' companies and the early joint stocks

---

[1] The English version of partnership, the *societas*, is said to have been more permanent than the European *commenda*; Holdsworth, VIII, pp. 196-7; Cooke, *op. cit.*, pp. 46-7. Partnership as a phenomenon in early English economic history would repay investigation.

[2] Holdsworth, *op. cit.*, VIII, pp. 215-18.

are remarkable for their similarity. The first example in England of the union of incorporation and joint ownership of capital is the Muscovy Company. Its charter, issued in 1555, gives no indication of the joint-stock character of the company.[1] Nor do the charters granted by Elizabeth I and James I to the East India Company.[2] On the other hand these charters contain many vestiges of gild-practice. Monopoly of the East Indian trade was vested, not in the shareholders, but in the freemen of the company named in the original charter, who were given power to add to their number. In the early history of this company, each 'voyage' was separately financed, the freemen having the option of subscribing to a given 'voyage' but not being obliged to do so.[3] The possession of the freedom of the company was thus distinct from financial participation in particular commercial ventures. Even in the later seventeenth century, when in practice the distinction had almost disappeared, the concept of a freedom of the East India Company was retained, entry to it being in one of the traditional ways, apprenticeship, inheritance or purchase. Those who bought East India stock were required to prove that they were free of the company, or else to purchase the freedom with a fine.[4] No doubt this arrangement was continued chiefly as a money-raising expedient. Similar clauses were written into the charter of the Royal African Company, but in practice were not observed.

The common ground between the 'regulated' and joint-stock companies was not confined to the legal instruments which brought them into existence, or to the methods of entry. In theory a 'regulated' company consisted of individual merchants, each trading on his own account, while in a joint-stock company capital was pooled and all trading done on a common account. In practice many companies which are classified as joint stocks permitted their own members to engage in private

[1] Charter in Hakluyt, *Principal Voyages* (Everyman), I, p. 318. See also T. S. Willan, 'Trade between England and Russia', in *English Historical Review*, LXIII (1948), pp. 316–20.

[2] Sir W. W. Hunter, *History of British India*, 1900, II, p. 129.

[3] *Ibid.*, I, pp. 259–64.

[4] Those holding less than £100 of stock were exempt from payment of this fine; *Calendar of Court Minutes of the East India Company, 1671–1673*, p. 40.

trade.[1] Although the history of the Muscovy Company is obscure it is possible that private trade was allowed, at least for a time.[2] In the history of the East India Company, especially after the Restoration, numerous instances are recorded of permission to export goods to India on private account. In certain commodities trade was open to non-members as well as to members on payment of a fee. This private trade is reputed to have reached very large proportions.[3] In Holland and France, as well as in England, the practice of licensing entire cargoes to be sent on private account within the limits of the monopoly of a joint-stock company must be regarded as normal.[4] Companies might grant such licences to members or non-members for a number of reasons. In the first place it was often possible to charge a heavy fee. If a company was in straitened financial circumstances, the sale of licences not only raised money but also kept in being a trade which might otherwise be lost to the nation and which, if things improved, might later be resumed. In view of the hostile criticism directed

---

[1] The terms of the union in one stock of the Assada Adventurers and the East India Company in 1649 are notable: 'It is "conceived" that, when the company is fully settled and the adventurers known, if any of them shall propose a new voyage to the generality and they dislike it, "it was not unlikely but that upon good caution liberty would be given to such persons to prosecute the same on their owne accompt" '; *Calendar of Court Minutes of the East India Company, 1644–1649*, p. 378. During 1653 and 1654 a section of the freemen of the company proposed, and eventually petitioned the Council of State, that private members should be given liberty to trade on their own account. Discussions within the company as to whether the trade should be carried on in a joint stock or regulated form led to the setting up of a committee to investigate. By 11 votes to 5, the committee decided in favour of the joint stock. Hunter, *op. cit.*, II, pp. 119–22; *Calendar of Court Minutes of the East India Company, 1650–1654*, pp. 283, 304–5, 314. As to the private trade actually permitted, see *Court Minutes, 1664–1667*, p. 18. All persons could export jewels and other 'things of great value but small bulk' on payment of 2 per cent. Likewise 'fine goods' could be imported from the Indies at the rate of 2 per cent. for freemen and 4 per cent. for others. Licensed private trade in 1675 was said to amount to £150,000 in exports and £300,000 in imports, compared to £430,000 and £860,000 on joint account. These figures are unconfirmed.

[2] T. S. Willan, 'Trade between England and Russia', in *English Historical Review*, LXIII (1948).

[3] Above, n. 1.   [4] Heckscher, *op. cit.*, I, p. 407.

against many of them, it was important that joint-stock companies should, even at the cost of temporarily forgoing their monopoly, preserve the interests of the country in the trade committed to them. Again, the judicious granting of licences might serve to silence embarrassing opponents of monopoly.[1] It is not surprising, therefore, that many joint-stock trading companies were at times constrained to allow private persons a share in the benefits of monopoly. Normally licences were granted for single voyages, but on at least one occasion a joint-stock company leased part of its monopoly to another joint-stock company. This was in 1668 when the company of Royal Adventurers trading to Africa farmed the trade of the north parts of Guinea to the company of Gambia Adventurers for a term of seven years.[2]

Between a joint-stock company and a partnership in the sixteenth and seventeenth centuries the legal distinction was much clearer. A joint-stock company was incorporated and a partnership was not. From the point of view of the economic historian, however, the difference is not so sharp. Size is certainly no true guide, for some companies consisted of very few members. In recent times limited liability has become one of the principal differences between partnerships and companies. But in the seventeenth century limited liability was enjoyed by shareholders of joint-stock companies only in a restricted and qualified form.[3] In some companies, the Elizabethan company of Mines Royal for example, the members owned, not shares of fixed nominal value, but fractions of the whole enterprise.[4] In order to retain their shares they had to meet all the calls which the majority of shareholders voted to impose. Thus at the time when an investor undertook a share in the company his ultimate liability was unknown and unfolded itself only as the capital needs of the enterprise became clear. Even after shares had

---

[1] Hunter, *op. cit.*, II, p. 282.   [2] G. F. Zook, *op. cit.*, p. 23.
[3] Holdsworth, *op. cit.*, VIII, pp. 203–5; Cooke, *op. cit.*, pp. 77–8; Carr, *op. cit.*, p. xviii, n. 1; K. G. Davies, 'Joint-Stock Investment in the Later Seventeenth Century', in *Ec.H.R.*, 2nd Series, IV (1952), pp. 293–4; H. A. Shannon, 'The Coming of Limited Liability', in *Economic History*, II (1931), No. 6.
[4] Scott, II, p. 385.

come to be generally expressed in nominal values, limited liability does not seem to have had much real meaning outside the brains of lawyers. Individual shareholders could and did find themselves coerced by the majority to contribute money beyond the fully paid up value of their stock or else to lose their holdings.[1] Until companies began, in the last decade of the seventeenth century, explicitly to renounce the power to make 'leviations' or calls of this kind,[2] the gulf between the partnership and the joint stock was not, in this respect, a great one. The assignability of shares was common to both, the difference being that in practice shares came to be transferred more widely in companies than in partnerships. Some of these difficulties of classification disappeared during the first hundred years of joint-stock development, but others remained to bedevil the law and practice of capital association in the eighteenth century.

The truth seems to be that the joint-stock company of the seventeenth century was as remarkable for its differences from the joint-stock company of the twentieth century as for its similarities; only misunderstanding can result from regarding them as exactly the same. The reasons for the creation of these early companies, the considerations which suggested that commercial organization should take this form rather than any other, were also different. At the present time four main forms of ownership of business enterprises (other than public ownership) can be distinguished: the sole trader, who has been driven from most spheres except retail trading and farming; the partnership, which can still be found in trade and industry but which is confined chiefly to the professions; the private limited liability company; and the public company. With certain important exceptions (such, for instance, as limited liability companies formed in order to secure tax concessions) the prime factor determining the form of ownership in modern business enterprises is capital requirement. It is indeed not uncommon for a business to have passed in the last hundred years from the first or second of these stages through the third to the fourth, expansion being accompanied by increasing capital needs which have caused the enterprise to outgrow one form of organization

[1] See authorities cited on p. 30, n. 3.   [2] Scott, I, p. 344.

and adopt another. In the seventeenth century the private limited company did not exist: the other three forms of ownership were present, but growth and development from one form to another was rare. No doubt sole traders took partners, but partnerships did not turn into public companies. The great joint stocks of the sixteenth and seventeenth centuries, the Muscovy Company, Mines Royal, Mineral and Battery Company, Levant Company, East India Company, New River Company, Royal Fishery, Royal Adventurers, Royal African, Hudson's Bay Company and Bank of England, did not so much evolve as result from specific creative acts: they were joint-stock companies from the beginning.

The history of the early joint-stock company is more complicated than a simple response to the need for more capital in one trade and less in another. The requirement of large sums of capital certainly was a consideration: when the East India Company was first launched with a permanent stock in 1657 its nominal capital was £739,782 10s., of which half was paid up. It is extremely unlikely that £369,891 5s. could have been raised at this time by any means other than a joint stock. The same is true of the Bank of England's capital of £1,200,000. But examples can readily be found, especially in the early years, where the joint-stock form was applied to enterprises in which the aggregate capital brought together was so small as to be well within the capacity of a partnership or even a sole trader to provide. The Hudson's Bay Company, for instance, set out in 1670 to exploit the trade of several million square miles of Canada with a capital of only £10,500. There is no doubt at all that this sum was well within the reach of many London merchants in the reign of Charles II. Indeed, until the last decade of the seventeenth century very few companies had share-capitals of more than £100,000. If their evolution had to be explained solely in terms of the size of capital requirements, some of them would appear as so many steam hammers employed to crack nuts.

If the mere size of capital needs fails to provide a complete explanation of the adoption of the joint stock, it becomes necessary to consider whether the type of capital required or the work which the capital was expected to do offers any aid to further understanding. In the field of foreign trade it is remarkable that joint-stock companies are found only in long-distance commerce, the Levant, Russia, the East, Africa and Canada; they are not found in English trade to the Low Countries, Northern Germany, France or Spain. Yet it is well known that in the seventeenth century the bulk of English overseas trade was with Europe, and the opportunities for the employment of large sums of capital must have existed. Not only are there no joint-stock companies in English trade with the Continent: we do not even hear of serious proposals for the erection of such companies. Yet in English trade with Africa, where trading capital needs were no greater, a succession of joint-stock companies is found. One reason for this difference lies in the different functions that capital had to perform in one trade or another. The capital employed in trade with the Continent was absorbed chiefly by stocks of goods awaiting sale or by credit given to manufacturers and purchasers. Warehouses and shops were probably rented, and the number of fixtures was small. In other words the capital invested was floating not fixed, and it could be withdrawn without great difficulty. Much the same is true in the organization of, for example, the seventeenth-century textile industry. Fixed capital was needed, for the cottages in which weaving and spinning took place, but it did not necessarily have to be supplied by the employer; and other fixtures were few and simple. It was, therefore, feasible to engage either in Continental trade or in domestic industry and still to preserve what moneyed men valued very highly in the seventeenth century, liquidity. In the Indian, African or Canadian trades, on the other hand, investment of a more permanent kind proved to be inevitable. Forts had to be built for defence and large funds came to be locked up in 'dead stock'; liquidity was impossible. By some historians, Heckscher for example, the necessity of investing in 'dead stock' has been regarded as decisive in stimulating joint-stock associations.[1] That it was important is clear from the history of long-distance trades in which the joint stock appeared and subsequently vanished. In the sixteenth century both the Levant and the Russian trades were organized on joint-stock lines. No large

[1] Heckscher, *op. cit.*, I, pp. 388, 408.

D

investment in 'dead stock' proved necessary and eventually the joint-stock companies were dissolved and replaced by associations of private merchants or 'regulated' companies.

The necessity of making permanent investments in fixed assets may also be taken to explain the use of joint stocks to finance water supply and drainage projects; such ventures inevitably meant the sacrifice of liquidity. It does not, however, fully explain the use of joint stocks in such fields as mining, whale fishing, or, for that matter, in the African trade before forts and settlements began to be built. A more complete understanding may be forthcoming if, for the moment, the distinction between the partnership and the joint-stock company is set aside and an attempt made to explain what was common to both, the association of capital. While it would be wrong to reject altogether the size of capital requirements as a cause of associations of capital, we have already seen that in certain joint-stock companies it cannot be regarded as decisive: this is even clearer in the case of partnerships. Although in the seventeenth century they are to be found in many branches of economic activity, it was in the business of shipowning that partnerships were most commonly adopted. All or nearly all seagoing ships appear to have been owned by syndicates of eight, sixteen, thirty-two or more persons. Yet the capital outlay required to build or purchase even a large vessel was not great; few merchant-ships can have cost more than £10,000, and most cost very much less.[1] Such sums could have been provided by individual capitalists; that they were not can probably be ascribed, at least in origin, to the factor of risk. Capitalists who wished to invest heavily in shipping, and there were some, did not acquire entire ships but bought small shares in a large number of ships.[2] Thereby they spread their risks as widely as

---

[1] A thirty-second share in the *Golden Fleece*, which made six voyages to the East Indies and must therefore have been larger than most merchant-ships, cost Sir William Turner £325 in 1671. A thirty-second share in the *Society* of 550 tons and a one-sixteenth share in the *Alexandre* cost £247 5s. and £147 10s. respectively. City of London Guildhall Library, MS. 5105.

[2] Sir Henry Johnson, probably the greatest shipowner of the seventeenth century, was part-owner of 38 ships; V. Barbour, 'Dutch and English Merchant Shipping in the Seventeenth Century', in *Ec.H.R.*, II (1930), p. 263, n. 1.

possible. During the seventeenth century the hazards of ship-owning were being reduced: on the one hand English sea power was able to give more effective protection to merchant vessels, and on the other hand marine insurance provided the means of covering, though not fully, some of the risks of the sea. Nevertheless the partnership continued to be the characteristic form of ownership in the shipping industry: whether because it was a well-established convention, or because it was a convenient way of mobilizing small savings, or because it was useful for sharing the risks that remained, it is difficult to say.

Risks, or men's assessment of them, can indeed be regarded as a powerful incentive to capital-associations which took the form of joint stocks as well as those which became partnerships. The trade of Africa or Canada was riskier than the trade of Spain or the Baltic. Mining, in the absence of geological knowledge, was risky.[1] All new ventures, such as colonization or the introduction of new industries, carried with them the danger of total loss. Scott's enquiry revealed that there were thirty-six important companies formed in England before 1680.[2] Of these ten were for long-distance trades, nine for colonization, three for fisheries, three for the introduction of new metallurgical industries and two for mining. In all these enterprises there must have been an important element of risk. Of the remainder, four were concerned with water-supply, two with drainage, two with the colonization of Ulster, and one with insurance. Here the element of risk is less obvious than the need for permanent investment.

The connexion between risks and the associations of capital is one which has, to a large extent, to be inferred; it is difficult to obtain documentary proof. It is not, however, an unwarrantable inference that where a man is prepared to invest £10,000 in a reasonably safe enterprise, he will invest no more

---

[1] The risks of mining are aptly summarized by Sir Bevis Bulmer: 'Whosoever is a menerall man must of force be a hasserd adventurer not greatly esteeming whether it hit or miss soddainly, as if he were a gamester playing at dice or such unlawful games.' Quoted by H. M. Robertson in 'Sir Bevis Bulmer', in *Journal of Economic and Business History*, IV (1931–2), p. 119.

[2] Scott, III, pp. 462–72, omitting the subsidiaries of the Virginia Company.

than £1000 in a risky venture. The connexion was certainly appreciated by Lewes Roberts:

> The only meanes to settle the Commerce and Traffike of a Nation into forraigne Countries by sea, in the which the best purses will not bee drawne to hazard themselves in the Enterprise, is to compell the Merchants which trade at sea to one and the selfe certaine place and countrey to joyn one with another in a corporation and Company and not to make their Traffike by themselves asunder . . . if in making a joynt Company or Society, the Gaine should turne to be the losse, yet it is ever more assured.[1]

The argument here was chiefly for the regulated company, but it applies equally or more strongly to joint-stock organization.

If we wish to explain why, for example, the £10,500 which in 1670 was thought appropriate for the trade of the Hudson's Bay was raised in penny-packets by an association of capitalists, instead of by one, part of the answer seems to lie in the presence of risks. Plenty of capitalists had £10,500 to invest; none would risk so much on such a project. There is, however, still another consideration which played an important part in the formation of this and other companies. Just as today there are attractive advantages to be gained by forming small limited companies, so in the seventeenth century there were great benefits in being incorporated by royal charter. There were, for example, questions of convenience: an incorporated body with a common seal could transact business much more expeditiously than a partnership, each member of which would have to subscribe every act. But far more fundamental than mere convenience was the matter of the additional privileges which might accompany the grant of a royal charter, and above all the privilege of monopoly. Until the Act of 1624 monopolies could be granted to individuals, though in the field of foreign trade they seldom were; after 1624 only a corporation could be given a monopoly. Thus if the courtiers and business men who mooted the Hudson's Bay project in the 1660's wanted to obtain a monopoly (and it may be taken as axiomatic that they

---

[1] *The Treasure of Traffike* in J. R. McCulloch's *Early English Tracts on Commerce*, reprinted 1952, pp. 85–6.

did) they had to be incorporated as the Governor and Company of Adventurers of England trading into Hudson's Bay.

Four explanations of the adoption of joint-stock organization have now been suggested: the need for amassing sums of capital beyond the capacity of individuals or partnerships (rarely decisive until the end of the seventeenth century); the necessity of locking up capital in the provision of schemes of defence in countries outside the orbits of both governmental control and diplomatic influence; risk, which prompted a large number of small investments instead of a small number of large ones; and, finally, the need to be incorporated as a condition of obtaining a monopoly. To disentangle one of these factors from another in particular examples of companies is not here attempted. As the seventeenth century drew to a close other reasons for the growth of joint-stock companies began to present themselves. Until 1690 the only joint-stock company with a really large capital had been the East India Company; between the Revolution of 1688 and 1720 several companies came into existence with funds many times greater than the old East India stock. In the formation of the Bank of England, the New and the United East India Companies, and the South Sea Company the joint stock was being used (almost for the first time) to amass huge aggregates of capital which no single capitalist or even small group could bring together. This was not an entirely spontaneous development: the capital raised by these companies was needed not only for financial or commercial operations but also in order that large loans could be made to the state. To satisfy these needs the joint stock was the only possible expedient. The stimulus did not prove to be permanent. After the crash of 1720 the policy of devolving ownership of the national debt upon giant corporations was reversed, and the necessity for joint stocks to undertake this particular function became less acute.

At the same time the joint-stock company had in the course of the seventeenth century shown itself to be an important channel of investment at a time when the existing opportunities for investment were few and not very varied. By the end of the seventeenth century, if not earlier, the potentialities of the joint stock as a vehicle for passive investment had come to be appreciated. Indeed the extraordinary outburst of company promotion between 1690 and 1720 could not have been achieved without the active co-operation of investors who were so hypnotized by the joint-stock that they would subscribe to any project however fantastic and misbegotten. The East India Company, it must be inferred, had generated such confidence in the joint-stock form as only a very severe crisis could break. Not for the last time investors forgot the failures with which the history of the joint-stock company is littered; they forgot, too, or never knew by how narrow a margin the East India Company itself had escaped disaster. It was for reasons such as this that the joint-stock company proliferated in the early years of the eighteenth century until the Bubble crisis and the Bubble Act restored a juster sense of proportion.

3. The Company of Royal Adventurers

The history of English trade in West Africa before the foundation of the company of Royal Adventurers in 1660 can be recounted briefly. Clearly it was of small proportions. Even at its height, in the eighteenth century, the African trade derived its importance not from its absolute volume but from its connexion with the commerce of the West Indies and America. Until 1630 or 1640 this connexion did not exist. No doubt much remains to be learned about the subject, but it is unlikely that these general conclusions will be invalidated.[1] So far as the English were concerned the African trade was probably roughly on a footing with trade to Morocco, and affords similar interesting and picturesque evidence of the broadening of England's commercial interests.

Although there may have been earlier attempts, the first well-documented English voyage to West Africa was in 1553. Then and for several years afterwards expeditions were dispatched which obtained gold, ivory and Guinea pepper or

---

[1] J. W. Blake, 'The Farm of the Guinea Trade', in *Essays in British and Irish History*, shows that material exists for elucidating some of the problems of this early period. It remains doubtful if the results would be commensurate with the effort.

malaguetta. They were financed, not by incorporated companies, but by partnerships and as yet there was no monopoly. The commerce continued in the early years of Elizabeth's reign, and indeed the Queen herself invested in it by the provision of ships.[1] The Portuguese, however, were not easily reconciled to English participation, and it was probably partly as a result of Portuguese discouragements that the promise of the 'fifties and 'sixties remained unfulfilled. The slave-voyages of Hawkins between 1562 and 1569 might have marked the entry of England into a new branch of the African trade; unfortunately for Hawkins his efforts coincided with a more rigorous policy of excluding foreigners from the only American colonies where negroes could be sold, those of Spain. After the disaster of Hawkins' last slave-voyage it is unlikely that English trade to West Africa ceased altogether, but it probably languished.[2] The next important landmark is in 1588 when a charter was issued to the Senegal Adventurers. There were only eight original members and they were not, apparently, incorporated:[3] they received a monopoly of the trade between the Senegal and the Gambia for a term of ten years.

Very little is known of the Senegal Adventurers after the first few years. The trade soon sank once more into an obscurity from which it did not emerge for thirty years, though, again, it is probable that commercial activity did not entirely cease. In 1618 a new company was formed under the name of the Governor and Company of Adventurers of London trading to 'Gynney and Bynney', i.e. to Guinea and Benin, designations which were probably meant to embrace the whole of West Africa. In one form or another this body lasted until the Restoration. It was the first explicitly incorporated company in the African trade; it had thirty-seven original members; and it was granted a monopoly.[4] In 1624 this monopoly was declared a grievance by the House of Commons though, at a time when Parliament was searching for grievances, this does not necessarily testify to its importance.[5] Despite an exhaustive investi-

[1] E. P. Cheyney, *A History of England from the Armada to the Death of Elizabeth*, 1914, I, Ch. xviii.

[2] *Ibid.*, I, p. 418.   [3] Scott, II, p. 10.   [4] *Ibid.*, p. 12.
[5] *Commons Journals*, I, p. 794.

gation of some aspects of the history of this company it is still a little difficult to evaluate its achievements.[1] Both before and after its reconstruction in 1631 it suffered from a shortage of capital, from the competition of interlopers, and from the rivalry of traders of other nations. But it was during the term of this monopoly that the first permanent English establishment was made on the African coast, at Kormantin probably in 1631. Another important achievement was the development of the trade in redwood (used for dye) of Sierra Leone and Sherbro. Gold, the original objective of the company, was not forthcoming in any large quantity, except in 1636 when a single ship brought home £30,000 worth. Scott very properly contrasted this fortunate event with the company's rather dismal record at other times, and inferred from it the uncertain and fluctuating nature of the trade.[2] It is during this period, also, that Englishmen began to engage in the slave-trade in a regular way, and it is probable that the company played some part therein. In the absence of the company's own records, however, knowledge is fragmentary and incomplete. Exactly what were the respective contributions of the company, the private merchants whom it licensed to trade, and the interlopers who infringed its monopoly, to the growth of English interests in the African trade can probably never be discovered.

That the Guinea company, either in the form it assumed in 1631 or in some other, was still in being during the Interregnum is proved not only by the renewal of its monopoly in 1651, but also by evidence of its activity on the Gold Coast in 1649 and 1650. Many years later, in 1686, the Royal African Company was involved in a dispute with Denmark about the land lying near Cape Coast on which both the principal English fort and a Danish fort called Frederixborg then stood. Amongst the documents brought forward by the English were two affidavits sworn by Thomas Crispe in 1655 and 1665.[4] Crispe deposed that in 1649 he was chief factor on the Gold Coast for Rowland Wilson, Maurice Thompson, John Wood and Thomas

---

[1] J. W. Blake, 'The Farm of the Guinea Trade', in *Essays in British and Irish History*.

[2] Scott, II, p. 15.　　　　　[3] *Ibid.*, p. 16.

[4] T. 70/169, fos. 35–6d.

Walter, whom he refers to collectively as the Guinea Company.[1] The English at that time had a factory at Cape Coast, but it consisted only of a native house. At the invitation of the King of Fetu, Crispe went to Cape Coast on 20 April 1650 and received permission to build there. As he understood the transaction he bought the land for goods worth £64, 'whereupon the people gave severall greate shouts, throwing the dust up in the aire and proclaimed that this was Crisp's land'. Four days later a ship arrived in the service of the Queen of Sweden. Despite the promise that none but the English should trade there, the merchant 'Henrick Carliff'[2] promptly obtained leave from the same king to build on the land already promised to Crispe. The English factors were turned out and the Swedes began the building of a castle which, Crispe said in 1655, 'is now in doing'. This was Cabo Corso or Cape Coast Castle which came into English hands a decade later.

The Restoration was a time for new beginnings, and the African trade was taken up with a fresh enthusiasm and unprecedented publicity. Prince Rupert had visited the Gambia in 1652, and it may be that it was through his keenness that so many members of the royal family and Court became interested in the trade. In December 1660 a charter was granted to a company known as the Royal Adventurers into Africa.[3] At first its finances were extremely haphazard; no fixed sum was set for the capital required and subscribers put in as much as they chose. The whole venture was more reminiscent of an aristocratic treasure-hunt than of an organized business: indeed its principal objective was the search for gold.[4] Two years later, however, when the dimensions of the trade had been more accurately taken, better methods of raising money were adopted, and in January 1663 a new charter was obtained. Significantly the slave-trade was mentioned for the first time as an objective of the company. Even after reorganization,

[1] Blake, 'Farm of the Guinea Trade', in *op. cit.*, mentions three of these merchants as prominent in the African trade.

[2] In 1658 Hendrick Carloff, this time with a commission from Denmark, attacked and took Cape Coast from the Swedes; G. F. Zook, *op. cit.*, p. 7.

[3] Printed in C. T. Carr, *op. cit.*, p. 172.

[4] *Ibid.*, pp. 173–9; Donnan, I, No. 48; below, p. 64.

however, the finances were chaotic. The capital eventually subscribed amounted to £120,000, but about one-seventh of this (including £6,000 promised by the King) was never paid.[1] In intention the stock was a terminable one, though of a different kind from the early East India Company. The accounts of each voyage were not, apparently, kept separately but at the end of seven years and thereafter every three years a valuation was to be made of the company's assets and each adventurer entitled to receive the appropriate value of his holding.[2]

The new company's inheritance on the African coast was probably small, but during its tenure of the trade several notable advances were effected, though not all of them were permanent. In 1661 an expedition under Robert Holmes expelled a small settlement of Courlanders from St. André in the mouth of the Gambia. An island in the river, given the name of James Island, was occupied and fortified. Further south, it is probable that some settlement was made by the Royal Adventurers in the region of Sierra Leone and Sherbro; certainly the company traded there. On the Gold Coast the company had Kormantin and was successful in establishing other smaller outposts.[3] From the first, however, the Dutch put every obstacle in the way of English commerce. Between April 1661 and January 1662, although the countries were at peace, six English ships were taken.[4] Recourse to diplomacy proved ineffective and relations between the two nations steadily deteriorated. Nor were the English passive victims of aggression: in 1664 Holmes captured the Dutch settlements at Cape Verde, and later in the same year the castle at Cape Coast and other Dutch possessions on the Gold Coast. Retribution, however, came swiftly. Before commercial rivalry had merged into open war, as it did in 1665, De Ruyter had swept the Gold Coast clear of English settlements, Cape Coast Castle alone excepted.

During the years before the outbreak of war the company had made a promising start in the slave-trade. Although the records are much less complete than for the later Royal African Company, we know that in the seven months beginning August

---

[1] T. 70/76, fos. 25, 25d. [2] Zook, *op. cit.*, p. 17.
[3] *Ibid.*, p. 46. [4] *Ibid.*, p. 36.

1663 there were delivered at Barbados 3,075 negroes.[1] Had this flow been maintained the company would have easily met the needs of the English West Indian colonies. As it was, the war and mounting financial difficulties curtailed supplies and aroused the bitter hostility of the English colonists. Numerous protests against the monopoly of the company were made to the English government and Parliament;[2] for the next forty years the planters (with only occasional instances of wavering) were to be ranged against the policy of a restricted labour-supply. Another cause of the company's unpopularity in the Plantations was its attempt to obtain a share of the trade in negroes to the Spanish colonies. In 1663 a contract was made with the agent of the *Asiento* to supply 3,500 negroes a year.[3] This was an ambitious undertaking which, even without the Dutch war, could have been fulfilled only by starving the English colonies: in the event very few negroes were delivered on this contract. The company had further troubles in the Plantations where great difficulty was experienced in obtaining payment for slaves supplied on credit.

In January 1665, with the Dutch war about to begin, the company was already in financial difficulties. Most of its assets were not realizable: at home apart from its obligations to shareholders it owed £100,000 to creditors.[4] The war put the finishing touch. In 1667 the practice began of selling licences to private individuals to trade within the limits of the monopoly, and for the next five years the greater part of English trade with West Africa was to be in the hands of private persons, though the company retained possession of Cape Coast and may even have re-established some of the factories on the Gold Coast. In the north-western parts of Africa, Gambia, Sierra Leone and Sherbro, the policy of granting licences was set aside: instead there was constituted a kind of daughter-company, known as the Gambia Adventurers. Its capital was £15,000 and it appears that all the shareholders were also members of the parent-body. To this new company was leased the trade of north-west Africa for seven years from 1 January 1669 at a rent of £1,000 a year.[5]

[1] *Ibid.*, p. 82. [2] *Ibid.*, p. 78 ff. [3] *Ibid.*, p. 93.
[4] *Ibid.*, p. 20, n. 44. [5] *Ibid.*, pp. 22–3.

It is impossible to distribute accurately the responsibility for the failure of the Royal Adventurers. Apart from the Dutch war and the losses then sustained, there are grounds for thinking that the company was not very well organized. The peers and courtiers who owned so much of the capital, especially in the early years, were probably inexperienced in business matters. The haphazard growth of the share-capital is one example of mismanagement; another is the contract with the *Asiento*. By 1665 a number of prominent London merchants had entered the company, but any talent they may have possessed came too late to save the Adventurers. The losses in the war were followed by the grant of licences and the formation of the Gambia Adventurers; and in 1670 the discussions began for the reconstruction of the company which matured in schemes for winding it up.[1]

From the ashes of the Royal Adventurers arose the Royal African Company. Its operations, like those of any business connected with the slave-trade, extended over three continents: it would be difficult, therefore, to describe and explain them coherently in their natural, chronological sequence. In the following pages the company's history has accordingly had to be divided into compartments suggested by subject or region. In the opening chapters two aspects are discussed in chronological order, the company's finances and its struggle to retain the monopoly granted in 1672. These are followed by accounts of the company's internal organization and shipping. Its operations in West Africa and the West Indies form the subjects of the remaining chapters. A complete picture of the company between 1672 and 1713 will, therefore, be long in emerging, and for this reason a brief summary is given here.

The primary problem of any African company was a shortage of liquid capital. Although the capitalization of the Royal African Company proceeded on more businesslike lines than that of most earlier joint stocks, the sum raised soon proved unequal to the demands made upon it. The turnover of capital was naturally slow, and was made slower by the necessity of extending long credit to the planters who bought slaves. In addition permanent investment was undertaken in the building

---

[1] Below, pp. 57–9.

of new forts on the West African coast and in the strengthening of old ones. To meet these needs the company was forced to borrow heavily, the interest on the debt becoming in time a major item of expenditure.

The trade itself can be divided roughly into two branches: the purchase of African products such as gold, ivory, dyewood, hides and wax for disposal in England, and the buying of slaves for sale in the West Indies. To carry on these trades on a scale large enough to earn profits, the company needed to export from England goods to the value of about £100,000 a year. In this it never succeeded in the period 1672 to 1713, though in a few years it came close to the mark. The exports themselves were extremely miscellaneous: the greater part consisted of cloth of many kinds, metal goods and firearms, but, in addition to these English manufactures, goods of foreign origin were indispensable constituents of an African cargo. Cheap textiles from the East were re-exported in considerable quantities, as was Swedish iron. Spirits of some kind were also necessary; until the growth of a trade in rum between the West Indies and West Africa, French brandy was commonly included. The task of mobilizing these cargoes and the provision of shipping was a heavy one.

On the African coast the north-western region, Gambia, Sierra Leone and Sherbro, yielded mainly goods for sale in England, though some slaves were obtained. Further south, on the Gold Coast, where most of the company's settlements were located, the trade was chiefly in gold and slaves. East of the Volta, in the Bight of Benin and south to Angola, slaves were the only significant product. The African goods intended for England were, except gold, generally shipped home directly, while the slaves were distributed amongst the English West Indian islands of Barbados, Jamaica, Nevis, St. Christopher's, Antigua and Montserrat, with small consignments to Virginia. In these colonies the company employed agents who saw to the sale of slaves, collected the proceeds and arranged for remittances to England.

Like all monopolies based on the royal prerogative the African Company aroused hostility. It was criticized by English manufacturers for artificially limiting their markets, by the

West Indian colonists for delivering insufficient slaves, and by merchants who wished to trade to Africa themselves. Despite active royal support, it never succeeded in checking infringements of its monopoly by inferlopers who, with lower overhead costs, traded more profitably. The Revolution of 1688 put the company in an extremely vulnerable position, and criticism, hitherto restrained, became open and violent. There was little real likelihood of Parliament's confirming the monopoly, and in 1698 the African trade was thrown open to all on payment of a duty of ten per cent. on exports. This duty was intended to assist the company in meeting the charges of the forts in Africa which Parliament believed were essential to the preservation of English interests. The company's own trade and finances had suffered in the war of 1689–97, and further heavy blows were received in the war of 1702–13. The separate traders or ten per cent. men also suffered, but the more flexible system of competitive enterprise emerged triumphant. In 1712 the ten per cent. Act expired and was not renewed. Henceforth the trade was free to all without restriction and the last vestiges of the company's monopoly were swept away.

From this brief account it will be seen that the company's organizational problems were many. It had to raise money, buy goods, hire ships, recruit men for Africa, build forts, make agreements with natives, negotiate with representatives of other European nations, ward off onslaughts on its monopoly and account for its actions to the Crown and Parliament. These were tasks which would try a modern corporation: the African Company had to face them without modern means of communication.

2

CAPITAL AND FINANCE

1. Credit and Investment

IN the commercial world of Restoration England credit was an accepted feature of the economy with an essential part to play in the lives of all merchants, most manufacturers and many farmers. Medieval prejudices against the taking of interest, if not dead, had been worn away by the forces of economic change. A man proposing to live by money-lending no longer needed to justify himself to any important body of public opinion. But if the idea of credit had by the seventeenth century been partly modernized, the practice was more reminiscent of the later Middle Ages than suggestive of the nineteenth or twentieth centuries. Its principal characteristic was a lack of system and organization. Specialists in the provision of credit had, it is true, made their appearance in London, but in the country at large credit flowed, not along broad and clearly defined channels, but in many small rivulets which seemed to spring from the ground, crossing and recrossing one another before vanishing as mysteriously as they had arisen. Credit remained to a large extent what it had long been, a series of personal and intimate arrangements between borrowers and lenders.

The traditional credit arrangements which the seventeenth century inherited from earlier times, and which it handed on, if not intact at least recognizable, to the eighteenth century, had one obvious defect. The scope, both for giving and getting credit, was limited. Until banks became the normal agency for putting borrowers in touch with lenders, the range of credit operations open to the individual tended to be confined to the

47

circle of his family and to his social and business acquaintances. The merchant borrowed in the first instance from his relatives or friends because they knew of his desire to borrow and his capacity to repay, and he knew of their willingness to lend. Credit was intimate and personal, not only in the sense that borrower and lender dealt directly with one another but also in the sense that they were likely to be friends, associates or kinsmen. In the course of the seventeenth century, however, it is clear that the demand for credit and the capacity to meet that demand were becoming too large and too diverse to be contained within the limits of personal acquaintanceship. The rise of specialists such as the goldsmiths and the scriveners is itself evidence of this. Their functions were to cater for borrowers and lenders, notably the State, whose operations were too big to be fitted into the existing machinery of credit. Nevertheless the traditional solutions to the problem of how to get credit, the loans between neighbours, friends, business acquaintances and relatives, were only impaired; they were not supplanted. They survived, especially in the provinces, to play a critical role in the finances of the Industrial Revolution.

The accepted interpretations of much of the economic history of the centuries before the Industrial Revolution assume a shortage of capital. Whether this is a wholly valid assumption or not (and it must be admitted that 'shortage of capital' is a highly relative term) it would be a fallacy to deduce that capital was so generally and permanently scarce that investors were always able to place their investments where they liked and on terms which they regarded as favourable. In the seventeenth century this was certainly not the case; 'shortage of investment facilities' was at least as marked as 'shortage of capital'.

Investments may be divided into two main classes: *active* investments in which the owner of capital supplies not only the funds but also the time and skill needed for the successful prosecution of the enterprise, and *passive* investments in which the owner of capital supplies only the money and leaves its employment to some other person or body. Both kinds existed in the seventeenth century. The facilities for *active* investment were already extensive and were becoming larger. Although many restrictions on the freedom of merchants and manufacturers still existed, the peak of regulation had been passed. At home new industries were less encumbered than old, and new centres of population less amenable to control than ancient boroughs. In overseas trade the second half of the seventeenth century saw no repetition of earlier attempts at the comprehensive regulation of England's European commerce.

The range of *passive* investments open to the moneyed man, however, was limited, and few of the opportunities that did exist could have been always and entirely satisfactory. The main channels of passive investment may indeed be reduced to six: real property, loans to private persons or to corporations, shipping, deposits with a banker, and shares in a joint-stock company. Other channels existed but were probably negligible.

Investment in property, whether direct in the form of purchase of land or buildings or indirect in the form of loans on the security of real estate, had long been favoured by merchants. The important question of the yield of direct investment in land, as compared to other types of investment, must still be regarded as an open one, but the other attractions, social standing and political influence, are beyond doubt. Many successful merchants are known to have bought country estates, though it is less clear to what extent, having thereby acquired the incidental benefits which landownership conferred, they went on buying land purely as an investment. Landownership for profit can indeed scarcely be regarded as a passive investment; it must have placed greater demands on the time and skill of the practising merchant than he would normally be able to give. Regarded simply as an investment the attraction of land may have lain in its security rather than in the return on capital which it afforded. What is known of the yield suggests that in the seventeenth century it was not much above five per cent., at least in areas within easy reach of London.[1] Those who hoped for better returns had either to look further afield, and perhaps thereby incur greater management difficulties, or to seek an alternative investment. Indirect investment in land through loans on mortgage demanded less personal attention but did not carry with it the incidental attractions of direct ownership.

[1] H. J. Habakkuk, 'The Long-term Rate of Interest and the Price of Land in the Seventeenth Century', in *Ec.H.R.*, 2nd Series, V (1952).

E

During the Restoration period, the yield of mortgages may have been slightly higher than that of direct investment in land but was little different from the interest on loans on personal security.[1] Having regard to security, yield and facilities for disinvestment, it would probably be safe to say that mortgages were amongst the most attractive of the available passive investments.

Answering a different need from investment in land, loans to private individuals on the personal security of bonds had been a feature of English life for centuries. From the Restoration to the Revolution such loans generally carried the statutory maximum rate of interest of six per cent., and in this respect compared favourably with land.[2] Apart from other disadvantages, however, one of the obstacles in the way of making an investment of this kind was the problem of finding a borrower worthy of credit. A prominent merchant could probably expect to find amongst his own acquaintances sufficient would-be borrowers to absorb a good deal of his investible capital, but if large sums were to be invested in this way it might be necessary to look further afield. To some extent the difficulty was overcome by the multiplication of financial intermediaries, scriveners and others, who made it their business to bring together potential borrowers and lenders and charged a fee for their services.[3] Loans on bond, though generally contracted for short terms of three or six months, were commonly renewed for

---

[1] This hypothesis is suggested by the records of the loans on bond and mortgage of Sir William Turner, covering the years 1672 to 1693. In January 1687, for example, he had outstanding loans of £3000 on mortgage and £700 on bond to Sir Arthur Harris; £2500 on mortgage and £1000 on bond to the Earl of Berkeley; £1000 on mortgage to Lady Williams; and other obligations on bond totalling several thousand pounds. All debts, on bond and mortgage alike, were at six per cent. except one (on bond) at 5½ per cent. City of London Guildhall Library, MS. 5105.

[2] Turner MSS. Habakkuk, *op. cit.*, p. 33, n. 3, quotes various authorities suggesting a slightly lower rate.

[3] The juxtaposition of the notions of lending and the payment of a commission for negotiating the loan is illustrated by an Act of 1660, 12 Car. II c. 13. This Act regulated both the rate of interest chargeable, six per cent., and the commission to be charged by scriveners, brokers, scriveners' brokers, etc. for bringing together borrower and lender, one-quarter of one per cent.

further periods or allowed to continue without renewal.[1] Compared to land, therefore, they represent a more flexible type of investment with the advantage of good facilities for rapid disinvestment. Nevertheless loans to private individuals were not without certain drawbacks. The security might become worthless and, if the borrower failed, the loan would probably be lost. On the other hand unexpected and unwanted repayment would oblige the lender to look for a new investment which might mean capital lying temporarily idle. The death of either party might be a source of confusion or loss.

Many of these disadvantages could be avoided or mitigated by lending to corporations. The quality of perpetual succession which the corporation enjoyed was especially desirable for an investor who sought a steady and reliable income over a term of years. For most of the seventeenth century the greatest corporation of all, the State, was not a good enough security to provide a normal channel for the investment of savings, but other corporations attracted a good deal of investible capital. Chief amongst these were the City of London and the livery companies. In the early seventeenth century the City had been more of a lender than a borrower, but after 1640 it was always in debt.[2] Its reputation and seeming security were generally such as to enable it to borrow on very favourable terms: in the year 1680–1, for example, its new loans totalled £14,750 and were all contracted at four per cent., the normal rate which a private borrower had to pay being six.[3] The records of certain livery companies show that they, too, borrowed extensively, partly in order to repair their finances after losses in the Civil War and partly for rebuilding after the Great Fire.[4] These loans were sometimes contracted at rates of interest below the statutory maximum, and from time to time companies such as the Goldsmiths and the Drapers were offered capital sums which private persons were anxious to invest for long periods in

[1] Many of the loans of Sir William Turner (*loc. cit.*) were prolonged for five or ten years. See also *Ec.H.R.*, 2nd Series IV, (1952), pp. 289–90, n. 1.

[2] M. C. Wren, 'The Chamber of London', in *Ec.H.R.*, 2nd Series, I (1948).

[3] City of London Records Office, Chamber Accounts.

[4] For example, the Goldsmiths, Drapers, Mercers, Fishmongers, Merchant Taylors, Girdlers, Blacksmiths, Brewers.

return for an annual income.[1] Joint-stock corporations also, notably the East India and Royal African Companies, were often able to borrow large sums on terms advantageous to themselves.[2] It does not, therefore, seem unreasonable to infer that the pressure of investors on the borrowing capacity of the better-known corporations forced down the rate of interest payable to a level no higher, and in some cases, lower, than the yield of land.

Investment in shipping was facilitated by the practice whereby seagoing vessels were owned by syndicates of four, eight, sixteen or thirty-two partners, each with only a small interest. Thus the total investment made by a single individual might be spread over a number of vessels and rendered more secure. While very high returns might be obtained, shipping, as an investment, appears to have had two disadvantages. In the first place, until marine insurance became more general and more effective than it appears to have been in the seventeenth century, the risk of loss was a real one. Secondly, despite the existence of syndicates and sleeping partnerships, profitable shipowning like profitable landowning must have depended to some extent on personal management. Hirings had to be secured, contracts made, charter-parties drawn up and accounts scrutinized. An investor ignorant of mercantile practice and law might easily be at a disadvantage; he would certainly have to rely on his more active and knowleddgeable partners. Thus while moneyed men other than merchants may have invested in shipping it does not seem probable that they did so in large numbers at this date. It is not unlikely that, when this subject has been more fully investigated, we shall find that most of those who invested in shipping normally risked only a small fraction of their capital.[3]

How far the rise of the specialist bankers influenced the pattern of seventeenth-century investment is not yet clear.

[1] W. S. Prideaux, *Memorials of the Goldsmiths' Company*, 1896, I, p. 245; II, pp. 123, 126, 127, 145; A. H. Johnson, *History of the Worshipful Company of the Drapers of London*, 1914–22, IV, p. 221.

[2] *Ec.H.R.*, 2nd Series, IV (1952), pp. 290–1.

[3] Sir William Turner, while holding shares in five ships, never adventured more than about one-thirtieth or one-fortieth of his total capital in this type of investment. City of London Guildhall Library, MS. 5105.

Some part of the money they handled consisted of temporary deposits made in order to enjoy the benefits of a current account. The practice of making longer-term deposits with goldsmiths was, however, well established and must have appeared to some to be a satisfactory use for idle funds. On the other hand the Stop of the Exchequer in 1672, in which the assets of many who had deposited with bankers were immobilized, may be thought to have made investors more careful. Moreover, the bankers had as yet given no proof that they would turn into institutions with perpetual succession, and for this reason deposits with them were open to some of the same objections as loans to private individuals.

Property, loans on mortgage or bond, shares in shipping and deposits with bankers, these were the conspicuous passive investments of the Restoration period. Together they satisfied the needs of a variety of investors. Each, however, had demerits, chief of which was the low yield of property, mortgages, loans on bond and deposits with bankers. None of these investments commonly returned more than six per cent., and some yielded less. Shipowning might produce a greater return but was risky. There was, therefore, room for a type of passive or semi-passive investment which, while being safer than shipping, might be expected to yield more than loans or land; and this appears to have been the status of the joint-stock share. Dividends on capital invested in joint-stock companies were not subject to the law restricting the maximum rate of interest, and it cannot be doubted that the fall in this legal rate from ten per cent. to eight in 1625 and from eight per cent. to six in 1651 gave some kind of fillip to joint-stock enterprise. Had the Royal African Company, for example, been formed fifty years earlier, its expectations of profit would have had to be of the order of twelve per cent. per annum in order to attract capital away from investments of greater security which yielded ten. In 1672, with the legal rate at six per cent., a company could be floated on much lower expectations. Joint-stock shares were of course open to objection on various grounds, and in the event many of them proved to be neither safe nor profitable. But it seems reasonable to infer that in the years after 1660 some real demand existed for investments of the joint-stock type. It is indeed difficult to explain parts of the history of the African Company, to say nothing of even less profitable ventures, without invoking some such assumption.

The means of satisfying such demand as existed were strictly limited. Few joint-stock companies existed, and there was little competition amongst them for the type of capital that might be invested in them. Of the companies in being in the reign of Charles II, the greatest, the East India Company, far from seeking to increase its share-capital, went to some lengths between 1670 and 1690 to avoid doing so.[1] As a general rule seventeenth-century joint-stock enterprises sought additional share-capital, less in order to finance an expanding trade, and more in order to redeem losses that had already been incurred. The managers of the highly successful East India Company preferred to keep the number of shares as small as possible and thus to maximize the dividends paid to the fortunate shareholders. Additional capital was raised, as required, not by fresh appeals to the public, but by borrowing at fixed rates of interest. No appeal for share-capital was in fact made by the East India Company between 1657 and 1693. Most of the other joint-stock companies of the Restoration were small and the demands which they made on the capital available were not such as to engender shortages. The capital invested by shareholders in the Royal Fishery Company does not appear to have exceeded a few thousand pounds; that of the Hudson's Bay Company was only £10,500; and the majority of the other companies of the Restoration period were on the same, or a smaller, scale.[2] If any demand existed for joint-stock shares, the way was certainly open for a new corporation to take advantage of it.

In a mercantile and financial world as imperfectly formed as that of Restoration London it is idle to search for any barometer which would indicate changes in business prospects and conditions. The term 'money-market' applied to the credit arrangements of the period would still be an anachronism, and capital was subject to stresses and influences other than supply and demand. English governments played no part in the financial life of the City comparable to that which they were to

[1] *Ec.H.R.*, 2nd Series, IV (1952), p. 291.   [2] Scott, III, pp. 470–4.

assume a century or even half a century later. The King borrowed as and where he could, but his credit was not such as to enable him to borrow large sums for long periods at reasonable rates of interest. Consequently no conspicuous investment existed, such as Consols were later to become, in the fluctuations of which the ebb and flow of business prospects might to some extent be mirrored. Any assessment of such highly intangible factors as business prospects or expectations must therefore be tentative.

A few pointers may nevertheless be mentioned which, taken together, perhaps provide some partial explanation of the success with which the Royal African Company was floated in 1672. Three factors in particular may be noticed, all of which have been taken by some historians as tokens of economic buoyancy. In the first place the Great Fire and the immense damage thereby caused, like the war-damage of recent years, set off a boom in public and private building such as can seldom if ever have been paralleled in this country before the nineteenth century.[1] Scores of churches and other public places and thousands of private houses had to be rebuilt, and the resultant demands for materials and labour were unprecedented. Money, some of which may previously have been hoarded, was transferred to the pockets of artisans, labourers and other persons with a strong propensity to spend. Once the immediate dislocation had been overcome something nearer to full employment than was commonly to be found in Restoration London must have existed. The repercussions of this building boom would, of course, be noticeable chiefly in industries producing consumers' goods such as brewing and textiles. But it is not impossible that even in the seventeenth century buoyancy in these industries may have been communicated to other sectors of the economy.

Secondly, the years between 1663 and 1692 contained an abnormally large number of good harvests.[2] There were in particular two long runs of cheap years, from 1664 to 1672 and from 1675 to 1691. The decennial average of the price of wheat

[1] T. F. Reddaway, *The Rebuilding of London after the Great Fire*, 1940.
[2] Thorold Rogers, *A History of Agriculture and Prices in England*, 1887, V, pp. 216–31, 276.

for 1663–72 was the lowest since the first decade of the century, and though higher prices in 1673 and 1674 sent up the average for the 'seventies, it fell again in the 'eighties to the lowest of the century. Good harvests, like heavy building, may have meant fuller employment than was generally the case, with a consequent transfer of spending power from farmers to farmworkers. Since farmers can have been little affected by the various developments of the seventeenth century which helped to mobilize and apply savings to productive purposes, good harvests were probably instrumental in putting into circulation (through wages) money that would otherwise have been idle.

Finally the growth of banking, especially after the Restoration, must have contributed something to the greater mobility of capital. Each citizen who took even a part of his savings from a hole in the floorboards and opened an account with a banker helped to make idle money productive, as did each noble or gentleman who trusted Backwell or Vyner with what would earlier have gone into the iron-bound chest of his ancestors. It does not matter very much whether such deposits were long-term investments or merely temporary: useless funds were being put to work and were helping to make capital more available.

Some doubt has been raised as to whether the tendency of the rate of interest to fall in the seventeenth century may be taken as a cause of economic progress.[1] It is not, however, necessary to regard this falling rate either as a cause or as a symptom of *general* economic progress in order to see the favourable repercussions which it must have had upon joint-stock enterprise. We have already noticed that the fall in the legal rate of interest permitted companies to come into existence which could not be expected to earn more than ten per cent. but which might earn more than six. But the falling rate had an even more direct bearing on company formation. By 1672 it had already become the common practice of joint-stock companies to supplement their share-capital by borrowing large sums on the security of their seals. The Royal African Company soon followed the same policy and, as a borrower, drew important benefits from the low price of money.

[1] H. J. Habakkuk, *op. cit.*, p. 44, favours the view that the falling rate was a cause of economic progress.

These are general considerations, and it would be wrong to attach the same weight to them in the context of the seventeenth century as might be permissible at a later date. They do not, for example, appear to have been instrumental in easing the birth and early career of the Royal Fishery Company formed in 1661, which never succeeded in obtaining all the capital promised to it and seems to have been doomed to failure from the first. Nevertheless they may perhaps be taken as providing at least subsidiary reasons why the reception accorded to the Royal African Company in 1671 and 1672 was more favourable and less discriminating than it might have been thirty or forty years earlier or later.

2. The Formation of the Company

The Company of Royal Adventurers trading to Africa, crippled by losses in the Second Dutch War, by debts, and by the non-payment of subscriptions, had virtually abandoned trade on a joint-stock basis in 1668.[1] During the next four years licences were granted to individuals to trade to Africa and a large and important part of the monopoly was leased to an offshoot of the parent-company, the Gambia Adventurers.[2] The Royal Adventurers were thus reduced to little more than a holding company in which English trade to Africa was formally vested, and they might have continued in this capacity for some time had it not been for the pressure of their creditors. Some £57,000 was owed, and there were no liquid assets available to meet the liability. The government, too, was anxious for the trade to be put upon a proper footing.[3] Under these circumstances the General Court of Adventurers debated in 1670 and in the first half of 1671 how the company's affairs might be redeemed.[4] The first formal proposals for reconstruction were drawn up in May 1671, the intention being to raise a new subscription of at least £100,000 and to continue the trade under the existing charter. Each adventurer was to be credited

---

[1] Scott, II, p. 18, and G. F. Zook, *The Company of Royal Adventurers Trading to Africa.*
[2] Above, p. 43.   [3] T. 70/75, fo. 95.   [4] *Ibid.*, fos. 101, 103, 103d, etc.

in the new stock with ten per cent. of his holding in the old, the other ninety per cent. being written off. Each creditor was to receive one-third of his debt in cash; the remaining two-thirds were to be paid in old stock, which would then be written down to ten per cent. of its nominal value and incorporated in the new stock.[1]

Negotiations with the creditors went forward on this footing in the summer of 1671, and on 11 September fuller proposals were laid before the General Court.[2] The creditors, who were naturally reluctant to agree to this scheme, were told that, if they did not do so, the charter would be surrendered and they would lose all.[3] When the subscription book for the new capital was opened on 10 November 1671 the plan was still to carry on trade under the old charter and to put into effect substantially the proposals of the previous May. A number of the adventurers subscribed under the formula: 'I will make up my present stock'; the implication being that they would put in sufficient cash which, when added to the sum already credited to them, would make up their holdings in the new stock.[4] Before any of this capital could be called up, however, and probably as a result of pressure from the creditors, fresh plans were put forward, adopted, and eventually carried through. The complicated scheme for writing down the old stock and grafting part of the old debt on to the new stock was abandoned. Instead, there was to be a new company which would purchase for the sum of £34,000 all the assets of the Royal Adventurers. With this money the old company was to pay its shareholders 2s. in the £ and its creditors 8s. in the £, both in cash.[5] In all essentials this simplified scheme was carried into effect, and there was thus a more formal break between the two companies than would otherwise have been the case. The Royal African Company had a distinct capital, a new name, and eventually a fresh charter. On the other hand, there was much informal

---

[1] T. 70/75, fos. 110d–111d.   [2] Ibid., fo. 110.   [3] Ibid., fo. 112.
[4] The autographed subscriptions are in T. 70/100.
[5] A copy of the Preamble, setting forth these arrangements, is preserved in the Shaftesbury Papers, Public Record Office, G. D. 24/49, No. 18. Since both Shaftesbury and John Locke were original subscribers to the company, this copy probably belonged to one of them. See also T. 70/100, pp. 1–7.

continuity, the premises, many of the shareholders, and some of the officials of the new company being the same as the old.

The subscription book of the Royal African Company lay open from 10 November to 11 December 1671, in which time two hundred persons underwrote stock to the value of £111,600. Ten of these subscribers paid no part of their subscriptions, and the stock thus vacated was (all but £500) taken up by other persons. In the end, therefore, the company went forward with a subscribed capital of £111,100, the target having thus been exceeded by more than ten per cent. To obtain the promises of owners of capital was, however, not the same as to get their money. In the past, several joint-stock companies, including the Royal Adventurers, had suffered from a cooling of the enthusiasm of their subscribers and had found difficulty in collecting outstanding subscriptions. But, with the exception of the £500 already mentioned, every penny promised to the new company was paid up, though not in all cases by the original subscriber. The intention had been to call up the capital in ten instalments between January and August 1672, but the outbreak of the Third Dutch War in February caused a change of plan. One-twentieth was called in January 1672, one-twentieth and two-tenths at the end of the same year, three-tenths in 1673, and the remaining four-tenths in 1674. This delay was due to the restrictions placed by war upon trade and not to any difficulties in the collection of subscriptions. It says much for the opinion which investors had formed of the prospects of the new company that virtually all of them responded within a few days to each call.[1]

The response made to any appeal for capital depends on many factors, and in considering the formation of the Royal African Company it is possible to identify only a few of them. The company began with a number of advantages of which all investors were aware. It is true that its predecessor, the Royal Adventurers, had been a total failure, but this could plausibly be attributed to the Second Dutch War and the losses thereby sustained, rather than to any inherent defect in either the African trade or the joint-stock form of organiza-

[1] The power to fine those who were late with the payment of their instalments had to be invoked only twice.

tion. The new company was to deal chiefly in negroes, for which there appeared to be an expanding demand in the English colonies. The Royal Adventurers, moreover, had secured a sub-contract for the *Asiento* and thus the promise of entry, albeit indirect, into the Spanish colonial market. African products, mainly gold and ivory, were valuable supplementaries to the negro trade, and sugar, in which remittances from the West Indies were expected to be made, still commanded a reasonable price.[1] The African Company could, therefore, be said to have been formed to meet genuine demands which there was every prospect would continue.

The company, when in being, was to be given a monopoly of the African trade, and so far Charles II had shown no disposition, as his father had, to play fast and loose with the charters of trading corporations. On the contrary there were excellent prospects that the African Company would be favoured by the Court, for the Duke of York, several ministers and a number of prominent courtiers were known to be interested in it. This promise was amply fulfilled. Throughout his reign Charles supported the company wholeheartedly, and it was to suffer not from lack of royal favour but, after the Revolution of 1688, from being too closely identified with and dependent on the royal cause. In 1671, however, such fears were distant.

These expectations were probably uppermost in the minds of those who subscribed to African stock in November and December 1671. But there were other considerations, both favourable and unfavourable, which should not be overlooked. The national finances were in a deplorable state. Revenue had been anticipated to such an extent that, even with French subsidies, provision for the coming war against Holland was inadequate. Within a few days of the closing of the company's subscription book and before any money had been paid in, the Stop of the Exchequer was ordered and a large current debt owed chiefly to goldsmith bankers was immobilized. The effects of this action on the world of business and finance are debatable; they do not, on the whole, appear to have been as serious

[1] At the first sales of sugar held by the company in 1674 prices were about 24–25*s*. per 100 lb. They fell fairly steadily until 1687.

as was once thought. Charles did not repudiate the debt; he declared his inability for the time being to pay interest on it or to repay any part of the principal. Some people undoubtedly were hard hit, chiefly men and women who had made deposits with the goldsmiths, and whose money, possibly unknown to themselves, had been lent to the Crown. Amongst them the Stop of the Exchequer may well have produced a reluctance to invest in any project of a partly speculative nature. But the wider psychological effects of the Stop, which in the eighteenth or nineteenth centuries would have been of greater moment than the direct consequences, were not apparently conspicuous. The bad state of the Crown's finances was well known, and the Stop cannot have come as a complete surprise to the City. However this may be, so far as the African Company was concerned, the Stop had no visible results and very few of those who had underwritten stock in 1671 defaulted in the following year.

The prospects of the new company were at least as closely connected with foreign affairs as they were with economic trends, and here a situation of unusual complexity confronted the investor. The facts were not only difficult to interpret, but to many were unknown. In 1671 English foreign policy was regulated by the 'secret' treaty of Dover by which Charles II had undertaken, in return for cash, to join France in an attack upon the United Provinces and, in his own time, to declare himself a Catholic. Such a policy would clearly have important consequences for a company trading to Africa, for the Dutch were more strongly entrenched on the Gold Coast than any other European power. The Second Dutch War had been very largely the product of Anglo-Dutch rivalry in West Africa, and its outcome had been fatal to the company of Royal Adventurers. We had, in Pepys' phrase, been 'beaten to dirt . . . to the utter ruine of our Royall Company'.[1] Africa played no significant part in the events leading up to the Third Dutch War of 1672–4, but it must nevertheless have appeared certain that a renewal of hostilities in Europe would have important effects on the Gold Coast. Whether these repercussions would follow the same course as in 1665 was a matter for specu-

[1] *Diary*, ed. H. B. Wheatley, IV, pp. 312–13.

lation. There was some hope that they would not. For the greater part of the Second Dutch War, France had been the not entirely passive ally of the United Provinces. If war should come again, and Charles was deeply committed to it, this situation would no longer obtain; on the contrary France would lead the assault and England would follow. If the Dutch could be contained in Europe by the navies of the aggressors, there might be rich pickings in Africa.

Some such interpretation of the foreign situation in the second half of 1671 may have occurred to those who were in the secret. In the months that followed the signing of the treaty of Dover, England's contract to fight became known to an increasing number of people connected with the Court.[1] By the time that the African Company's subscription book opened on 10 November 1671 all the chief ministers and a good many others, secretaries, relatives and dependants, must have been fully aware that England was being led into war. It is therefore not without interest to find that a number of persons who knew of the secret treaty subscribed to African stock. Foremost amongst them were Clifford, Arlington, Buckingham and Ashley, four of the five ministers who formed the Cabal. To them may be added the Duke of York, Prince Rupert, Sir William Coventry and Sir Joseph Williamson. There were others who through connexions at Court or friendship with a minister may have known that war was probable: John Locke, Sir George Carteret, Sir Peter Colleton, the Earl of Craven and Thomas Povey had all been associated with Ashley in his earlier colonial schemes.[2] Others, Lord Hawley, Lawrence du Puy and Mathew Wren, were close to the Duke of York. All these men subscribed to African stock, and most, if not all, understood the risk.

The majority of investors, however, had only rumour and gossip to help them. Already the signs were pointing to war. In the summer of 1671 the war-party amongst Charles' ministers was gaining the upper hand; French influence at Court was growing; and in July 1671 Sir William Temple was recalled

---

[1] K. Feiling, *British Foreign Policy, 1660–1672*, 1930, pp. 311–15.

[2] L. F. Brown, *First Earl of Shaftesbury*, American Historical Association, 1933, pp. 130, 151–2.

from The Hague to be replaced by Downing whose hostility towards the Dutch was well known.[1] When the war would begin, how it would be fought, and above all what effects it would have on the African Company, were questions which must have occurred to would-be investors but to which no answer could be given. On the whole optimism was probably the prevalent mood, for it is difficult otherwise to explain why, floated under the shadow of war, the subscription to the African Company should have been as successful as it was.

In the event, the Third Dutch War fulfilled neither the hopes nor the fears of any who may have considered its effects on the African Company. For England it went badly, and we were glad to escape from it in February 1674. If anyone reaped rewards in Africa, it was not the English but the French, who succeeded in expelling the Dutch from Goree in 1677. While England was engaged in the war the African Company wisely abstained from active trading operations. Little more than half the capital was called up until peace had been signed and few ships were sent out until the end of 1673. Charles' foreign policy, dishonourable, furtive and vacillating as it was, proved no bad thing for trade. From 1674 until 1678 England enjoyed the rare experience of neutrality while her chief colonial and commercial rivals fought one another. During these years English trading interests were extended and consolidated,[2] and in Africa the company was able to begin its operations under favourable circumstances. So far as dividends were concerned, the months immediately preceding the Franco-Dutch treaty of Nymwegen in 1678 were the best in its history.

3. The Shareholders

The owners of the capital of the Royal African Company were on the whole better qualified to assess business prospects than to forecast political events. They contrast sharply with those who had been concerned in the first of the Restoration African Companies. More than half of the thirty-two bene-

---

[1] Feiling, *op. cit.*, p. 329.
[2] Suggested by the rising yield of Customs duties.

ficiaries of the charter granted to the Royal Adventurers in 1660 were peers or members of the Royal family.[1] They included the Duke of York, the Princesses Maria and Henrietta, Prince Rupert, the Dukes of Albemarle and Buckingham, and the Earls of Bath, Ossory, Pembroke, St. Albans and Sandwich. The second charter of 1663 had brought some changes of personnel, but there were still twenty shareholders of the rank of peer or above, and as late as 1667 a list of the Adventurers shows that, against forty-nine untitled shareholders, there were the King and Queen, one prince, four dukes, eight earls and seven barons.[2] Amongst the commoners who invested in this company were some of the greatest mercantile figures of Restoration London, Sir Robert Vyner, Edward Backwell, Sir John Robinson, Sir Philip Frowd and Sir Andrew Riccard. But their knowledge of business came too late to save the company, and probably all of them lost money by its failure.

By 1672 the enthusiasm of the Court and the peerage for investment in the African trade had sensibly cooled, and in the new company the mercantile element was from the first predominant both in the provision of capital and in the conduct of business. The Company of Royal Adventurers was not the last such body to be 'top heavy with titles', and in 1675 an anonymous memorialist wrote with satisfaction of the change: 'The English Company now consisteth of most merchants, that conduct the company businesse better and will most certainly comply with any contract they make.'[3] Nevertheless, the shareholders of the Royal African Company included a number of very prominent ministers and courtiers, amongst them Shaftesbury and Arlington. Such men were obviously assets of great value to a company in process of formation. They could expedite the grant of the charter and their presence as shareholders advertised the good prospects of the stock. But once a company was well-established they were of less consequence, for they were generally unable or unwilling to give time to the

---

[1] C. T. Carr, *Select Charters of Trading Companies* (Selden Society), pp. 172–7.
[2] Donnan, I, No. 48.
[3] Brit. Mus., Egerton MS. 2395, fo. 501.

day-to-day problems of management.[1] After the first few years of the African Company's existence the number of prominent politicians and men of affairs amongst its shareholders became steadily smaller. In the twenty years after 1672 a total of fifteen peers and other persons of note were associated with it, though not all at the same time. A few, the Earl of Bath, Sir William Coventry, Prince Rupert and Lord Hawley, withdrew .before the capital had been fully paid up. Death removed Clifford in 1673 and Buckingham in 1687. Shaftesbury sold out in 1677, Arlington in 1679, Sir Joseph Williamson in 1687 and Lord Berkeley in 1688.[2] By the Revolution only three such persons remained, King James, who sold his stock in 1689, the Earl of Craven and Lord Powis, neither of the last two being large investors.[3] No one of comparable calibre or distinction was recruited, and African stock passed steadily out of the hands of the aristocracy and the Court into the hands of the mercantile community. The aggregate capital invested by these distinguished men was, apart from James' £3,000, small, and at no time after 1674 can it have amounted to more than six or seven per cent. of the stock.

Below this group of prominent persons, and often associated with it, came such men as Sir George Carteret, Sir Peter Colleton, Thomas Povey, John Locke, Sir Edmund Andros and Ferdinando Gorges. Apart from Povey none of these was a merchant, but all had interests or experience in the colonies. Colleton owned a large plantation in Barbados; Andros was a former governor of New York; Locke's interest in colonies and colonial constitutions is well known; Gorges came from a family with estates in New England; Carteret was a Lord Proprietor of Carolina and a member of the Committee of Trade and Plantations.[4] With them may be mentioned courtiers and

[1] For example, Sir Joseph Williamson, Secretary of State, a member of the Court of Assistants in 1676–1677–1678, attended only nine of 253 meetings held in those years. Lord Falconberg, an Assistant in 1677, 1682 and 1683, attended only eighteen out of the 215 meetings.

[2] Clifford held £400 of stock, Buckingham £500, Shaftesbury varying amounts between £600 and £1600, Arlington £500, Williamson £500 and Berkeley varying amounts between £400 and £1,600.

[3] James' stock was £3,000, Craven's £600 and Powis' £100.

[4] Locke held £400 of stock and sold in 1675; Colleton £1000, reduced to £400 in 1683; Gorges £1,000, sold in 1679; Carteret £500.

F

dependants such as Tobias Rustat,[1] Yeoman of the Wardrobe, Lawrence du Puy, the Keeper of the Mall, William Ashburnham, Cofferer of the Household, Mathew Wren, secretary to the Duke of York, and Eusebius Mathews. This group, like its patrons, diminished through death or withdrawal. Most of their holdings were small and altogether they accounted for no more than about five per cent. of the total capital of the African Company.

A few holders of minor civil offices, a few widows, and a small number of country gentlemen complete the non-mercantile element in the stock. Among the officials were a Controller of Prizes, a Cashier to the Customs and two revenue officers. The widows were for the most part relicts who had inherited holdings of African stock from deceased merchants; their number increased over the years and by 1688 fifteen of them were shareholders. Amongst the country gentlemen, Sir John Lowther of Lowther, Sir John Lowther of Whitehaven, Sir Anthony Craven of Buckinghamshire, Broom Whorwood of Oxfordshire, George Garth of Surrey and Francis Farnaby of Kent are the most easily identified. None of the gentlemen and few of the widows owned as much as £1,000 of stock, and in aggregate their investments were of small significance. The ownership of African stock was continually changing hands, but it is safe to assume that all the shareholders from outside the business world, ministers of the Crown, peers, courtiers, officials, widows, and gentry, at no time held more than about one-quarter of African stock.[2]

The remainder of the stock belonged to men who, if not 'merchants' within the traditional definition of the term, made their livings by buying and selling, importing and exporting, banking and moneylending. In a mercantile community such as that of Restoration London these functions were still largely performed by non-specialists: bankers dealt in commodities and merchants were money-lenders. A rigid classification of the business element in the African Company's stock would not therefore be meaningful. All that can be attempted is an in-

---

[1] The benefactor of Jesus College, Cambridge; his stock was £400.

[2] It has proved impossible to identify a small number of shareholders, but insufficient materially to affect this conclusion.

dication of the business activities for which some of the company's shareholders were best known. Foremost amongst these activities was overseas trade, and 'merchants' in the sense of exporters and importers were the backbone of the company. More than one-fifth of the shareholders in 1675 were practising members of the Levant Company; they held nearly a quarter of African stock.[1] Another prominent group was made up of merchants trading to the Baltic and North Germany. They included Sir John Lethuillier, Governor of the Merchant Adventurers in 1676,[2] Peter Joye, importer of metals and timber and contractor to the Admiralty,[3] John Morice, Thomas Westerne the ironmonger, and Thomas Vernon. Colonial, and especially West Indian, merchants were represented by John Gardiner, afterwards an active enemy of the company, Thomas Ducke, Mark Mortimer, Jacob Lucy and John Hill.[4] So far as can be ascertained investors known chiefly for their activity in overseas trade held more than half the company's capital, the part played by the Levant merchants being particularly remarkable. It is well known that the formation of the East India Company in 1600 owed much to Turkey merchants, and, while their part in the establishment of the African Company was less direct, it was just as real. The Levant trade ranked high in the overseas commerce of Restoration London,[5] and was still able to fertilize other branches of England's trade.

Beyond and above these practising merchants were the great figures of the City, elder-merchants with fortunes derived mainly from trade, bankers and revenue-farmers, who formed the mercantile aristocracy of the day. Upon them the African Company leaned heavily not only for its capital but also for the management of its affairs. Fifteen of the Lord Mayors of London between the Restoration and the Revolution, and twenty-five of the Sheriffs were shareholders in the company, as were thirty-eight of the men elected or appointed aldermen

[1] *Ec.H.R.*, 2nd Series, IV (1952), p. 299.
[2] Public Record Office, C.8/270/50.
[3] J. Ehrman, *The Navy in the War of William III*, 1953, pp. 61–2.
[4] For John Gardiner see *T.R.H.S.*, 5th Series, II (1952), pp. 105–6.
[5] In 1668–9 a table of London's imports and exports of English products placed Turkey fourth in importance. Brit. Mus., Add. MSS. 36785.

between 1672 and 1690.[1] Such notable figures as Sir John
Banks, Sir Josiah Childe, Sir John Moore, Sir Gabriel Roberts,
Sir Samuel Dashwood, Sir Robert Clayton, and Sir William
Prichard[2] gave the company a more solid backing than the
ephemeral enthusiasms of a Shaftesbury or an Arlington.
Some, like Sir William Turner, were retired merchants who
lived on their investments and had time for City politics and
company-management.[3] Others like Clayton were still in the
full flood of fortune-making.[4] They came and went, and increased and decreased their holdings of stock, but at least until
the Revolution the number of prominent City men in the company was maintained. And, even after the Revolution, there
were still some to be found amongst the shareholders and
managers.[5]

The presence in the stock, and especially in the management,
of notable mercantile figures such as these was calculated to
inspire confidence in others and helped the company to appear
a better prospect than in fact it was. The individual holdings
of such men, though in aggregate amounting to a large proportion of the total capital of the company, were seldom large;
few owned as much as £2,000 of stock which, by comparison
with some of the giant holdings of East India stock, must be
accounted small.[6] The modest size of the holdings of even the
wealthiest members of the African Company gives some indi-

---

[1] From A. B. Beaven, *Aldermen of the City of London*, 1908–13.

[2] Banks: banker, landowner, Governor E.I. Co. Childe: the greatest
shareholder and personality in E.I. Co. in 1680's and 1690's. Moore: Lord
Mayor 1681–2, M.P. London 1685, Director E.I. Co. Roberts: Director
E.I. Co., Deputy-Governor Levant Co. S. Dashwood: M.P. London, Com-
mnr. of Excise, Director E.I. Co., Asst. Levant Co. Clayton: the great
scrivener, M.P. London, Lord Mayor, Director Bank of England. Prichard:
Lord Mayor 1682–3, M.P. London, Director E.I. Co. See below, p. 159,
n. 1, and p. 160, n. 1, for other distinguished figures of the City of London
who were associated with the African Company.

[3] City of London Guildhall Library, MS. 5105.

[4] D. C. Coleman, 'London Scriveners and the Estate Market in the later
Seventeenth Century', in *Ec.H.R.*, 2nd Series, IV (1951), p. 222.

[5] For example, Davenant's discussion of the company's Court of Assistants in *Works* (1771), V, pp. 264–9.

[6] For the large holdings in the East India Company see *Ec.H.R.*, 2nd
Series, IV (1952), pp. 296–7.

cation of how such experienced merchants and financiers viewed its prospects. Neither in 1671 nor at any time thereafter did they plunge into African stock. Until the quadrupling of the capital in 1691 a majority of all shareholders held £400 of stock or less, and the bulk of the capital was owned by men and women whose individual holdings were under £1,000. In 1675 only fourteen out of more than two hundred owned more than £1,000 and in 1688 only four held more than £2,000. The attitude of the investor in African stock may therefore be described as cautious optimism. While many were prepared to risk small investments, few or none would stake large sums. Experience was to show that this assessment was sound.

With this purely mercantile element in the company's stock may be joined such men as Benjamin Newland who bought goods at the company's sales, John Gourney, Thomas Aldworth, Thomas Nichols and Peter Proby who supplied it with goods for export and may be described as wholesalers, Sir Humphrey Edwin, company promoter,[1] Sir John Buckworth, a commissioner of the Mint,[2] and Sir George Waterman, the City Auditor. All these, if not 'merchants', were members of the business community of London. Harbingers of a new feature in English social life were Sir William Langhorne, Sir Jeremy Sambrooke and Streynsham Master, who on their return from service in India invested part of the proceeds in African stock. They were not 'nabobs' by eighteenth-century standards, but Sambrooke had £18,000 in East India stock and £700 in African, and Langhorne £19,000 in the former and £4,000 in the latter. At the market prices prevailing just before the Revolution these investments must have been worth about £40,000 and £50,000 respectively. The investments of retired servants of the African Company itself, Abraham Holditch and Henry Nurse, former Agents at Cape Coast, and Alexander Cleeve, former Agent in the Gambia, were on a more modest scale.

The picture of the African company's shareholders that emerges from this enquiry suggests that at least two-thirds of the capital and probably more was in the hands of business

[1] Roger North, *Lives of the Norths*, ed. A. Jessopp, 1826, III, p. 203.
[2] Sir J. Craig, *The Mint*, 1953, pp. 176–7.

men, of whom the majority were or had been overseas traders. The part played by ministers of the Crown, courtiers and other non-mercantile elements appears to have been more spectacular than substantial. Only in a small way can the company be said to have mobilized capital which would otherwise have been excluded from foreign trade. Rather it drew capital out of older established branches of England's commerce and applied it to a trade that was still undeveloped.

The terms upon which African stock was issued were set forth in a Preamble or prospectus, printed at the end of 1671.[1] A penalty was imposed of two per cent. per month on subscriptions unpaid after the date at which they were called; this had to be imposed only twice. Any member who defrauded the company or traded to Africa on his own account was liable to forfeit his entire stock or to pay such fine as the General Court should determine. The stock of each shareholder was also made liable for debts owing to the company. A dividend of twenty per cent. was to be declared 'if it shall please God at any time the stock shall be augmented fifty per cent.', and all dividends were to be paid in cash. Apart from the article restricting dividends, which proved difficult to interpret, the terms of the Preamble were generally observed in the first twenty or thirty years of the company's history, including those concerning the liability of the stock for the debts of individual shareholders. In 1676, for example, Samuel Sambrooke was refused permission to transfer any part of his stock until he had given the company satisfaction for goods he was alleged to have embezzled.[2] In 1677 William Walker's stock and accrued dividend were detained on suspicion that he had been concerned with interloping,[3] and in 1678 Captain Abraham Holditch's stock was immobilized for the same reason.[4] Similar practices obtained in the East India Company, holdings of stock being regarded as pledges for the good behaviour of members.[5] Many shareholders had separate business relationships with these companies either as buyers or sellers, and their accounts for stock and goods, though kept separately, were not

---

[1] Above, p. 58,   n. 5.   [2] T. 70/76, fos. 71d, 72, 84.
[3] T. 70/77, fos. 34, 43d.   [4] Ibid., fo. 77.
[5] Calendar of Court Minutes, 1664–1667, p. 133, n. 1; 1668–1670, pp. 71, 313.

regarded as entirely distinct. Thus, when the East India Company declared a dividend, shareholders who were indebted to it received, instead of a cash payment, credit for the appropriate sum,[1] and before the Court of Assistants approved a transfer of African stock the accountant had to state all accounts depending between the company and the shareholder concerned.[2] Even in these comparatively large companies the notion of the shareholder as an anonymous provider of capital was a long way off.

Apart from the questions of indebtedness to the company or infringements of its monopoly, there were few restrictions on the transfer of stock. Purchasers were required to take the oath of fidelity, and the approval of the Court of Assistants was needed before a transfer could be registered. Both parties to a transfer were required to sign in a book kept by the company's accountant, and proxies were accepted only in exceptional circumstances, as when James II transferred his stock by deed of assignment dated at St. Germain on 10 January 1689.[3] It is possible, however, that these formalities were not observed in every instance and that stock passed through several hands between the registered vendor and the registered purchaser. Holdings were certainly used as collateral securities without notification to the company.[4] Such transactions cannot be computed, but the volume of transfers actually registered is surprisingly high and suggests an active market in the stock from the beginning.[5] Between 1672 and 1690 the equivalent

---

[1] *Calendar of Court Minutes, 1660–1663*, p. 320; *1664–1667*, p. 130.

[2] T. 70/76, fo. 49.   [3] T. 70/187, between fos. 33 and 34.

[4] T. 70/76, fo. 14d. For the use of East India stock in this way, Maidstone Record Office, Aylesford MSS., Journal C of Sir John Banks, account of East India stock, 24 March 1675/6. For shares passing through several hands at a later date, see *The Villainy of Stock-Jobbers Detected* (1705).

[5] *Transfers of Stock in the Royal African Company 1672–1691*

1672	£18,700	1680	£11,400
1673	£11,300	1681	£20,250
1674	£13,500	1682	£15,600
1675	£24,500	1683	£14,900
1676	£19,800	1684	£18,600
1677	£17,800	1685	£9,250
1678	£12,350	1686	£15,550
1679	£9,900	1687	£22,850

of the whole capital changed hands three times, and after 1690 the turnover was much faster. A substantial proportion of these transfers concerned a fairly small number of investors who, it seems, raised or lowered their holdings in accordance with their expectations of short-run changes. John Bull, for example, was an original subscriber for £500; he bought a further £400 in 1674 and sold his entire holding in the next eight months. He bought again in 1675 and 1676 only to resell immediately. From 1679 to 1685 he engaged in similar transactions. Altogether he was concerned in thirty-eight transfers. There were several other investors, the Earl of Berkeley, John Cudworth, Nicholas Hayward and Thomas Hall, who manipulated their holdings in the same way.

The price at which African stock changed hands is extremely difficult to discover until the publication of newspaper quotations after the Revolution. The highest price found is 191 in January 1689, and the lowest 125 in April 1677,[1] and it is unlikely that the price went far outside this range until 1690. That the stock should have sold at a premium at all is sufficiently remarkable. The record of dividend payments shows that in the first twenty years of its existence the company paid an annual average of about seven per cent. Dividends were paid in guineas and the aggregate return to shareholders was

1688	£22,800	1690	£10,400
1689	£22,500	1691 to 30 July £82,350	
		1691 from 1 August (in the quadrupled stock) £261,550.	

Compiled from the Transfer Books and Journals T. 70/185–8.

[1] The only reliable prices of African stock that have so far come to hand for the period 1672–92 are as follows:

Sept. 1674	130	Oct. 1677	170–6	July 1681	136
April 1677	125	July 1678	148–50	Jan. 1689	191
June 1677	125–6	July 1680	150	June 1689	173
Sept. 1677	145	July 1680	132		

The first eight quotations are from City of London Guildhall Library, MS. 5105; the next from Maidstone Record Office, Aylesford MSS, Journal C of Sir John Banks; the last two from T. 70/101, fo. 24d. and *Whiston's Merchant's Weekly Remembrancer*, 17 June 1689.

132 guineas or £142$\frac{3}{20}$ per cent.[1] This must be regarded as a poor yield from an investment which was more than a little speculative. The fall in the yield of securities of other kinds between 1670 and 1689, though noticeable, does not seem great enough to warrant prices of 140 or 150 such as were paid for African stock. No dividend was declared until September 1676; the four dividends of ten guineas per cent. paid between that date and December 1677 sent the price of the stock up to 170. This high level was not maintained, but even so the quotations that are available suggest that it was never below par and usually well above it.

These inflated prices of the company's stock were in part artificial; to some extent they testify to the imperfections of the contemporary market for shares. Few companies existed, too few to provide facilities for all who wished to invest, and investors in African stock appear to have been over-optimistic about the possibilities of future dividends and capital appreciation. The latter was certainly an important consideration affecting joint-stock investment at this time. Successful manipulations of purchases and sales of East India stock could probably bring greater returns than were paid in dividends and even in African stock there were windfall profits to be made.

[1] The complete list of dividends paid by the company is as follows:

21 September	1676	10 guineas per cent.		
20 December	1676	10	do.	do.
20 July	1677	10	do.	do.
15 December	1677	10	do.	do.
31 January	1679	10	do.	do.
15 July	1680	10	do.	do.
30 August	1681	10	do.	do.
3 September	1685	10	do.	do.
9 November	1686	10	do.	do.
9 August	1687	10	do.	do.
18 September	1688	10	do.	do.
28 April	1691	10	do.	do.
4 October	1692	3	do.	do. (on the quadrupled

stock, equivalent to 12 guineas per cent. on the original.)

The date is the date on which the warrants for payments were pased by the Court of Assistants. In the first dividend the guinea was valued at 22s., in all others at 21s. 6d. Compiled from T. 70/77–83.

All the original subscribers to the African company who sold their holdings before 1691 must have made satisfactory if not spectacular profits as a result of capital appreciation. James II, for example, held fully paid-up stock of £3,000; he received in dividends £3,480 and sold for about £5,730. Thus his total profit was £6,210 spread over seventeen years, the equivalent of an annual return of twelve per cent. There were others in the same happy position. It is, however, important to notice that even in the 'prosperous' period of the company's history from 1672 to 1691 it was capital appreciation alone that hoisted the profits on a holding of African stock well above the yield of other and more secure investments, and that this capital appreciation lowered the yield to all except the original subscribers. The losers were those who bought stock above par and held on after 1691; their capital losses, as will presently be shown, easily cancelled out any dividends they may have received.

4. *The Growth of the Debt 1675–1692*

The capital of £111,100 swiftly proved insufficient for the needs of the company. The Royal Adventurers had been promised £34,000 for the surrender of their charter and assets, and they were paid £29,000, the remainder being withheld on the grounds that some subscribers to the old company had never fully paid up on their stock and were therefore not entitled to be bought out.[1] After buying out the Adventurers, therefore, the African Company was left with only £82,100 to meet all expenses. This was inadequate, not so much for the reason given by Scott that the company had to sink most of its capital in the re-establishment of forts and factories, though some expenditure was incurred under this heading;[2] more important was the need, if the company was to supply the Plantations with sufficient negroes, to spend about £100,000 a year on goods to be sent to Africa. As will be seen in a later chapter, the company achieved this volume of exports only once, in 1723, but between 1680 and 1688 it dispatched trading goods worth on average £68,000 a year.[3] Thus the equivalent of

---

[1] T. 70/76, fos. 18, 25, 25d.   [2] Scott, I, p. 303.   [3] Appendix I.

nearly the whole capital was exported annually. On top of this the company had to meet very heavy freight charges, maintain its forts and factories in Africa, pay salaries and wages both at home and abroad, and defray various other charges. Each of these items of expenditure will be considered separately in later chapters, but it may be noted here that the company spent £20–£25,000 a year on hired ships alone.[1] Thus in the later 'seventies and in the 'eighties the company spent each year on the purchase of goods for export and on shipping a sum appreciably larger than what was left of its share-capital after the Adventurers had been bought out.

It might have been possible to carry on a short-distance trade of such dimensions with the attenuated resources at the company's disposal. But the turnover of capital in the African trade was exceedingly slow. This was due partly to the length of the voyage and partly to the time which had to be spent on the African coast.[2] But most of all it was due to the necessity of extending credit, sometimes for years, to the purchasers of the end-product of the slave-trade.[3] A large debt owed by the West Indian planters had been inherited from the Royal Adventurers, and by 1690 this had so far increased that the company was owed in Barbados, Jamaica and the Leewards no less than £170,000 and could justly claim that the equivalent of its whole capital and more was locked up in the colonies.[4] Even if all these Plantation debts had proved good, which many did not, the consequence of giving long credit was to slow down the turnover of capital until a gap often of years intervened between the sowing of the seed, in the form of exports to Africa, and the reaping of the harvest, in the shape of returns from the West Indies.

Whether this under-capitalization was accidental or involuntary or deliberate it is impossible to say. It may be that the heavy costs of freight and the necessity of piling up credits in the West Indies were not foreseen, though the Royal Adventurers had experienced both. It may be that no more capital could be obtained in 1671 than the sum actually raised: the subscription book lay open for a month and all who wanted to

---

[1] Below, p. 204.   [2] Below, pp. 186–8.   [3] Below, pp. 318–19.
[4] T. 70/101, 14 January 1691.

invest must have had the opportunity to do so. On the other hand the advertised target had been only £100,000, and this had been exceeded. It is even possible that the issued share-capital was deliberately kept at a minimum in order to concentrate profits in as few hands as possible. If so, it was done on two assumptions, one of which proved correct and one of which did not. The first was that the African Company would be able to borrow as much money as it needed at a fixed and reasonable rate of interest in order to supplement the share-capital. The second was that profits could be made out of the African trade large enough to liquidate or at least to service the debts thus contracted, leaving the remainder of the earnings to be distributed amongst a comparatively small number of ordinary shareholders. These assumptions were certainly implicit in the policy of the directors of the East India Company in the 'eighties of the seventeenth century; they could easily have taken up more capital by the issue of fresh stock but instead they resisted, as long as they were able, the public demand that they should do so. The East India Company, however, had a capacity to earn large profits which had been proved, while the African Company was still untested. There is no evidence to suggest that limitations were imposed on subscriptions to African stock or that additional contributions would not have been welcomed had they been forthcoming. On the whole it seems likely that the target of £100,000 was set in the belief that the trade would be lucrative enough to manufacture fresh capital out of undistributed profits.

Borrowing began in 1675, only six months after the last instalment of the subscribed capital had been called up and little more than a year after the company had begun active trading. In three months £10,000 was taken up on the security of the company's bonds at six per cent. interest.[1] In form and probably in intention this borrowing was short-term, three or six months being the periods for which the loans were contracted. Little difficulty, however, was experienced in persuading lenders to renew their bonds; money for those who were unwilling to do so was found by the contraction of new debts. Long before the initial debt of £10,000 had been

[1] T. 70/76, fo. 35d.

liquidated, more bonds had been issued. As the company's commitments became clearer and its trade expanded the debt steadily increased, a process facilitated by the reduction in the rate of interest payable from six per cent. to five in 1677.[1] Five per cent. was the ruling rate until January 1683 when six had once more to be paid on new and existing debts.[2] In June of the same year the rate returned to five, only to rise once more to six in January 1684.[3] In 1685 the cheaper rate was restored and continued until after the Revolution.[4]

In 1675 £12,300 was borrowed, in 1676 £18,850, in 1678 £26,850; by 1682 and 1683 the yearly totals of new debts had reached £48,565 and £50,947.[5] Periodic efforts were made to curtail borrowing, but with little success. Much of the money thus borrowed was provided by shareholders, particularly in years when the rate of interest paid by the company appears to have compared favourably with the yield of comparable securities. Thus in the years 1675–7, when the company was paying six per cent., members of the Court of Assistants provided £32,100 and other shareholders £6,650 of the £51,650 borrowed. Later on, the debt owed to outsiders increased, but until the Revolution about half the total sums taken up were from persons already financially concerned in the company.

Though bonds were periodically redeemed the process of repayment was never fast enough to get rid of the incubus of debt which grew alarmingly in the early 'eighties until the interest upon it was transformed from an insignificant sum into a major item of the company's expenditure. The following figures show the annual debt-charges in various years between 1678 and 1693:

1678	£1,095	1687	£4,665
1679	£1,630	1688	£6,238
1680	£1,010		
		1692	£9,204
1682	£2,383	1693	£9,428[6]
1683	£4,094		
1684	£5,965		

[1] T. 70/77, fo. 31d. [2] T. 70/80, fo. 9. [3] *Ibid.*, fos. 24, 47.
[4] T. 70/81, fos. 12, 41.
[5] Totals compiled from the company's Cash Books, T. 70/216–20.
[6] Compiled from the company's General Home Ledgers, T. 70/601–8.

Thus, soon after the Revolution, the company had accumulated a debt on which the annual charge was the equivalent of a dividend of eight or nine per cent. And this liability had grown up, not in poor years, but in some of the best years for English trade in the half-century that followed the Restoration.

Capitalizing the debt charge of 1692 at six per cent. (the rate then paid) the company owed more than £150,000 and had no prospect of liquidating its debts. In this chapter no attempt will be made to examine the profits and losses of the different branches of the company's trade. But in order to understand the internal financial history it is necessary to know something of the assets that had been built up. The debt was, on paper, fully covered by assets in Africa and the West Indies. The value of the dead stock, the forts and factories, was variously computed but may reasonably be put at £20,000, while the debts owing to the company in the West Indies exceeded what the company itself owed in London. In 1693 the company put its assets at £375,000, of which £30,000 consisted of worthless debts or claims, £140,000 of debts owing in the Plantations, £20,200 the estimated value of the forts and £90,000 the value of goods awaiting sale in Africa.[1] Though some of the other assets were real enough, these four items accounted for three-quarters of the total and each of the four was suspect. In the West Indies some of the planters' debts were bad, the time for payment of many was uncertain or distant, and the legal processes for the recovery of all were extremely unfavourable to creditors.[2] The investment which the company had made in the forts in Africa, though real, was subject to a depreciation which does not seem to have been allowed for, and could not in any case be realized without dissolving the company. The unsold goods in factories were in part book assets, for many of them had rotted or perished while others had been embezzled.[3]

The question of whether the company earned true profits between 1672 and 1692 thus resolves itself largely into a matter of accounting. By modern accounting canons the company cannot be regarded as having made real profits large enough to justify the dividends it had distributed. Profits were made only in the sense that a collection of doubtful or desperate debts and

[1] T. 70/101, fos. 38d–40.   [2] Below, pp. 316–25.   [3] Below, p. 261.

decayed goods together with some real assets in cash and kind were given a paper value greater than the company's liabilities on stock and seal. From this, it can be argued that during its 'prosperous period' the Royal African Company was in effect borrowing money in order to pay dividends. The total sum distributed in dividends between 1672 and 1692, £157,927, does indeed bear a striking resemblance to the debt outstanding in the latter year, £153,413. Some such interpretation occasionally occurred to the Court of Assistants which voted in 1679 to pay no more dividends until 'the present debts owing be all satisfyed'.[1] It is hardly necessary to add that this good intention was not implemented.

5. The Stock 1691–1708

The direct effects of the Revolution of 1688 upon the Royal African Company will be considered in another chapter.[2] But the political and dynastic changes were clearly mirrored in the subsequent history of the company's finances. Until 1689 the company may be said to have just succeeded in keeping its head above water, or at least in sinking in a way that was barely perceptible. The Revolution greatly increased the difficulties which had to be faced and exposed weaknesses hitherto concealed. Monopoly based on royal charter was discredited and the company lost the protection and favour which it had formerly enjoyed. Competition in the African trade, previously restrained, became open and in 1698 received statutory recognition. The rivalry thus engendered between the company and the separate traders ate up such profits as had accrued through the possession of monopoly.[3] Simultaneously the war with France which began in 1689 brought to the company in the next twenty-five years a series of disasters in Africa, the West Indies and on the high seas.[4] These mounting difficulties and losses were reflected in the company's finances more clearly than anywhere else. For a quarter of a century it staggered from one internal crisis to another, falling deeper into

[1] T. 70/78, fo. 55d.   [2] Below, pp. 122 *et seq.*   [3] Below, p. 139.
[4] Below, pp. 205–12.

debt until nothing but the most drastic reorganization, coupled with the intervention of Parliament, could restore even the semblance of solvency. After 1692 the price of African stock began a fall that continued almost without interruption for twenty years.[1]

It has already been suggested that the comparative ease with which capital was attracted to a project such as the African trade was due in part to the small number of joint-stock companies available as channels for investment. After 1689 this situation changed rapidly. Charters were granted more freely; many new companies were formed; and the shares on offer to the public increased in number and variety.[2] For thirty years after the Revolution the attitude of English governments to company-promotion was largely one of *laissez-faire*, varied only by occasional interventions to check excessive speculation. All the greater corporations formed in this period received charters and Parliamentary sanction, but some of the smaller undertakings were brought into existence without any formal signification of governmental approval. Inevitably there were abuses, and the Bubble Act terminated the experiment in freedom by insisting that shares should be sold only by companies which had received charters. While it lasted the period was marked by bursts of extraordinary activity in the joint-stock sphere which must have served to turn the attention of some investors away from the less successful of the older companies.

The boom in the promotion of projects of domestic interest which began in 1692 has, through Houghton's *Collections*, long been known.[3] But the forces which generated this boom do not appear to have been without effect upon the older-established foreign-trading companies; indeed the effects can be discerned in the East India, Royal African and Hudson's Bay Companies as early as 1691. Very little is known of the course of prices of these stocks at this time, but the volume of transfers suggests an unusually active market. The equivalent of the entire stock of the East India Company is said to have changed hands in two years, and a surviving transfer book suggests that this is more

[1] Scott, II, pp. 34–5. [2] Scott, III, pp. 474–9.
[3] Scott, I, Ch. xvii.

likely to be an understatement than an exaggeration.[1] Transfers in the stock of the Hudson's Bay Company in the single year 1691 were equal to more than the nominal capital, whereas until 1689 they had averaged one-third or less.[2] Even more remarkable is the history of African stock. For the first four months of 1691 the market was quiet, in March and April abnormally so. In May dealings were well above average and continued brisk for the first three weeks of June. Then on 23 June £8,500 of stock was transferred, almost as much in a single day as in some whole years in the 'eighties. There followed five weeks of feverish activity in which transfers totalled £70,450, the equivalent of nearly two-thirds of the company's nominal capital. This phenomenal rate of turnover was not long maintained, but from the beginning of August to the end of the year the equivalent of another sixty per cent. of the stock changed hands. Altogether in this single year the aggregate of transfers equalled 130 per cent. of the nominal capital of the company.[3] The spur to this activity in African stock was a scrip dividend of three hundred per cent., authorized by the General Court of the company on 30 July 1691.[4] Whether the intention to make a bonus issue was published openly or whether it leaked out accidentally does not appear from the company's records. Buyers and sellers must have known of it several weeks before the General Court gave its approval, and, though we have no quotations for this period, the price of African stock was probably rising.

The practice of declaring scrip dividends seems to have been begun by the East India Company in 1682. When that company had been formed in 1657 only half of its nominal capital had been called up. In 1682 the whole of the capital was declared to be fully paid, so that in effect a one-for-one bonus was issued.[5] This example was followed by the Hudson's Bay

---

[1] Scott, II, p. 154. No continuous series of East India transfer books is preserved for the later seventeenth century, but certain volumes have survived including one for the months of June to September 1691 at the Bank of England Records Office, Roehampton.

[2] Hudson's Bay Company Transfer Book, A. 43/1.

[3] £82,350 in the old stock and £261,550 in the new.

[4] T. 70/101, fo. 28d.   [5] Scott, II, p. 145.

G

Company in 1690, when a two-for-one bonus was given to shareholders.[1] In both cases it is possible to argue that nominal capital was being brought into line with the value of the assets of the companies. But when the African Company presented its members with a three-for-one bonus, no such justification could be argued. Before the nominal capital was quadrupled African stock seems to have stood at about 200, and when regular quotations begin to be recorded early in 1692 the price was about 50.[2] The largest bonus that could be justified, therefore, was one-for-one, and, as has already been suggested, these prices were far higher than either the earning capacity or the real value of the assets warranted. The minutes of the General Court which resolved to quadruple the nominal capital record no explanation other than 'the great improvement made upon the stock of this company'. At earlier General Courts figures had been produced which suggested that the company was piling up valuable assets in excess of its nominal capital, but these have already been shown to be misleading.[3] And even they could not be made to justify a scrip dividend of 300 per cent. Only by accounting so dubious as to be worthless can Scott's assumption that the bonus payment betokened the existence of considerable capital reserves be accepted.[4]

The reasons for this action must remain a subject for speculation. There may have been a deliberate intention to increase the number of shares and thus to lower the cost of purchasing the smallest unit in which transfers were normally made, £100 nominal. This might have been intended to assuage critics of the company's monopoly who complained that the benefits of the trade were restricted to too few persons. Alternatively the Assistants, by advising this step, may have hoped to give some nominal recompense to shareholders starved of dividends, and, by manufacturing activity in the company's stock, to divert attention from the languishing condition of the trade. Dishonest practice cannot be entirely ruled out, but if there was such it was well concealed and cannot now be disinterred. Only two members of the Court of Assistants, from which the

[1] Scott, II, p. 232.   [2] *Ibid.*, p. 34.   [3] Above, p. 78.
[4] Scott, II, p. 26.

suggestion of a bonus emanated, were unusually active in share-dealings in the weeks preceding 30 July.

Whatever the explanation may be, the results recorded in the transfer books were remarkable not only for the unprecedented turnover of stock but also for the first appearance of the stock-jobber. Until this time many shareholders had indulged in a certain amount of buying and selling, but none on a scale large enough to be called jobbing. Now in the weeks preceding 31 July 1691 the stock-jobber materialized in the person of William Sheppard. In a little over a month he was party to 67 transactions in African stock, buying £9,150 and selling £6,600. After the stock had been quadrupled he continued his activities; in the second week of August, for example, he bought £12,300 and sold £7,000. At the same time he was dealing extensively in other stocks. In 1691 he bought £3,100 of Hudson's Bay stock and sold £3,000, and in 1692 he bought £4,800 and sold £4,400.[1] These were small sums, but the nominal capital of the company was then only £31,500, so that in two years the equivalent of a quarter of its stock passed through his hands. As might be expected his dealings in East India stock were on a larger scale than in either of the other two. In a little over three months, from 4 June to 19 September 1691, he bought £70,200 of India stock in 182 lots and sold £65,650 in 207 lots.[2] The evil influence of the stock-jobbers (of whom William Sheppard was at this time the greatest) was probably much exaggerated by contemporaries who mistook the symptom for the disease.[3] Jobbing meant a rapid turnover of stock, improved facilities for investment and disinvestment, and a swifter readjustment of prices to prospects. No doubt there were abuses but, putting the worst construction on the alleged misdoings of the jobbers, they gave the public no more than it wanted. Very little, if any, of the responsibility for the African Company's financial collapse can be laid upon them.

As the company's financial position deteriorated, the need for fresh funds became acute. This requirement was met between 1691 and 1708 partly by calls for more capital and partly by borrowing. Though the two methods of raising money were

---

[1] Hudson's Bay Company Transfer Books, A. 43/1–2.
[2] Above, p. 81, n. 1.   [3] Scott, I, pp. 356–8.

closely connected, so tangled are the company's finances in this period that it is necessary to consider them separately.

In 1693, less than two years after the quadrupling of the nominal capital, a fresh issue of stock was made. The purpose of the issue was frankly to raise money for carrying on the trade in the attenuated form that war conditions permitted, not to expand it. It was on this occasion that the General Court was presented with the valuation of assets to which reference has already been made.[1] Gross assets were put at £375,034 1s. 1d. so that, the debt owed at interest being £151,870, nett assets were taken as £223,164. The original stock valued at 160 (or the quadrupled stock valued at its current price of 40) amounted to £177,760. By the company's own accounting, therefore, an issue of £45,000 of new stock at par (nett assets minus present valuation of stock) or its equivalent at 40 might appear to be justified. In fact the company went much further. No appeal was made to the general public, but existing shareholders were offered new stock up to a maximum of half their present holdings. It was not a compulsory call, and the shareholders' response, though satisfactory, was not overwhelming. Had they all taken up their permitted allotments, £222,000 of new stock would have been issued and the company would have received £88,880 in cash or 40 per cent. of the issue. In fact £180,850 of stock was taken up, bringing in £72,340 in cash.[2]

The comparative success of this transaction was not matched by an improvement in the company's fortunes, and none could be expected as long as the war continued and the future of the monopoly remained uncertain. In 1697, with the war ending, a recovery seemed possible. In any case an effort to achieve solvency had to be made in order to convince Parliament that the company was a worthy trustee of the African trade. As part of a reorganization of the company's affairs, therefore, a further issue of stock was resolved upon in September 1697.[3] Elaborate plans were laid for reducing the debt and for extinguishing part of the stock 'if it shall please God that at any time it shall be augmented'. Again the new issue was confined to existing shareholders, each being offered as much of the new stock as he already possessed of the old. The issue was made at

[1] Above, p. 78. [2] T. 70/1186, p. 137. [3] T. 70/85, fos. 3–4.

12, substantially below the ruling price of African stock which in 1697 fluctuated between 17 and 13.[1] Moreover, shareholders were allowed to pay for each £100 of the new stock with £9 in cash and £3 in the company's bonds. These were very favourable terms and, despite the company's worsening prospects, the issue met with much the same reception as that of 1693. Out of a possible £625,250 of new stock, £475,800 was taken up, the yield to the company being £42,802 in cash and £14,924 in its own bonds.[2]

At this point it may be convenient to summarize the history of £100 of the original stock, supposing the holders to have taken full advantage of the two issues just described:

	Stock Held	Cash Paid
1672–4	£100	£100
1691	£400	£100
1693	£600	£180
1697	£1,200	£252

At the lowest market-price recorded in 1698, namely 15, this holding was worth £180, and therefore already showed a substantial capital loss. In 1692, with only £100 paid, it could have been sold for £208. No dividend had been paid between these two dates, and it is in these years that the stock of the African Company slumped to depths from which it never recovered. They were years of unmitigated disaster for the company, but it is one of the objects of this book to show that most of the basic causes of the financial collapse were present and at work before the war began. The war hastened the company's downfall by exposing its failure to earn true profits and consolidate its finances before 1689.

With attenuated capital resources, supplemented wherever possible by indiscriminate borrowing, the company made a notable effort at recovery between 1698 and 1704. Exports in those years, in proportion to available funds, were at a very high level. But the effort came to nothing and between 1702 and 1708 the company plumbed the depths of joint-stock finance. The desperate expedients then adopted cannot be described as fresh issues of stock; they were rather calls or 'leviations' on the existing capital. The first call of £6 a share

---

[1] Scott, II, p. 34.   [2] T. 70/1186, p. 137.

was made in December 1702. The holder of £100 of the original stock, now carrying a nominal value of £1,200, thus had to pay £72.[1] A second call of £7 a share was made in June 1704;[2] a third of £4 in April 1707;[3] and a fourth of £4 in April 1708.[4] Thus in six years the company demanded £21 on each £100 of stock.

In the form in which they were enacted these calls were obligatory on every shareholder. In 1705, after the second call, the Committee of Eight recommended and the Court of Assistants agreed that shareholders who did not pay their calls should not be permitted to transfer any part of their stock,[5] and this was confirmed by the General Court in 1707.[6] Thus shareholders were led to throw good money after bad. In fact a number wisely refused to do so. At the time of the first call there were 11,010[7] shares of nominal value of £100 each.[1] On that occasion the call of £6 a share was paid in respect of 10,691⅔ shares and realized £64,150; in 1704 £7 was paid on 10,587½ shares yielding £74,112 10s.; in 1707 £4 was paid on 9544½ shares bringing in £38,178; and in 1708 £4 was paid on 8031 shares realizing £32,124.[8] Thus while the number of shareholders who paid the calls was surprisingly high, by 1708 the owners of more than a quarter of the capital preferred to risk sequestration.

The financial inducements which accompanied these calls varied. In 1702 the shareholders who met the call were promised a 'dividend' of £1 a year for every share on which they had paid. No term was set for the continuation of these payments, so that at the end of six years the call would presumably be extinguished and the shareholder would receive some compensation for his forbearance. Subsequent calls were even less attractive. In 1704, though £7 was requested instead

---

[1] T. 70/101, fos. 83–83d.   [2] Ibid., fos. 88–88d.   [3] Ibid., fos. 95–95d.
[4] Ibid., fos. 98d, 99.   [5] T. 70/102, 1 February 1705.
[6] T. 70/101, fo. 95d.

[7] This figure is arrived at as follows: in 1672 there were 1,111 shares of £100 each, increased to 4,444 in 1691. In 1693, 2,222 new shares were offered, but only 1,808½ taken up. In 1697, 6,252½ shares (i.e. 4,444 plus 1,808½) were offered, and 4,758 taken up. This gives the total number after 1697 of 11,010½ shares.

[8] T. 70/1186, pp. 137, 141.

of £6, an annual 'dividend' of only 10s. per share was promised, and in the third and fourth calls only the 'usual interest', whatever that may mean. The fourth call is particularly notable; the 'dividends' currently owed by the company on earlier calls were accepted as part payment, and those who did not pay were not only to be barred from transferring their stock but also were to be denied 'dividends' to which they were entitled on the first, second and third calls.[2] In all, the calls yielded £206,998 10s., and between 1703 and 1708 the company disbursed in 'dividends' a total of £67,628.[1]

6. The Progress of the Debt 1692–1708

There seemed, in the first decade of the eighteenth century, to be no limit to the almost heroic devices for enlarging and exploiting the share-capital of the African Company. But during the same period obligations were being contracted which were much less susceptible to manipulation. At the end of 1692 the debt owed on bonds under the company's seal exceeded £150,000. The fortunes of the company in the following sixteen years are summarized in the history of this debt:

THE COMPANY'S DEBT 1692–1708[3]

	At Interest	Book Debts
31 Dec. 1692	£151,870	not stated
do. 1693	£131,300	£8,500
do. 1694	£115,460	£20,000
do. 1695	£96,950	not stated
do. 1696	£107,975	£11,234
do. 1699	£113,105	£8,959
do. 1700	£125,794	£12,173
do. 1701	£146,620	£14,493
do. 1702	£176,275	£12,279
do. 1703	£161,665	£15,795
do. 1705	£221,628	£16,633
do. 1708	£301,195	£11,429

It will be seen from this table that from 1692 until the end of

[1] T. 70/101, fo. 95d.   [2] T. 70/175, reverse, p. 53.
[3] Compiled from the annual reports presented to the General Court of the company, T. 70/101.

the war the debt was reduced by as much as one-third. For this there are two explanations. In the first place the embargoes and restrictions imposed upon trade curtailed the company's activities. The reduced volume of exports (about £30,000 a year against £65,000 before the war) meant that less borrowing had to be undertaken. Such credit as the company required, however, was not easily come by. In January 1695 the Court of Assistants sanctioned the issue of interest-bearing bills to creditors who were prepared to accept them as payment for goods or services.[1] This was not immediately followed by a rise in the debt; indeed the total owed at interest fell in that year by nearly £20,000. But it was a bad precedent. The second explanation of the reduction was the more realistic policy adopted by the company towards its debt. In July 1695 the Court of Assistants voted that £20,000 of the effects to hand should be applied to the redemption of bonds, and in January 1697 the expedient of accepting bonds in payment for goods sold at the company's auctions was adopted.[2]

By this time however the company was experiencing some difficulty in borrowing in the ordinary way. The financial exhaustion of the country through war, coupled with the bad state of the company's own finances, made it imperative that some better security than a seal, and some higher rate of interest than the legal maximum of six per cent., should be offered. An issue of bottomry bonds was accordingly resolved upon in August 1696.[3] A loan on bottomry in the strict sense was an advance made on the security of a ship at sea, repayment being conditional upon the safe return of the vessel.[4] On this occasion, and in subsequent issue of bottomry bonds, ships in the company's service were specified as part of the security. But the obligations entered into by the company, though referred to as bottomry bonds, were at the same time *respondentia* contracts for which not only the ships but also the goods

---

[1] T. 70/84, fo. 41.

[2] The first sale at which this practice was adopted was on 28 January 1697, when payment in bonds was accepted for one-quarter of purchases, T 70/84, fo. 83. The practice continued until 1710, the proportion payable in bonds varying between one-quarter and the whole.

[3] T. 70/84, fo. 75.   [4] G. Jacob, *A New Law Dictionary*, 1729.

carried in them stood as security.[1] In this issue each adventurer was invited to pay in £3 per share on the inducement of receiving £4 when ten ships then at sea, or any of them, should return to England. The loan was in any case to be repaid within twelve months and it was not obligatory upon shareholders. The proceeds of future sales were thus mortgaged to those members of the company who were willing to advance money at a rate of interest of 33 per cent. per annum.[2] Nearly two-thirds of the shareholders responded, £3 being lent on 3,878¾ shares and £11,636 being raised.[3]

In July 1699 a fresh issue of bottomry bonds was made.[4] Again £3 a share was requested from shareholders but the date for repayment was eighteen months hence instead of a year and the interest 15s. instead of £1. Interest was thus at the annual rate of 16⅔ per cent. Following the capital issue of 1697 there were now 11,010½ shares of nominal value of £100; £3 was lent on 10,435¾ shares yielding £31,307.[5] Further issues of bottomry bonds were made in 1702 when £40,803 was raised, in 1705 (£42,374) and in 1706 (£41,426).[6] The frequent use of this expedient is an indication of the depths to which the company had now sunk. Raising money by bottomry or *respondentia* was a well-established and legitimate device. But it must be remembered that the company was at the same time borrowing money on ordinary bonds and buying goods with promissory bonds. Imports of gold, sugar, ivory and other commodities from the West Indies and Africa were being made to stand security for both bottomry and ordinary bonds. In February 1699 and in April 1700, for example, the company authorized the issue of bonds at six per cent. interest to anyone who would take them up, three-quarters of the money accruing from sales being appropriated to discharging these bonds in the order in which they had been issued.[7] The

[1] Sir W. Holdsworth, *History of English Law* (2nd edition), VIII, pp. 261–2.

[2] Because the lender participated in the risks of the sea, loans on bottomry were not within the statute of usury.

[3] T. 70/1186, p. 137.   [4] T. 70/85, fo. 69d; T. 70/101, fo. 73d.

[5] T. 70/1186, p. 137.

[6] T. 70/101, fos. 82–82d, 92–92d; T. 70/102, 26 July 1705.

[7] T. 70/85, fo. 52; T. 70/86, pp. 30, 208; T. 70/102, 25 January 1704.

holders of bottomry bonds presumably had first claim on the company's income and the holders of ordinary bonds the second. Anything left over went to pay the 'dividends' on the calls made between 1702 and 1708. The chance of a dividend in the proper sense was remote indeed.

In these ways the company accumulated, between 1699 and 1708, debts which it could never repay. What is remarkable is that creditors proved so indulgent. Even in 1706 when the company appealed to its own shareholders for £40,000 to 'circulate' outstanding bonds, almost the whole sum was raised.[1]

7. Insolvency and Reconstruction

On paper the company could make out a reasonable claim to solvency as late as 1708.[2] Its debts now exceeded £300,000, but it valued its 'quick' assets at £278,550 and its 'dead' assets at £152,500. As always, the debts owed to the company in the West Indies were an important item on the credit side. About £80,000 of the sum outstanding there was now reckoned too desperate to be regarded as an asset, but a further £78,000 of new debts were owed by the planters, the company's agents in the West Indies being legally bound to make good any deficiency. Goods in forts and factories in Africa and aboard ship, with an allowance for profit, were valued at £130,000, ships at £21,000, and there were sundry other minor assets. Significantly, cash in hand, bills of exchange awaiting payment, gold and silver in London, all the truly liquid assets, amounted together to no more than £5,805. The same criticisms can of course be applied to these figures as to those put forward by the company on earlier occasions. The 'dead' stock was overvalued; the debts in the West Indies, even if guaranteed by the company's agents, were not liquid assets; while the trading goods in the pipe-line were subject to depreciation through long storage and losses from enemy action. The company was, in short, bankrupt in every sense except the technical one, and the

---

[1] T. 70/102, 12 September and 24 October 1706; T. 70/101, fo. 93.
[2] T. 70/101, 6 October 1708.

moment for the winding-up of its affairs had come, if indeed it had not long passed.

But while, as we have seen, numerous obstacles had to be surmounted in the seventeenth century before a company could come into existence, they were slight compared to the difficulties facing a company seeking to liquidate its affairs. The problems encumbering the liquidation of the Company of Royal Adventurers in 1671 have already been noticed. Then the stock to be wound up had been little more than £100,000 and the debts owed only £57,000. Now the nominal capital was over £1 million and the debts £300,000. In the early eighteenth century, despite the need for it, there was no standing legal machinery by which a company in the condition of the Royal African could satisfy its creditors and pass out of existence. While there may have been some amongst the shareholders who hoped and believed that a drastic surgical operation could give the company a fresh start, it is probable that one of the main reasons why the company eked out another forty years of miserable existence, to be finally dissolved in 1750, was that this was the only way in which even a token satisfaction could be made to creditors.

The first meeting between the company and its creditors was held at the beginning of May 1709,[1] hurried on by the fear that a few creditors, by putting outstanding bonds in suit, might possess themselves of all the negotiable assets and leave nothing for the others.[2] Several meetings were held in an effort to obtain unanimity, and a joint committee of shareholders and creditors was appointed to dispose of such of the company's effects as might come to hand.[3] Another committee of bond-holders was appointed to examine the books, which they later reported were 'very regularly kept'.[4] Under the circumstances only one solution seemed possible. If the creditors could not have cash, they must be given stock; the questions to be decided were how much they should have and what proportion their allocation was to form of a new nominal capital. Four separate schemes were needed before the 'Coalition' between adventurers and bond-holders could be consummated.

[1] T. 70/101, fo. 112d.   [2] *Ibid.*, fos. 113, 113d.
[3] *Ibid.*, fos. 116–116d.   [4] *Ibid.*, fos. 117–117d.

First Scheme for uniting Adventurers and Bond-holders in one Stock
August 1709[1]

(1) The existing 11,000 shares (of £100 each) to be written down
to 1,100 and charged (a) with any arrears of former calls,
(b) with a new call of £20 each, thus producing £22,000 in
cash. Each new share would then be of the nominal value of
£100.

(2) The stock of the Coalition to comprise 4,100 shares of £100
each, of which the above 1,100 would form part.

(3) The remaining 3,000 shares to be allocated to the creditors
after the rate of one £100 share for £100 principal debt.

(4) Interest due on the debt to be cast up to Michaelmas 1709 and
be paid on the following Lady Day (presumably in cash).

The arrangement was approved, *nem. con.*, by the General
Court of the company and by a general meeting of creditors,
and was drafted into the form of an instrument to be subscribed
by all parties. More than five hundred creditors, agreeing with
their chairman, Sir Edward Gould, that the 'Adventurers had
made very great concessions, and as much as could be desired',
eventually signed.[2] But some stood out. Seven times the final
date for subscribing the instrument was extended, on the last
occasion until 28 February 1710. The legal position was
doubtful; counsel advised that the company had the right to
make a bill of sale of its effects to such creditors as subscribed
the instrument but thought that everything possible should be
done to obtain unanimous agreement.[3] The company accordingly brought forward a second scheme.

Second Scheme for uniting Adventurers and Bond-holders in one Stock
May 1710[4]

(1) The existing 11,010 shares of £100 each to be written down to
1,101 and to be charged with (a) arrears of former calls, and
(b) £30 per new share, thus producing £33,030 in cash. Each
new share would then be of nominal value of £100.

(2) Creditors to receive £100 of new stock for £100 of principal
debt. Interest to be cast up to Michaelmas 1710, and new
stock to be allocated for it at the same rate.

---

[1] T. 70/101, fos. 118–118d, 119d–120.   [2] *Ibid.*, fos. 120d–121.
[3] *Ibid.*, fos. 123–123d.   [4] *Ibid.*, fos. 133–134d.

(3) The agreement to become binding as soon as so many creditors had subscribed it as to leave no more than £20,000 in
bonds outstanding.

Thus the negotiations proceeded. In these new proposals the
shareholders had advanced their call from £20 per share to
£30; but the creditors were being asked to accept stock in payment of interest as well as principal. Consequently the scheme
made little progress. By the middle of June only a hundred
persons had subscribed it,[1] and the date for completion had to
be set a long time thence, 1 May 1711.[2] It was deemed
advisable to offer creditors and stock-holders an inducement of
£2 per share if they would 'make it their business to effect the
union'.[3]

At this juncture the company's predicament was exposed by
a curious lawsuit. For a long time it had been fighting a rear-
guard action against recalcitrant creditors who sought to tear
its estate 'to peices to the benefitt of nobody' but themselves.[4]
Now it found itself defendant in an action brought in the name
of the Crown. The Receiver-General for the County of Wor-
cester, Thomas Albert, had, it appeared, embezzled sums of
money which he had received in virtue of his office. Seeking for
an escape from the position in which he found himself, he hit
upon the device of purchasing at a substantial discount a number of the company's bonds and presenting them for repayment
at par as a debt owing to the Crown. With the help of his
brother, Fletcher Albert, he obtained bonds to the face value
of some £11,000, bought at a large discount, and instituted proceedings for the recovery of the debt. He failed to obtain an
extent against the company from the Barons of the Exchequer,
but, under colour of one granted by the Chancellor of the Exchequer the company's house in Leadenhall Street was entered
in December 1710 and certain books and papers seized.[5] The
company promptly petitioned for a stay of execution,[6] and in
May 1711 a petition to the same effect was drawn up by 150 of
the creditors.[7] The case was argued up to the House of Lords

[1] Ibid., fo. 135.   [2] Ibid., fo. 136.   [3] Ibid., fos. 137, 137d.
[4] Ibid., fo. 112d.   [5] T. 70/170, fos. 66d–68.   [6] Ibid., fo. 66d.
[7] Ibid., fos. 66d, 67.

where in the session of 1711–12 the company's appeal was dismissed, with costs against the company.[1]

Meanwhile a third attempt was being made to find an acceptable basis for agreement:

Third Scheme for uniting Adventurers and Bond-holders in one Stock
February 1711[2]

(1) The nominal value of the existing shares to be written down from £100 to £5. Arrears of calls to be paid, but no new call to be made.

(2) Creditors to receive stock at par for their principal debt and for interest to Christmas 1710.

(3) A new subscription of not less than £50,000 to be raised.

Like their predecessors these proposals came to nothing and presumably for the same reason. Evidently it was felt that unanimity, or something very near it, amongst the creditors was essential. Especially was it necessary if, as in the third scheme, a new cash subscription was proposed. For no outsider would put in money if it was to be applied to paying off creditors who stood out from the agreement. Anything less than unanimity seemed to require legislation, and after these three abortive schemes this was the solution finally adopted. In 1711 a bill 'for making effectual such agreement as shall be made between the Royal African Company of England and their creditors' became law.[3] It enacted that that if agreement between the adventurers and two-thirds of the creditors was reached before 20 December 1712 it should be binding on all.

The company was at last free to act, though for the moment all its energies had to be applied to countering a bill put forward by its competitors to regulate the trade to Africa in their own interests. This being successfully defeated, fresh proposals for the union were drawn up in July 1712.

Final Scheme for uniting Adventurers and Bond-holders in one Stock
July 1712[4]

(1) A call of £3 on each of the 11,010 shares, with discounts of 15s. per share if paid within 40 days, 10s. within 60 days, 5s.

---

[1] *House of Lords Journal*, 12 December 1711, 17 and 29 March, 7 April 1712; W. R. Ward, *The English Land Tax in the Eighteenth Century*, 1953, pp. 49–50.

[2] T. 70/101, fos. 139–40.   [3] 10 Ann. c. 34.   [4] T. 70/101, fos. 144–147d.

within 80 days. After 120 days, stock on which the call had not been paid to stand forfeited.

(2) These 11,010 shares would then be written down to 1101 and would each be of nominal value of £100 in the new stock.

(3) Creditors to receive new stock at par for principal and interest to Michaelmas 1712.

On 16 December 1712, four days before the expiry of the time-limit set by the Act of 1711, an advertisement was placed in the *London Gazette* signifying that, as provided in that Act, agreement had been reached between the company and two-thirds (both in number and value) of its creditors.[1] On 29 January 1713 the General Court was informed that most of the money due on call had been paid, and on 26 February it received an assurance from the directors that the trade was being prosecuted to best advantage and that no further call was contemplated.[2] By these drastic measures the company was brought back to life, or more accurately was put into such condition that, after a few months of activity, it could relapse into a state of moribund somnolence in which it was less of a nuisance to the government, to Parliament, and to the nation, than it had been in the first decade of the eighteenth century.

In concluding this examination of the capital of the Royal African Company it may be of interest to summarize the history of an original subscription of £100 over the whole period from 1672 to 1713. The following calculation assumes that the investor took up all the new issues of stock to which he was entitled and paid all his calls.

Date	Cash Paid	Stock Credited	Cash Returned in Dividends
December 1671	—	£100	—
1672–4	£100	£100	—
1676–91	£100	£100	£129 5s.
August 1691	£100	£400	£129 5s.
1692	£100	£400	£142 3s.
1693	£180	£600	£142 3s.
1697	£252	£1,200	£142 3s.
1702, 1st call	£324	£1,200 ⎤	£142 3s. plus an
1704, 2nd call	£408	£1,200 ⎟	indeterminate sum
1707, 3rd call	£456	£1,200 ⎟	in 'dividends',
1708, 4th call	£504	£1,200 ⎦	probably about
			£72 = £214 3s.
1712	£540	£120	£214 3s.

[1] *Ibid.*, fo. 148.　　　[2] *Ibid.*, fos. 149d, 151d.

After the reconstruction of 1712, £100 of African stock sold at 60. The subscriber of £100 of the original stock who sold in 1713 would thus have paid in £540, received in dividends about £215, and sold his holding for £72. His total loss would thus have been about £253. But to this must be added the loss of the five or six per cent. he would have earned if his money had been invested in a good fixed-interest security, something over £350 at five per cent. simple interest.

Although the finances of the African Company appear at times to have been handled with criminal dishonesty, it is much more probable that the disaster should be attributed to ignorance, to lack of experience in the science of capital-management, and perhaps above all to the lack of any ordinary means by which a company's affairs could be wound up. No charge of dishonesty was ever brought against the Assistants by a General Court and the independent committee of creditors which examined the books in 1709 found them in order. The directors were not, on the whole, the kind of men to practise embezzlement themselves or to condone it in others. Rather we must conclude that the company staggered from capital issue to issue and from debt to debt because there was little else that it could do. Even in 1712 when the company was patently insolvent agreement for reconstruction was reached only after four years of negotiation and the intervention of Parliament. In 1704 or 1705, when the company was still active, agreement would have been impossible.

3

MONOPOLY AND COMPETITION

1. The Charter

THE charter of the Royal African Company passed the great seal on 27 September 1672, nearly a year after the capital had been subscribed. Legal recognition was thus accorded to the new body and its powers and privileges defined.[1] In many respects the terms of the charter were similar to those granted to contemporary joint-stock companies trading to other parts of the world. The title of the English Crown to 'Guinney and Binney' was asserted and the failure of the Royal Adventurers through debts, inadequate privileges and war losses was recited. Surrender of the charter of the Adventurers was accepted,[2] and a new company, to be known as the Royal African Company of England, was incorporated and granted the lands and trade between Cape Blanco in the north and Cape de Bona Speranza in the south for the term of one thousand years. The constitution of the company was defined as a Governor, Sub-Governor, Deputy Governor and twenty-four Assistants; these were named and provision made for annual elections. Power to administer oaths to officers, members and employees was granted, and the assignment of stock was authorized provided the vendor was not indebted to the company. The remaining clauses of the charter dealt with the trading monopoly and the company's administrative powers.

---

[1] C. T. Carr, *Select Charters of Trading Companies* (Selden Society, Vol. 28), pp. 186–92.

[2] Thus making extraordinary the remark of the Lord Keeper in Curson *v.* Royal African Company that the old charter had not been surrendered. 1. Vern. 122.

97

No subject of the Crown other than those now incorporated was to visit West Africa except by permission of the company, which was empowered to seize the ships and goods of all who infringed its monopoly. Gold, silver and negroes were mentioned as the company's objectives, and an optimistic proviso about the mining of gold which had figured in the charter to the Royal Adventurers in 1662 was repeated. The King, if he chose, could bear two-thirds of the cost of mining and thereby entitle himself to two-thirds of the profits. Finally, the company was authorized to establish and govern forts, factories and plantations in Africa, to make war and peace with any heathen nation there, to raise troops, and to execute martial law.

Thus far the charter was little more than a reissue of the grants to earlier African companies. The Royal Adventurers, however, were believed to have failed partly because of insufficient privileges, and in the charter of 1672 something was done to remedy the supposed defects. Apart from small changes of detail there were three innovations. In the first place, any twelve shareholders were entitled to demand the summoning of a General Court at which a Governor or Assistant could be removed from office on conviction of a misdemeanour. This provision, which was invoked at least once,[1] was presumably intended to give the ordinary shareholder a greater control over the company's affairs and thus to make the stock more attractive to investors. The other innovations were both designed to tighten up the monopoly. Officers of the English Customs were forbidden to accept entries of goods exported to or imported from Africa other than as permitted by the company. So far as exports were concerned, something, but not much, could be hoped for from this clause: interlopers seldom declared their intentions to the Customs but registered their cargoes for other destinations. Imports of such characteristic African products as redwood and ivory might, however, be recognized as originating from the area of the company's monopoly, and it is possible that this provision made smuggling a little more difficult.

These were minor alterations, but the charter of 1672 strengthened monopoly in the African trade in another and

[1] In 1699. T. 70/85, fos. 79, 79d.

more effective way: it sanctioned the erection of a court of judicature to sit on the African coast to hear and determine cases of seizure of interlopers and other mercantile suits. The court was to comprise two merchants and one person learned in the civil law, all to be nominated by the company; cases were to be judged according to equity, the law and custom of merchants, and such rules as the King himself might make. The existence of such a court did not of course make any easier the task of catching interlopers; its chief purpose was to take away the appearance of robbery from the act of seizure and to substitute a semblance of legality. Thereby the company might hope to avoid lengthy and expensive suits in other courts by parties who believed themselves to be injured. No other trading company enjoyed a comparable privilege at this time, though the East India Company was authorized to erect similar courts in 1683.[1] In effect the Crown was sanctioning a court with power over the property of English subjects and leaving its composition to be determined by a body which would be an interested party in every important matter that came before it. The King could scarcely have given a more emphatic demonstration of his favour towards the African company.

The charter made no reference to saving the rights of the Gambia Adventurers who, under a lease from the company of Royal Adventurers, enjoyed the trade to the northern parts of West Africa for seven years from 1 January 1669 at a rent of £1,000 a year.[2] Nevertheless, the Royal African Company honoured the obligations of its predecessor; it was not itself yet ready to enter upon the whole trade of West Africa and the rent, when it could be collected, was useful.[3] The lease, due to expire at the end of 1675, was evidently prolonged for two further years,[4] and it was not until 1 January 1678 that the Royal African Company finally entered into the full and sole possession of its monopoly. The Gambia Adventurers, under their original lease, were entitled to compensation for the goods

---

[1] Sir W. Hunter, *A History of British India*, II, p. 288; H. J. Crump, *Colonial Admiralty Jurisdiction in the Seventeenth Century*, 1931, Ch. x.

[2] G. F. Zook, *Company of Royal Adventurers Trading to Africa*, p. 23.

[3] T. 70/76, fos. 31d, 35, 44, 63d.   [4] T. 70/77, fo. 35d.

in their factories at the time of the surrender, and these they valued at over £12,000.[1] The African Company disputed the figure and a lawsuit ensued, as a result of which the Gambia Adventurers were awarded all that they claimed with accrued interest.[2] As late as 1684 the differences between the two companies had not been finally adjusted.[3]

It will be convenient to mention here another, and more permanent, qualification of the company's monopoly. It extended to West Africa only, and, while West Africa was easily the greatest market for the purchase of slaves in the seventeenth century, at least one alternative source of supply existed. When, as frequently happened, the planters of the English West Indian colonies felt themselves to be insufficiently supplied with negroes by the African Company, it was to Madagascar that they turned. Between 1675 and 1690 numbers of Malagasy slaves were brought to the English colonies, and the company was powerless to stop the trade.[4] Madagascar lay within the limits of the charter of the East India Company, but that body had no interests there and turned a deaf ear to appeals for help in restraining interlopers.[5]

Equipped with this charter the company was launched into the political and commercial world of Restoration England. Whatever excuses might be made for the failure of the Royal Adventurers, the charter of 1672 gave the new company all that it could reasonably expect. The last and greatest of the joint-stock monopolies in the African trade was also the most privileged and the most favoured. In this chapter the company's efforts to preserve this monopoly, and its failure to do so, will be discussed. The narrative may conveniently be divided into four periods: from 1672 to 1689, when the royal charter was in force and the monopoly nominally intact; from 1689 to 1698, when the charter was recognized to be partly or wholly defective but no fresh basis for the African trade had been devised; from 1698 to 1712, when under Act of Parliament

[1] *Cal. S.P. Col.*, 1677–80, No. 822.
[2] T. 70/78, fo. 107; T. 70/80, fos. 10, 32d.   [3] T. 70/80, fo. 61d.
[4] *Cal. S.P. Col.*, 1675–6, pp. 349, 465; T. 70/1, fo. 48; T. 70/10, fos. 9d, 22; T. 70/12, fo. 6d; *Cal. S.P. Col.*, 1681–5, No. 136.
[5] T. 70/77, fos. 26, 56d., 57d.

private persons were permitted to trade to Africa on payment
of a duty to the company for the upkeep of its forts; and after
1712, when the necessity of paying this duty lapsed and the trade
was open to all without restriction. In the space of rather more
than forty years, therefore, it is possible to observe in the same
field monopoly, anarchy, a form of licensed freedom, and
finally complete liberty of trade. Within the same compass of
time and space, the joint-stock company and the private trader
or small partnership were pitted against one another. It may
be hoped that a study of the African trade in this period can
contribute something to an understanding of different forms of
commercial organization and the comparative merits of free
trade and monopoly in the seventeenth and eighteenth centuries.

2. Before the Revolution

From the closing years of Elizabeth I to the Revolution of
1689, monopoly was one of the great issues in which political,
constitutional, economic and social antagonisms were fused.
Contemporaries, discussing the question in its constitutional
and legal aspects, commonly saw it as a contest between the
royal prerogative and the common law. This contest was made
to appear as one between the royal power to make rules affecting the processes of manufacture and distribution, and the
common law doctrine of the liberty of every man to practise his
own trade without interference.[1] Constitutional issues, however, seldom arise spontaneously. Behind the question of
prerogative *versus* common law, as forcefully debated on the
constitutional plane in the case of the East India Company *v.*
Sandys in 1684 as in the Parliaments of James I, lay all kinds of

[1] Sir George Treby's argument in the East India Company *v.* Sandys: 'I
shall chiefly insist upon two cases in one book, Coke 11 Rep., the Taylor of
Ipswich's case, fol. 53, and Darcy and Allen's case, called the Case of
Monopolies, fo. 86. It is the main ground of both these cases that at com-
mon-law no man could be prohibited to exercise his trade, for that is an
avoidance of idleness, it helps to provide sustenance for a man and his
family; and it is a service to the King: and the consequences of restraining
trade are pernicious, as raising prices of commodities and impoverishing
men, bad commodities &c.' Cobbett's *State Trials*, X, p. 387.

political, economic and personal tensions and ambitions. For example, assaults on monopolies were launched by those who were chiefly concerned to displace the monopolist and to put themselves in his place.[1] At other times criticism of monopolies was part of an attack on a court favourite or unpopular minister.[2] Yet again, and especially after the eleven years' personal rule of Charles I, monopolies were under fire as a remunerative though exceedingly inefficient means of raising non-parliamentary revenue. In most cases the opponents of monopoly took their stand on legal principles, and also painted harrowing pictures of the suffering consumer groaning under intolerable burdens. These evocations need not be taken too seriously. The Long Parliament, which attacked monopolies so bitterly, imposed excise duties which, from the consumer's point of view, produced the same effect, an increase in price of essential purchases. Whatever form the battle over monopolies might take, and whatever the real issue behind that battle, the interests of the consumer for the most part had to take second place, to be paraded or ignored as opportunity served.

The Civil War and the Restoration did not settle the question of monopolies, and as soon as Charles II was back on the throne patents began to issue from the great seal, not only to inventors but also to trading companies. Charles did not, however, grant them indiscriminately as his father had done. Most of those of consequence were given to companies engaged in overseas trade, and their repercussions upon the life of the ordinary citizen were, therefore, less direct than those bestowed upon domestic industries. Constitutionally, monopolies in overseas trade were less offensive, for the Crown's power to regulate foreign commerce had always been admitted to be more extensive and more justifiable than its power to control industry or internal trade. And, while the Crown did from time to time in the Restoration period draw tangible financial benefits from the companies it had created, they were not on such a scale as to threaten the parliamentary method of raising money.[3] Nor

[1] E.g. the rivalry between the Westminster and London soap companies under Charles I. W. H. Price, *English Patents of Monopoly*, Ch. XI.

[2] *Ibid.*, p. 32.

[3] Charles II received gifts from the East India Company.

could the Restoration trading companies be criticized as artificial creations designed merely to advantage royal favourites. Both the East India Company and the Royal African Company contained many members, the majority of whom had no connexion with the Court; and both could plausibly be represented as engaged upon trades which were useful, or indeed essential, to the economic well-being of the country. Moreover, the abolition of the prerogative courts rendered monopoly in practice less of a grievance than it had been. It can scarcely be doubted that if Charles II and his brother had had Star Chamber to hand, they would have used it to support the monopoly of the African Company. Its procedure and methods would have been well suited to the punishment of interlopers; the Privy Council, with its restricted judicial functions, was no substitute.

Grounds of objection to monopoly could, nevertheless, still be found after 1660. In the first place, the status and powers of the Royal African Company derived from one source alone, the royal prerogative. Its motto, 'regio floret patricinio commercium, commercioque regnum', was aptly chosen. While prerogative was unchallenged, the company was safe; when prerogative was attacked, the company was in danger; when prerogative was overthrown, the company was doomed. All the chartered companies of the Restoration were in some measure identified with royal power, and in some of them the connexion was drawn closer by the personal participation of the royal family: Charles II in the Royal Adventurers; Prince Rupert in the Hudson's Bay Company; the Duke of Monmouth in the Royal Fishery; and James, both as Duke of York and as King, in the East India and Royal African Companies. But it is safe to say that in no instance was the identification between the royal family and a trading monopoly so close as in the African companies. James, for many years the Governor and the largest shareholder in the Royal African Company, was also the Lord High Admiral whose courts chastised those who infringed its privileges. The future of the company's monopoly was indeed heavily staked on the undisturbed continuation of the Stuart line, and more than any other single event the Revolution of 1688 hastened its downfall. It would have failed in any case; its financial policy before, and its war losses after, 1689 would have ensured this. But the shock of the Revolution, the sudden withdrawal of the royal support, so long and generously given that it had come to be relied on, exposed the company to a storm of criticism and attack for which it was ill prepared, and in a moment the monopoly derived from the royal prerogative was gone for ever.

This involvement of the African Company in the political tensions of the day may have been deepened by the political affiliations of many of its members. Of the twenty-three share-holders who were elected to Parliament after the adoption of the political labels of Whig and Tory, twenty sat as Tories, the majority for the City of London.[1] Between 1681 and 1702 there were sixteen successful Tory candidates in City elections to Parliament, and all but two were financially interested in the African Company. And when, between 1683 and 1687, the City's charter was in suspense and the Crown filled up vacancies amongst the aldermen with its own nominees, nearly a half of those appointed were shareholders.[2] Such men, prominent in civic and national affairs, were equally to the fore in the management of the company's business, and they must have helped to spread the belief that it stood or fell with James II.

The principal victims of some of the monopolies of the early seventeenth century must have been the poor, or at least the unrepresented and generally inarticulate lower strata of society. Their sufferings could be used for the sake of argument; but were unlikely to be pressed very hard. Against the monopoly of the Royal African Company, however, the voice of the consumer was raised loudly and in the end effectively. From the first, the monopoly was under fire from those who were at its receiving end, not the suffering poor but the planters of America and the West Indies. In the years that followed the Restoration, the West Indian colonists, exploiting the critical position which they occupied in the imperial economy, were laying the foundations of a most efficient pressure group and parliament-

---

[1] A. B. Beaven, *Aldermen of the City of London*, 1908–13, I, pp. 261–316; K. Feiling, *History of the Tory Party, 1640–1714*, 1924, pp. 494–8.

[2] Beaven, *op. cit.*, II, pp. 109–15.

ary lobby.[1] If the number of negroes which the company supplied fell short of what they judged to be necessary, ample means existed for publicizing this fact. By petitions to Crown or Parliament, pamphlets, lawsuits, and retaliatory measures in their own legislatures, a public sentiment long hostile to monopoly could be whipped into a formidable opposition.

After the Revolution, when the monopolies of the overseas trading companies were brought up for trial, one of the noisiest and not the least effective of the witnesses for the prosecution was the manufacturing interest, now beginning to be a power to be reckoned with. Manufacturers had of course raised their voices against monopoly in the past, often in the name of their employees who had been rendered workless. By the end of the century they were stronger and more numerous. How the clothiers and their satellites stoked the fires of opposition to the East India Company's import of cheap textiles is well known. For different reasons they campaigned against the monopoly of the African Company. This company was a purchaser of English woollens and other manufactures, and the volume of its exports was thus a matter of concern to manufacturers. Monopoly allowed only one buyer, while free trade meant many. Monopoly kept exports at an artificially low level; free trade would send them soaring.[2] Thus ran the arguments, and with few exceptions the articulate manufacturing interest ranged itself behind the opponents of monopoly in foreign trade.

Finally there were the merchants who wished to trade to Africa themselves and were prevented from doing so by the company's monopoly. How numerous they were, and whether they were Londoners or provincials, are questions which cannot easily be answered. All that can confidently be stated is that such persons existed and believed that the African trade was one in which they could profitably engage. Two proofs of their existence may be mentioned. In the first place, from about 1667 to 1671 the greater part of the African trade had been in the hands of private merchants. When the ques-

---

[1] L. M. Penson, *Colonial Agents of the British West Indies*, 1924.

[2] Below, pp. 126, 149, for examples of petitions from manufacturers against monopoly.

tion of the African Company's monopoly was under discussion in Parliament in 1694, Mr. Dockwra, a former Searcher in the Customs House, testified that in four years of open trade 103 ships had gone out to Africa with licences from the Royal Adventurers and 32 more without licences.[1] And secondly, even after 1672 when the trade was once more confined, the private merchants or interlopers never ceased to infringe the company's monopoly.[2] The case against monopoly was thereby strengthened, for the existence of an alternative means of organizing the trade could not be denied.

Between 1672 and 1689 opposition to the African Company's monopoly, apart from the regular hammerings of the privileged sugar-growers, had for the most part to be silent, expressing itself in action rather than in words. There was little that foreshadowed the spate of pamphlets and parliamentary enquiries which followed the Revolution. The real challenge to the company is to be found neither in Parliament, nor in the press, nor in the law courts, but in the Atlantic ocean, on the African coast and in the West Indies. Once only was the company given a foretaste of what was in store for it. Charles' second Parliament assembled in March 1679, with a strong and vocal majority bent on excluding the Duke of York from succession to the throne. After some delay the Commons began on 27 April to debate the business in hand, the apprehension of Popery and the danger of a Catholic King. The following day a committee was set up to examine into 'miscarriages relating to his Majesty's Navy . . . and likewise the information that hath been given in touching the Ship called the Hunter'.[3] The *Hunter* was a man-of-war which, under the command of Captain Dickinson, had been lent to the African Company in 1676 for a cruise to West Africa.[4] Two interlopers had been there seized and the proceeds, some £2,800, had been divided according to the charter, one-half to the King and one-half to the company.[5] This practice of hiring warships to private

---

[1] Stock, II, pp. 92–3.   [2] Below, pp. 113 *et seq.*

[3] *Commons Journals*, IX, p. 606.   [4] T. 70/76, fo. 76.

[5] T. 70/77, fos. 75, 81. Two ships were taken, the *John & Mathew* and the *Anne*. The company gave £700, half of its share of the proceeds, to Captain Dickinson. Royal African Company v. Dockwra, Colles 327 (1703).

persons or bodies was an old one, and it is not clear whether the Commons' enquiry was intended to reveal any abuses other than the loan of a royal ship to support a monopoly which critics of the royal prerogative held to be illegal. There are certainly grounds for thinking that the appointment of this committee was part of a campaign which, if it had been allowed to proceed, would have developed into an assault on the company as well as on the prerogative which sustained it. The committee immediately demanded from the African Company copies of the instructions given to the commanders of the *Hunter* and the *Constant Warwick*, a man-of-war employed for the same purpose in the West Indies.[1] The company began hastily to improvise defences: a special committee was appointed, members of Parliament were lobbied, a printed defence ordered, counsel's opinion taken, and a petition drawn up and submitted to the Commons.[2] This petition, praying that the company might be heard in its own defence, was read on 27 May.[3] On the same day Parliament was prorogued, later to be dissolved. The company expressed relief at its deliverance by voting thanks to two members of Parliament and leaving it to the Sub-Governor to 'dispose of fifty pounds for the Companyes service as he sees fitt'.[4]

The danger was now past, and, though there were hints of trouble in the next two years, nothing serious materialized.[5] The company was determined not to be again caught unprepared. In September 1679 the Court of Assistants commissioned five members to prepare a paper showing the necessity for carrying on the African trade in a joint stock.[6] The inten-

[1] T. 70/78, fo. 54d. [2] *Ibid.*, fos. 55d, 56d.
[3] Stock, I, p. 420. [4] T. 70/78, fo. 56d.
[5] Complaint was made to the King and Council in June 1679 against Captain Heywood, commander of H.M.S. *Norwich*, also lent to the company, for taking an interloper in Guinea (T. 70/78, fo. 59d). The Sub-Governor was authorized to retain the Solicitor-General on behalf of the company, and various members of the Court of Assistants attended the Earl of Shaftesbury, presumably to ask him to leave the company alone (*Ibid.*, fo. 59d). There were petitions against the company in December 1680 from Joshua Brooke and others, and in January 1681 from Samuel Nash and others (Stock, I, p. 422). But an early dissolution again relieved the situation.
[6] T. 70/78, fo. 68d.

tion was to present this to Parliament, but the opportunity never came, and it probably served as the basis for a pamphlet, *Certain Considerations Relating to the Royal African Company*, published in 1680. The arguments employed, the necessity of forts for defending the trade, the need to make stable agreements with natives, the example of other countries which traded in joint stocks, were to become familiar, and indeed threadbare, after the Revolution.[1] This, the first recognition of the need to justify the African monopoly to public opinion, shows how seriously the company took the events of May 1679. They had good reason to do so: two interlopers off Sierra Leone at the end of 1680 'made great braggs of assistance that they expect from Parliment' and claimed that 'the Parliment gives permission to goe trade at Guynia'.[2] For its deliverance the company had to thank the royal prerogative of dissolution.

During this period the African Company was concerned in many lawsuits, both in England and in the colonies, and in a number of them the validity of the monopoly was brought into question. Though unfavourable decisions were to be expected in the common law courts of the West Indies, it appears that the charter was generally accepted in the English courts. The company was not involved in any major action such as the East India Company *v.* Sandys in 1684, but it undoubtedly drew encouragement from this great, if temporary, victory of royal monopoly. In the Sandys case the royal prerogative to grant monopolies to overseas trading companies was put on trial and vindicated in the judgment of Lord Chief Justice Jeffreys.[3] Yet the success was barren. Persons with grievances against the

---

[1] This pamphlet is chiefly remarkable for a classic statement of the 'mercantilist' theory of foreign trade: 'No man ever doubted but that Forreign Trade and Commerce is the great Concern and Interest of every Nation, because the Increase and Wealth of all States is evermore made upon the Forreigner, for whatsoever is gained by one Native from another in one part of this Kingdom must necessarily be lost in another part, and so the publick Stock nothing thereby Augmented. But Trade and Commerce cannot be maintained or increased without Government, Order, and regular Discipline; for in all confused Traffique it must necessarily happen that while every single Person pursues his own particular Interest the Publique is deserted by All and consequently must fall to Ruine.'

[2] T. 70/1, fo. 42d.   [3] Cobbett's *State Trials*, X, pp. 371 ff.

African Company's monopoly, knowing that under Charles II and his brother they had no hope of redress, did not abandon or forget the injuries done to them but cherished and nursed them, often for years, until the political climate should change. When, in 1689, it did so, the African Company was faced not only with the loss of its monopoly but also with a bill for having exercised it in the shape of numerous claims for compensation by former interlopers.

Even while the monopoly of 1672 remained in force nothing would be further from the truth than to suppose that English trade to and in Africa was conducted solely by the Royal African Company on a joint-stock footing. Breaches in the monopoly were of two kinds, authorized and unauthorized. In principle, the company was opposed to private trade by its shareholders, who were required upon admission to swear not to trade to Africa in any way other than the joint stock. This principle was generally upheld, and twice at least a shareholder was refused permission to transfer his stock or receive his dividend on suspicion of being concerned with infringements of the monopoly.[1] There was no counterpart to the extensive legitimate trade on private account already noted in the East India Company, and this must have helped to make African stock less desirable. Yet, like so many other distasteful decisions or rules which the company had to adopt, this was unavoidable. There was little demand for the goods of 'great value but small bulk' which East Indian ships carried on private account, while for returns, there was gold, but never in sufficient quantity for the company to wish to share it with others.

At first the company was willing to concede to its servants, both ships' captains and factors in Africa, what was denied to its shareholders. Thus in 1674, captains of vessels sailing in the company's service were given a personal allowance of private trade.[2] This promptly led to abuses, and in the following year ships for the Gold Coast and the Bight of Benin were forbidden to carry any goods on private account.[3] From then onwards

---

[1] William Walker's case in 1677, T. 70/77, fos. 34, 43d, and Abraham Holditch's case in 1678, *Ibid.*, fo. 77, and T. 70/78, fos. 35, 35d.

[2] E.g. T. 70/76, fo. 3, Captain Utber allowed £62.

[3] T. 70/76, fos. 35, 43d.

the company and the crews of its hired ships were at war. Such safeguards as the appointment of searchers or the writing into charterparties of clauses against private trade were ineffective. The steady trickle of concealed exports and imports which came to light suggests that the practice was very widespread. Sometimes it was flagrant: the master of the *Marygold* was found at Barbados to be carrying 62 more negroes than he admitted to.[1] As might be expected, it was on the Middle Passage that deception was easiest.[2] Slaves, written off in the ship's journal as dead, could be landed at the West Indian islands before the company's agents came aboard. Captain Bennett, for example, of the *Lucitania* lay off Barbados till nightfall and landed thirty of the choicest negroes under cover of darkness.[3] In such matters the company had to rely on the honesty of its captains, and as a result was often defrauded. Later it capitulated and restored a private trading allowance,[4] but there can be little doubt that this allowance was generously exceeded.

By the later seventeenth century private trade by the employees, as well as the shareholders, of the East India Company had reached formidable proportions. The day of the nabobs returning from the East with swollen fortunes had not yet arrived, but already comfortable riches were being brought back to England by time-expired agents and factors. Though an attempt was made to keep homeward private trade within reasonable limits, the lucrative port-to-port or country-trade of the Far East was subject to few restrictions. The salaries which the East India Company paid its employees on foreign stations, never large, came to matter less and less, spare-time trade more and more. Provided the company's affairs were properly managed, this development was not unhealthy. There was plenty of trade to be had and the chance of sharing in it must

[1] T. 70/1, fos. 13–14d.

[2] Company to Agents at Antigua, 23 August 1687: 'We have good grounds to beeleeve that there are few or none of them [ships' captains] but doe, or attempt to, run negroes.' T. 70/57, fo. 9d. Cf. Royal African Company *v.* Doegood, P.R.O., C. 9/99/3.

[3] T. 70/57, fo. 15. Cf. Royal African Company *v.* Gowing *et al.*, P.R.O., C. 9/425/10.

[4] T. 70/85, fo. 30d; T. 70/86, pp. 16, 79.

have induced able men to take service in the East. Very different were Africa and the African trade. There was no country-trade to speak of and little enough trade of any kind; profits had to be struggled for in the face of keen international competition, and the African Company soon discovered that it could not afford to extend to its servants the liberty that was enjoyed in the Far East. At first a modest scale of private trade, ranging from £300 for the Agent-General down to £30 for a junior factor, was permitted.[1] But in 1680 this was stopped and the company resolved to pay higher salaries in lieu.[2] The employees, as might perhaps have been foreseen, accepted the extra salary and continued their private trade, obtaining goods and remitting profits by interlopers. Often these abuses were exposed only by the death of the offender. 'It is a proverbe', runs a letter to Agent Nurse, 'that death brings a man's debts and sinns to light, soe wee see that severall of our factors were concerned in private trade which it's like you would not have been able to have discovered had they lived.'[3]

It is impossible to estimate even approximately how much the company lost by the frauds of its agents and factors. The cases which were disclosed were probably only a small fraction of the abuses committed, and of the cases brought to light the number in which the company obtained any satisfaction, either from the offenders, their securities or executors, was very small. Had trade been plentiful and profitable enough, the company could have indulged its servants; had it been able to indulge them, it might have attracted to Africa men of character and ability who, while looking to their own interests, could at the same time have discharged their obligations to the company. As it was the company could only make sour comparisons between the loyalty and efficiency of the East India Company's servants and its own.[4]

Despite its early recognition that profits would not be great enough to be divided with its employees, the company either chose or was obliged to share with others what was probably

---

[1] T. 70/76, fo. 64d.
[2] T. 70/78, fos. 100d, 101. Occasional exceptions to this rule were allowed.
[3] T. 70/50, fo. 3d.   [4] T. 70/51, p. 120.

the most consistently rewarding branch of its African commerce. This was the trade of the Windward Coast, lying to the
west of the Gold Coast. Until 1689 it was the company's
general practice to allow the owners of ships hired for this trade
a share of one-half or one-quarter in the cargo.[1] The owners
supplied no goods and had no voice in the disposal; they simply
paid their portion and at the conclusion of the voyage received
their profits. The reason for this arrangement is not clear;
possibly it induced owners to accept lower freight rates and,
since the master was generally himself an owner, gave him an
interest in the success of the voyage. In some years the shares
allowed to owners amounted to as much as £6,000 and the
sums distributed to them in profits equalled a nett return of
two per cent. on the company's capital.

The African Company was able to defer adoption of the
practice of licensing private ships to make voyages to Africa
until 1686, but, once launched, it flourished until some years
after the Revolution when it was swamped by uncertainty as
to whether the company had any monopoly from which it was
necessary to purchase a dispensation. As in the case of the
Windward cargoes, the company at first supplied the goods for
the voyage, demanding and receiving premiums on their value
of up to forty per cent.[2] In taking this step the desire to allay
criticism of the monopoly was probably of less importance than
the need for ready cash and a certain profit. Without question,
by granting licences to private traders in this way the company
gave a powerful argument to its enemies. Trade under licence
could be, and later was, taken to denote, first that the joint-
stock system was not indispensable in the African trade, and,
secondly, that the company was no longer able fully to exploit
its privileges and had taken the unpopular and unwise step of
using its monopoly as a tax on private enterprise.[3] Both these
charges contained some truth. As in the history of most,
though not all, joint-stock trading monopolies, the issue of
licences was a token of weakness and a prelude to collapse.

[1] Below, p. 200.
[2] T. 70/81, fos. 46d, 73, 77, 89, 89d; T. 70/82, fos. 19, 25; T. 70/61, fos.
69d, 70; Stock, II, pp. 93–4.
[3] In the House of Commons in 1690. Stock, II, p. 33.

Private trade, both authorized and illicit, shares allotted to owners of hired ships, commissions in negroes to captains, and the grant of licences, were all cracks in the company's monopoly and in the joint-stock system. Some were of small account, but added together they were considerable. Yet if these were cracks, the breach torn in the company's privileges by the interlopers was a crevasse. As in all forms of smuggling, the incidence of interloping between 1672 and 1689 defies measurement. But the records of Chancery and Admiralty, Privy Council, the Plantations, and the company itself unite to tell of the persistent, resourceful and successful challenge which from first to last had to be met from this quarter.

The earliest records of the company show that the problem of interloping was present from the beginning. Thereafter it is impossible to ascertain how constant the volume of illicit trade was; probably it was fairly steady except in the brief periods when the company was able to mount effective countermeasures. A few instances will suffice to indicate the approximate dimensions and consequences of this running sore. In 1679 the company's Agent at Cape Coast wrote that four interlopers had sailed past the castle in a single day;[1] in 1682 he reported that eighteen had been at Kommenda within two months;[2] while in the same year the Governor of Jamaica was informed that there were no fewer than seventy on the African coast.[3] This last statement was certainly an exaggeration, and a more accurate idea can be formed from the arrivals of interlopers reported by the company's Agents in the West Indies. In four years, 1679 to 1682, thirty-two are mentioned, eleven at Barbados, ten at Nevis, nine at Jamaica and two at Antigua.[4] Of these only four were seized by the company, the remainder landing and disposing of their slaves. Certain defects in the records make it possible that the true total was somewhat higher; it seems likely, therefore, that while the interlopers were delivering fewer slaves to the Plantations than the company the margin between them at this time was not as great as might be supposed. In the same period the number of company's ships arriving in the West Indies was about seventy,

[1] T. 70/1, fo. 26d.
[2] T. 70/10, fo. 51.
[3] *Cal. S.P. Col.*, 1681–5, No. 668.
[4] From T. 70/1 and 10.

though in the normal way they would be larger and would carry more slaves than those of the interlopers. Thus while the monopoly did undoubtedly curb the private trader, and probably increased his costs, it was far from extinguishing him.

Of the damage done by interlopers to the company's trade there can be no doubt. Competition from other nations was fierce and the English interlopers made worse an already difficult situation. The company itself in its petitions to the King painted a black picture,[1] and its Agents in Africa and the West Indies wrote to the same effect. In 1680, for example, the Agent at Cape Coast wrote that the company's affairs were in a sinking condition owing to interlopers who carried off the greater part of the trade;[2] and in 1682 an Agent at Sherbro reported that the trade in ivory had been ruined in the same way.[3] Interlopers were evidently regular and dependable customers since native traders were said to keep slaves for them.[4] In the West Indies the company's sales of negroes were wrecked by the arrival of interlopers who glutted the market.[5] Little indication has been found of the comparative prices at which the company and its rivals bought and sold. In 1682 an interloper was buying ivory at twice what the company would pay,[6] and in 1678 interlopers were said to be selling slaves in Barbados well below the company's prices in order to reinforce the widespread demand for free trade.[7] That the interlopers were apparently able to sell level with, or even undercut, the company is in itself sufficiently remarkable in view of the artificial disadvantages under which they had to trade. Between 1672 and 1688 the authority granted to the company by its charter to seize ships infringing the monopoly was wholeheartedly backed up by the Crown. Governors of Plantations were instructed to help the company in every possible way;[8] proclamations against interlopers were periodically issued;[9] ships suspected of heading for Africa were stayed on the order

---

[1] *A.P.C.* (Colonial Series), 1613–80, pp. 655–6; *Ibid.*, 1680–1720, p. 8; T. 70/169, fo. 23d; *Cal., S.P. Col.* 1685–8, No. 914.

[2] T. 70/1, fos. 53–6.   [3] T. 70/16, fos. 27, 27d.   [4] T. 70/10, fo. 48d.

[5] T. 70/12, fo. 6d.   [6] T. 70/16, fos. 27, 27d.   [7] T. 70/1, fo. 7d.

[8] *Cal. S.P. Col.*, 1675–6, Nos. 841, 1179, 1181, and many other references in this series.

[9] *A.P.C.* (Colonial Series), 1613–80, pp. 614–16; *Ibid.*, 1680–1720, p. 80.

of the Privy Council;[1] five ships of the Royal Navy, the *Phoenix* in 1674, the *Hunter* in 1676, the *Norwich* in 1678, the *Orange Tree* and the *Mordaunt* in 1684, were sent to prey on interlopers on the African coast;[2] and commanders of naval vessels in the West Indies were ordered to do the same in the Caribbean. Charles II, even more than his brother, responded to the appeals which the company made to him, and its failure can in no way be attributed to him. The measures which he took were within limits effective;[3] they made interloping more hazardous and costly and interlopers more wary. But they were not enough to crush illicit trading.

Besides the risk of confiscation, the interlopers had to contend with a major problem in securing suitable cargoes with which to buy slaves. The goods normally included in an African cargo were East Indian textiles, English woollens, cowries, iron bars and beads; a ship loading with such things, and especially with cowries, in an English port might be suspected of interloping.[4] Thus, while interlopers undoubtedly did sail from English ports, declaring their cargoes to be destined for the Canaries or the West Indies,[5] the greater risk of interception and confiscation forced part of the interloping trade away from England to the colonies. It is likely that the traffic in rum between the West Indies and West Africa, which in the eighteenth century reached notable proportions, had its origins in the interlopers' search for a cargo that was at once suitable for West Africa and obtainable in the West Indies. Certainly it was the example of the interlopers that suggested

[1] E.g. *Cal. S.P. Col.*, 1677–80, Nos. 217, 497.

[2] H.M. ships *Phoenix*, T. 70/76, fo. 6; *Hunter*, *Ibid.*, fo. 76; *Norwich*, T. 70/77, fo. 81d; *Orange Tree*, P.R.O.Adm. 106/66 under date 26 October 1686 (I owe this reference to Mr. J. H. Collingridge of the Public Record Office); *Mordaunt*, T. 70/169, fos. 21d–22d, *Cal. S.P. Col.*, 1685–8, No. 554. 554.

[3] The *Hunter* seized two interlopers, above, p. 106, n. 5; the *Norwich*, *Deptford*, *Mordaunt*, *Constant Warwick* and *Orange Tree* at least one each. T. 70/1, fo. 41d; T. 70/11, fo. 10d; *Cal. S.P. Col.*, 1681–5, No. 545.

[4] E.g. the *Mayflower* in 1674 was the subject of a petition to the Crown on suspicion of lading with goods 'only proper for Guinea'.

[5] A memorial of 1691 notes three interlopers entered for the West Indies, and one each for the Canaries, Cadiz and the Straits. T. 70/169, fos. 88d, 89.

to the African Company that the rum-trade might be made into a profitable sideline.[1] Before the Revolution the company did little; but under the stresses of war-risks in European waters the rum-trade was developed until between 1703 and 1709 thirty-one ships were dispatched from the West Indies by the company.[2] But it was the private trader, obliged to improvise, who had first seen the possibilities of this commerce.

The persistence of interloping in the face of these difficulties and risks argues that the private trader was contriving a profit while the company was not. It must, however, be acknowledged that the interlopers were aided in their work by a number of factors over which the company had no control. Interloping was not, as has sometimes been suggested, a quasi-piratical venture. Between 1672 and 1689 the company's own records have yielded only one case of alleged piracy by interlopers.[3] Pirates there certainly were on the west coast of Africa in the later seventeenth century, but they were a danger equally to the interlopers as to the company. The great majority of interlopers went to Africa for normal trading purposes. The company, so long as its charter was held to be of full force, could seize the ships and cargoes of those who infringed its monopoly, but neither the owners nor the captain nor the crew were liable to criminal proceedings in common law courts. They might attract royal displeasure, but this did not necessarily prove fatal in England, let alone in the colonies. Interloping could of course entail the commission of offences cognizable in common law courts: false declarations might have to be made to Customs officials, or negroes landed at places other than ports. These were criminal acts and could be punished as such. But merely to be concerned in an interloper was neither a crime nor a cause for shame or embarrassment. On the contrary, interlopers in the West Indies were respected as leaders of the assault on a hated monopoly and as the indispensable means of forcing down the company's prices. Some of the greatest men in the Plantations favoured or engaged in illicit trade: Christopher Codrington, owner of 'the greatest

---

[1] T. 70/16, fos. 49, 80; T. 70/80, fo. 23.   [2] T. 70/951–6.
[3] E. Pierce at Sierra Leone to the company, 5 January 1681: 'under the pretence of trading these only come to robb and steale'. T. 70/1, fo. 42d.

individual fortune in the West Indies';[1] in Barbados, the Chief Justice, a Commissioner of Customs and two members of the Council;[2] in Nevis a Councillor and the Speaker of the Assembly;[3] in Jamaica a Councillor and other notable figures.[4]

The popularity of interlopers in the colonies was such that in actions upon seizure the company was unlikely to obtain a favourable verdict from a jury in a common law court.[5] In 1682, for example, damages of £1,627 were awarded to an interloper whose ship had been seized by the company's agents in Jamaica.[6] The judge's decision in this case rested upon an unconvincing technicality which three English lawyers, including Holt, found to be bad law.[7] Naturally the company sought to have actions upon seizure heard in Admiralty courts where, especially when the Duke of York was Lord High Admiral, its charter might be heeded, while the interlopers put their trust in the common law. This conflict of jurisdictions was clearly exhibited in the case of the *St. George*, an interloper seized at Jamaica in 1676. The company's suit for condemnation in the Vice-Admiralty court was dismissed on the ground that an Act of the Jamaican legislature made the water where the seizure occurred part of the parish of St. Dorothy; the action was therefore not within Admiralty jurisdiction.[8] Such was the animus against the company's monopoly in the West Indies that more damage could be done to interlopers by having them prosecuted for false entry under the Acts of Trade instead of for infringement of its privileges.[9] When, after the Revolution, the company lost confidence in the validity of its own charter, general instructions to this effect were sent to the colonies.[10]

Unless an interloper could be taken before landing his negroes there was no chance of the company's drawing financial benefit from a seizure. The costs of the action, even if suc-

[1] V. T. Harlow, *Christopher Codrington*, 1928, p. 11; T. 70/10, fo. 6d.
[2] *Cal. S.P. Col.*, 1677–80, No. 266. [3] T. 70/1, fo. 17d.
[4] *Cal. S.P. Col.*, 1685–8, No. 586. [5] *Ibid.*, No. 1773.
[6] T. 70/16, fo. 38. [7] T. 70/169, fos. 7d–8d.
[8] J. H. Smith, *Appeals to the Privy Council from the American Plantations*, New York, 1950, pp. 127–8.
[9] *Cal. S.P. Col.*, 1681–5, No. 13; T. 70/10, fo. 29d; T. 70/12, fo. 6.
[10] T. 70/57, fos. 38, 56, 57d.

cessful, would be barely covered out of the proceeds of the sale of the ship. Thus the *St. Paul*, an interloper, was seized at Barbados and sold by the company: the hulk, stripped of everything of value, realized only £55 and, after deducting the costs of the suit for condemnation and the King's share, the company was left with only £2 14*s*.[1] Once an interloper's negroes were sold and dispersed, the company was helpless. The Attorney-General decided in 1683 that the transfer of illicitly imported slaves from one owner to another did not bar the right of seizure;[2] the Jamaican assembly countered by passing an Act in the following year under which purchasers of illicitly imported negroes were rendered liable to forfeit £5 for each negro, but made it conditional upon the company's transporting to the island each year almost as many slaves as it was able to deliver to Jamaica, Barbados and the Leeward Islands together.[3]

Orders to give encouragement to the Royal African Company formed a regular article in the instructions given to Governors of West Indian colonies at this date.[4] The company, too, was at pains to get on good terms with them, providing 'treats' or purses of money before they left England.[5] Nevertheless, their support was not always forthcoming. Some Governors, such as Sir William Stapleton of the Leeward Islands, issued warrants for the seizure of interlopers on demand;[6] but others, notably Sir Jonathan Atkins and Sir Richard Dutton of Barbados, were reluctant to do anything for the company. Atkins was sharply rebuked by the King in 1676 for neglecting to punish an interloper who forcibly and successfully resisted seizure,[7] and Dutton would not condemn interlopers as such.[8] Their unwillingness to accept the company's charter as law is understandable. Many of the colonists with whom they had to work favoured interlopers and hated the company. Besides, there was real uncertainty as to whether the

---

[1] T. 70/939 under date 19 July 1681.   [2] *Cal. S.P. Col.*, 1681–5, No. 908.
[3] *A.P.C.* (Colonial Series), 1680–1720, pp. 64–6.
[4] *Cal. S.P. Col.*, 1669–74, Nos. 1186, 1398; 1675–6, No. 1176; 1681–5, No. 227.
[5] T. 70/76, fos. 6d, 19; T. 70/77, fo. 67d; T. 70/81, fo. 72d.
[6] *Cal. S.P. Col.*, 1677–80, No. 1455.   [7] *Ibid.*, 1675–6, Nos. 841, 1179.
[8] T. 70/12, fo. 8.

right or seizure implied power to use force in overcoming resistance. This question was put more than once, but no authoritative answer was ever given.[1] Force certainly was used or offered by interlopers in defence of their property. At least one murder was committed, and once the company's agents, armed with a warrant for seizure, were met by six men 'standing with their swords pointing to our breasts, and some their pistolls, swearing bitterly that they would kill that man that did offer to seize a negroe'.[2]

The indifference or hostility of colonial Governors, whether spontaneous or not, made the company's task of defending the monopoly more difficult. The West Indies might have been the place where illicit trade could be most readily intercepted. Had Governors been willing or able to carry out their instructions, the interlopers could have been denied their natural market. As it was, they were encouraged to go on with their trade in the confidence that the risk of confiscation in the West Indies was slight. In the event, it seems probable that the company scored better success in Africa, though there too the campaign against interlopers was waged under difficulties. The long coastline had no strategic points where illicit traders could be intercepted, such as the straits of Sunda or Malacca in the East; the company's settlements were few; and traders of other nations often encouraged and protected English interlopers, just as the company encouraged Dutchmen.[3] Nevertheless, the collection of a cargo of slaves was a task that neither the company's ships nor the interlopers could commonly complete in less than a month, and an armed patrol of the coast between Whydah and the Calabar rivers would at any time have yielded prizes. The ships of the Royal Navy lent to the company did in fact make a number of seizures.[4] And, once an interloper was taken, the only court in Africa empowered to hear the suit for condemnation was that constituted by the company itself. But, just as royal intentions were often negatived in the West Indies by the disobedience or lack of interest of colonial officials, so in Africa the work of the Navy was partly neutralized by the company's

---

[1] T. 70/1, fos. 65, 65d; *Cal. S.P. Col.*, 1677–80, No. 1418.
[2] T. 70/1, fos. 30d, 31. [3] T. 70/11, fo. 20d.
[4] The company made some seizures of its own. T. 70/11, fos. 16d, 20.

own servants who, when they did not trade with interlopers, fraternized with them. Agent Bradley, for example, caused a scandal by entertaining an interloper at Cape Coast over the Christmas of 1680.[1] Not all the company's servants behaved like this,[2] but there are enough examples to suggest that the hatred of interlopers displayed by the Court of Assistants was not always shared by their subordinates in Africa. In any case the company was seldom able to afford the expense of a vigorous campaign: as an interloping captain put it to a Parliamentary committee in 1694, 'Any person may trade within a mile of Cape Coast Castle; and the negroes will come off from thence by stealth.'[3]

The neutrality or secret approval of many colonial officials, the enthusiastic patronage of planters, and the lukewarm attitude of the company's servants in Africa all contributed something to the success of the interlopers. But with Charles II so stoutly supporting the monopoly, and with the comparatively large capital, the permanent settlements and the staff at the company's disposal, the odds appeared heavily against the interlopers. Yet they must be presumed to have succeeded. An explanation of this phenomenon is of some importance, for the struggle between the company and the interlopers, and later the separate traders, is an interesting phase in the seventeenth-century contest between monopoly and free trade and between large-scale commercial organization and the small partnership or private merchant. No single reason why the outcome should have been the defeat of the African Company and its monopoly can be adduced. Many factors, political as well as economic, combined to bring it about. Financially the company's policy was often unwise; politically it was unfortunate in losing the support of the Stuarts in 1689; structurally it was weakened by its failure to attract to its foreign service sufficient men of integrity and ability. These broad aspects of the company's failure should not, however, be allowed to

[1] T. 70/1, fos. 57-59.
[2] E.g. an interloper, the *Dorothy*, was fired on when she anchored off Cape Coast castle. P.R.O., H.C.A. 24/121, No. 97. But cf. T. 70/1, fos. 37d, 38, 50d.
[3] Stock, II, p. 92.

obscure a more immediate cause of the success of the interlopers. Any disadvantage under which the private trader had
to operate was compensated by the expenditure which the
company itself incurred in the maintenance of its settlements on
the African coast and in the paying of the three hundred men
who lived in them. The question of the economic advantages
deriving from settlement will be discussed in a later chapter;[1]
but we may notice here that in the slave-trade itself the company's forts were of little value. The principal markets for the
purchase of negroes lay between the Volta river, at the eastern
end of the Gold Coast, and the Congo, and on this stretch of
coast no European nation in the seventeenth century maintained an establishment worth the name of a fort. Several
ephemeral factories are known to have existed on the Slave
Coast,[2] and permanent factories were settled by Dutch, English
and French at Whydah, one of the chief slave-marts.[3] The
slave-trade remained, however, very largely one in which
captains of slaving ships, company and interlopers alike, had
to do their own buying as best they could. The African Company parted with nearly one-third of its initial capital to obtain,
amongst other things, the forts on the Gold Coast and the
Gambia, and each year it spent about £20,000 on maintaining,
improving and staffing them.[4] For this expenditure it obtained
very little direct advantage in the slave-trade. Some negroes
were purchased every year in the Gambia or on the Gold Coast,
where the company's principal settlements were sited, but
many had to be fetched from the Slave Coast and the Bight of
Benin.[5]

---

[1] Below, pp. 259–64.

[2] At Ophra in the kingdom of Ardra, where the company had a factory
in 1678. T. 70/10, fo. 6.

[3] Whydah, which in the eighteenth century became an international
slave-market of great importance, was the scene of the most audacious blow
aimed at the company in this period. About 1680 one Petley Weyborne
settled there as a factor for interloping slave-ships; T. 70/169, fos. 5, 5d,
23d. For four years he kept up his illicit trade until finally the company
obtained an order from the Privy Council for his return to England. *Ibid.*,
fo. 24. The company later employed him at Whydah as its factor. P.R.O.,
C.9/425/6.

[4] Below, p. 259. [5] Below, pp. 226–7.

The interlopers and separate traders, with no forts to keep up, were thus able to compete successfully with the company in the slave-trade. Indeed the possession of forts and settlements may be taken as a positive handicap to the profitable conduct of the African trade by the company, for they rarely paid for their own upkeep.[1] In a broader sense, they had their uses as an insurance that English traders would not be molested or expelled by other nations, but in day-to-day trade they were of doubtful value. Nor was the company free to recover such heavy costs as building and maintenance by increasing the price of negroes to the planters. High prices would certainly be brought to the notice of the English Government by the planters and would strengthen the case of the opponents of monopoly. In a sense the company may be regarded as a public utility, a corporation charged by the government with supplying labour to the colonies, a function recognized on every hand to be vital to the economic well-being of England and her empire. It was a monopoly endowed with privileges; but it had responsibilities too. The company was expected not merely to supply the colonies with negroes, but also to supply them at a price low enough to enable the English plantations to compete with other nations in sugar production. The colonists believed that it was incapable of fulfilling this function and they worked to foment opposition to the monopoly. Until 1689 this opposition was held in check by royal support. Once the barrier was down a flood of hostility burst over and overwhelmed the company.

3. The Downfall of Monopoly

By the Revolution of 1688 the Crown suffered a heavy defeat; yet it is remarkable how few were the formal limitations imposed by the revolutionary settlement upon royal authority. Prerogative was curbed; but in constitutional theory, and for some time in practice, it remained a powerful force in the government of the country. In miniature, the monopolies which had derived from this prerogative underwent a similar

---

[1] Below, p. 260.

experience. The Bill of Rights did not mention them and no legislation specifically declaring them to be invalid was passed. Indeed an Act of 1689 which permitted the free export of English woollens contained a clause saving the privileges of the Levant, Eastland, Russia and African companies.[1] Nevertheless the flight of James II, which marked the end of arbitrary royal government, was recognized by the Royal African Company to be the end also of royal monopolies. On 11 December 1688 the King left Whitehall. Seven days earlier, the secretary of the company had written out a commission in the usual form to Captain Rickard of the *Alexander* empowering and requiring him to seize any interlopers he found trading within the limits of the company's monopoly.[2] It was the last of hundreds to be issued. Without any recorded decision of the Court of Assistants, still less a decision of Parliament, the claim to seize interlopers in virtue of the royal charter of 1672 was swiftly and silently abandoned. Henceforth, the campaign, in so far as it was carried on at all, was conducted strictly on the basis of the Acts of Trade.[3] Outwardly the company might pretend that its charter was still in force, but since it did not itself believe this it could scarcely hope to convince others. Early in 1691 its agents at Barbados, Nevis and Montserrat, who years earlier had been commissioned to seize interlopers, were instructed that 'they doe not by any powers to them derived from our charter seize or detaine any shipp or goods whatsoever till further orders'.[4] Just as the passing into law of measures such as the Triennial Act set down on paper the constitutional victory which had already been won, so in the case of the African trade a certain time was to elapse before the destruction of the royal monopoly was formally enacted. But the real change occurred in December 1688.

If monopoly based upon royal charter was discredited and nullified, there remained the chance that the African Company might secure a monopoly founded upon Act of Parliament. This had been attempted once before, in 1671. A bill had been introduced into the House of Lords for confirming the charter of the Royal Adventurers, which at that time it was still hoped

---

[1] 1 Wm. & Mar. c. 32.   [2] T. 70/61, fo. 76d.
[3] T. 70/57, fos. 38, 39d, 58.   [4] *Ibid.*, fos. 56, 57d.

could be revived.[1] This bill had not been proceeded with, and no further move had been made until the Revolution. In January 1690 the attempt was renewed, and there began a series of Parliamentary debates and enquiries into the African trade lasting on and off for the next twenty years.[2] Before the company could proceed very far in this direction, however, it was obliged to settle accounts with those interlopers whose ships had been seized before the Revolution. As early as July 1689 it had to bail two former employees who had been arrested at the suit of owners of confiscated vessels.[3] In April 1690 three petitions were presented to the House of Commons by aggrieved parties whose ships had been taken more than ten years earlier.[4] In May 1691 the Court of Assistants empowered its treasurer to make what compositions he could with persons having actions pending against the company:[5] £4,000 was paid to one claimant, £2,750, £2,630 and £1,100 to others.[6] As late as 1703 the company was involved in litigation concerning an interloper seized by the *Hunter* in 1676.[7] There is little doubt that the company was compelled to disburse more in compositions with interlopers after the Revolution than it had gained from the original seizures, and at a time when it needed all its money to support the trade.

Pending a Parliamentary settlement the company continued to apply the term interloper to those who competed with it, even though they were no longer molested. Despite the dangers from French privateers after the outbreak of war in 1689, it is probable that the number of interlopers was as great as in peace.[8] The company was left to improvise such measures for restraining them as appeared to be legally possible, notably laying information of false entries in the Customs records. In 1691, for example, a list was drawn up of six ships 'amongst many that are this yeare gon for Guynie but cleared out for

---

[1] Historical Manuscripts Commission, Appendix to *Ninth Report*, Part II, p. 9.

[2] The African trade was before Parliament in 1690–1, 1693–4–5–6–7–8 and 1708–9–10–11–12–13.

[3] T. 70/82, fo. 63.   [4] Stock, II, pp. 20–1, 22–3.

[5] T. 70/83, fo. 13d.   [6] *Ibid.*, fos. 32, 36d, 46, and Colles 327.

[7] Royal African Company *v.* Dockwra, Colles 327.

[8] T. 70/11, fos. 21, 25, 26, 38, 63d; T. 70/50, fo. 132.

other parts', and an Order-in-Council was obtained directing the Commissioners of Customs to examine the complaint.[1] This, with other evidence, suggests that some of the private traders still had enough respect for the company's monopoly to conceal their intentions of infringing it. The situation was indeed paradoxical and badly needed Parliamentary clarification. Few seizures were in fact made for breaches of the Acts of Trade, and the company was forced back to economic weapons. An attempt was made to foil the interlopers by buying up all the trade in regions where they were expected.[2] But the interlopers appear to have met with at least as much success as the company and probably more.[3] The apathy towards them previously shown by agents and factors on the African coast was already turning into a friendliness which infuriated the company at home, and from this time an increasingly querulous note became apparent in letters from London to Africa.

In the years following the Revolution the practice of selling licences to private traders was for a while continued. It was at once an anticipation of and a precedent for the Parliamentary settlement of 1698.[4] Its extension after 1689 was due to a number of causes. In the first place, the company was already in a steadily worsening financial plight, and the sale of a licence brought in badly needed cash. Secondly, since the company could no longer restrain its competitors, it probably seemed better to try to come to terms with them. The disadvantages of the licensing system have already been suggested: temporary financial relief was obtained by giving to the opponents of monopoly one of their most telling arguments. In 1689 the company's prospects were dark but not hopeless. An Act of Parliament, such as was awarded to the Hudson's Bay Company in 1690, did not seem beyond the possibility of achievement. Until Parliament made up its mind, there were still men wishing to trade to Africa who preferred to purchase licences rather than go as interlopers. For a while the company was able to profit from this uncertainty, but its gains steadily diminished. In 1687 licences had been granted at a premium

[1] T. 70/169, fos. 88d, 89.   [2] T. 70/50, fo. 132.
[3] T. 70/11, fos. 26, 59; T. 70/51, p. 6.
[4] *Some Considerations Relating to the Trade of Guiney* (n.d. ?1691–4).

of forty per cent. on the goods which the company itself
supplied and valued.[1] By 1690 the premium had dropped to
twenty-five per cent. on cargoes supplied by the company and
fifteen per cent. on cargoes supplied by the licensee.[2] In 1693
it was fifteen per cent. on the company's cargoes.[3] Generally
licensees were restricted to trading on the coast east of the
Volta river, in effect to the slave-trade; in 1695 the company
voluntarily threw open the trade of this region to any Englishman on payment of 20s. for each negro transported.[4] Most
of the licensed ships sailed from London, but in 1690 proposals for a ship fitting out from Bristol were approved by
the company and in 1696 a licence was granted for a voyage
from Barbados.[5] Thus two of the main points at issue, participation in the African trade by the English outports and the
West Indian colonies, were quietly conceded.

The licensing system could be no more than an interim solution to the problems of the African trade. For a permanent
settlement, both the company and its opponents turned to
Parliament. On 27 January 1690 the company took the
initiative with a petition to the Commons in which its achievements over the past eighteen years were set forth, and a bill to
secure its trade requested.[6] The early dissolution of Parliament
prevented further discussion, and on 31 March following a fresh
petition was presented in the same terms.[7] The resultant bill
was read a second time on 15 April and referred to a committee
of the whole House. Petitions against it were heard from the
planters and merchants interested in and trading to Jamaica
and Barbados, and from the clothiers of Essex and Suffolk.[8]
Thus the three chief elements in the opposition to the African
company were established: the colonists, the separate traders,
and the manufacturing interest. The clothiers on this occasion
complained that a joint-stock monopoly minimized exports of
English woollens and, as the campaign proceeded, more and
more manufacturers joined the battle for free trade with the
same argument. At the end of the seventeenth century, the

---

[1] T. 70/81, fo. 89d; T. 70/82, fo. 19.   [2] T. 70/82, fo. 83d.
[3] T. 70/83, fo. 82d.   [4] T. 70/84, fo. 49.
[5] T. 70/82, fo. 81d; T. 70/57, fo. 121.   [6] Stock, II, p. 16.
[7] Ibid., p. 18.   [8] Ibid., pp. 20, 21, and Commons Journals, X, p. 382.

level of exports was still regarded as the most convenient and revealing indicator of the health of the national economy, and the argument was an effective one.

Nothing further was achieved in this session of Parliament, and on 17 October 1690 the company reopened the subject with a petition in the usual terms.[1] In a way that was soon to become common form, the merchants and planters of Jamaica and Barbados and the clothiers of Essex and Suffolk reacted with petitions for either free trade or a regulated company.[2] They were joined on this occasion by the city of Exeter, and by the cutlers of Hallamshire who objected to the company's monopoly of the importation of ivory.[3] Both the supporters and the opponents of monopoly appeared before a Parliamentary committee which reported to the House of Commons on 26 November. As presented in this report, the company's case stood on three main points: first, that forts were essential for the preservation of the trade and a joint stock necessary for the preservation of the forts; secondly, that its own exports amounted to £80–£100,000 a year and that the trade available was not sufficient to warrant any more, 'their ships oftentimes bringing back part of their cargoes'; and finally, that the Dutch and other nations had forts and joint stocks. The petitioners against the company replied that its forts were weak, few, and far between, there being 4,000 miles of coast between Capes Sallee and Good Hope where no English settlement existed. They admitted that forts might be useful as certain, known, fixed markets, but claimed that interlopers carried on their trade in greater safety and just as profitably on board their ships. They complained of having to pay the company £40 per cent. for licences to trade to Africa, looked back longingly to the good times of 1665 to 1672 when licences had been cheap and negroes plentiful, deprecated the consequences of monopoly upon English exports and the labour supply of the Plantations, and concluded by asking for a regulated company empowered to raise dues from its members for the upkeep of the forts.[4] The committee made two recommendations: that the African trade should be vested in a regulated company, and that forts were

[1] Stock, II, p. 28.　　　　　　　　　　[2] *Ibid.*, p. 29.
[3] *Commons Journals*, X, pp. 449, 459.　[4] Stock, II, pp. 32–5.

necessary for the preservation of the trade. Both these recommendations were embodied in resolutions and agreed to by the House.[1] A bill was duly brought in upon them, but the adjournment of Parliament in January 1691 put a stop to further proceedings.

The company had done its best to make friends in Parliament,[2] but thus far the outcome had been a signal though not necessarily decisive defeat. For the next three years the struggle was confined mainly to pamphlet warfare, the company awaiting the opportunity to reopen the question and its opponents seemingly satisfied with the victory they had won.[3] The company's chance came in 1693 when John Booker, its agent in the Gambia, captured the French settlements on the Senegal and Goree. In the favourable atmosphere thus engendered, the company on 24 January 1694 once more petitioned Parliament dwelling on its triumph over the French, and at the same time pointing out the difficulty of maintaining the forts without the compensation of monopoly.[4] On this occasion a petition from the city of Exeter against the company was matched by a petition from the clothiers of Witney in favour of monopoly.[5] These petitions were referred to a committee of the Commons, and on 2 March another full report was presented in which, once again, the case of the company and its opponents was set forth. The company began by offering to open the trade south of Cape Lopez, thus leaving the coast of Angola free to its competitors. Four former employees were brought to testify that forts were essential, and two claimed that the Portuguese, who had no forts on the Gold Coast, were obliged to pay a twenty-five per cent. duty to the Dutch for liberty to

---

[1] Stock, II, p. 35.   [2] T. 70/82, fo. 80d.

[3] Examples of pamphlets and broadsheets in this period are *Some Considerations Relating to the Trade to Guiney* and *The Case of the Royal African Company of England*. Neither contributed anything fresh to the subject. Although the fate of the African trade had now passed into the hands of Parliament, the King by Order-in-Council dated 29 August 1693 directed the Attorney-General to inquire into the company's position. The company put in a memorial giving the value of its exports from 1691 to 1693 and claiming that since January 1691 it had granted permission to trade for only three ships 'to particular persons'. T. 70/169, fo. 105.

[4] Stock, II, pp. 88–9.   [5] *Commons Journals*, XI, pp. 96, 100.

trade there. In support of the argument that forts could not be maintained without a joint stock, the company's witnesses cited the capture and plunder of Cape Coast castle by natives in 1669 as an instance of the probable consequences of open trade.[1]

Against the company there appeared Edward Lyttelton,[2] Mr. Gardner,[3] Mr. Hethcot, Mr. Dockwra,[4] Melisha Holder, and a number of ships' captains with experience in the African trade. Gardner argued that the African Company had already ceased to exist, being dissolved for non-payment of a tax imposed on joint-stock companies.[5] Dockwra, a former searcher in the Customs House, asserted that in four years of open trade under Charles II 135 ships had gone out to Africa compared to only 45 in the first four years of the company's monopoly. Other witnesses developed the now familiar arguments, the iniquities of the licensing system, the uselessness of forts in the negro trade, and the shortcomings of the company from the point of view of both manufacturers and planters.[6] These arguments did not prevail, and the committee's report concluded by recommending that the African trade could best be carried on by a joint stock. The company had thus timed its appeal with skill and won a victory which more than wiped out the defeat of 1690. Yet the one was as barren as the other. The House of Commons did not vote on the committee's recommendations, and no further action was taken during the session.

This episode is chiefly notable for the naming of some of the company's opponents. As might be expected, they were a heterogeneous collection with diverse aims, planters seeking cheap slaves, merchants seeking unrestricted entry into the African trade, sea-captains seeking full employment. Yet, though their methods of doing so are hidden, they welded themselves into an effective coalition. Between 1690 and 1713 about a hundred petitions were presented to Parliament in

[1] Stock, II, pp. 90–1.

[2] Presumably the author of *Groans of the Plantations*, 1689, a well-known pamphlet in which the inadequate supply of negroes had been blamed for much colonial distress.

[3] Presumably John Gardner or Gardiner, a prominent West Indian merchant and commission agent.

[4] The owner of an interloper seized by the company in 1676.

[5] Stock, II, pp. 92–4.   [6] *Ibid.*

K

favour of free trade to Africa, as against fewer than twenty (apart from those of the company itself) which supported monopoly. Similarly, the pamphlets published against the company out-numbered those in its favour. The opponents of monopoly had, of course, a case with a wider appeal and one which was easier to argue and defend, and no doubt many of the petitions and pamphlets which backed them up were spontaneous. It is, however, difficult to see that the concern of such places as Whitehaven, Minehead, Kingsbridge, Modbury and Crediton in the Africa trade was very deep; that in the end they, and many others, were brought to petition for free trade is probably due to the efforts of the separate traders to build up a solid, almost national, opposition to monopoly.

In the next session of Parliament the proceedings of 1694 were repeated in almost precisely the same form. A petition by the company was countered by petitions from the West Indian interest, the planters of Jamaica using the disasters of the recent earthquake and invasion as an added argument for a free labour supply. The inevitable committee was appointed and reported, again in favour of the joint-stock form, but, as in 1694, the House postponed consideration of the report until prorogation.[1] For the time being the fate of the English African trade was submerged in discussions of the Scottish Darien Company which in 1695 obtained a charter from the Scottish Parliament including a perpetual monopoly of trade with both Africa and Asia. In intention this venture was Anglo-Scottish. Half of the twenty directors were to be English and half of the capital of £600,000 was offered for subscription in London on 6 November 1695 and taken up in the following fortnight.[2] The threat to the Royal African Company was not, however, serious; its opponents in England and the colonies were for the most part genuinely determined to abolish the joint-stock monopoly in the African trade and the question of their using the Darien Company as a stalking-horse does not seem to have arisen. In any event, English participation in the Scottish scheme was swiftly nipped in the bud by Parliamentary action and the threatened impeachment of the English directors.[3] The

[1] Stock, II, pp. 101–3, 109.
[2] G. P. Insh, *The Company of Scotland*, 1932, p. 47.   [3] *Ibid.*, pp. 48 ff.

African Company was summoned to attend an enquiry by the House of Lords in December 1695 and delivered a memorial in which the opportunity was taken of publicizing its own difficulties: the Scots, with a joint-stock exclusive trade, would capture the trade from the disorganized English, while the freedom from Customs duties which the Scots had been granted would enable them to undersell all competitors.[1] This memorial was followed by another paper in which the company suggested that if the Scots were to enjoy such privileges the proper course would be to re-establish an exclusive company in England with like powers.[2] The hint was not without effect. In reporting on the Darien Company, a committee of the House of Lords proposed that a bill should be prepared to establish an English African Company with powers and privileges sufficient to obviate the inconveniences that might arise from the Scottish Act.[3]

It was in the House of Commons, however, that the battle for the African trade had to be decided, and on 2 January 1696 the company renewed its efforts there with a petition in which the capture of Gambia by the French in 1695 was represented as reducing the company to its last extremity.[4] Counter-petitions were presented by the Jamaican interest, and, for the first time, by the merchants and planters interested in Virginia and Maryland; the weavers and dyers of Kidderminster, on the other hand, supported monopoly.[5] The Darien incident appears to have swayed opinion for the time being in favour of a strong, privileged body as the only possible reply to Scottish designs, and the report of the committee of the whole House recommended the adoption of the joint-stock form. It went on, however, to propose that the trade in negroes should be open to all and that a new subscription of not more than £200,000 should be raised, regard being had to the real value of the assets of the existing company.[6] Thus the atmosphere favourable to a joint-stock company created by the challenge from Scotland appeared likely to benefit, not the Royal African Company but its successor, and the recommendations of the committee read

---

[1] T. 70/169, fos. 114, 114d; *House of Lords MSS.*, 1695–7, p. 13.
[2] T. 70/169, fos. 116, 116d; *House of Lords MSS.*, 1695–7, pp. 18–19.
[3] Stock, II, p. 143.   [4] *Ibid.*, p. 145.   [5] *Ibid.*, pp. 160–2.   [6] *Ibid.*, p. 165.

like an order for winding-up. A bill was brought in to implement them and reached its second reading on 20 March. The African Company was ordered to give an account of the value of its stock, but, apart from a petition from Bristol asking for consideration in the settlement of the trade, no further action was taken in this session. Once again the African trade was thrust aside by more urgent matters.

By now the end of the war with France was in sight and the settlement of the African trade was itself becoming an urgent matter. Yet the session of 1696–7 brought no solution. In September 1696 the General Court of the company resolved to try once more for confirmation of its charter.[1] Following the usual petition and counter-petitions, the Commons ordered another account of the value of the company's stock; this was presented to Parliament on 1 December 1696. Assets were estimated at £286,751 7s. 3d., including the forts in Africa valued at £40,000; liabilities other than on issued stock were £113,788 7s. 8d.[2] In the following weeks meetings were held between representatives of the company and its opponents in an attempt to reach a solution.[3] More petitions followed, until on 11 March 1697 the company took the desperate step of praying the Commons that its forts should be maintained by those who traded to Africa, or else that it should be given leave to sell them to any persons in amity with the Crown.[4] This petition was at once rejected by 77 votes to 55, and the session ended without any progress made.

A fresh approach was now tried. On 30 December 1697 the company petitioned the King, claiming that it had suffered losses of £400,000 in the war; a new stock had been raised, but without some encouragement it was impossible to venture upon the trade.[5] A few days later a memorial was presented to the House of Lords in which the company put forward proposals for a compromise. The northern parts of West Africa, from Cape Blanco to Cape Mount, were to be reserved to itself: these regions yielded chiefly hides, wax, ivory and dyewood, and only few negroes. The whole of the remainder of the coast, from Cape Mount to the Cape of Good Hope, including the

---

[1] T. 70/101, fos. 54, 54d.   [2] Stock, II, p. 185.
[3] T. 70/84, fos. 80, 80d, 85.   [4] Stock, II, p. 202.   [5] T. 70/170, fo. 5.

Gold and Slave Coasts, was to be open to all on payment to the company of a levy of fifteen per cent. on exports and 15*s.* a head on negroes imported into the Plantations or elsewhere.[1] Before anything could be done in the Lords, however, the Commons took up the question in earnest and ordered a bill for settling the African trade.[2] Whereas in previous years the opposition to the company had consisted of only two or three petitions, now the whole strength was mobilized. The merchants and planters of Maryland and Virginia, the merchants and planters of Jamaica, the merchants and planters of Barbados, the city of Bristol, the artificers and tradesmen of Bristol, the dyers of London, and the clothiers of Somerset and Wiltshire all entered petitions, some praying for free trade, others opposing the Commons' bill as placing too many restrictions on freedom.[3] On the other side, the planters of the Leeward Islands and the inhabitants of Montserrat petitioned on behalf of the company.[4] Probably these last two petitions were stimulated by the company's agents. Nevertheless they are important as the earliest signs of a partial reaction in favour of the company in some of the colonies: the Montserrat petition in particular complained of the high prices and short credit in the negro trade since private merchants had gained entry to it. None of these petitions had any effect, and, in contrast to the earlier difficulties and delays in devising a settlement, the bill went through both Houses of Parliament with remarkable speed. It passed its third reading in the Commons on 23 May 1698,[5] and, despite a final volley of petitions both for and against it, got through the Lords in a little over a month, the royal assent being given on 5 July.[6]

During the eight years in which the African trade had been before Parliament, opinion had swayed back and forth between the conflicting claims and merits of the private traders and a strong, privileged corporation. As we have seen, the company, by its association with the exiled Stuart line, began at a disadvantage and the early decisions of Parliament went against it. Its successes against the French in 1693, transient as they

---

[1] *Ibid.*, fos. 5–6.   [2] Stock, II, p. 216.
[3] *Ibid.*, p. 217; *Commons Journals*, XII, pp. 133, 185.
[4] Stock, II, pp. 222–3.   [5]*Ibid.*, p. 235.   [6] *Ibid.*, p. 245, n. 82.

were, followed by the challenge of the Scottish Darien Company, served as reminders of the merits of strength and privilege and kept the issue in the balance for a number of years. Indeed, if the African Company had been in better shape in the later stages of the war of 1689–97 it might possibly have gained, if not confirmation of its charter, at least better terms than it received. It is remarkable that, while Parliamentary committees had more than once declared in favour of joint-stock organization, the House of Commons itself had never passed a resolution in favour of the existing company. This reluctance to commit a trade of such importance to a body that was already close to bankruptcy is understandable.

Parliament had never wavered from its original resolution in 1690 that the forts and settlements of the company were necessary for the preservation of the trade, despite the doubts thrown upon their value by the separate traders. All the petitions of the company and its opponents, however urgent their appeal, had been referred to the leisurely consideration of committees, save on one occasion: when the company had prayed in 1697 for permission to sell its forts to any friendly person or power, the request had been immediately rejected by a vote of the House. The Act of 1698 was first and foremost a provision for the upkeep of the forts to which so much importance was attached.[1] It began by declaring that the forts and castles were 'undoubtedly necessary', and that all those who traded to Africa ought to contribute to their maintenance. The trade of the whole of West Africa, from Cape Blanco to the Cape of Good Hope, was thrown open to all subjects of the Crown from 24 June 1698. Responsibility for the upkeep of the forts was placed on the company, but the separate traders were to pay a duty of ten per cent. *ad valorem* on all exports to Africa. In addition, imports to this country from the northern parts of West Africa between Capes Blanco and Mount were to be charged with a similar duty of ten per cent., except redwood which was to pay five per cent. Imports from other parts of Africa were free of duty, as were negroes, gold and silver, wherever obtained. The owners of any ship cast away or returning with unsold cargoes were to be entitled to export to

[1] 9 & 10 Wm. III c. 26, printed in Donnan, I, pp. 421–9.

an equivalent value without further charge. Officers of the Customs were to collect the proceeds of the duty and pay them to the African Company for the sole purpose of maintaining the forts, and the company was to account annually to the Cursitor Baron of the Exchequer. In return private traders were to enjoy the same protection and privileges at the forts as the company's own servants, and they were further empowered, if they chose, to settle factories of their own. One final clause was added, that no Governor, Deputy Governor, or judge in the colonies should act as factor for negroes of either the company or the private traders. The Act was to last for thirteen years and thereafter to the end of the next session of Parliament.

Neither side could be satisfied with this measure. The company had shown, especially in recent years, a disposition to compromise, but the utmost limit of the concessions it had offered had been an open trade beyond Cape Mount and a duty of fifteen per cent. On the other hand the company's opponents had as good or better reason to be disappointed with the Act, as is shown by their petitions against it in the spring of 1698. By this date a number of private merchants must have become used to trading freely to Africa without paying anything for permission, and in doing so they had broken no law. Now they were saddled with a duty which, as they pointed out, would render them unable to compete on equal terms with traders of other nations, and in return they were given benefits which they did not want. In all, the Act was a poor result of eight years of argument and deliberation, and from the point of view of the participants in the trade it represented an uncomfortable compromise which left both sides with a sense of grievance.

4. The Separate Traders

The Act of 1698 endured till 1712. This period may itself be subdivided: from 1698 to about 1706 the war between the company and the separate traders was fought principally on the coast of Africa and with purely economic weapons. By 1706, though the separate traders were not unscathed, the company had been fairly conclusively defeated, and thenceforth concen-

trated its efforts towards securing such modification of the Act
of 1698 as would encourage the investment of fresh capital. In
this later phase the battle with the separate traders was fought
chiefly before the Lords Commissioners of Trade and Plantations, in Parliament and in the press.[1]

When the Act came into force the company's course was
clear. The Act had to be implemented, the ten per cent. duty
exacted to the full, and the separate traders given their rights,
and at the same time the company had to make a supreme
effort to win in Africa the victory which had eluded it at Westminster. To these tasks the company vigorously addressed
itself. Collection of the duty was in the hands of Customs
officials, but agents in the West Indies were ordered to keep a
careful record of vessels clearing for Africa for purposes of
checking.[2] In Virginia, Maryland and New England, where
there were no permanent agents, attorneys were appointed to
receive the money.[3] It is of course impossible to say how far
these and other measures prevented the company from being
defrauded of the duty. The oaths prescribed by the Act seem
an inadequate safeguard, and many traders to Africa had had
years of experience of evading the Customs authorities. One
abuse, however, was quickly detected and apparently curbed.
In the autumn of 1698 the company began an enquiry into
English ships going from foreign ports to Africa.[4] One ship, the
Africa, which had taken in goods in Ireland was seized at
Jamaica,[5] and information of two others which had laded at
Venice was placed before the Commissioners of Trade.[6] These
were the most flagrant abuses, and it would be surprising if
there were no other frauds.[7]

As to granting the separate traders their rights under the
Act, two days after the royal assent was given the company
wrote to its agents in Africa: 'it is our desire that they be protected and treated civilly, but we positively expect you should

[1] For the names of some of the separate traders see Appendix VI.
[2] T. 70/57, fo. 143.   [3] T. 70/86, pp. 4, 6, 18.
[4] T. 70/85, fo. 38d.   [5] T. 70/57, fo. 151.
[6] *Cal. S.P. Col.*, 1699, Nos. 619, 963i; *A.P.C.* (Colonial Series), 1680–1720,
p. 345.
[7] C. Davenant, 'Reflections on the Constitution and Management of the
Trade to Africa', in *Works* (1771), V, pp. 99–100.

not assist them in buying or selling goods'.[1] Further clarification was provided by an order to all agents, factors and
commanders.[2] Under the Act all natural-born subjects of
England were authorized to trade, and the company instructed
its servants not to 'insist too nicely on the words naturall born
if they be subjects of England and come from England or our
Plantations'. The protection to be extended was defined as
follows:

> That in case of any war between the Europeans and Natives, or
> amongst the Europeans or Natives only, or any commotion or
> other calamity unforeseen, which shall or may happen, whereby
> the traders not of the company may be distressed so as to want
> security or preservation for their persons or effects, you must
> receive, defend and protect them as if they were of and did belong
> to the company. You are also to give them no molestation in
> respect of their being seperate traders, but 'tis conceived that it is
> not the meaning of that clause of the Act that the company's forts
> & castles are to be either the common habitations of or ware-
> houses for the seperate traders except in the cases aforesaid, or
> such like, wherein we must leave much to your discretion.[3]

Having provided as best it could for the implementation of
the Act, the company turned to the more important task of
competing with the separate traders. A great effort was called
for, and, to the full extent of the resources available, was made.
In the four years from 1694 to 1697 only twenty-three ships had
been sent to Africa by the company; in the four following
years fifty-nine were dispatched. While from 1694 to 1697
exports had totalled only £80,000, between 1701 and 1704 they
were double this figure.[4] These efforts were made at a time
when the company was extremely short of money and they are
a creditable achievement. But, for the period 1672 to 1713,
they represent the company's last stand. Departures of ships
fell to ten in 1705, to seven in 1706, and to two in 1708, and
exports sank to £15,000 in 1708 and to below £10,000 in
1709.[5] While they lasted, the company's exertions did not seem

---

[1] T. 70/51, pp. 5, 9, 11–12.   [2] T. 70/170, fos. 7, 7d, no date.
[3] *Ibid.*   [4] Appendix I.
[5] Between Michaelmas 1709 and Michaelmas 1710 the separate traders
dispatched 24 ships from London, 20 from Bristol, 2 from Liverpool, 2 from

without hope of success. In a letter written to the Chief Merchants at Cape Coast on 15 January 1700, the plan for defeating the separate traders was outlined.[1] First, agents were to send immediate notice of goods in demand on the coast and the company was to dispatch them without delay. Factors were to buy up all the African commodities available and were to tell the natives that the company would supply them with better goods than the separate traders, and at the same prices. No encouragement was to be given by the company's employees to their rivals, and above all no price-agreement was to be made.[3] Finally, the swiftest possible dispatch was to be given to all ships in the company's service. In other words, the company proposed to try once more to exploit the advantages of permanent settlement in order to defeat the casual trade of its competitors. At the same time the natives were to be convinced of the superiority of the company's goods over those of its rivals.[2]

Such was the hope and such the intention. The struggle between the company and the separate traders now entered a crucial phase, for at last they were competing on something like equal terms. The private merchant was free to trade without any fear of confiscation, but the company had succeeded in shifting part at least of the cost of upkeep of the forts on to his shoulders. The issue was not in doubt for long. In the very first season of open trade the separate traders scored a signal victory. In September 1699 the company wrote to the Chief Merchants on the Gold Coast:

> you quite lost us the last year's trade and give encouragement to
> 10 per cent. men to return in greater numbers than last year. . . .
> So that the company hath been at 20*l*. per cent. charge without
> a trade and the others at 10*l*. per cent. with a trade, by which

Jamaica and 3 from Barbados. In the same period the company sent out 3 from England and 2 from the Plantations. *Cal. S.P. Col.*, 1710–11, No. 544.

[1] T. 70/51, pp. 71–2.

[2] The company's servants in Africa continued to deal unofficially with the separate traders as they had with the interlopers, and on an even friendlier footing. T. 70/51, pp. 45, 322–3; Donnan, II, pp. 2, 101; Davenant, *op. cit.*, in *Works*, V, pp. 177, 189.

[3] T. 70/51, p. 95. The separate traders were alleged to have imitated the company's mark. T. 70/86, p. 52.

you may judge the difference, and how much their affairs have been better mannaged than ours.[1]

To excuses that trade was lacking the company sourly replied that its competitors found no such want.[2] Two years later, in July 1701, the disappointments of the fruitless campaign were reviewed:

> It's a great dissatisfaction to us when we reflect upon the great advantages we might reasonably expect from settled factories and magazins well stored with goods and finde the quite contrary effect thereof. Not a person of the 10 per cent. men with 500*l*. stock but makes his returns once a year with farr greater advantage than any person in the joynt stock of 5000*l*. value.[3]

In the years that followed the separate traders did not always enjoy victories over the company as complete as those of 1698 and 1700. Like the company they suffered losses at the hands of French privateers, and there were moments, even as late as 1706, when Sir Dalby Thomas, Agent-General on the Gold Coast, could write that the only ships there, apart from one belonging to the Dutch, were those employed by the company.[4] Such occasions, however, were rare, and the final outcome of the struggle was little in doubt. The separate traders even when contributing to the upkeep of the forts could still afford to outbid the company. Under the stress of competition, the price of slaves in Africa rose to £8, £12, and even £16 a head,[5] so that in 1710 Dalby Thomas was obliged to negotiate an agreement with a separate trader whereby neither should pay more than £12 for men slaves and £8 for women.[6] Long before this, however, the company's factors in Africa had been driven to trade with the ten per cent. men by lack of goods from England. In 1706 Thomas himself announced that rather than allow Ashanti merchants to see the English settlements bare of goods he was going to buy from a separate trader.[7] In 1710 he finally admitted defeat by offering to the company's chiefs at Dixcove, Sekondi, Kommenda, Winnebah, and Shido, liberty to trade with the ten per cent. men on their own

---

[1] T. 70/51, p. 45; cf. p. 55. [2] *Ibid.*, p. 92. [3] *Ibid.*, p. 197.
[4] T. 70/5, fo. 9d. [5] *Ibid.*, fos. 32, 48d, 53d.
[6] *Ibid.*, fo. 67. [7] *Ibid.*, fo. 23d.

accounts provided they would assume financial responsibility for the upkeep of their forts and factories. This, he wrote, 'as things went & as things was with us I lookt upon as trading for your Honours by taking of a dead charge from you'.[1]

It remained only for the company at home to acknowledge defeat by seeking to change the Act of 1698. At the end of 1705 the Committee of Eight took the company's affairs into serious consideration and in framing its conclusions laid down the lines upon which, with certain additions, the company's case was to be presented to the English Government, to Parliament and to the public in the next seven years.[2] Any suggestion that the separate traders had won a fair fight was of course carefully avoided; instead, arguments were selected which would excuse the company's failure and hold out the promise that, given a fresh start, success might yet be achieved. In the first place, the company claimed that the ten per cent. duty did not cover the charge of maintaining the forts and that it had therefore to bear a disproportionate share of overhead costs; and secondly, it was alleged that excessive and ruinous competition in Africa had greatly worsened the terms of trade and rendered the native merchants 'so insolent that they are not to be dealt withall under any reasonable terms'. Slaves, which formerly cost 40 or 50s. and sold in the Plantations at £12 or £14 a head, now cost £12 or £14 in Africa and could not be sold for less than £30. The trade, it was concluded, 'under the present establishment is onely advantagious to the natives of Guinea and prejuditiall to the company & Plantations and in great hazard of being totally lost to this nation'.

After more than a year's delay, these conclusions were embodied in a petition to be presented to the Lord Treasurer.[3] They were reinforced by various accusations against the separate traders of making false entries of goods liable to the ten per cent. duty, of gun-running, and of confederating with the company's servants to perpetrate frauds. In the company's submission, the high price of negroes in the Plantations could be remedied only by the restoration of monopoly, coupled with a guarantee to furnish annually a certain number of negroes at

---

[1] T. 70/2, pp. 26–7.   [2] T. 70/102, under date 18 December 1705.
[3] T. 70/170, fos. 64–5.

a reasonable price. The fate of this petition is unknown, but another in the same terms delivered to the Queen in November 1707 was referred to the Commissioners of Trade and Plantations who, for the next five years, had the African trade almost continuously under their notice. The Commissioners spared no pains to arrive at the truth, and time and again both the company and the separate traders were ordered to produce papers or to appear before the Board. It is unnecessary to follow the day-to-day deliberations, since the findings of the Commissioners were set out in periodic reports.

The company's attempt to limit discussion to the yield of the ten per cent. duty and the evils of competition did not succeed. Between November 1707 and April 1708, the Commissioners of Trade and Plantations steadily widened the scope of their enquiry, taking evidence of the improvement in supplies of negroes to Maryland and Virginia since 1698,[1] and of the financial state of the company.[2] The separate traders answered the company's charges, and made counter-proposals for a regulated company.[3] In the original petition of November 1707 the company had offered to prove its allegations, and on 23 January 1708 the Deputy Governor and others came before the Commissioners to do so.[4] They claimed that between 1698 and 1707 the ten per cent. duty had yielded only £53,731, whereas the cost of maintaining the forts had been £273,172.[5] The Act of 1698 had given no precise indication of what services the duty was expected to cover: the company, in arriving at the figure given to the Commissioners, had added in the freight of stores from England to Africa, as well as the salaries of the Agent-General, soldiers and artificers.[6] The company's total expenditure on its African establishment may be taken as about £20,000 a year:[7] but this included the cost of services of a purely commercial nature to which Parliament can scarcely have intended that the separate traders should contribute.

---

[1] *Journal of the Commissioners of Trade and Plantations*, 1704–9, p. 430.
[2] *Ibid.*, pp. 436, 438–9.   [3] *Ibid.*, pp. 446, 447, 449.
[4] *Ibid.*, pp. 452–4.   [5] *Ibid.*, Donnan, II, p. 51.
[6] T. 70/102, 18 December 1705; *Journal of the Commissioners of Trade and Plantations*, 1704–9, p. 453.
[7] Below, p. 259.

It does not seem possible from the material available accurately to estimate whether the ten per cent. duty met the company's expenditure on what might legitimately be regarded as defence, such as building and repairing forts, cannon, and soldiers' wages; on the whole the likelihood is that it did not, though the margin by which it fell short was certainly much smaller than the company alleged. As for the malpractices of the separate traders, the best evidence the company could bring forward was an incident which had occurred in 1703. A separate trader had carried off a number of negroes without paying for them; the company, it was claimed, had recovered them from Barbados and returned them to their owner.[1] For the rest, the company's representatives were able to do little more than repeat what had already been said in the petition, and when the Commissioners began to put awkward questions about the company's financial state and the spending of the proceeds of the duty they were unable to give satisfactory replies.[2]

The company now turned to Parliament, and on 10 March 1708 initiated discussions which over the next four years were to prove even less fruitful and even more dreary than those of the previous decade.[3] It was immediately confronted with counter-petitions from the separate traders and an unfavourable report from the Commissioners of Trade.[4] Nothing further was done in Parliament in this session, and the Commissioners were left to proceed to the crux of their enquiry, the supply of slaves to the Plantations. On 15 April 1708 a circular letter was addressed to all colonial Governors requesting a return of imports and prices of negroes since 1698, distinguishing the company's from those of the separate traders. Governors were further asked to sound opinion in their colonies as to the best means of carrying on the trade.[5] The question of the future of the

---

[1] *Journal of the Commissioners of Trade and Plantations*, 1704–9, p. 452, and *Cal. S.P. Col.*, 1708–9, No. 331. This was probably the *Guinea Hen* (see T. 70/51, p. 361, though the story is differently told there). Davenant searched hard for examples of depredations by the separate traders, but he cannot be said to have found many. *Works*, V, pp. 170 ff.

[2] *Journal of the Commissioners of Trade and Plantations*, 1704–9, p. 454.

[3] Stock, III, p. 189.   [4] *Ibid.*, pp. 190–1, 195–6.

[5] *Cal. S.P. Col.*, 1706–8. No. 1434.

African trade was then deferred until replies to this enquiry had been received.

When they came, these replies put certain facts beyond reasonable doubt. In the first place, the separate traders so far as could be ascertained had imported into the colonies about 75,000 negroes since the Act of 1698 had come into force, as against approximately 18,000 by the company.[1] To Antigua the separate traders had brought more than twice as many as the company, to Barbados nearly three times, to Jamaica five times, to Virginia nine times. Despite the war, they had transported more negroes than the company had ever been able to do in any corresponding period. To that extent the claims of free trade were vindicated and monopoly discredited. Equally clear, however, was the fact that, despite these plentiful supplies, prices of negroes had risen sharply. In Virginia, for example, slaves now cost £20 to £35, whereas before 1698 the price had never exceeded £23.[2] Nevertheless, and despite the fact that the company still sold cheaper than the separate traders, the Governor of Virginia expected that the feelings of the planters would be solidly against any restriction, and the Governor of Maryland took the same view.[3] In Barbados prices had similarly risen and, despite the comparative figures of imports of negroes by the company and the separate traders,

---

[1] The returns may be summarized as follows:

Colony	Period (from 24.6.1698)	By separate traders	By company	Unknown	Reference in Cal. S.P. Col. 1708–9.
Jamaica	to 14.6.1708	35,718	6854	1804	No. 142
Barbados	to Dec. 1707	25,577†	9006*		No. 94
Antigua	to 25.12.1707	4,945	1805*		No. 109
Montserrat	to 25.12.1707	1,604	599		No. 192
Nevis and St. Christopher's		not available			No. 109
Virginia	to 12.10.1708	5,928‡	679		No. 215
Maryland	to 25.12.1707	2,290	—		No. 197
New England	to 25.12.1707	—	—	c. 200‖	No. 151

* The company claimed more.
† Naval Officer's returns, others being imperfect.
‡ Including 236 from Barbados.
‖ Supplied from the West Indies.

[2] *Cal. S.P. Col.*, 1708–9, No. 215.   [3] *Ibid.*, No. 197.

opinion there favoured the revival of a joint-stock monopoly.[1] Jamaica, on the other hand, was as fiercely opposed to monopoly as ever.[2]

The explanations suggested for this rise in prices were various and it is not easy to distinguish which were effective. Clearly the war played some part. Freight charges were high and losses had to be covered; but the participation of the separate traders in the African trade must bear some of the responsibility. Though the war may have kept their number lower than it would have been in peace, there were probably more of them on the coast after 1698 than before. And there is convincing evidence that, competing amongst themselves and with the company, they drove up the cost of negroes and all other African products.[3] Because they traded from ships and did not have to maintain expensive settlements, the separate traders could afford to pay more than the company; being small traders they were especially anxious to complete their cargoes and recklessly outbid one another without caring for the consequences. They were not solely responsible for the price-rise, but some of the blame must be attached to them. The rise in prices, once begun, continued in the eighteenth century, and the planters were the chief sufferers. Thus the effects of monopoly and competition, in this particular context, were somewhat different from the expectations of their respective advocates and critics. Monopoly, imperfect as it was, resulted in inadequate supplies at low prices, while free trade was followed by much larger supplies at higher prices; and, as the eighteenth century proceeded and competition in the slave-trade was intensified, prices rose to still greater heights.[4]

Apart from the dissatisfaction with prices, the enquiry of 1708 exposed important defects in the distribution of negroes in the colonies, and to these must be attributed the *volte-face* of

---

[1] *Cal. S.P. Col.*, 1708–9, No. 94.   [2] *Ibid.*, No. 243.

[3] Donnan, II, pp. 6–7, 9; Charles Davenant, 'Reflections on the Constitution and Management of the Trade to Africa', in *Works* (1771), V, pp. 176, 181, 182, 184, 190, 192, 196; T. 70/5, fos. 32, 48d, 53d.

[4] There are other explanations for the rise in negro prices. The colonial demand was probably increasing; and prices in Africa were being forced up by French competition and the establishment of a factory at Whydah in 1704. See below, p. 274.

Barbados. Only nine years earlier the Assembly of that colony had condemned the 'oppressions, avarice and rapinous desire' of the Royal African Company;[1] now, in 1708, the colony was said to favour a return to monopoly.[2] Nor was Barbados alone: some of the inhabitants of Nevis and Montserrat complained of insufficient supplies from the company and separate traders alike.[3] Until 1698, the planters of the West Indies and America, almost to a man, had looked to free trade in negroes to solve their problems. Jamaica, Virginia and Maryland still did so: they accepted higher prices as an inevitable concomitant of plentiful supplies. Barbados and the smaller colonies, on the other hand, found themselves faced with higher prices and, so they claimed, supplies that were still far from adequate.

This crack in the solid front of colonial opposition to the African Company went to the root of the conflicting merits and demerits of monopoly and free trade. As has already been suggested, the company until 1689 was in some sense a public corporation which could be held responsible for its actions and omissions. It was, moreover, a single body with a single management, and it could plan or be made to plan the supply of negroes to the colonies in accordance with their needs. In doing this it was, of course, exceedingly inefficient; the machinery of distribution was subjected to the continuous stresses of profit-making and was prevented from functioning properly by an insufficient aggregate supply of slaves. Jamaica especially had never been adequately supplied by the company. Nevertheless, a more even distribution of the negroes available was possible under a system of monopoly than in the free trade period to 1713. Nevis provides the clearest evidence. Between 1674 and 1681 the company had sold between 400 and 1,000 slaves there each year, a total of nearly 5,000. In the two years previous to August 1708, the company had delivered none and the separate traders only 180.[4] Early in 1706, the French had devastated the island and carried off a great number of negroes.[5] Slaves were therefore urgently needed for resettlement and on

---

[1] *Cal. S.P. Col.*, 1699, No. 954iii.
[2] *Ibid.*, 1708–9, No. 94; 1710–11, No. 541; Stock, III, pp. 202–3, 223, 224.
[3] Stock, III, pp. 205, 207, 225, 284. [4] *Cal. S.P. Col.*, 1708–9, No. 109.
[5] V. T. Harlow, *Christopher Codrington*, p. 186.

L

easy terms. The separate traders, who were scarcely susceptible to official scrutiny or regulation, could be put under no obligation to extend charity to the stricken colony. They delivered their negroes where they expected to get the largest profits, and at this time that place was Jamaica.

The experience of Barbados provides further clarification. According to the figures available some 36,000 negroes were brought to this island between 1698 and 1708, a supply very nearly, if not quite, sufficient to keep up the numbers of its slave-population.[1] But two-thirds of these had arrived in the first three or four years of open trade and almost all in the first eight years. Between January 1706 and August 1708 the separate traders had imported no more than 570, as against nearly 2,000 by the company.[2] Neither side had delivered enough, but the company, crippled as it was, had transported nearly four times as many as the separate traders. 'Any little discouragement', wrote the Governor of Barbados in August 1708, 'to private traders may occasion their desisting, and then the Collonies must suffer.'[3] The 'little discouragement' in this case is identifiable as an Act passed by the Assembly of the colony in 1706 'to supply the want of cash and to establish a method of credit'.[4] The expressed intention of this measure was to remedy the chronic shortage of ready money, and this it did by permitting owners of real estate to obtain paper credit in respect of one-quarter of their property.[5] It was one of the earliest of many similar experiments in paper currency in the American and West Indian colonies. The home Government promptly disallowed the Act,[6] but not before the signs of inflation and a general dislocation of trade had manifested themselves.[7] The Act damaged the interests of the company and the

---

[1] Below, pp. 304–6.

[2] In the case of the company I have been able to supplement the figures of slave-imports for Barbados compiled by the Naval Officer (Donnan, II, p. 30) from the company's own records. Four company's ships arrived in this period which are not mentioned in the Naval Officer's list. I have not of course been able to correct any omissions in the case of the separate traders.

[3] *Cal. S.P. Col.*, 1708–9, No. 94.   [4] *Ibid.*, 1706–8, No. 405.

[5] *Ibid.*, No. 542i.   [6] *Ibid.*, No. 546.

[7] *Ibid.*, Nos. 961i, 1071, 1257, 1483.

separate traders alike, since they and all other creditors were obliged to take depreciated paper currency not only for the slaves they sold but also for outstanding old debts. The company petitioned against the Act,[1] but continued to send slaves to Barbados in the following years. The separate traders remained silent, but quietly cut off supplies to the offending colony.[2]

It is of course possible, and indeed likely, that the company's action in continuing to supply Barbados was the result less of a sense of responsibility and more of inefficiency. Even so the implication is clear. The separate traders responded silently, efficiently and at once, to the threat to their pockets, and there was really very little that could be done to persuade them to do anything else. The company continued to supply the colony, and the planters did not ask why; hence the reaction, incomplete and ineffective as it was, in favour of joint-stock monopoly. The whole episode underlines the vicissitudes of a trade from which a profit could be extracted only by perpetual vigilance, swift action and good luck. Beyond a certain point, the advantages of a large capital and large-scale organization began to be outweighed by the disadvantages of cumbersome administration, inadequate supervision and slow responses to changing needs. All these defects can be discerned in the African Company, and it laboured under the further handicap of an enforcible responsibility to the public to trade and go on trading whatever the profit might be. The separate traders were under no such obligation; they traded or refrained from trading as they chose.[3] They were not even bound to stay in the business. If they suffered losses and elected to sail close-

[1] *Ibid.*, No. 529.

[2] For general comments on this point, *Cal. S.P. Col.*, 1708–9, p. 211.

[3] The figures of exports by the separate traders during the lifetime of the Act of 1698 are defective. But they seem sufficient to expose this feature. From 1702 to 1704 the company was exporting at the rate of £30–40,000 a year; thereafter the figure fell away to only £4,000 in 1709 after which exports ceased. In other words it traded until it could trade no more. Exports by the separate traders offer a somewhat different picture. Of the 66 chief exporters, 27 sent consignments in only one of the eleven years 1702–12, 8 in two years, and 15 in three years. None made consignments in all eleven years, only 3 in ten years and 5 in nine years. Appendix VI.

hauled for a while, they were free to do so, or they could abandon it altogether. Probably a good many who entered the trade after 1698 were experimenting in a new branch of commerce, and if they failed they could not be expected to continue. This was one of the more convincing arguments which Charles Davenant, easily the ablest writer on the African trade in this period, levelled against the separate traders.[1] 'Whenever', he wrote, 'they should come to find their profit not answerable to their expectation, they would quickly draw their necks out of the collar, and give over the trade by degrees.'[2] The figures of ships clearing from England to Africa which he cited showed a steady drop from 145 in 1699 to 27 in 1708 and seem to prove his point.[3] The fall can in part be ascribed to overconfidence and ignorance, and Davenant was probably right in supposing that many ten per cent. men were only too glad to get out of the African trade. But it must also be attributed to war conditions which bore heavily on the separate traders. Moreover, Davenant wrote at the lowest ebb in their fortunes. In 1707–8 more ships were sent out than in the previous year, and as the end of the war came in sight the improvement was maintained.[4] The company's fortunes, on the other hand, continued to decline. By 1713 a good many of Davenant's arguments had been exploded, and most of the remainder dissolved in the course of the eighteenth century.

Although so little is known of the separate traders, they seem at this date (though not necessarily earlier or later) to have enjoyed at least four advantages over the large company in the African trade. They could personally supervise their own businesses. They were more manoeuvrable and could adapt themselves more easily to changing conditions within the trade. They were not committed, as the company was, to remaining in this particular branch of commerce and trading on until overwhelmed by loss and debt. And they were virtually impervious to direction by public authority. It may also be argued that the system of small private firms was at this date more

[1] 'Reflections on the Constitution and Management of the Trade to Africa', in *Works* (1771), V.

[2] *Ibid.*, p. 130.   [3] *Ibid.*, pp. 280–1.

[3] Donnan, II, pp. 63, 72–3, 92–5, 116–18.

fitted to the African trade than the large corporation just because of the risks and losses which were an intrinsic part of it. For when the African Company lost a ship or a cargo or suffered some other setback, its capacity to export in the following year was by that much diminished; reduced exports meant reduced returns and a further drop in export capacity. Every loss had a cumulative effect and left a permanent mark on the system of large-scale trading. In theory these risks and losses could have been met and covered by a capital much larger than that employed by the company; but the trade available in Africa did not justify investment on such a scale. If, on the other hand, a private trader encountered a loss, he alone was the sufferer. If the reverse was serious, he slipped into the oblivion of bankruptcy, and in time another trader with fresh and unencumbered capital rose to take his place. Individuals were wiped out or deterred; but the system endured.

The replies to the enquiry of the Commissioners of Trade and Plantations about supplies of negroes trickled in at the end of 1708 and the beginning of 1709. Before they had all come to hand, the Commissioners were required to report to the House of Commons upon the state of the African trade. On 20 January 1709 the company had renewed its assault on Parliament with a petition along familiar lines.[1] This was followed by a flood of counter-petitions from other interested parties greater than any previously recorded. In less than a month, twenty-five petitions were presented, sixteen for free trade, six for the restoration of monopoly, and three, from Barbados, Nevis and Montserrat, complaining impartially of both systems. Against the company was the usual alignment of forces, the separate traders themselves, Virginia, Maryland and Jamaica, Bristol and Liverpool, Birmingham and other manufacturing towns, reinforced on this occasion by five Scottish burghs which claimed that the revival of monopoly in the African trade would constitute a violation of the Act of Union. For the company a less impressive set of interests was mustered, most of those who petitioned for monopoly being artisans of London.[2] Clearly the balance of opinion lay with the separate traders, and their

---

[1] Stock, III, p. 202. [2] *Ibid.*, pp. 203-9.

cause was strengthened by the report which the Commissioners of Trade and Plantations submitted to the House of Commons on 27 January.[1] This report summarized the arguments and allegations of both sides and the results so far to hand of the enquiry about supplies of negroes. Local and temporary scarcities of slaves were admitted, but these were attributed to the war, and, in the case of Barbados, to the Paper Act; they did not alter the fact that more negroes were now being brought to the Plantations than in the time of the company's monopoly. The argument that other nations traded to Africa in joint stocks was neatly turned by citing the example of the Portuguese whose open trade was said to have resulted in their transporting more negroes than any other nation. The Commissioners concluded that the present establishment of the African trade was unsatisfactory and conducive to disputes and quarrels. On the basis of this report, a committee of the whole House declared in favour of a regulated company with provisions for preserving the forts.[2] A bill brought in on these proposals obtained a second reading only to disappear in the prorogation that followed immediately.[3]

When Parliament reassembled for the session of 1709–10 much the same sequence of events was enacted. On this occasion the separate traders took the initiative with a petition accusing the company of remaining 'only in a capacity to oppress the petitioners'.[4] The usual volley of petitions was loosed off, thirteen for free trade and four for the company. The Commissioners of Trade once more reported in terms unfavourable to monopoly.[5] The separate traders and the company appeared before the Commons and made their threadbare proposals, and a committee of the whole House rendered the usual report.[6] A certain variety was provided when the committee's recommendation of a regulated company was negatived, but the outcome was not in the least affected, for nothing was done. The only interest attaching to this session is to be found in some fresh suggestions put forward by the

---

[1] *Cal. S.P. Col.*, 1708–9, No. 331. The report is printed in full in Donnan, II, pp. 49–81.

[2] Stock, III, p. 217.   [3] *Ibid.*, p. 219, n. 32.   [4] *Ibid.*, pp. 222–3.

[5] *Cal. S.P. Col.*, 1708–9, No. 913.   [6] Stock, III, pp. 227–9.

separate traders in February 1710.[1] They proposed the nationalization of the forts with a duty upon trade to maintain them, compensation for the company, and a system of licences to supply Spanish and Portuguese America with negroes. They might have saved themselves the trouble.

In each of the next four sessions of Parliament, the African trade was under consideration, but little interest can be stimulated by debates and resolutions which were so utterly barren of consequence. The Commissioners of Trade continued diligently to collect evidence, and submit reports, all to no purpose. Nearly fifty more petitions were presented, hours of Parliamentary time, days and weeks at the Board of Trade were consumed, reams of paper were covered and hundreds of printed pages published, before the African trade was allowed to escape from the notoriety which surrounded it. The Act of 1698 expired at the end of the Parliamentary session of 1711–12, little regretted. A desperate last-minute effort was made to put the trade on a statutory footing by the erection of a regulated company. A bill was drafted and passed its second reading. But, true to the history of similar measures in the past, it failed to go through and was heard of no more.[2]

5. Free Trade

Though wrangling continued, both within and without Parliament, until 1714, the expiry of the Act of 1698 really marks the end of a fifty years contest between monopoly and free trade. The last shreds of the fabric of monopoly, already torn to pieces by the interlopers and the separate traders, were swept away. The company was not entirely destroyed: it even claimed that the expiry of the Act of 1698 restored its monopoly and threatened to proceed against the separate traders.[3] This was pure bluff. But, as a result of internal reorganization in 1712 and an Act of Parliament to relieve it from its creditors, the company was able to make one more effort to win back lost ground. In 1713 fifteen ships were sent to Africa, more than

[1] *Commons Journals*, XVI, pp. 317–20.
[2] Stock, III, pp. 288, 289, n. 47.   [3] *Ibid.*, p. 298.

in the previous four years together. The *Asiento*, after ruining almost everyone who had ever been associated with it, had at last been gained by England and committed to the care of the South Sea Company. Pending arrangements for securing its own slaves, the South Sea Company contracted with the African Company for this purpose, and in 1713 and 1714 several ships were dispatched under orders to deliver their negroes where the South Sea Company should direct.[1] But this effort proved no longer lasting or successful than that which had followed the Act of 1698. The company had now to maintain the forts entirely out of its own resources, and so great a burden precluded effective competition with the separate traders in the slave-trade. The castles, which the House of Commons had on seven occasions resolved were necessary for the preservation of the trade, were left to decay until in 1730 the nation came to the rescue with a subsidy. The regulated company, three times voted the proper method of carrying on the trade, did not appear until 1750.

Free trade, then, won a notable triumph, no less convincing through being negative, more than sixty years before the publication of the *Wealth of Nations*. Smith, in belabouring the African Company, wrote of the dead. The victories of 1698 and 1712, indeed, owed little to theorists. The vast number of pamphlets generated by the struggle were almost without exception statements of fact or alleged fact already rehearsed in Parliament or elsewhere. They contribute little fresh to an understanding of the problems at issue.[2] Free trade was given its chance by one of the least ideological of all revolutions, and it won on merits that were severely practical. The most striking, though not immediately visible, consequence of its triumph was the ending of the dominion of London and the rise to prominence in the slave-trade of Bristol and Liverpool. Already, by 1713, Bristol was challenging; a new chapter in the history of the trade had begun in which the monopoly of the African Company would have no place.

[1] Donnan, II, pp. 156–7; tables of ships dispatched in T. 70/63.
[2] Davenant's 'Reflections' (*op. cit.*), despite some bad history and some knockabout comedy in Part III, is an exception to this generalization.

4

THE COMPANY IN ENGLAND

1. Courts and Committees

THE history of the Royal African Company has thus far
appeared as the melancholy record of defeat and ruin
which the followers of Adam Smith would expect. And
it must be admitted that many of the strictures which Smith
laid upon joint-stock enterprises apply to the company. About
its financial history, he was substantially right. He was right,
also, to emphasize its failure to compete with the private
traders. Various reasons for this lack of success have already
been suggested, but so far the explanation favoured by Smith
has not yet been examined. To him, waste and inefficiency
were implicit in any business where the ownership of capital
was separated from management. The directors of a joint-
stock company 'like the stewards of a rich man are apt to
consider attention to small matters as not for their master's
honour, and very easily give themselves a dispensation from
having it. Negligence and profusion, therefore, must always
prevail, more or less, in the management of the affairs of such
a company.'[1] The purpose of this chapter is to explain the
internal structure of the company in England and those aspects
of its affairs which were most immediately under the supervision of its directors, the provision of exports to Africa, and
the disposal of imports.

The constitution of the African Company, as defined by its
charter, conformed to the customary pattern of the seventeenth-
century joint-stock company. A Governor, Sub-Governor and
Deputy Governor were named as the chief officers, with a

[1] *Wealth of Nations* (Everyman), II, p. 229.

Court of twenty-four Assistants, all to be chosen by annual elections at General Courts of the whole body of shareholders. Any twelve of the adventurers could demand the calling of a General Court at which a Governor or Assistant could be removed from office on conviction of misdemeanour. The charter thus defined the basic institutions of the company, while leaving many important questions, such as voting rights, to be settled at discretion. For information about this and other matters, the prospective investor could refer to the company's Preamble or prospectus, issued in its final form just before the first call-up of capital in January 1672.[1] Many of the stipulations of this document were subsequently embodied in the by-laws of the company, and with minor alterations remained intact until the eighteenth century. The terms of issue and the obligations contracted to the Royal Adventurers were set forth. Voting rights at the General Courts were fixed at one vote for each £100 of stock, with no limit on the number of votes which any shareholders might exercise. The qualification for election to the Court of Assistants was put at £400, and the Deputy Governor was always to be a merchant.

In one important respect the Preamble was not implemented. It envisaged a small standing committee of five persons elected from the Assistants which would meet at least three times a week and have discretionary powers in all matters in which the intentions of the Court of Assistants or General Court were unknown. It appears from this that the direction and control of the company's day-to-day affairs were meant to be in the hands of this committee of managing directors (who were to be paid 20s. for each attendance), with the Assistants meeting only once a month as an overseeing board. Such an arrangement would have been in sharp contrast to the overgrown Court of Assistants of the Royal Adventurers, which had numbered thirty-six. It did not, however, materialize, though something very like it, a Committee of Eight, was instituted in 1699. Why the Committee of Five was abandoned or displaced does not appear, owing to the loss of the first minute-book of the Court of Assistants. When the second minute-book begins in 1674, the Assistants had already assumed the effective direction of the

[1] P.R.O., G.D.24/49/18.

company's business, with full meetings twice a week and sub-committees meeting at least as often.

According to the Preamble, there were to be two General Courts a year, one for the election of officers, and the other for hearing a statement of the company's stock 'by an exact Ballance of the Books and an indifferent valuation of all remaining effects, that thereby the Adventurers may know the true condition of their Stock and Trade'. Ordinary members of the company were entitled to attend and speak at meetings of the Assistants, but not to vote. Other articles of the Preamble dealt with oaths for members and officers, and provided for the sale by auction of all goods except gold and silver. The stock of each member was liable to confiscation either for indebtedness or for infringement of the monopoly. Finally, a clause was included which stated that if and when the stock should be augmented by fifty per cent. a dividend of twenty per cent. should be paid; it is hardly necessary to add that this condition was not observed.

Such was the constitution foreshadowed by the charter and the Preamble; its practical working will now be examined. Nominally, supreme power over the company's affairs was vested in the General Court, but the part played by this body in normal times was no greater than that of a modern annual general meeting. It met three times a year, twice in January and once in February. From time to time extraordinary meetings for special purposes were summoned, and after 1700 General Courts met much more frequently and exercised a greater influence; they alone could take the grave decisions necessitated by the company's plight. As long as the company's affairs were in tolerable order, however, the business of the General Courts seems to have been of a formal nature. The first Court of the year was to elect the Governor and to hear the 'state of the stock' from the Sub-Governor. This statement usually took the form of a crude analysis of the company's assets and liabilities, which seldom distinguished between liquid and other assets, or between good and bad debts.[1] Though elaborate account books were kept by the company for cash, freight, bills and other items, as well as general and

[1] Examples can be found in T. 70/100–1, Minutes of General Courts.

stock ledgers, no serious attempt seems ever to have been made to digest or summarize the information they contained, until pressure from outside forced the company to draw up more realistic statements. The crudeness of the early statements may have helped to keep alive the belief that the company was a profit-making concern long after it had ceased to be one. The accounts published to shareholders were always statements of assets and liabilities, never analyses of income and expenditure. After 1692 more elaborate capital accounts were presented, but they were still often misleading and groundlessly optimistic.

The election of a Governor was a formality: from 1672 until his flight from England in December 1688, James, as Duke of York and later as King, was the automatic choice. His close association with the company has already been mentioned,[1] and there can be no doubt that he helped it in many ways. Frequently matters were referred to him by the Court of Assistants, and in June 1677 he was voted a purse of 500 guineas for extraordinary services.[2] His service on this occasion is unknown, for his work was always done behind the scenes. In the Company of Royal Adventurers, he had attended meetings regularly and helped to direct the daily business. He attended no meetings of the Royal African Company, and probably this was a more satisfactory arrangement for everyone. With James' departure in 1688, the company tried to repair the damage by electing in succession William of Orange, Prince George of Denmark, Queen Anne, and George I. But where James had been a Governor, his successors were at most patrons, and in no way identified, as he had been, with the fortunes of the company.

At the second General Court of the year, the Sub-Governor, Deputy Governor, and the twenty-four Assistants, were elected by the shareholders on the basis of one vote for each £100 of stock. The absence of any limit on the number of votes which one man might exercise did not lead, as it did in the case of the East India Company, to the predominance of the over-mighty investor.[3] The accumulation of large blocks of shares in the

[1] Above, p. 104,   [2] T. 70/100, p. 72.
[3] Sir Josiah Childe and seven others owned more than a quarter of the stock and enjoyed corresponding voting rights in 1691.

African Company was uncommon, and probably at any time between 1672 and 1691 the members with less than £1,000 of stock could comfortably outvote those with more. Initially a maximum term of three consecutive years as an Assistant was imposed, but, following the quadrupling of the stock in 1691, this restriction was abolished, and at the same time the qualification for election was raised from £400 to £1,000 of new stock.[1] Since this represented no more than £250 of old stock, it was a step towards enabling smaller investors to become Assistants.

Though elected annually, the Sub- and Deputy Governors normally served for two years, at the expiry of which the Deputy Governor was generally elected Sub-Governor for a further two years. Assistants were elected for one year, but, even before the abolition of the limit of three successive terms in 1691, some members remained in office for long periods. An Assistant of three years' standing, though not eligible for re-election in that capacity, could be nominated for one of the governorships, at the conclusion of which he could be once more elected an Assistant. In this way Sir Benjamin Bathurst was continuously in office from 1677 to 1695, thirteen times as Assistant, twice as Deputy Governor, and four times as Sub-Governor. Such long service must have been largely its own reward, for the official remuneration was very small. Annually until 1700, £750 was divided amongst the two Governors and the twenty-four Assistants according to the number of meetings which they had attended. In 1680, for example, each received 7s. 11d. per appearance, the Governors (whose attendances counted double) receiving about £60 each, and the more assiduous of the Assistants about £30.[2]

The full Court of Assistants met at least once a week, and more frequently if necessary. In 1677 it met 98 times, in 1685 51 times, and in 1692 79 times. The sub-committees of the Court met almost as often; in 1684 the Committee of Accounts met 76 times. Each Assistant normally served on at least one sub-committee, and many on two or more.

[1] T. 70/101, fo. 28d. Under the new rule at least eight of the old Court retired each year.

[2] T. 70/107, p. 25.

It is difficult to find an historical measure of efficiency, but if it can be expressed in terms of assiduous attendance at Courts and committees, Adam Smith's criticism is unfounded in so far as it was applied to the African Company. As an outstanding example, Sir Gabriel Roberts was absent from only two out of 290 meetings of the Court of Assistants between 1685 and 1690. In 1679 there were 84 Court meetings: fourteen Assistants attended over sixty of them. In 1688 there were 51 meetings: four Assistants attended them all, and fifteen others attended over forty. After the Revolution there was more absenteeism, but many Assistants still came regularly to meetings. If, on the other hand, efficiency is measured in terms of attention to the *minutiae* of business, Smith's charge of negligence against the directors is equally baseless. No subject seems to have been too insignificant for consideration by the Court. Its business was first to read and discuss letters which had come in since the last meeting; any necessary action thereupon was decided, or if a problem was complex it would be remitted to the appropriate committee. Reports from committees were next examined and usually accepted, and letters drafted by the Secretary or the Committee of Correspondence were approved. The business of examining candidates for the frequent vacancies in Africa was followed by the scrutiny and sealing of charterparties. Finally, transfers in the stock and warrants for all money disbursed by the company were approved. These were the items of business appearing on the agenda of practically every meeting; many others such as the conduct of lawsuits, the disposal of goods imported from Africa and the West Indies, organizing pressure on members of Parliament, drafting petitions, interviewing men back from the Coast, and examining samples of exports, occurred frequently.

With such a diversity of business, the use of sub-committees was essential. Originally there were four, for correspondence, for the purchase of goods, for the provision of shipping and the prevention of private trade, and for accounts. Others were added later to supervise the trade of the northern parts of West Africa, and for the prosecution of lawsuits; and in 1693 the duties of the company's Treasurer were transferred to a committee. After 1700, the part played in the company's affairs by the Court of Assistants diminished, and many of its functions were remitted to a steering Committee of Eight. Most of these committees had a formal existence and kept their own records; in addition *ad hoc* committees were appointed to deal with particular problems. The management of the company's affairs can indeed be described as business-administration by committees. A Court of Assistants of twenty-four members was large for effective discussion and decision: by electing so many directors, it was possible, first, to carry a few impressive figureheads, and, secondly, to man the numerous committees which must have been the real policy-making organs.

Election as an Assistant, therefore, was a heavy burden to undertake, and the virtually unpaid service in this capacity of some of the leading figures of the City of London is not easily explicable.[1] They were of course all shareholders whose hopes of dividends depended upon efficient management. But none of them owned as much as £5,000 of the stock, and most of them much less. In few instances can their holdings have represented more than a small fraction of their total wealth. Sir William Turner, for example, served as an Assistant for six years, but never had much more than one-twentieth of his wealth invested in African stock.[2] Sir Robert Vyner's holding of £4,000 could not have signified a great deal to a man who grappled with hundreds of thousands. Most of the company's Assistants had business interests of their own to attend to, and many had civic or parliamentary duties as well. Yet at least

---

[1] For example, Sir Robert Vyner, the goldsmith, Assistant 1672–4; Sir John Robinson, Lord Mayor, M.P. for the City, Deputy Governor of Hudson's Bay Co., Director of East India Co., Assistant 1673–5; Sir James Edwards, Lord Mayor, Deputy Governor of East India Co., Assistant 1676; Sir Arthur Ingram, Director of East India Co., Alderman of London, Assistant 1673–5, 1679; Sir Henry Tulse, Lord Mayor, Director of East India Co., Assistant 1675–7, 1680–2, 1685–7; Sir Thomas Bludworth, Lord Mayor, M.P. for Southwark, Director of East India Co., Assistant 1675–6; Sir John Lethuillier, Sheriff, Governor of Merchant Adventurers, Director of East India Co., Assistant 1681–3; Sir William Turner, Lord Mayor, M.P. for the City, Assistant 1676–8, 1681–3, 1688, 1691. The names of all Governors, Sub-Governors, Deputy Governors, and members of the Court of Assistants of the Royal African Company are given in the index to this book.

[2] City of London Guildhall Library, MSS. 5105.

until the Revolution the company was able to attract some of the greatest merchants of London to its board of directors. Even after 1700 it could still secure the services of prominent men.[1] Charles Davenant, reflecting on the management of the African trade, supported his case for the company by naming the Assistants for the year 1708. They included two M.P.s, the Lord Mayor of London for the previous year, the City Chamberlain, and ten men with experience in the East India trade as well as representatives of other interests.[2] Davenant did not disclose that by this date the Court had become largely a formal body with infrequent meetings, power in the company having passed to the Committee of Eight. Nevertheless, the Eight were not men of straw, and it is remarkable that such persons should consent to be associated with a company verging on bankruptcy.

For this phenomenon there are several possible explanations. In the first place, the African Company did not begin to look like an obviously bad investment until some time after the Revolution. At one time in 1678, with dividends totalling $43\frac{1}{2}$ per cent. in fourteen months, it must have looked very attractive. It was secure in royal favour; demand for gold and slaves was steady; and a surprising volume of exports was maintained. These expectations were not entirely belied by events. Probably all who subscribed to the original issue of stock and sold out before 1691 made capital gains. Not until 1691 or 1692 did the stock begin to appear obviously weak; thereafter it never recovered. But even then there remained the possibility that Parliament would come to its rescue and grant a new lease of life. The most plausible explanation of the appearance, in the company's later history, of prominent business men amongst the Assistants is that they hoped that the stock might be trans-

---

[1] For example, Sir William Withers, Lord Mayor, M.P. for the City, Director of New and United East India Co.s, Assistant 1697–8, 1706, Sub-Governor 1707–8; Sir John Fleete, Lord Mayor, M.P. for the City, Governor of East India Co., Assistant 1693–4, 1699–1702, Sub-Governor 1697–8; Sir Thomas Cooke, Sheriff, M.P. for Colchester, Governor of East India Co., Assistant 1690–2, 1701–2, 1703–8; Sir Samuel Stanier, Lord Mayor, Assistant 1686–8, 1691–2, 1698–9, 1702, Deputy Governor 1693–4.

[2] 'Reflections on the Constitution and Management of the Trade to Africa', in *Works* (1771), V, pp. 264 ff.

formed into a thing of value by some *deus ex machina*. Such optimism probably appeared less unfounded then than it does now.

Patronage, economic and otherwise, in the eighteenth-century East India Company was a powerful incentive to the purchase of stock and the acceptance of office. The Royal African Company had nothing comparable to offer; but there was no point in letting even the £100,000 which it annually disbursed go to strangers. It is likely that some at least of the London merchants who accepted election as Assistants of the company did so in the hope of doing profitable business with it. Very few of the company's purchases of English manufactures were obtained from its own members; very few of its members were manufacturers. But throughout the first thirty years of its existence, the goods of foreign origin for dispatch to Africa were obtained chiefly from importers who were also shareholders.[1] In particular, supplies of commodities from Eastern Europe, iron, copper, textiles and amber, and of such Asiatic goods as were not bought from the East India Company, were provided by merchants who were not only shareholders and Assistants, but often also members of the Committee of Goods which distributed the company's contracts. This practice does not necessarily imply dishonesty. London merchants engaged in foreign trade were well represented in the company and had special knowledge which could be useful to it. The company as a whole was well aware of these purchases and sought to regulate rather than abolish them. In 1683, for example, the Court of Assistants left it to the Committee of Goods to ensure that the company paid no more for goods bought from members than from others.[2] In 1690 purchases from merchants who were themselves members of the Committee of Goods were required to have the previous sanction of the Court.[3] A committee appointed in 1697 to frame new by-laws recommended that members having interests in goods to

---

[1] In the first five years the company bought bar metals, German textiles and East India goods (other than from the East India Company) to the value of about £40,000; nearly three-quarters (£27,855) was purchased from its own shareholders.

[2] T. 70/80, fo. 27.   [3] T. 70/127, 21 January 1690.

M

be bought or ships to be hired should declare them, on penalty of forfeiture of their stock.[1]

The hope of selling goods to the company, however, affected only about a quarter of the Assistants, though a particularly active quarter.[2] Shipping provided another possible source of profit. Many of the ships which the company employed were owned in part by members and employees.[3] Jobs, though numerous, were not attractive: a few modestly paid appointments in London and a multitude of situations in Africa, never filled for long, which must have been suitable only for the most impoverished or desperate of relatives.

Other considerations may have encouraged some shareholders to accept office. The company in its day was one of the leading corporations in the City of London: service to it was as honourable as, and not less profitable than, office-holding in a livery company. Before the Revolution, some Sub-Governors received knighthoods during their term of office.[4] There was no social side to speak of, but there must have been opportunities to gain useful information and to make business connexions. Dudley North, the Turkey merchant, is said by his biographer to have entered the African Company and accepted office in it in order to learn the method of trading in a joint stock, hitherto unfamiliar to him. Thereby he made himself and his talents known to others.[5]

Scott believed that the joint-stock company owed much to the mixture of mercantile and non-mercantile elements in its management,[6] but this was not the experience of the African Company. Its shareholders were chiefly business men, and it was to business men that the task of management was entrusted.

[1] T. 70/101, fos. 58–62.

[2] Seven of the twenty-four Assistant selected in 1683 were engaged in selling to the company.

[3] Forty out of a very incomplete list of 150 owners of ships hired by the company between 1672 and 1689 were shareholders.

[4] Gabriel Roberts, Benjamin Newland, Benjamin Bathurst and Dudley North.

[5] Roger North, Lives of the Norths, ed. A. Jessopp, 1826, III, pp. 106–7.

[6] 'The combination of the specific and detailed knowledge of the trader with the broad outlook of the man of affairs tended towards a greater efficiency.' Scott, I, p. 444.

The Company of Royal Adventurers, as we have seen, contained a large non-mercantile element, and this may have contributed to its early downfall; in 1665 its Court of Assistants was composed largely of the royal family and members of the peerage. These men may have given something of value to the company, but the enterprise demanded patience, application, and business experience, qualities for which the Restoration court was not especially notable. The Royal African Company did not make the same mistake; its affairs were committed to City men who combined in themselves a knowledge of business and of the world beyond business. Only a handful of Assistants came from outside the mercantile community, and only one, the Earl of Shaftesbury, was elected to a governorship. George, Lord Berkeley, the first peer of the realm to collect directorships,[1] was nine times an Assistant. Both he and the Earl of Craven attended meetings regularly. But others such as Lord Falconberg did not. He attended no more than twenty meetings in five years. Occasionally a courtier was elected, perhaps as a compliment to the Duke of York, but the company did not gain much thereby. Tobias Rustat, an Assistant for three years, attended only sixteen meetings,[2] and the record of Lawrence du Puy, the Duke's barber, was not much better. The truth is that courtiers and prominent men of affairs had rarely the time or the patience to do the routine work which an Assistantship entailed. No doubt it was useful to have Sir Joseph Williamson, the Secretary of State, as a member of the Court, but his contribution to the efficient running of the company's day-to-day business was negligible.[3]

Only the virtually unpaid services of shareholders made it possible for the company's affairs in England to be managed so cheaply. For the first few years, there were only six salaried officials in regular employment, a Treasurer, a Secretary, and

---

[1] Governor of the Levant Company 1673–96; Director of the East India Company for 37 years; and an active member of the Hudson's Bay Company.

[2] Rustat, the benefactor of Jesus College, Cambridge, was Housekeeper at Hampton Court. (Luttrell, *Brief Historical Relation of State Affairs*, 1857, III, p. 285.)

[3] Davenant took a different view (*Works*, V, pp. 268–9), but the 'mixture' of which he wrote was a weak one.

an Accountant, each at £100 a year, a Husband at £80, a Surveyor of Shipping at £50, and a Housekeeper at £15.[1] Casual labour was employed as necessary, but the total cost of the home establishment, including the rent of £100 for the African House in Throckmorton-street, could not have been more than £1,500 a year. Later the number of officers was increased and higher salaries paid, but at its greatest extent the establishment consisted of not more than twenty officials. The voluminous accounts which have survived were the work of the accountant and two juniors; most of the other records were compiled by the Secretary and one junior. In 1678 additional expense was incurred by the removal of African House to Leadenhall-street, where premises were taken at £230 a year.[2] But it is unlikely that salaries, gratuities, payments to Assistants, and rent, exceeded £2,500 a year, a small sum in view of the work to be done.

Each of the four principal sub-committees of the Court of Assistants was attended in an executive capacity by a senior official, the Committee of Correspondence by the Secretary, the Committee of Goods by the Husband, the Committee of Shipping by the Clerk of Shipping, and the Committee of Accounts by the Accountant. In this way contact was kept between policy-makers and executives, though not infrequently the policy-makers implemented their own decisions.

The salaries paid to the permanent officials were small and the appointments were no sinecures. Those whose business lay at African House had to attend daily from 8.30 a.m. to noon and from 3 p.m. to 6 p.m., and all employees including those on outside business had to be available when the Court was sitting.[3] Nevertheless, the chief posts were filled by men of some substance. Samuel Heron, Secretary for twenty-seven years, subscribed £600 to the original stock,[4] and later lent the company £2,000. Colonel John Pery, his successor, was likewise a man of good standing. At the time of his appointment in 1699, he had been a shareholder for twenty-five years, and six

---

[1] These salaries were supplemented by gratuities which were later increased to the equivalent of the annual rate of pay.

[2] T. 70/77, fo. 89d.   [3] T. 70/76, fo. 29.

[4] He withdrew upon being appointed Secretary.

times an Assistant. Between them, Heron and Pery held the secretaryship for forty-eight years. The company was less fortunate in its selection of other officers. Robert Williamson, appointed Treasurer in 1682, embezzled about £25,000 during his ten years of office, partly by direct theft and partly by giving promissory notes to the company's creditors and appropriating the cash voted to them. This fraud was a tragedy for the company, being exposed at a time of acute shortage of liquid assets, and materially weakened its efforts to survive. To prevent a recurrence, the treasurership was put in commission, with a paid cashier responsible to five Assistants.[1] Two years later the cashier, Nicholas Gilbert, also absconded; on this occasion the company wisely accepted a composition of £2,500.[2]

To what extent such defalcations may be attributed to inadequate supervision it is impossible to say. They occur in the best regulated companies. They do not, in any case, alter the general impression that, at least until the Revolution, the African Company was able to call upon the services of able men, both as officials and as Assistants. After the Revolution a deterioration was to be expected; nevertheless the quality remained surprisingly high. Errors of judgment were certainly made. But the lethargy and dishonesty which characterized the company's affairs in Africa are not to be found in its domestic arrangements. Its failure, in so far as it was due to structural weaknesses, must be ascribed to the difficulty of controlling from London far-flung and complex interests in Africa and the West Indies. Too much had to be left to the discretion of employees abroad, who for the most part followed their own concerns to the detriment of the company's. They, and not the Assistants or staff in London, were the weak links.

2. Exports

Chief amongst the many functions of the Court of Assistants was the provision of goods for export. Unless a sufficient volume of suitable goods was pumped into Africa every year, trade would languish; the fluctuations in its exports provide

[1] T. 70/83, fo. 69.   [2] T. 70/84, fo. 54d.

perhaps the most sensitive indicator of the company's general health and expectations.[1] Between 1672 and 1713 goods to the value of about £1,500,000 were dispatched to Africa, an average of about £40,000 a year.. During the years of comparative prosperity, until 1689, the average was higher; in the first decade of the eighteenth century it sank below £25,000. The highest figure recorded, in 1682, was £88,000; the lowest, in 1711, was nil. The relationship of these figures to total English exports cannot easily be established, no accurate or complete statistics of English trade having yet been devised for the second half of the seventeenth century. The records of the Inspector-General which begin in 1696 are complete, but are notoriously difficult to interpret. It is not, therefore, possible to state with any precision the proportion which the exports of the African company bore to the aggregate exports of the nation; but it was probably never more than three per cent. and often less.

The place of the African trade in the economy of England in the later seventeenth century cannot of course be expressed simply by a statistical formula. There were other considerations which led contemporaries to set such store by it. West Africa, for instance, was the only gold-producing region to which England had either pretensions or access, and gold was still widely and properly regarded as a commodity to be esteemed above all others. When, in the mid-seventeenth century, Englishmen began to go to Africa for a different cargo, slaves, the trade took on a new significance without losing the old. The potential wealth of the West Indies was universally recognized, and their development was believed to depend upon a sufficient supply of negroes. The African trade was converted into an appendage of Barbados and Jamaica, and partook of the esteem in which the West Indian colonies were held. Sugar transformed the trade, from a desirable if dangerous branch of English commerce, into an essential instrument of imperial expansion.

Such considerations as these help to explain the attention lavished upon the African trade by parliaments, governments and pamphleteers. But at the same time the exports of the African Company have a significance of their own in the wider

[1] Appendix I.

theme of the growth of English overseas trade in the seventeenth century. In many ways they reflect and embody the commercial trends which were transforming the country into a great trading nation.

Though obscured by the general lack of statistical evidence, three main developments can be discerned in English commercial history in the seventeenth century. In the first place, there was a slow but certain growth of trade between England and countries beyond the limits of Europe. This had been initiated in the middle years of the sixteenth century with the beginnings of English trade to Russia and Africa, but by the death of Elizabeth I very little progress had been made; English trade was still closely linked to the Continent.[1] While it is not possible to observe in any detail the changes which followed, it appears that in the next sixty or seventy years the re-orientation of English trade proceeded more swiftly. By the close of the seventeenth century, the new pattern is clearly visible; one-fifth of all our exports and more than one-third of our imports depended on regions outside Europe.[2] This trend was closely associated with the growth of English colonies and largely explains the increasing emphasis laid upon sea power. English commercial interests at the beginning of the eighteenth century were scattered far and wide, and the price to be paid for them was the responsibility of empire and the expense of a navy.

Contemporaries fully understood and often exaggerated the importance of this development.[3] Long voyages meant large ships and the training of many sailors. But the dispersal of English trade across the world had a deeper significance. In the old world of Europe before the Industrial Revolution, trade ran along lines that were largely, though not entirely, determined by natural factors. The export of corn or wine, both

---

[1] L. Stone, 'Elizabethan Trade', in *Ec.H.R.*, 2nd Series, II, p. 51.

[2] Based upon the Inspector-General's statistics for 1697–1702.

[3] 'Wee ought to esteem and cherish those trades which we have in remote or far Countreys, for besides the encrease of Shipping and Mariners thereby, the wares also sent thither and receiv'd from thence are far more profitable unto the Kingdom than by our trades neer at hand.' Mun, *England's Treasure by Forraign Trade*, reprint, 1949, p. 10.

European staples, depended on the possession of an appropriate soil and climate; the manufacture of cloth was conditional upon the availability of suitable raw materials; shipbuilding upon timber; and so on. The limits imposed by nature could be broken down; the Dutch were in many ways poorly endowed for the commercial supremacy which they won. But England in the sixteenth century had never looked likely to succeed to the economic dominion of Antwerp, and, once the Dutch had established themselves, her chance of doing the same or better disappeared for a long time. English trade to the Continent laboured under other handicaps besides nature; relations with European countries were at any time liable to be disrupted by religious differences or political crises. This had been especially true in the reign of Elizabeth I, when Englishmen first began to give serious consideration to the Discoveries. The two Richard Hakluyts, in formulating the first comprehensive theory of an economically self-sufficient empire, had argued that Europe was more trouble than it was worth.[1] Disturbances in the Netherlands, quarrels with the Hanseatic towns, the persecution of English sailors in Spain, made our trade with the Continent precarious and dangerously dependent upon the whims of other nations. The Hakluyts proposed that England should cut loose and leave Europe to stew in the juices of religious and political squabbles. All our essential imports, now obtained at great trouble and expense in Europe, could be produced without difficulty and more cheaply in America, and the Indians would buy our cloth. The New World was to be called in to fill the gap left by voluntary isolation from the Old. It was a pleasing picture which never became a reality. America proved less immediately productive and more costly to exploit than the Hakluyts had expected. Moreover, with the death of Elizabeth, English relations with the Continent took a turn for the better, and for a time the arguments for imperialism lost some of their force. Nevertheless, the Hakluyts had been right to stress the potentialities of colonies, and the spectacular growth of tobacco and sugar in

[1] 'A Discourse of Western Planting', in *The Original Writings and Correspondence of the two Richard Hakluyts*, ed. E. G. R. Taylor, II (Hakluyt Society, 2nd Series, LXXVII, 1935).

the seventeenth century proved that imperialism could be profitable.

Of the distant regions with which English commercial relations were developed in the seventeenth century, West Africa was not the least important.[1] Success in trade there owed little to the natural endowments of the countries participating. It was a prize to be competed for, if necessary to be fought for, and when secured to be cherished.

The second main trend in English commercial history in this period was the appearance and growth of triangular or rectangular trades in which exports were exchanged, not against imports, but for some commodity to be resold elsewhere. The value of exports could thereby be augmented by the performance of carrying services. This development is naturally an elusive one, since only the first and last stages of a voyage can be discovered from English Customs records. But there is evidence of its growth in the Mediterranean, where English merchants shipped corn from Sicily to the Levant and carried wine and dried fruits from Greece and the Aegean Islands to Italy.[2] Similarly, trade between England, the fishing banks of Newfoundland, and the countries of southern Europe, was an important branch of English commerce in the seventeenth century.[3] This was particularly esteemed, because the export which set the triangular process in motion was chiefly English labour. In the Far East, the port-to-port or 'country trade' of the East India Company and its servants developed rapidly. But of all the triangular and polyangular trades, none was more famous than the trade in negroes, in which English exports were believed to increase in value by being exchanged for African slaves.

The growth of triangular trades was analogous to another seventeenth-century contribution to English commercial development, the rise of London as an *entrepôt*. In both, Englishmen handled and made profits out of the products of other

[1] In 1699–1702 about 11 per cent. of English exports to non-European countries went to West Africa.

[2] H. Koenigsberger, 'English Merchants in Naples and Sicily in the Seventeenth Century', in *English Historical Review*, LXII (1947).

[3] H. A. Innis, *The Cod Fisheries*, New Haven, 1940.

countries. In the mid-sixteenth century, re-exports had accounted for only an insignificant fraction of English trade,[1] and as late as 1640 the proportion had been no more than five or six per cent.[2] By the end of the century, more than a quarter of all our exports were of foreign production or manufacture.[3] To this spectacular and richly promising development, the African trade made a contribution which, though small, is not entirely without interest. About half of the company's exports were of foreign origin, and the processes by which these various goods were assembled in London for shipment to Africa throw some light upon the methods of English trade at this time.

Chief amongst the company's re-exports were East Indian cottons, calicoes and prints, which, because of their cheapness and bright colours, commanded a ready sale in Africa. They were normally bought at the East India Company's sales,[4] but also, and especially during the war of 1689–97, from private traders. In good years, £20,000 worth of East India goods went to Africa, mainly in the form of fabrics, but also in cowrie-shells which continued to serve as the local currency in parts of Africa until recent times. To some extent, the African trade vindicated Mun's defence of the East India Company: bullion exports to the East purchased goods which, when re-exported to Africa, might be exchanged for gold. Cheap Asiatic textiles which might otherwise have competed with home-produced manufactures were headed off to the safety of West Africa. Thus the African trade fulfilled many of the requirements of contemporary economic thinking.

Amongst the African Company's re-exports, iron and copper from Sweden and Germany were next in importance after East

[1] One per cent in 1564–5; L. Stone, 'Elizabethan Overseas Trade', in *Ec.H.R.*, 2nd Series, II, p. 57.

[2] F. J. Fisher, 'London's Export Trade in the Early Seventeenth Century', in *Ec.H.R.*, 2nd Series, III, p. 154, permits a rough calculation to be made for London. It is unlikely that the national figure would be very different.

[3] Just over 26 per cent. between 1697 and 1702 according to the Inspector-General's records.

[4] £10,000 worth of goods were commonly bought from the East India Company each year; in 1682 the figure was £25,000.

Indian goods. Iron was practically indispensable in the African trade; thus in 1685, of 35 ships dispatched all but six carried iron. Copper was less in demand and exports never exceeded £4,000 a year. So far as it has been possible to ascertain, no iron or copper of English manufacture was exported by the company in this period, requirements of both metals being met by English merchants trading to the Baltic, many of them Merchant Adventurers.[1] For a time the company had a buying agent in Stockholm, but normally it relied upon the London importers. The biggest suppliers of iron were Thomas Westerne and Peter Joye; and of copper, Thomas Vernon and Godfrey Lee. All four were shareholders in the company and all served as Assistants. Much of the metal, which was invariably supplied in the form of bars, was bought on forward contracts which enabled the importer to place firm orders with his correspondent in Sweden or Hamburg. The terms of one such agreement have been preserved:

> Contract of Agreement made between the Royal African Company of England and Peter Joy of London for 450 tuns of voyage Iron that the said Company have agreed with the said Joy to pay him for, at the rate of fourteen pounds per tun (besides any New Imposition on Iron if any should be laid) and the Barrs to be of the usual lenght with Mark or Marks on each Barr and the Number to be from 75 to 80 Barrs at the least in each tun, and the said Joy does promise and Agree to deliver unto the said Company By Gods Blessing wind and weather permitting the Iron abovesaid, vizt.
>
> 100 tuns part of the said Iron by the Middle July 86 or sooner
> 100 tuns more part of the said Iron by the Middle Augt. 86
> or sooner
> 100 tuns more part of the said Iron by the Middle Sept. 86
> or sooner
> 100 tuns more part of the said Iron by the Middle Oct. 86
> or sooner
> 50 tuns more the remainder of the abovesaid Iron in the Monts of November and December following provided that the Company have occation for the said 50 tuns, or shall want any more Iron before the Summer following.

[1] For instance, Sir John Lethuillier, Governor of the Merchant Adventurers, James and John Banckes, Godfrey Lee and Francis Boynton. See P.R.O., C.8/270/50.

And the said Company doe promise to pay unto the said Joye for all the afforesaid Iron within one Month after the delivery or tender of the same at the rate of 14*l.* per tun as afforesaid.

Farther Mr. Peter Joy does contract and agree with the abovesaid Royal African Company to deliver them next yeere Copper Barrs at the rate of six pound and five shillings per cwt. not exceeding 40,000 Barrs to be delivered:

>   10000 Barrs in July or sooner
> More 10000 Barrs in Augt. or sooner
> More 10000 Barrs in Sept. or sooner
> More 10000 Barrs in Nov. and Dec. if the Company thinke fitt to receive the last 10000 Barrs, and the Company to pay the New Imposition if any.[1]

Two other commodities were imported from the Baltic, amber and sletias (silesias, a German textile). African demand for amber was sporadic and shipments irregular. To begin with, the company bought in Holland; but in 1686 Peter Joye was asked by the Committee of Goods to write to his friend at Danzig to supply a sample of the best amber available.[2] If satisfactory, a regular order was promised. As a result of this connexion, 900 lbs. (at £1 a lb.) was exported in 1688, and Joye became the principal contractor. Sletias reached London from Germany by way of Hamburg, and the company obtained the bulk of its supplies from London importers, some of whom dealt also in copper.

At the foundation of the Royal African Company, the Dutch were not only the chief carriers of Europe but were also themselves deeply concerned and experienced in the African trade. Most of the commodities needed for the trade could be obtained in Amsterdam, and throughout the period of its active trade the company maintained an agent there.[3] Through this agency was obtained, especially in the early years, a great variety of goods, iron bars, copper basins, knives, cheap textiles, trumpets, amber, coral and crystal beads. Sheets in particular, generally described as 'old sheets', were bought in large quantities for re-export; in twenty-four years over half a million were shipped

---

[1] T. 70/126, 17 November 1685.   [2] *Ibid.*, 24 June 1586.
[3] From 1674 to 1685 Henry Daems; thereafter Meulenaer & Magnus.

to Africa.[1] Occasionally East India goods, cowries especially, were bought in Holland.[2] Firearms, for which the African demand fluctuated with the alternations of war and peace on the Coast, were a Dutch speciality, and guns of English manufacture proved difficult to sell in the company's early years.[3] The London gunsmiths were invited to copy the Dutch pattern, but their price, 9s., against 6s. 6d. nett for the Dutch, was too high. In 1684 the gunsmiths protested against imports from Holland, naming the company as the chief offender. Their complaint was upheld in a report from the Ordnance Office.[4] To avoid further criticism, the company hired a ship to be laden in Holland with a cargo of guns and gunpowder, to proceed direct to Africa.[5]

The remaining European products which were re-exported to Africa can be briefly summarized. Between two and three thousand gallons of French brandy were exported annually until West Indian rum proved to be a cheaper and equally efficacious substitute. In a good year about £3,000 worth of glass and other types of beads was dispatched. At first these were bought in Holland; after 1680 they were obtained either directly from Venice where they were made, or from English importers. The beads were manufactured in many shapes, sizes and colours, large red, small coral, speckled, speckled white, large and small garnet, rangoes, some threaded as pendants, some loose. Orders were placed from patterns supplied to the company by the importers.

The trends in English commercial history so far observed, the growth of long-distance and triangular trades and the rise of London as an *entrepôt*, all have their origins in the late sixteenth and early seventeenth centuries when the lines of future growth were being drawn.[6] In each of them, English merchants competed and clashed with the Dutch. In 1650 the Dutch were at

---

[1] The Africans used sheets for wrapping themselves in at night. Barbot in Churchill's *Voyages* (1746), V, p. 274.

[2] T. 70/76, fo. 3d; T. 70/79, fo. 87d; T. 70/85, fo. 28d.

[3] In 1684 the company had five thousand English handguns on its hands unsold. T. 70/169, fos. 29d–30.

[4] *Ibid.*, fos. 27–28d.   [5] T. 70/80, fo. 58.

[6] F. J. Fisher, 'London's Export Trade in the Early Seventeenth Century', in *Ec.H.R.*, 2nd Series, III.

the height of their power. They dominated the Baltic and were active in the Mediterranean; their East and West India Companies prospered; much of the trade of central Europe was in their hands; their ships covered the world. Like Antwerp a century earlier, Amsterdam was a market for everything under the sun, and she won and held her position by virtue of efficiency and low costs. It was cheaper for the French to buy goods of Baltic origin in Amsterdam than to fetch them from their source.[1]

Against this impressive economic and financial power, England began in the second half of the seventeenth century to mount an offensive which, gathering speed after 1700, eventually achieved what in 1650 must have seemed impossible, the substitution of London for Amsterdam as the centre of world trade. In this trade-war, the part played by English Governments is well known. By measures such as the Navigation Acts and by maritime war, England formally challenged the Dutch hegemony. But the policy of open aggression did little more than sketch the course of future developments; its positive achievements were few. Unless seconded and implemented by English merchants and manufacturers, its successes would have been slight. The contest for world trade was decided not so much in war or Parliament, but in counting-houses, factories and cottages.

One of the most solid achievements of the Royal African Company was the encouragement which it was able to give to English merchants and manufacturers to compete with the Dutch. As has already been suggested, the company in its early years looked to Amsterdam for many of the goods which it needed to send to Africa, textiles, beads, iron, metal goods such as knives and swords, and firearms. Some, principally sheets, it continued to buy there throughout its history. But, one by one, the other items disappeared from the company's imports from Holland, to be replaced by supplies obtained elsewhere. Before 1680 consignments of Swedish iron were purchased in Amsterdam; after 1680 never. Until 1686 amber was obtained only from Holland; thereafter English merchants imported the

[1] V. Barbour, *Capitalism in Amsterdam in the Seventeenth Century*, pp. 21–2, 95–6.

company's requirements from the Baltic. Beads were supplied from Amsterdam, until in 1681 the Court of Assistants ordered a consignment from Venice.[1] Thenceforth the needs of the African trade were met either by direct purchase from Italy or through English merchants in the Italian trade.

Even more striking is the switch from imports of Dutch products to English-manufactured substitutes which took place in the first thirty years of the company's existence, Amongst the normal constituents of an African cargo was a cheap fabric known as annabasses or 'annabas clouts'. When the company began to export them in 1676 it was obliged to buy in Amsterdam: 17,000 were imported in two years. But in August 1677 the Court of Assistants instructed the Committee of Goods to promote the manufacture of annabasses in England 'that this Company may be supplied with our own manufactory provided they be as good as those' from Holland.[2] The stimulus was entirely successful: between 1680 and 1688 nearly 20,000 anna-basses were shipped to Africa each year, all of English manu-facture. At the same time, the Committee of Goods was ordered, 'for the promoting the English manifacture', to institute the production of scarlet cloths with broad lists suit-able for the Angola trade.[3] Later, boysadoes, a heavy and expensive cloth previously imported from Holland, were manu-factured in England to the company's order.[4]

It was not only in textiles that the company was able to find adequate substitutes in England for imports from Holland. In 1675 it bought knives and sheaths in Amsterdam through its agent, Henry Daems; later they were obtained in Birmingham. Even the Dutch-type guns, which in 1684 English manufac-turers had been unable to rival, were being turned out in thousands by John Sibley & Co. at the beginning of the eighteenth century. The company could and did look back with satisfaction upon these achievements. In its disputes with the separate traders, it obtained certificates from English manu-facturers to the effect that it had been solely responsible for introducing new industries, and in a letter to the Commis-sioners of Trade and Plantations in 1707 it claimed:

[1] T. 70/78, fo. 152.
[2] T. 70/77, fo. 46.
[3] Ibid., fo. 54.
[4] T. 70/126, passim.

to have gained this trade from the Dutch who were before this Company in a manner the sole traders to Guiney, from whence the Company was at first forced to buy the greatest part of their cargoes, vizt. Leyden sayes, 'scarlett cloth, fustians, knives, musketts, boysadoes, annabasses, and for many yeares past they have manufactured all these commodities in England.[1]

These encroachments upon Dutch omnipotence were, of course, straws in the wind rather than significant gains to English trade. And credit for them belongs chiefly to the manufacturers who were able to produce at competitive prices. The company, however, provided the opportunity and took the initiative. In so doing, it contributed something to the establishment of English commercial supremacy in the eighteenth century.[2]

A wide range of goods of English manufacture, apart from those already mentioned, was exported, woollens being easily the most important. Exports to Africa formed only a small fraction of the aggregate export of English manufactured cloth, and the significance of the African market is limited to certain types and localities; only in a few regions did it acquire even a marginal importance. Obviously certain types were unsuitable. Broadcloth was too heavy and too expensive for general sale, and the little that was exported was intended chiefly as gifts to African notables. Similarly, bays, hollands, isinghams, kersies, velvets, and other common English textile products, were exported only in small quantities. What was needed was a fabric that was cheap, durable, and not too heavy, requirements which at this date were best met by serges. The perpetuana, as its name suggests, was hard-wearing, and at 1s. to 1s. 4d. a yard it was reasonably cheap. In the twenty-seven years for which figures are available, more than 170,000 pieces were exported;[3] even in years of depression when the export of

---

[1] T. 70/175, p. 17.

[2] Exactly the same phenomenon has been observed in French trade to Africa at a somewhat later date. S. Berbain, *Le Comptoir Français de Juda (Ouidah) au XVIIIe Siècle*, Paris, 1942, pp. 82–8.

[3] In 1683 the company specified that perpetuanas should be 20–21 yards in length and about 9 lbs. in weight, T. 70/126, 19 July 1683. After the Revolution perpetuanas were made in singles weighing about 5½ lbs. and doubles about 11 lbs.; T. 70/129, fo. 160d.

every other commodity was reduced, perpetuanas continued to be dispatched in large quantities. Another serge, the say, was exported at the rate of two or three thousand pieces annually for the first twenty years of the company's existence; thereafter it declined in favour and disappeared.

All the company's serges, apart from some says imported from Holland in the early years, were manufactured in Devonshire,[1] the company buying either through an agent at Exeter or from a London intermediary. Purchases made at Exeter were paid for by bills drawn on the company, and the goods were transported by sea.[2] Of the perpetuanas bought in London, a large number was supplied by William Warren, himself a shareholder and for ten years a member of the Court of Assistants; in nine years he sold the company more than 25,000 pieces, receiving on average £1 apiece. Almost always, serges were bought undyed and undressed, the company employing a number of dyers, setters, pressers and packers to finish and prepare them for shipment. In this and other ways, the African trade provided direct employment for London artisans.

Most of the other types of English woollens which the company exported were bought from London merchants, but the quantities were quite small. Apart from woollens, consignments to the value of between £1,000 and £2,000 a year each were made of brassware, gunpowder, guns, ironware, knives, pewter and swords. Guns, as a result of local wars in Africa, were in great demand at the beginning of the eighteenth century; in four years, 1701–1704, the company sent to the Coast 32,954 muskets, carbines, pistols, snaphances, fowling-pieces and fuses, enough to equip a fair-sized army. Many of these goods were purchased on contract. At the end of 1685, for example, the company had outstanding contracts for the supply of tallow, Welsh plains (a simply woven woollen cloth), pewter, gunpowder, spirits, iron, copper, firearms and beads.[3] Tallow

---

[1] For the Devon serge industry see W. G. Hoskins, *Industry, Trade and People in Exeter, 1688–1800*, 1935.

[2] In the first two years of the company's life, its agents bought about £8,000 worth of perpetuanas in Exeter.

[3] T. 70/126, 9 February 1686.

was contracted for at 1*s.* a barrel below and pewter at 2¼*d.* a lb.
below the price current, the other commodities being at fixed
prices. In 1696 a contract was made with Richardson & Co.,
gunpowder makers of Hounslow, for 200 barrels at 95*s.* a
barrel, with the proviso that if the price current rose before
delivery the company was to pay no more than the stipulated
sum, but if it fell the company was to have the benefit.[1] Thus
the company was able to gain advantages by large orders
placed in advance.

Knives and swords were bought either in Holland or from
London merchants until 1690, when the company began to
obtain its requirements from Samuel Banner of Birmingham,
who earlier had supplied the Hudson's Bay Company.[2] The
Birmingham knives were cheap: less than 2½*d.*, and only 1½*d.*
for wooden-hafted varieties; the swords were 3*s.* each, all prices
inclusive of carriage by wagon to London. Between 1690 and
1701 Banner supplied the company with over 400,000 knives
and 7,000 swords. During much of this time, the war and consequent embargoes on sailing made it difficult to plan cargoes
in advance, and many orders were for delivery 'as soon as he
can', 'per first oppertunity', 'with all possible speed', as the
embargo was lifted or ships became available.[3]

The remaining products of English manufacture which
found a place in the African trade may be briefly mentioned.
About £1,000 worth of pewter basins, jugs and tankards, £1,500
worth of brass basins, pans and kettles, small quantities of
carpets, a few tons of manillas,[4] spirits, a miscellany of clothing,
some trumpets, scissors, mirrors, and other trifles were exported
in most years. In addition, food and drink for the garrisons,
provisions for slave-ships, and building materials for the forts
were sent out from England. The almost complete dependence
of the company's employees upon supplies from home is
illustrated by Agent Bradley's request in 1679 for:

> all sorts of necessaryes for finishing the Castle, except bricks and
> Lime which wee make here, as Timber Baulks, Planks, Deales,
> Sparrs, all sorts of nayles, locks, Crows, Shovells, Pitch, Tarr,

[1] T. 70/129, fo. 8d.
[2] *Minutes of Hudson's Bay Company*, 1679–82, pp. 174, 175, 209.
[3] T. 70/128–9, *passim.*   [4] Brass half-rings.

Tarris, and Plaister to Parris, Rigging for ships that are here, sheathing board, Twine, some small spare Anchors, Pick Axes, and workmen, vizt. Bricklayers, Smiths, Armorers, Carpenters, and Chirurgeons to be sent to other places and a mate for this . . . . Borax for soldering, 30 or 40 sheets of good lead . . . two pair of bellows for the smith and Hides to mend them, four dozen of good sheepskins for spunges, and staves for ditto, four or five dozen of sayle needles, 1,000 of ten inche tyles, good quantityes of all sorts nayles . . . quills, inke, penknives, two quire paper bookes, and other and good writing papers, wax and wafers, parchment skins for drum head and cords for ditto.[1]

3. Imports and Sales

Though much less miscellaneous than exports, the company's imports were still numerous. From Africa came gold, ivory, dyewood, wax, hides, gum, malaguetta and palm-oil; from the West Indies, sugar, tobacco, cotton, indigo, cocoa, ginger, logwood and silver.[2] The sale of these commodities, like the provision of goods for export, was under the management of the Committee of Goods and supervised by the Court of Assistants. By its Preamble, the company had obliged itself to sell all goods except gold and silver 'by inch of candle', and this rule was generally kept. There were, therefore, no contracts to be distributed, and the task of the Committee was merely to warehouse the company's goods, and to arrange and advertise the sales on days appointed by the Court. At the beginning of the eighteenth century, if not earlier, notice of forthcoming sales was sent to Amsterdam.[3] They were not, however, on anything like the scale of those of the East India Company, where goods to the value of several hundreds of thousands of pounds were offered. Auctions were held at Africa House about six times a year until 1689, and thereafter whenever sufficient goods had been accumulated. In 1682, for example, there were six sales; in 1704 four; in 1711 none.

The African Company derived a larger proportion of its income from the sale of goods of African origin than is generally supposed, probably about two-fifths. The growth of the slave-

[1] T. 70/1, fos. 23d, 24.   [2] Appendix II.   [3] T. 70/86, p. 95.

trade since 1640 did not make the products which had first attracted Englishmen to Africa any less sought after. Indeed, bitter experience in the English West Indies caused the company to prefer dealing in African goods to engaging in the slave-trade. In 1695, as we have already seen, the company voluntarily threw open the slave-trade to its competitors, and in the following year its proposals for a compromise settlement with the separate traders envisaged the retention of monopoly only between Capes Blanco and Mount, that is, in the regions producing chiefly commodities and but few slaves.[1] For the company, as we shall see, the negro-trade was the source of endless frustration, bitter hostility, and substantial losses.[2] For example, long credit had to be extended to planters; African products brought directly to England were sold at once for cash. Another consideration was that the company's monopoly, even when nominally in force, ended when the slaves had been sold in the colonies. On the third side of its triangular trade, therefore, the company was exposed to the cold winds of competition. Almost certainly it was the largest single importer of English West Indian products; but equally certainly its imports represented only a small fraction of all the sugar, ginger, cotton and tobacco reaching this country in the later seventeenth century.[3] No effective control could, therefore, be kept over the supply, distribution and prices of colonial goods.

Imports from Africa were in a different position. The company's charter not only excluded all but itself from visiting Africa, but also contained an injunction forbidding Customs officials to admit to this country goods of African origin, other than those imported by the company. And the governments of Charles II and James II were ready to enforce this prohibition. In 1684, for example, the company complained to the Commissioners of Customs that 500 tons of red sanders wood (used for making dyes) had been imported from Holland. This wood was found on investigation to be the product of the East Indies not of Africa; nevertheless it competed with African redwood and, when the company took its case to the King in December 1684, an Order-in-Council was obtained forbidding

[1] Above, p. 132.   [2] Below, 'The Company in the West Indies'.
[3] Below, p. 338.

further importation.[1] Redwood, originating chiefly from Sierra Leone and the Sherbro river, was one of the most profitable commodities in which the company dealt. Before and just after the Revolution, it could be bought in Africa for goods to the value of about £3 a ton and sold in London for £40 or more. In 1693, the company departed from its usual practice of selling by auction, and concluded a contract with a group of salters for redwood at £60 a ton.[2] The selling-price in London went even higher in the following years, but when competition from the separate traders began to take effect the purchase-price in Africa rose about four-fold and the profit margin was narrowed. In the thirty-two years for which the figures are available, 2,313 tons were brought to England by the company.

For the first thirty years of the company's existence, all gold obtained in West Africa was delivered to the Mint, and there coined into guineas stamped with the elephant. After 1700 small quantities were sold privately, but the bulk appears still to have gone to the Mint. In all, 548,327 guineas were coined for the company between 1673 and 1713.[3] While this trade in gold was vitally important to the company as a source of income, its importance in the monetary system of the nation has probably been exaggerated. Between 1677 and 1689, when the company was bringing home more gold than at any other time in its history, it was responsible for about seven per cent. of the total of gold coined by the Mint.[4] After the Revolution, and indeed as late as 1736, the company continued to import gold, but its contribution to the monetary stock of the nation became steadily less significant. The use of the company's emblem upon the guineas which were thus put into circulation provided an unusual and picturesque form of advertisement which has probably been responsible for the excessive importance sometimes attached to West Africa as a source of precious metal. Silver imports from the West Indies were even less remarkable. They came mainly from Jamaica in the form of Spanish pieces-of-eight, and totalled about £66,000 in forty

---

[1] T. 70/169, fos. 16d, 17d, 25, 25d.   [2] T. 70/84, fo. 7d.

[3] Appendix II gives yearly totals.

[4] For totals of gold coined, see Sir J. Craig, *The Mint*, 1953, Appendix I, pp. 415-17.

years. Much the greater part, both before and after the recoinage of 1696, was sold privately, the Mint price presumably
being unattractive.

Ivory could be purchased almost anywhere along the African
coast, though the greater part of the company's imports derived
from the Gambia and the Windward Coast. It ranked second
to gold, and in the forty years for which records are available
over 17,000 cwt. was imported, of which 9,300 cwt. arrived in
the decade 1680–89. Ivory varied so much in quality that no
average price can usefully be assigned to it. Generally, larger
tusks fetched much better prices than smaller ones. At a sale in
1679, for example, the highest price paid was £6 13s. a cwt. and
the lowest £4 7s. Higher prices were often paid for the best
quality, £10 or £12 a cwt. being commonly recorded. Wax,
from north-west Africa, was less variable in quality and kept a
steadier price at £4–£5 a cwt. In forty years the company
imported 6,600 cwt., but, as in the case of ivory, the bulk of it
(5,000 cwt.) arrived in the 'eighties. The curtailment of trade in
both commodities after 1689 must be attributed chiefly to the
wars with France, the effects of which were especially severe in
north-west Africa.

The remaining products of Africa were of small account.
Gum was valuable, but was obtainable only in the Senegal
region where the French were too strongly entrenched for
the English to be able to obtain the supplies they would have
liked.[1] Hides were plentiful in north-west Africa, but were not
esteemed by the company. Those that were bought, the company accepted as an unprofitable burden, undertaken in order
that other and more valuable commodities might be secured.
Malaguetta was used principally as a physic for negroes, and
palm-oil was not imported in any quantity until well into the
eighteenth century.

Of the West Indian commodities in which the company
dealt, sugar was easily outstanding, 30,000 tons being imported
in thirty-five years. An account of the company's sugar trade
will be given in a later chapter.[2] By this date the English West
Indies had already gone far towards specializing in a single
crop, and the quantities of tobacco, cotton, ginger, indigo and

[1] Below, p. 219.   [2] Below, p. 335 *et seq.*

logwood which the company imported were small.[1] All these commodities, and most of those from Africa, were sold by auction, the buyers being often brokers who purchased for resale. Generally they paid a deposit within a day or two of making a purchase, the balance being paid later. Three per cent. discount was allowed for payment within twenty days.[2] Prominent amongst the brokers was Robert Woolley, who paid the company £65,000 in ten years. The destination of the company's goods, once they had passed through his hands, cannot be discovered: presumably the West Indian commodities went chiefly to London refiners and eventually to grocers and confectioners; the ivory to furniture makers and cutlers; and the dyewood to salters.

For twenty-five years from 1672 the company's sales proceeded uneventfully. In common with every other vendor, however, it had to meet the difficult monetary situation preceding and created by the recoinage of 1696. The guinea, which had been valued by the company for dividend purposes at 22s. in 1676 and had since been stable at 21s. 6d., rose in 1695 to 30s.[3] At its first sale in 1696, the company resolved to accept payment of one-half in guineas and the other half in 'good silver, banke notes, or such other notes as the Company should like'.[4] Later in the same year, one-half in banknotes was accepted and at the beginning of 1697 'old silver money at 5/2 an ounce'. This disorder subsided in 1698 when the recoinage was completed, but meanwhile the company had taken the decision to liquidate part of its debt by accepting its own bonds in payment for goods sold at auctions.[5] Thus at the sale of 20 December 1697, buyers were permitted to pay as to one-quarter in milled money or guineas and the other three-quarters in the company's bonds. This practice was continued until 1710, the company accepting payment as to one-quarter, one-half or three-quarters in bonds according to the size of its debt or the pressure of its creditors. Occasionally it was forced to take payment entirely in bonds. In the circumstances, the policy was sound and even honest. But as affairs drifted from bad to worse, unforeseen difficulties arose. Before the Revolu-

---

[1] Appendix II.   [2] T. 70/80, fo. 48.   [3] Craig, *op. cit.*, p. 184.
[4] T. 70/84, fo. 64.   [5] *Ibid.*, fo. 80.

tion, bonds such as the company had issued had seldom been assigned, though they may have been legally assignable. Now persons intending to buy at the company's sales began to acquire them, and inevitably they came to circulate at a discount.[1] The damage thereby done to the company's reputation was considerable.

Nevertheless, the company's sales were on the whole conducted with at least as much efficiency and dispatch as was usual at the end of the seventeenth century. Much the same can be said of all its affairs in England. Mistakes there certainly were, especially in financial policy; but knowledge of capital-management was still in its infancy, and what in the twentieth century appear to be foolhardy and impossible risks were in the seventeenth century taken cheerfully and without much realization of their possible consequences. In particular there seems to have been no appreciation of the value of a reserve of liquid or near-liquid assets stored up against unforeseen contingencies. Bad finance, however, though fundamental, is almost the only visible blot on the company's domestic record. Of the negligence, indolence and waste assumed by Adam Smith there are few signs.

[1] Above, p. 93.

5

SHIPPING

1. Voyages and Vessels

PROMINENT amongst the claims made by the Royal African Company upon the favour of Parliament and the nation were the stimulus given by its operations to the shipping industry and the employment and training provided for large numbers of seamen. They were not unreasonable claims. A voyage to West Africa and the West Indies called for ships and crews above the size commonly engaged in European waters, and afforded a wide variety of marine experience for masters and crews alike. Without benefit of the chronometer, voyages of six, eight or ten weeks were made out of sight of land. On the African coast itself there were peculiar navigational problems of winds and currents, while the Atlantic crossing, with tiny islands such as Barbados or Nevis as the objective, must have demanded skill. Socially there may have been little to be said for a slaving captain, but professionally he must have ranked high.

Although, as is well known, the slave-trade was triangular, the shipping employed by the African Company proceeded, not on one, but on five distinct routes or services. There was, first, the voyage from London to Africa and directly back, to collect products such as ivory, wax, dyewood, hides, and gum, which, because of their bulk, could not be economically consigned to England *via* the West Indies. The greater part of these products derived from north-west Africa, and it was therefore to Gambia, Sierra Leone, and Sherbro that such voyages were commonly made. The number of ships on this route was never large; in each of the years 1686 to 1688, for example, two went to Gambia and one to Sierra Leone and Sherbro. After 1690, when the company's operations were curtailed by war, one ship had to collect from all three places.

The duration of this voyage, as of all others to Africa, varied enormously, not only according to the speed of the ship, the weather, and the presence or otherwise of pirates and privateers, but also according to the work which had to be done on the coast. Much time might have to be spent loading and unloading, and a stay of 90 days for a ship loading ivory, wax, hides or gum and 120 days for slaves was thought necessary.[1] Sailing time from England to north-west Africa was probably between five and seven weeks: the *James*, for example, in 1675 reached Sierra Leone after a passage from the Downs of 45 days.[2] When possible, ships sailed in company, in peace as well as in war. The *James* sailed with East Indiamen as far as Madeira, and the *Carlisle* in 1680 joined a fleet of eleven, including an East Indiaman bound for Bantam, an African Company's ship for Angola, and eight other ships for the Canaries.[3] It does not seem to have been usual for a ship to perform the complete voyage, from England to Africa and back, more frequently than once a year, allowing for refitting and repairs. The *Delight* and the *Margaret* each sailed to the Gambia three years running, and the *Dolphin* in each year from 1680 to 1683. War probably lengthened the duration, for a ship on this route was hardly ever out of range of French privateers. Convoys might be arranged for outward-bound vessels, but the homeward run had almost always to be attempted alone. Thus, of nine ships beginning the out-and-home voyage in the years 1702 to 1704, only three completed it; one disappeared and five were taken by the French, all on the return passage.

The second route, from England to the African coast for slaves, and thence to the West Indies, was that followed by the majority of ships sailing in the company's service. In 1686, for instance, thirty-two ships departed from London for Africa: twenty-three were to discharge slaves in the West Indies, three to return directly to England, two to deliver slaves in Virginia, and four to remain as supply-ships on the African coast. The

[1] T. 70/1, fo. 19.   [2] T. 70/1211.   [3] T. 70/1216.

voyage from London to the West Indies *via* Africa, it must be understood, was quite distinct from the complete triangular voyage. Until the outbreak of war in 1689, no merchant-ship was hired by the company to perform the triangular voyage; invariably the contract terminated upon arrival in the West Indies. For this practice there were two reasons. In the first place, it was seldom if ever possible to realize the proceeds of the sale of a cargo of slaves in the West Indies quickly enough to provide that same ship with a return cargo of sugar. Planters demanded and were given several months to pay, and they frequently took several years. If they paid for their negroes in cash, there might be no goods available in which it could be invested, for slaves often arrived between harvests when sugar was scarce or of poor quality. Thus, unless the company was prepared to store sugar and run the real danger of deterioration, it could never guarantee to provide homeward cargoes for ships which had completed two-thirds of the triangular voyage.[1] Secondly, and more important, for reasons which will be discussed in a later chapter, the company did not always choose to make returns from the West Indies in the form of goods such as sugar, ginger, cotton or indigo, for which cargo-space would be required. During the 'eighties in particular, the price of all these commodities in London was extremely low, and there was little, if any, money to be made from them. Consequently the company often preferred to receive remittances from the Plantations in bills of exchange or specie.[2] Thus, the entire proceeds of the sale of a cargo of slaves might be returned to England in an envelope containing bills of exchange. In such circumstances a ship hired by the company for the whole triangular voyage would have made her homeward run in ballast.

The duration of voyages on this route depended chiefly upon the time spent on the African coast. Ships slaving in the Gambia, for instance, collected the whole of their complement

---

[1] On this and many other points in this chapter comparison may be made with eighteenth-century French experience in the slave-trade in Gaston-Martin, *Nantes au XVIIIe Siècle, L'Ère des Négriers, 1714–1774*, Paris, 1931.

[2] Below, pp. 336–40.

of negroes from the company's fort there and might hope to get away in four months or less. Ships slaving on the coast of Angola, on the other hand, had further to sail and had to collect their own cargoes. The *Sherbro*, having obtained her slaves from Sherbro, reached Barbados in November 1707, 218 days out from Plymouth; while the *Katherine* which sailed with her from England, but had to slave further south, was 327 days in reaching the same destination.[1] One of the fastest voyages on record was that performed in 1677 by the *Arthur*, which arrived in Barbados 160 days after leaving the Downs, despite having had to collect her own slaves in the Calabar river. She was 57 days from the Downs to Calabar, 38 days in purchasing her complement of negroes, 27 days from Calabar to Cape Lopez (where the ship was cleaned and provisioned), and 38 days from Cape Lopez to Barbados.[2] By contrast, the *James* spent nine months on the Windward and Gold Coasts, collecting trade and chasing interlopers, and did not reach Barbados until 414 days after leaving the Downs.[3]

The third route for the company's shipping was the homeward voyage from the West Indies to England. For reasons that have already been mentioned, it was seldom possible for the company's agents to provide a homeward-bound ship with a full cargo of West Indian goods. Complete cargoes could occasionally be found, but they were normally reserved for ships owned by the company. Usually, therefore, ships engaged for the homeward voyage carried only small or medium-sized consignments on the company's account and got the remainder of their cargo from other shippers. In 1677, for example, 43 ships were employed by the company to bring sugar from Barbados, Jamaica and Nevis; on average, each carried 32 tons. In wartime, prudence suggested even smaller consignments, and in 1706 86 ships were employed to carry an average of about 15 tons of sugar each. Ships which had completed the London-Africa-West Indies voyage and had discharged their negroes were eligible for re-engagement for the homeward voyage by the company's agents in the Plantations, but there was no guarantee or understanding that this would be done. In any case, since the company could seldom supply the whole

[1] T. 70/63.   [2] T. 70/1213.   [3] T. 70/1211.

return cargo, slaving ships, having discharged, had to become tramps and compete with other tramps for their freight.

The complete triangular voyage, the fourth route, was, for reasons already suggested, rarely performed by ships in the company's service until the outbreak of war. The few that undertook it were ships owned by the company, or those, like the *Orange Tree*, lent by the Royal Navy. After 1689 the triangular voyage came to be more frequently performed. The price in London of all West Indian products and especially of sugar, which until then had been abnormally low, rose sharply, and it began to be profitable to make returns from the West Indies in goods instead of in bills or specie. Thus, despite the contraction of every other branch of the company's trade as a result of war, imports of sugar were fairly well maintained or even increased.[1] In the three years, 1680 to 1682, for example, about 2,070 tons were brought from Barbados and Jamaica; in the years 1706 to 1708, notwithstanding all the disasters that had befallen the company, imports totalled 2,335 tons. Although far fewer negroes were being delivered in the West Indies, almost as much sugar, and in some years more, was brought to England. The difficulty of reconciling the company's shipping needs on the second and third 'legs' of the trade was thus somewhat eased, and the triangular voyage became a more feasible proposition.

The overall duration of the London-Africa-West Indies-London voyage is best exemplified by the history of the *Falconbergh*, a company-owned ship. Between 1691 and 1704 she performed the round trip eight times, more than any other vessel that ever sailed in the company's service. Of 320 tons, manned by a crew of 65 in war and 50 in peace, this remarkable ship delivered more than 3,500 negroes in the West Indies.

At the conclusion of her last voyage, the *Falconbergh* was cast away near Bristol. Her eight voyages were thus completed in thirteen years, an average of one trip in each twenty months. Allowing for time spent in refitting between trips, the voyages themselves can scarcely have exceeded fifteen or sixteen months. The fifth voyage, accomplished in less than a year, is particularly remarkable. Few ships on the triangular voyage

[1] Appendix II.

took less than nine months, and few, apart from those assigned to special duties on the African coast, failed to return to England within eighteen months of departure.[1]

The Voyages of the *Falconbergh*[2]

Departure from the Downs	Destination in Africa	Place of Discharge	No. of Negroes Delivered Alive	Return Cargo
31 Oct. 1691	Gold Coast, Ardra	Barbados	not known	19 tons sugar
29 May 1694	do.	do.	592	148 tons sugar, 1 ton cotton
8 Dec. 1695	do., Whydah	do.	491	158 tons sugar
8 March 1697	do.	do.	502	240 tons sugar
23 July 1698	do.	do.	471	228 tons sugar
27 Aug. 1699	Cape Coast	Antigua & Montserrat	339	274 tons sugar
10 March 1701	Cape Coast, Alampo	Barbados	375	6 tons cotton
28 Sept. 1703	do., Whydah	Jamaica	459	86 tons sugar

The fifth and final route for ships employed by the African Company was from the West Indies to Africa, and back to the West Indies. This voyage was seldom performed in the early years of the company's history, though small craft sometimes shuttled between Gambia and Barbados, carrying slaves in one direction and rum in the other. In the later 'eighties the commercial possibilities of rum in Africa came to be more fully appreciated, and war provided a further stimulus. The danger from privateers was always greater in the English Channel than in the Caribbean. Difficulties in getting seamen and permission to sail in wartime also encouraged the use of the West Indies for departures to Africa. In 1703, for example, the company wrote to Sir Dalby Thomas at Cape Coast that the *Davers* galley on arrival at Barbados was to be sent back to Africa: 'its so very difficult to procure seamen and get any shipps out of the river of Thames that we have thought of this expedient'.[3]

[1] Gaston-Martin, *op. cit.*, pp. 65 ff.
[2] Compiled from T. 70/61-2 and T. 70/946-52.   [3] T. 70/52, p. 11.

Between 1703 and 1709, thirty-one ships were dispatched from Jamaica, Barbados and Antigua, carrying rum to Cape Coast castle and returning with negroes.

Between 1672 and 1713 more than five hundred ships were sent out from England to Africa by the Royal African Company. During its most active period, from 1680 to 1688, departures totalled 249.[1] These were the ships engaged on the first, second and (more rarely) the fourth of the routes described. Over the same period of 1672 to 1713 the company employed a further 1,250 ships on the third route, the homeward voyage from the West Indies, though, as we have seen, on the majority of them the company was only one amongst several consignors.[2] While no accurate estimate has been made of the aggregate strength of the English mercantile marine in the later seventeenth century, the ships employed either wholly or in part by the African Company must represent a significant fraction of the ocean-going tonnage. Indeed, shipping was probably the branch of the English domestic economy upon which the African trade made its greatest impact. For ships had not only to be built and manned, but also repaired and refitted between voyages. Work was thereby provided for large numbers of artisans as well as seamen. Thus, when debates about the future of the African trade were at their height in 1708 and 1709, a petition in favour of the company's monopoly was presented to the House of Commons signed by 403 shipwrights, sailmakers and rope-merchants living in and about London. It was promptly answered by a petition in favour of the separate traders signed by 183 persons of the same occupations.[3]

The average burden of ships of all kinds in the English mercantile marine of the later seventeenth century was certainly well under 100 tons.[4] By such standards the ships engaged in the African trade were large. Yet the company employed few

[1] T. 70/175, reverse, p. 13. [2] T. 70/936-56.
[3] T. 70/175, pp. 61, 169-70.
[4] Ships engaged in trade between London and France in 1669-70 averaged only 54 tons and many coastwise trading ships would be even smaller. V. Barbour, 'Dutch and English Merchant Shipping' in,*Ec.H.R.*, II (1929-30).

really big vessels, comparable to the East Indiaman. Because of their exceptional size, the latter had generally to be built to the order and specification of the East India Company. In the later history of the slave-trade, ships were sometimes, though not invariably, specially designed or adapted for the transport of human cargo, but this does not seem to have been the common practice in the seventeenth century. Small modifications might be made, but the 'slaver' was not a distinctive craft. Thus, while the African Company did from time to time order the construction of ships for its service, such as shallow-draught sloops for river-navigation and the coastal trade of West Africa, it was generally able to meet its needs from the pool of ordinary ocean-going vessels which were built for the American and West Indian trades.

The tonnage of ships dispatched by the African Company is shown by the following figures of departures between 1680 and 1688 and between 1691 and 1713:

Tonnage	No. of ships clearing 1680–1688	No. of ships clearing 1691–1713
under 50	11	9
50–99	58	28
100–149	85	60
150–199	34	16
200–249	31	17
250–299	11	12
300–349	6	22
350–399	3	8
400 and over	10	12
Total	249	184[1]

It will be apparent that the two periods exhibit an important contrast. In the first, a period of peace, 249 ships of an average burden of 147 tons were dispatched. In the second, which was given over largely to war, 184 ships were sent out with an average burden of 186 tons. This seems to be only slightly lower than the tonnage of ships engaged in the African trade a century later.[2] The effects of war conditions, however, were not

---

[1] T. 70/175, reverse, pp. 11–14 for 1680–8; T. 70/61, fos. 165d, 166; and T. 70/62–3 for 1691–1713.

[2] Ships entering from or clearing to Africa at British ports in 1792 averaged 202 tons; C. E. Fayle, 'The Employment of British Shipping', in *The Trade Winds*, ed. C. Northcote Parkinson, 1948, p. 73.

simply to promote the use of larger ships, though the 'ship of force' was commoner in war than in peace. Even in war over half the total number of ships dispatched were under 150 tons. The most conspicuous effect of war was to reduce the number of medium-sized merchantmen of between 150 and 250 tons which were too large to escape the attention of privateers and not large enough to mount a heavy defensive armament. Presumably the smaller ships of under 150 tons were less conspicuous and cheaper to lose, and they continued to be employed in war as in peace, supplemented by more formidable armed merchantmen of 300 tons or over. While in peace only seven per cent. of ships clearing for Africa were of 300 tons or more, in war the proportion rose to nearly a quarter. The expectation that large ships could defend themselves and small ones escape notice was not always fulfilled. In 1694, for example, four large and four small ships were dispatched to Africa. The *Averilla* of 320 tons and 30 guns and the *Three Brothers* of 320 tons and 24 guns were both taken by the French, as were three of the smaller ships. In 1703, on the other hand, all the larger ships escaped capture, while eight of the eighteen smaller craft were taken. In time of war all the company's ships were armed, 'a ship of force' mounting from 24 to 36 guns and smaller vessels from six to ten.

The effects of war are equally apparent in increasing the size of crews manning the company's ships, though here the evidence is incomplete. Figures can be devised only for the years between 1691 and 1699 when the average ratio of seamen to tonnage was 1 : 5.2 tons. Between 1691 and 1696, despite the difficulties of obtaining seamen, the ratio was as high as 1 : 4.75, while in 1698 and 1699, two years of peace, it fell to 1 : 6.5 tons.[1] Even so it was probably above the national average, for the African trade differed from others in that the size of the crews was not determined solely by navigational requirements or even by the exigencies of defence against privateers and pirates. A ship of 150 tons manned by a crew of 28 might be intended to transport as many as 300 or even 400 negroes. A crew of this size would probably appear excessive for a ship in the Baltic or Mediterranean trades, but it was none too large for holding

[1] T. 70/61, fos. 165d, 166.

O

down hundreds of frightened and sometimes desperate slaves. It may well be that the advantage which the Dutch commonly held in operating their ships with fewer men, and thus more cheaply, was absent from a trade where the size of the crew was determined partly by the nature of the cargo handled.

When loading negroes on to a slaving ship, the object was to pack as many as possible between the decks and on the top deck consistent with such low standards of hygiene as prudence dictated. Samples from the available evidence suggest an average intended ratio of one negro to .5 tons, but this figure requires qualification. In the first place, it derives from the rough estimates of the size of the intended slave-cargo; the actual cargo occasionally exceeded but more often fell below expectations. Secondly, the number of negroes per ton carried on small ships was always greater than on larger vessels. For example, on four ships of over 300 tons the intended ratio was 1 negro to .59 tons, while on eight ships of under 150 tons it was 1 : .44 tons, a difference that seems small but probably meant a good deal in terms of human discomfort and mortality. These figures suggest that in respect of overcrowding, the slave-trade at the end of the seventeenth century may have been rather worse than a hundred years later. The Act of 1788 which regulated the number of negroes to be carried on slave-ships prescribed a ratio of 1 : .6 tons on ships of under 160 tons, and 1 : .66 for those of greater burden. These proportions were applicable to ships specially built or adapted for slave-transport, and ordinary ships were restricted to a ratio of 1 : 1. It is, however, unlikely that any such proportions had prevailed in the Liverpool slave-trade before the passing of the Act.[1]

2. The Cost of Shipping

Before the Revolution the company owned few of the ships which transported its goods. Thus of 165 sent out in the years

---

[1] 28 Geo. III c. 54; E. Williams, *Capitalism and Slavery*, University of North Carolina Press, 1944, p. 59. Comparisons of tonnages at the end of the seventeenth and the end of the eighteenth centuries may, however, be misleading, owing to variations in the meaning of the 'ton'.

1680 to 1685, 124 are known to have been hired ships, while a number of the remainder were small craft which were to stay on the African coast. This extensive use of hired ships does not seem to have been due, as might have been expected, to a shortage of capital, though large sums would have been needed had the company owned all the vessels it employed. It had no objection in principle to owning ships, and many of those engaged on the London-Africa-London route did in fact belong to it. Before 1689, as we have seen, the company found little difficulty in borrowing money, and there is no reason to doubt that, had it been so minded, it could have raised the money to build or purchase its ówn fleet. This actually happened at a later stage in the company's history, for between 1700 and 1709 111 ships were dispatched of which 64 were company-owned. And this heavy investment in shipping was undertaken when money was desperately short and borrowing difficult. The use of hired ships before 1689 must therefore be regarded as a deliberate policy rather than one enforced by lack of funds. It can probably be explained in terms already suggested. Had the company owned all or many of the ships engaged in carrying slaves to the Plantations, it would have been faced with the problem of finding homeward cargoes for them. Owing to the low prices of West Indian products in the 'seventies and 'eighties and the consequent practice of making remittances in bills or specie, company-owned ships would have been obliged either to return to London in ballast or to carry goods for other consignors, the first an unprofitable and the second a speculative and dubious business. Until the price of sugar rose, beginning just before the Revolution and continuing under the stimulus of war, it was more economical to hire ships for the voyage to Africa and the West Indies, and leave them there to make what arrangements they could for a return cargo. Thus while several company-owned ships completed the triangular voyage in the early eighteenth century, it is seldom that we find one doing so before 1689.

The ships which the company owned were mostly bought second-hand or ready to use, rather than built to order. As already suggested, ships employed in the African trade were not yet distinctive enough to necessitate special construction. The company did, however, have a number of yachts, sloops and smacks of 30 to 50 tons built to order for the trade of the African coast. In 1675, for example, Henry Johnson, the well-known ship-builder, agreed to construct a sloop 46 feet long and 15 feet in the beam, finding all materials except rigging, sails and sheathing, for £5 17s. 6d. a ton.[1] In 1699 £5 a ton was paid for building a ship of 90 tons and in the following year three ships of about 100 tons were ordered for the company at £5, £4 17s. 6d. and £4 15s. a ton each.[2] While other ships may have been built to order in this way, it is clear that the company generally bought such vessels as it needed second-hand. The initial cost of a merchantman in the later seventeenth century was not great, though fitting out and maintenance were expensive. In January 1675, for example, a ship of 180 tons, to be named the *James*, was bought for £1,300; preparing her for service took nearly a year and cost the company £814. Fitting out the *Freizland* in 1673 cost £480, and after one voyage she was sold for £650, so that her capital value was little more than the cost of making her seaworthy.[3]

It was, however, as a charterer that the company made its greatest impact upon the shipping industry, for, even after 1700, when company-owned ships predominated, many of the larger vessels employed were hired. In 1707, for example, nine ships were dispatched to Africa of which six were company-owned. But while all the smaller vessels belonged to the company, three of the four ships of more than 300 tons were on charter. All these hired ships appear to have belonged to syndicates of eight, sixteen or more owners, so that the number of persons thereby given an interest in the African trade was very large. Ship-owning at this date was seldom a specialized occupation but rather a form of investment favoured by merchants of most kinds and classes. The shipping interest was not distinct from, but co-extensive (or almost so) with, the mercantile interest. It is not therefore surprising that many of the owners of hired ships were shareholders or employees of the company.[4]

[1] T. 70/76, fo. 40d.   [2] T. 70/85, fo. 65; T. 70/86, pp. 72–3, 81.
[3] From Cash Book, T. 70/216.
[4] References to owners of ships hired by the company appear in the

The hiring of a ship was regulated by charterparty, pre-scribing the size of the crew, the number of passengers, cargo to be carried on each stage of the voyage, places of lading and discharge and the time to be spent at each, and the freight charges.[1] This agreement was strictly binding on the captain (who was often himself one of the owners), and breaches of charterparty, even of a petty or technical kind, provided grounds for damages.[2] More serious breaches resulted in the deduction of several hundred pounds from the ship's earnings.[3] Most, if not all, charterparties contained clauses relating to demurrage, a necessary precaution for owners of ships going to West Africa, where delays in the provision of slave-cargoes might result in serious loss of time. Demurrage rates varied from £2 10s. to £6 a day, and the company generally had to pay a few hundred pounds yearly in this way. Part of the loss was recovered by counter-demurrage clauses in the charter-party, whereby the company obtained an allowance for ships which completed their lading in less than the stipulated time.[4]

On the voyage from London to Africa and back, freight charges were generally calculated according to the tonnage of goods carried on the return passage. The same rate prevailed for Gambia as for Sierra Leone, and for all the principal pro-ducts of those regions, ivory, dyewood, wax, gum and hides. In peacetime it was from £5 10s. to £6 a ton; in war rather more than double, £12 to £13 10s.[5] The gross earnings of ships engaged on this route could, therefore, be large. The *Thomas & Elizabeth*, for example, which carried a cargo valued at

Minutes of the Court of Assistants on the occasion of the sealing of charter-parties, but never more than two or three names are mentioned, pre-sumably those of the more active members of the syndicate. Between 1672 and 1689, 150 owners, apart from captains, are mentioned in connexion with 174 hired ships. Of these owners 40 were shareholders or employees of the company.

[1] No copies of charterparties have been preserved, and the originals appear to have been returned to the owners at the end of the voyage. Details can sometimes be pieced together from other sources.

[2] See the company's Black Book, T. 70/1433.

[3] For example, £450 was deducted from the earnings of the *Arcana Mer-chant*; T. 70/963 under date 20 September 1683.

[4] Two examples in T. 70/50, fos. 120, 126.

[5] From the company's Freight Books, T. 70/962–972.

£1,768 from London to Sherbro in 1701 and returned with a consignment of ivory and dyewood, earned £867 in freight.[1] She was a vessel of only 120 tons and the basic cost of building her was probably not much more than she earned on this single voyage. From these gross earnings, however, would have to be deducted the very heavy cost of fitting-out, provisioning, repairs and upkeep, and seamen's wages. It is generally true that in the later seventeenth century ships were cheap to build and expensive to keep afloat. After 1701 the company ceased to hire ships for the out-and-home run, and either employed its own vessels or, occasionally, made consignments of dyewood and ivory *via* the West Indies.

On the slave run from London to the West Indies *via* West Africa a much more complicated method of payment for freight prevailed, unique indeed in the shipping industry. The charge for the whole voyage was calculated according to the number of negroes delivered alive at the port of discharge, no separate payment being made for the London-Africa run. Thus the company might agree to hire a ship to carry to West Africa a cargo of trading goods to the value of £5,000. Part of this cargo would be for delivery at Cape Coast or for the purchase of gold and ivory along the coast, but a sufficient proportion would be appropriated to buying an agreed number of negroes. However many negroes might eventually be taken aboard, and however many might die on the Middle Passage, the owners would be paid for the whole voyage at so much a head for those delivered alive in the Plantations. The obvious merit of this arrangement from the company's point of view was to give the owners (of whom the captain would normally be one) a direct incentive to keep the slaves alive. It may, however, have had the reverse effect of promoting overcrowding and consequent mortality.

From 1678, when records begin, to 1689 the prevailing rate for a voyage from London to Barbados *via* West Africa was £5 for each negro delivered alive, though rates as high as £5 10s. and as low as £4 were occasionally paid. Rates for the Leeward Islands were slightly lower, £4 to £4 10s., and for Jamaica slightly higher, £5 6s. 8d. being most common. War doubled

[1] T. 70/971.

these charges, rates for Barbados going to £10 or more and for Jamaica to £11 and £11 10s., with a return to pre-war levels in 1697. The opening of the African trade to private merchants in 1698, however, together perhaps with a general boom in trade in the brief inter-war period, appear quickly to have forced rates up again. In June 1701, for example, the company advertised for freight at £6 to £6 10s. a head, but received no offers under £8.[1] The outbreak of war in the following year may to some extent have limited competition, but rates quickly rose to £10 and £11 a head.

Another unusual practice in the African trade was the obligation laid by charterparty on owners of hired ships to take a proportion of their earnings in the form of negroes. In 1676 the Court of Assistants resolved to employ no hired ship the owners of which would not take at least a quarter of their earnings in slaves;[2] the proportion was subsequently increased to a half, and in 1678 to two-thirds. This proportion prevailed until 1703, when it returned to a half, and in 1708 it was further reduced to one-third. Negroes were valued for this purpose at the company's declared selling price of £15, £16, and £17, in Barbados, the Leewards, and Jamaica respectively, prices which, notably in Barbados, it was not always possible to get. After 1689, when prices of negroes began to rise, fresh valuations were made, so that by 1706 owners were taking one-half of their earnings in negroes at £28 a head. From the point of view of the owners of slaving ships, the practice was wholly disadvantageous. Instead of being paid entirely in sterling, they were obliged to make arrangements for the sale of the negroes thus acquired, probably to give credit to purchasers, and certainly to organize the remittance of the proceeds to England. In other words, they were forced to become dealers in negroes and probably also dealers in sugar, when they would have preferred to be paid in cash in London. From the company's point of view, the arrangement had merits and demerits. It removed the necessity of paying for part of the freight in London and thus relieved pressure upon the company's slender cash resources; it also shifted onto the shipowners part of the onus of collecting debts for negroes sold on

[1] T. 70/86, pp. 170–71, 217.   [2] T. 70/76, fo. 78d.

credit and the cost and risk of remitting the proceeds to London in sugar or bills. These were important considerations at a time when the West Indian trade was sluggish. On the other hand the company created competition for its own salesmen, and in 1684 the agents at Barbados complained that the disposal of freight-negroes absorbed all the ready-money buyers.[1] Despite this obvious disadvantage the practice continued, the company choosing to preserve its cash at home by passing over to ship-owners the disposal of nearly one-fifth of all slaves delivered in the West Indies.

A third feature of the relations between the company and the owners of ships hired for the London-Africa-West Indies route was the practice of allowing the latter an interest in part of the outward cargo. Such ships commonly carried three separate cargoes, each assigned to a distinct purpose. The price of slaves in Africa before 1689 was such that a ship from England destined to take in 450 negroes could carry the goods needed to purchase that number and still be much less than fully loaded. In order to make the most economical use of shipping, therefore, most ships carried one cargo for delivery at Cape Coast castle, a second to purchase negroes, and a third, the Windward cargo. This last was intended for the trade of the Windward Coast, immediately to the west of the Gold Coast, and it was in this branch of the African trade that owners of hired ships were given a share, generally of one-quarter, one-third or a half. The owners supplied no goods but paid their share of the invoice value of the cargo, recovering their capital at the conclusion of the voyage together with their portion of the net profit, all incidental charges having been deducted. In the event of a loss (which was rare) the owners shared in it. On the whole, this arrangement was advantageous to owners, and probably did something to counterbalance the obligation to receive part of their earnings in the form of negroes. In some years the company disbursed £2,000 to £3,000 to owners in the form of profits on these cargoes. With the contraction of the Windward trade after 1689 and the extended use of company-owned ships, the practice declined, and it appears to have died

[1] T. 70/12, fo. 3d.

out altogether when the African trade was opened to private enterprise in 1698.

The preceding paragraphs and the complicated system of freight-charges which they have attempted to describe may be made clearer by an example. In February 1683 a hired ship, the *Robert*, Captain Robert Bell, sailed from London in the company's service. She carried three cargoes, one of £1,905 for the trade of the Windward Coast, one of £236 for delivery at Cape Coast castle, and a third of £1,483 for the purchase of slaves at Ardra. The owners' share in the Windward cargo was £560. The *Robert* discharged 235 negroes at Barbados, on which she earned £5 a head, £1,175. Of this sum, two-thirds, £780, was paid in Barbados in negroes, 17 men, 26 women, 7 boys and 2 girls (52 at £15 each), leaving a balance of £395 payable in London. The Windward cargo showed a nett profit of 37 per cent., so on that account the owners recovered their capital investment with a profit of £207. In all, therefore, they received £602 in cash, paid in London, and 52 negroes delivered in Barbados.[1]

The conditions of hiring of all ships dispatched from England were arranged with owners by the Committee of Shipping, which reported to the Court of Assistants for the formal approval and sealing of charterparties. Shipping on the homeward route from the West Indies to England was, however, the responsibility of the company's agents in the Plantations who alone were in a position to know what effects had to be transported and what rates prevailed. With the outbreak of war in 1689 and the consequent shortage of shipping and seamen, it became necessary for the company to pre-contract in London for at least part of the cargo-space required on the West Indies-England route.[2] Freight rates on this route were at so much per ton of goods carried, the effects of war upon them being clearly shown in the table on the following page.

The most striking inference to be drawn from these figures is the profound effect of war upon freight-rates. By 1690 Barbados rates were three times what they had been in 1688, and by 1691 Jamaican rates were three-and-a-half times the pre-

[1] T. 70/912, T. 70/941 and T. 70/964.
[2] T. 70/57, fos. 55d, 114, 137, 167d, 168.

Freight Charges for 1 Ton of Sugar from Barbados and Jamaica to England 1678–1713[1]

(the date is the date of the invoice in the colony)

	Barbados						Jamaica						
Year	No. of quotations	Max. £	s.	Aver. £	s.	Min. £	s.	No. of quotations	Max. £	s.	Aver. £	s.	Min. £	s.
1678	13	6		5		4		7	7		7		5	10
1679	16	4	10	3	10	3		14	8		7		5	10
1680	13	4		3	15	3		7	8		7		5	
1681	10	4		3	15	3	10	19	7		6	5	5	10
1682–3	16	5		4		3	10	22	6		5	5	3	10
1684–5	22	6	10	4	10	3	10	29	6	10	5	15	4	
1686–7	19	6	10	4	15	4	10	32	6		5		4	
1688	11	5		4	5	3		12	5	10	5	5	4	10
1689	17	10		7	15	4		10	8		7	10	7	
1690	5	20		13	10	8		5	16		13	5	10	
1691	6	9	10	8		6	10	11	25		18	5	7	10
1692	1	8		8		8		4	10		10		10	
1693	3	8		7	5	7		4	12		12		12	
1694	10	9		8		7		2	16		16		16	
1695	12	13		10	10	9		6	22		18		16	
1696	9	14		13		11		5	25		23	5	16	
1697	8	13		11		10		2	25		22	10	20	
1698	14	5		4		3		4	10		9	15	9	
1699	5	3		2	10	2	10	5	10		10		10	
1700	12	4		3	5	2		4	7		6	10	6	
1701	16	5		3		2		7	8		7	5	7	
1702–3	26	10		8	5	3	10	11	18		14		10	
1704	10	13		10	5	7	10	3	18		17	5	16	
1705	8	10		8	5	6		4	23		10	10	12	10
1706	27	9		7	10	5		12	18		16	5	14	
1707	22	10		8		6		4	18		18		18	
1708	15	11		10		9		7	20		17	10	13	
1709	12	9		7	5	5		2	20		19		18	
1710	11	10		7	15	5		—	—		—		—	
1711	16	6		5	5	5		—	—		—		—	
1712–13	29	7		5	10	4		—	—		—		—	

(averages to nearest 5s.)

war figure. War did not, however, merely drive rates up and keep them up. Both periods, 1689 to 1697 and 1702 to 1713, exhibit sharp rises at the outbreak of war followed by almost equally sharp falls in 1691 in the case of Barbados, and in 1692

[1] Compiled from T. 70/962–72.

in the case of Jamaica, and less noticeable falls in both series in 1705. The surprisingly low rates prevailing in the middle of both wars were not maintained. The years 1694 and 1695 saw marked increases rising to a peak in 1696, the last full year of war; similarly rates rose in 1707 and 1708, though less sharply, falling once more as peace became probable. How much these fluctuations were due to the varying incidence of risk on the homeward route, and how much to the scarcity or plenty of seamen (and therefore to the higher or lower wages that had to be paid) consequent upon the claims of the Navy, cannot be precisely determined. The high rates prevailing in the later part of the war of 1689–97 certainly seem to reflect the heavy losses which prompted the merchants of Barbados to complain to Parliament in 1695.[1] On the other hand the scarcity of seamen was at times acute, not only in England but in the West Indies as well.[2] This is clear from the story of the *Averilla* which arrived in Barbados in June 1695 with a crew of sixty. Twenty-one seamen were there pressed for the Navy and, although four were redeemed, the undermanned ship was taken by the French on her homeward voyage with a loss of £25,000.[3]

The normal discrepancy of £1 or £2 per ton between the Jamaican and Barbadian rates, even in peacetime, is probably explicable in terms of geography and risk. The homeward course from Jamaica, northward and then east, was against the prevailing winds and took a ship dangerously near Spanish territory and the bases of privateers and pirates; in war, these risks were increased.[4] Freight rates from Antigua, Nevis and Montserrat were fractionally above those from Barbados in peacetime, and well above in war. Only in one year, however, 1690, did they rise above the Jamaican rates, and the lower shipping costs enjoyed at all other times by the Outer Antilles helped them to hold off as long as they did the challenge of Jamaica for supremacy in sugar-production.

[1] *House of Lords MSS*, II (New Series), 1695–1697, pp. 76 ff.
[2] Richard Pares, 'The Manning of the Navy in the West Indies, 1702–63' in *T.R.H.S.* (Fourth Series), XX (1937).
[3] *House of Lords MSS.*, II (New Series), 1695–7, pp. 97–8.
[4] L. F. Horsfall, 'The West Indian Trade', in *The Trade Winds*, ed. C. Northcote Parkinson, pp. 187–8.

In the finances of the Royal African Company, shipping ranked as an item of expenditure second only to the provision of goods for export. Owing to the employment, especially

Gross Expenditure on Hired Ships by the African Company

Year	Slave Ships	Others (from West Indies, Africa direct, Europe)	Total
	£	£	£
1681	13,325	5,745	19,070
1682	31,918	4,852	36,770
1683	23,693	3,787	27,480
1684	29,829	3,919	33,748
1685	21,128	5,436	26,564
1686	21,942	5,455	27,397
1687	30,195	6,018	36,213
1688	19,452	4,132	23,584
1689	9,520	2,186	11,706
1690	11,511	5,174	16,685
1691	4,423	2,478	6,901
1692	10,732	17,212	27,944
1693	18,014	951	18,965
1694	20,388	7,582	27,970
1695	22,113	4,936	27,049
1696	8,993	4,526	13,519
1697	427	5,653	6,080
1698	8,808	4,748	13,556
1699	5,012	4,047	9,059
1700	8,397	4,184	12,581
1701	5,812	2,223	8,035
1702	2,509	1,810	4,319
1703	10,953	3,612	14,565
1704	2,072	8,036	10,108
1705	8,224	6,684	14,908
1706	11,348	6,569	17,917
1707	20,912	8,460	29,372
1708	14,262	3,632	17,894
1709	—	5,221	5,221
1710	4,368	3,360	7,728
1711	—	1,089	1,089
1712	—	1,222	1,222
1713	—	1,968	1,968
Totals (1681–1713)[1] £400,280		£156,907	£557,187

[1] Compiled from the company's Freight Books, T. 70/962–72.

after 1700, of company-owned vessels, involving a vast number of unconsolidated cash payments, the total cost cannot readily be calculated.[1] Gross expenditure on hired ships, however, can be computed, and between 1681 and 1713 it exceeded £550,000. Of this total an important proportion was, as has already been shown, paid in kind in the form of negroes, but the strain on the company's cash resources must nevertheless have been heavy. If allowance be made for the period 1672 to 1680 (for which no figures can be devised), and for the purchase, equipping, maintaining and manning of the company's own fleet, expenditure on shipping between 1672 and 1713 cannot have amounted to less than three-quarters of a million pounds, or ten shillings for every pound's worth of goods exported from England.

3. War and Shipping

The wars of 1689–97 and 1702–13 had profound effects on almost every aspect of the trade of the African Company, and there can be no doubt that the blows which it received exposed its weaknesses and shortened its effective life. At home, a higher rate of interest had to be paid on loans, and the price of certain important components of African cargoes, such as gunpowder and East Indian textiles, rose sharply. In Africa and the West Indies, French forces inflicted serious damage on the company's interests in the Gambia, Sierra Leone, Sherbro, Jamaica and Nevis. It was, however, at sea that the consequences of war were most severely felt. From Land's End to the Bight of Benin and in the Caribbean, French privateers preyed on English merchant-shipping to such effect that the losses in goods and ships inflicted upon the African Company alone approached £300,000. The main threat came from the privateers of St. Malo and the Atlantic ports who cruised in the western

---

[1] The changeover from a predominantly hired fleet to a fleet of ships owned by the company is well illustrated by the accounts of the Clerk of Shipping. In the four years 1686–9 he disbursed less than £5,000 on seamen's wages, ships' stores, repairs, etc. In the four years 1703–6 he disbursed over £20,000. T. 70/255–7.

approaches and took ships outward bound for Africa or on the homeward voyage from the West Indies. In Africa itself privateers operated from the Senegal and Goree, and, after 1704, from Whydah. In the West Indies, Martinique and Guadeloupe provided bases from which English trade could be intercepted. Counter-measures taken by the Admiralty and by the company itself helped only a little, for the African trade was dispersed over far too wide an area for effective protection to be given all the time.

For the purpose of estimating the incidence of losses at sea, the company's ships may be divided into those dispatched from England for Africa either to return or to proceed to the West Indies, and those employed on the homeward voyage from Barbados, Jamaica and Antigua to England. Numerically losses amongst the second group were far heavier, sixty-four ships being lost between 1689 and 1697 and fifty between 1702 and 1708. The practice of loading mainly small consignments on ships from the West Indies, however, ensured that the resultant financial loss, though serious, was not as crippling as the number of casualties might suggest. Ships taken sailing to or from Africa, though fewer in number, were usually carrying more valuable cargoes on the company's account, so that the gross financial loss was almost as heavy as on the West Indies-London route.

Aggregate losses from enemy action amongst ships sailing to and from Africa exceeded fifty.[1] Of 183 ships dispatched from England in the years 1688 to 1697 and 1702 to 1712, forty-five or one-quarter were taken by the French. Twelve other ships were either lost at sea or condemned as unseaworthy before reaching England. In all, therefore, fifty-seven failed to return. In addition, there were losses amongst the coastal vessels stationed on the African coast and amongst the rum-ships dispatched from the West Indies. The war began badly for the company, five of the ships dispatched in 1688 being taken, no doubt having sailed unprepared for attack. In 1689, 1690 and 1691 only three ships were lost, but in the three following years nine were taken and one cast away out of a total of twenty-five

[1] These and the following figures of losses are taken from T. 70/175, reverse, pp. 34–7, and from T. 70/61–3.

leaving England. On both the outward and the homeward voyages, the years 1693 to 1695 were the worst of the war, and the loss of the *Ann* in Africa in 1693 with a cargo of gold, ivory, gum, wax and dyewood, valued at over £23,000, was the heaviest single casualty at sea ever suffered by the company.

Heavy blows were to come again at the beginning of the war of 1702 to 1713. In 1703 and 1704 the company was still actively competing with the separate traders, and forty-two ships were dispatched to West Africa. Of these, fourteen were taken by the French, and nine others either cast away or condemned. In one disastrous period of eighteen months, from January 1703 to June 1704, thirty-two ships left England, only ten of which are known to have returned. Three slaving ships were taken outward bound with cargoes worth £10,000; three others, with negroes aboard, were taken in Caribbean waters; four were taken on the return voyage from Africa to London; and two, carrying eighty tons of sugar, were taken between the West Indies and England. The company never recovered from these calamities which must be regarded as the immediate occasions of the rapid decline in exports after 1705 and the tortuous financial expedients adopted in an attempt to keep in being. In the later years of the war losses on voyages to and from Africa did not continue at so high a rate. The increasing use of Bristol and other western ports for departures and arrivals may, after 1705, have reduced the dangers of the western approaches, but the chief reason is that fewer and fewer ships were sent out. Even so, the company suffered three particularly severe losses. The *Maurice & George* (cargo, £5,815) was cast away at Spithead in 1705; the *Angola* (£5,682) was taken off Finisterre in 1706; and the *Barbados Merchant* (£6,600) was taken off Cape Palmas in Africa in 1707.

For evidence of losses on the homeward voyage from the West Indies, we have to rely on figures prepared by the company itself in 1709, in which no distinction is made between those resulting from enemy action and those caused by shipwreck. Many of the latter could, however, be justly regarded as the outcome of war conditions. The scarcity of seamen forced ships to carry a high proportion of unskilled landsmen amongst their crews, with a resulting loss of efficiency that caused ship-wrecks to be more frequent in war than in peace. Particularly on the homeward voyage from the West Indies, the delay caused by the necessity of waiting for convoy could mean sailing in the season of bad weather. Thus, in 1694 a West India fleet was detained for five months before sailing from England; it was correspondingly late leaving the West Indies and the returning ships met a hurricane in which five carrying goods for the company were lost.[1] This disaster can reasonably be regarded as the result of war conditions. The company's aggregate losses on the West Indies-England route for the periods 1689-97 and 1702-8 were 114 ships, though its own share in many of them was quite small. The worst years were 1694, 1704 and 1706 when sixteen, eleven, and twelve ships in which the company was interested fell to the French, the weather, or bad seamanship.

The financial consequences of these losses cannot be exactly gauged. The company itself made valuations which appear to be accurate: on voyages to and from Africa the 44 ships lost up to 1708 cost the company £124,652, while cargoes on ships lost on the West India run were valued at £136,641.[2] In addition, the company claimed losses of £45,000 resulting from the French assaults upon James Fort in the Gambia in 1695, 1702 and 1704; £12,500 for the French attacks on Sierra Leone in 1695 and 1704 and on Sherbro in 1705; £16,000 lost in the French invasion of Jamaica and the earthquake there; and £27,000 for the plunder of Nevis in 1706. The grand total for the years 1689 to 1708, with a few shipwrecks between the wars included, was £383,898 12s. 3d. Some part of the losses at sea, though not of those on land, was recovered by insurance. In peacetime, the company seems to have insured gold and silver, and sometimes sugar. In the war of 1702-13, it insured extensively, though seldom up to the full value of a cargo. Rates rose very steeply after 1689. In 1684, for example, in-surance was ordered on a ship carrying silver and sugar from Jamaica to London at premiums of 2½ and 3 per cent.[3] In 1696 a premium for gold from Barbados of 24 guineas per cent.

---

[1] *House of Lords MSS.*, II (New Series), 1695-7, pp. 77, 88.
[2] T. 70/175, reverse, pp. 34-7.   [3] T. 70/80, fo. 54d.

is mentioned.[1] Insurance, however, was not yet a comprehensive safeguard against war-risks. Thus, a search of the company's cash-books for the years 1695 to 1708, a period when many losses were suffered at sea, shows that only £5,536 was recovered from underwriters. In no case does the company seem to have insured to the full value of a cargo; and in no case did the underwriters pay more than 84 per cent. of the sum insured.[2] And even if a greater proportion of losses had eventually been recovered, the damage done to the company would still be formidable, especially as a result of the losses on voyages to Africa. With increasing frequency in the early years of the eighteenth century, the company's factors on the African coast were obliged, through lack of goods, to watch the separate traders and competitors of other nations take a growing share of the trade. If ships carrying goods from England were lost, slaves could not be bought; and if slaves were not delivered in the Plantations, the company's chances of recovering its monopoly were gone.

The effects of war upon the company's trade reached far beyond the material losses inflicted by the enemy. As a result of embargoes and restrictions imposed by the government, the company was unable to dispatch as many ships as were necessary to keep up the flow of exports, and those which were sent out were often delayed. Although general embargoes on the departure of merchant shipping were imposed in 1689 and 1702,[3] the governments of William and Anne were reluctant to take so drastic a step more often than was absolutely necessary for the manning of the Navy. For the African trade, as for the East Indian and Mediterranean trades, a system of rationing was devised whereby the ships to be dispatched and the seamen to be employed were brought under governmental direction.[4] In September 1690, for example, the company was given permission to send out ten ships and 350 men on condition that half the crews should be landsmen or foreigners.[5] This licence was superseded by a general embargo, and in November the

[1] T. 70/57, fo. 118.   [2] Details from Cash Books, T. 70/225–234.
[3] *A.P.C.* (Colonial Series), 1680–1720, pp. 117, 387 ff.
[4] J. Ehrman, *The Navy in the War of William III*, pp. 113–14.
[5] T. 70/169, fo. 78.

P

company was authorized to dispatch four ships instead of ten with 60 instead of 175 seamen.[1] The four ships eventually sailed in January 1691 manned by crews of 170 of whom only just over one-third were English seamen.

The African trade did not easily fit into the convoy arrangements provided by the Admiralty which were based mainly on the needs of ships sailing to and from the West Indies. This is made clear by a memorial delivered to the Lords of Trade and Plantations by the company in 1690.[2] Convoys had been ordered to depart for the West Indies in October, to return at the end of March. Ships bound for Africa could therefore be protected through the Channel and out into the Atlantic, but they could not be expected to complete their trade on the African coast and reach the West Indies in time to have the benefit of the homeward convoy in March. On this and on many other occasions, the company asked for special protection for the African trade by the allocation of a man-of-war for convoy and counter-attack on French shipping in Africa.[3] Ships of the Royal Navy were occasionally sent to cruise on the coast but not regularly enough to provide full protection. In 1704, after very heavy losses from ships proceeding without convoy, the company put forward a plan for two West Indian fleets a year, two warships to leave England in December and return with the first sugar-crop in March, and two to depart in March and return with the final crop in June.[4] Ships for Africa might then go out with the first convoy and return with the second. The ill-success attending this and all other proposals is, however, put beyond doubt by the figures of losses already quoted. The Admiralty was severely criticized by merchants for the inadequacy of the protection it afforded, but English trade was now dispersed over the whole world and the Navy's resources too slender for the task. The African trade, itself extending over three continents, had to take its chance with others, and it suffered accordingly.

[1] T. 70/169, fo. 80.

[2] *Cal. S.P. Col.*, 1689–92, No. 1052; *Cal. S.P. Col.*, 1699 and Addenda, No. 1203.

[3] T. 70/170, especially in 1704 and 1705; J. H. Owen, *The War at Sea under Queen Anne*, 1938, p. 58.

[4] *Cal. S.P. Col.*, 1704–5, No. 556.

The effects of war upon the cost of hired ships have already been noticed. Between 1681 and 1689, the company spent about £200,000 gross on the hiring of 170 ships; between 1690 and 1698, it disbursed £105,000 for only 42 ships. Thus it paid half as much for fewer than a quarter the number of ships. These rising costs may partly explain the increased use of company-owned ships, but the expense of running a merchant-fleet must also have gone up. Larger crews were needed in war than in peace, and seamen commanded higher wages. Guns had to be mounted, gunners employed, firearms, powder and shot issued to crews. The cost of ships' stores and of upkeep and repair increased as a result of naval demands. Obviously, some part of all these rising costs was passed on to the consumer: the selling prices of negroes in the Plantations and sugar in London were much increased. What proportion was in the end carried by the company it is impossible to say. What is clear is that the war made even longer the time that had to elapse between the making of an investment in the African trade and the final coming to hand of such profits as might be earned. Even if the increased prices of the end-product of this complex trade eventually compensated for increased costs, the initial invest-ment, at a time when the company could ill afford it, had to be larger than in peace.

Finally, the war at sea led to a recrudescence of piracy. Pirates were not unknown in Africa before the war. In 1683, for example, they plundered the company's ship, *Lisbon Merchant*, of 150 marks of gold, and were reported to have a fleet of seven vessels.[1] Further outbreaks occurred in 1685 and 1686 when the *James* was taken.[2] The most serious menace to shipping, however, came in the later stages of the war of 1689–97 and immediately afterwards, when the activities of Avery and others eventually induced the Admiralty to send a man-of-war to the African coast.[3]

War and the disastrous losses incurred were not, it must

---

[1] T. 70/12, fo. 2; T. 70/11, fos. 7d, 52d; T. 70/16, fo. 62d.

[2] T. 70/11, fo. 13d; T. 70/50, fo. 15d; T. 70/169, fos. 47d–48d, 50–1.

[3] T. 70/86, pp. 97, 133–4, 138, 169; T. 70/51, pp. 162, 186, 193; T. 70/170, *passim* in years 1700 and 1701; *A.P.C.* (Colonial Series), 1680–1720, pp. 331, 367, 376; *Cal. S.P. Col.*, 1699, Nos. 212, 213, 221, 286, 335.

again be emphasized, responsible for the failure of joint-stock trading to Africa. All the conditions necessary for eventual downfall had already been fulfilled before 1689. Nevertheless, the damage suffered at the hands of the French at sea and on land, the delays and interruptions of trade, and the scarcity of cash which they helped to engender, made important contributions to the *malaise* from which the company was suffering in the years between 1689 and 1712. As a result, the crisis came sooner rather than later and the French unwittingly proved the best allies of the separate traders.

6

THE COMPANY IN AFRICA

1. The Commercial Regions of West Africa

UNDER the charter of 1672, the Royal African Company was granted a monopoly of the trade of five thousand miles of the western coast of Africa, from Cape Sallee in the north to the Cape of Good Hope. Large parts of this enormous littoral appeared in the seventeenth century to hold out no prospect of profitable trade. In the north, the coast from Sallee to the Senegal river, and in the south the long stretch from Angola to the Cape of Good Hope were never considered by the company as possible fields for commercial exploitation. Even so, the company's activities in West Africa were dispersed over a very wide area, some two thousand miles lying between the northern and southern extremities of its trade. Within these boundaries lay not one but several regions, having certain common features, but each exhibiting a rich variety both of geographical characteristics and of commercial potentialities. Neither politically nor economically was West Africa a single unit; the term 'African trade' in the later seventeenth century was generic, embracing regions which, because of their divergencies, demanded distinct and appropriate commercial techniques.

At an early date Europeans had learned to associate certain parts of West Africa with particular commodities; hence the designations, Gold, Ivory, Slave, Gum and Grain Coasts. These terms may not, however, be taken as accurate descriptions of the distribution of African products. Slaves could be bought almost anywhere on the coast between the Senegal and Angola, though they were more plentiful in some places than

213

others. Ivory, likewise, was obtainable, not only on the Ivory Coast, but on the Gold Coast, in Angola, in the Gambia and elsewhere. Indeed, apart from the Gold Coast, these designations were little used by the Royal African Company. For all purposes, organizational as well as commercial, West Africa was divided by the company into six regions: 'the Northern parts of Guinea', the Windward Coast, the Gold Coast, Ardra and Whydah, Benin and the Calabar rivers, and Angola.

'The Northern parts of Guinea' consisted of the stretch of the west coast of Africa lying between the Senegal river in the north and Cape Mount, and in some ways it was the most distinctive of all the regions. Although the Gold Coast had been the objective of the earliest English voyages to Africa, the companies formed in the later part of the reign of Elizabeth I and under James I and Charles I appear to have concentrated their chief efforts on the Gambia river and the lands adjacent to it. For this choice there were two reasons. First, the Portuguese were more strongly entrenched on the Gold Coast than in the north. The English, arriving later than the Portuguese, and in less strength than the Dutch, had to content themselves with what was left. And, secondly, until the middle of the seventeenth century and the growth of the English West Indian colonies, the northern parts of West Africa appeared to offer commercial prospects not greatly inferior to those to be found further south. It was not until the second half of the century that the African trade began to be valued by the English and French primarily for the slaves which it yielded. Slaves could be, and were, purchased in the Gambia and elsewhere in the north-west, but better and cheaper supplies could be found in the south. Thus, first the English and later the French, under the stimulus of colonial demand for negroes, were constrained to extend their operations from the Senegal and the Gambia to regions more productive of slaves, while the Dutch, expelled from the island of Goree in 1677, henceforth concentrated chiefly on the Gold Coast and the slave-markets of Ardra and Whydah.

In 1672 England's concern in the trade of the whole of the 'Northern parts of Guinea' was in the hands of the Gambia Adventurers, a lessee of the now defunct company of Royal

Adventurers.[1] The lease had still some years to run and the Royal African Company did not obtain possession of the trade until 1678. Apart from the commercial monopoly which was then handed over by the Gambia Adventurers, the new company inherited one fairly substantial fort on James Island in the mouth of the river Gambia and two smaller settlements on Bence Island in Sierra Leone and York Island in the Sherbro river. James Island, formerly St. Andrew's Island, had been occupied in 1651 by Courlanders, or at least by men in the service of the Duke of Courland. In 1652 the fort had been constructed which, nine years later, passed into English hands.[2] The date of the beginning of continuous English occupation of Bence and York Islands is less certain; probably they both date from the early days of the Gambia Adventurers.[3]

The principal products of this region were ivory, wax, gum, hides, dyewood and slaves. Of these, two at least, ivory and slaves, originated chiefly from the lands lying well back from the coast rather than from the coastal lands themselves.[4] Until well into the eighteenth century, Europeans, both English and French, cherished a dream of an interior country, above the Senegal and Gambia, rich in gold. Gold was indeed mined, though in no great quantity, some hundreds of miles from the mouths of these rivers, but little of it reached the Atlantic coast. For centuries it had been carried to Timbuktu and thence across the desert to North Africa.[5] In the course of the seventeenth century, at least two Englishmen, Richard Jobson and Cornelius Hodges, reconnoitred the interior with the hope of deflecting this gold from its traditional course.

[1] Above, p. 99.   [2] J. M. Gray, *History of the Gambia*, Chs. v and vi.

[3] G. F. Zook, *The Company of Royal Adventurers Trading to Africa*, mentions neither of them. Zachary Rogers, whom the Royal African Company continued as agent at Sherbro, wrote in 1678 that he had been agent for the Gambia Adventurers since June 1668; T. 70/10, fo. 4. Mr. C. Fyfe has suggested to me that the settlement was elsewhere in the Sherbro and that York Fort was not occupied until later. Re-examination of the evidence causes me to think that he is right. The Royal Adventurers had a settlement in Sierra Leone on Tasso Island which De Ruyter plundered and destroyed; Churchill's *Voyages* (1746), V, 99.

[4] See in particular T. G. Stone, 'The Journey of Cornelius Hodges in Senegambia', in *English Historical Review*, XXXIX (1924), p. 89.

[5] E. W. Bovill, *Caravans of the Old Sahara*.

Jobson in 1621 sailed up the Gambia as far as Barra Kunda and traded for gold with a Moslem merchant, but no permanent results accrued from his journey.[1] Hodges' journeys, in 1681, 1688, and 1689, are poorly documented, but at his third attempt he reached a land where gold was mined.[2] Meanwhile, the French were exploring the upper waters of the Senegal with the same end in view, to ensure that traders bringing gold or slaves or ivory from the east should come down their river and no other. These explorations cannot be regarded as entirely fruitless; much was learned and some knowledge disseminated. But from the commercial point of view, no spectacular results were obtained.

The trade of the whole of this north-western region of Africa was dominated by its great navigable rivers, Senegal and Gambia, down which the products of the interior reached the sea. But it was not enough for European traders to wait at the mouth of one of these rivers for trade to come to them. If action was not taken, consignments of slaves or ivory might be diverted to another river or intercepted by competitors. 'Trade will not come without seeking', wrote an English agent at James Fort;[3] it had to be sought wherever it could be found. The Royal African Company's settlement at James Island had, therefore, to serve less as a magnet attracting trade, and more as a magazine for commercial operations extending northward as far as Cape Verde, eastward for several hundred miles up the Gambia and southward to Portuguese Guinea, the settlements at Cacheu and Bissao. To this end, two distinct methods of trading were adopted. In the first place, small outposts were settled at strategic points, especially upriver. At each, one or two Englishmen with a few slaves might be stationed with a supply of trading goods periodically replenished from the base. In 1672, the Gambia Adventurers were said to have three such posts,[4] and at various times after 1678 the Royal African Company established factories both in the river and along the coast, at Barra Kunda, Buruko, Sangrigoe, Furbroh, Rufisque, Portudal and Joal.[5] In this way a

---

[1] Richard Jobson, *The Golden Trade*, reprinted, Teignmouth, 1904.
[2] Gray, *op. cit.*, pp. 96, 184; Stone, *op. cit.*   [3] T. 70/11, fo. 41d.
[4] *Cal. S.P. Col.*, 1669–74, No. 936.   [5] Gray, *op. cit.*, pp. 92, 104.

permanent interest could be kept in the chosen districts and trade carried on all the year round. On the other hand, this method of trading demanded more men than the company's agent at James Island could generally spare. Moreover, these isolated factories could easily fall under the domination of local rulers who might impose prohibitive duties on trade, or even resort to confiscation and murder.

The second, and seemingly more widely adopted, method of trade was by shallow-draught sloops or yachts of forty tons or less which plied back and forth between James Island and the chief places of business. In 1684, for example, there were five such sloops engaged in fetching and carrying ivory and wax from Cacheu, the slaves, ivory, hides and wax which the Gambia itself yielded, and the slaves and hides of Joal and Portudal.[1] Between 1678 and 1703, thirty-one of these small craft were sent out from England to West Africa, the majority of them for the trade of the north-west. In the Gambia they were designed both for the interception of trade from the interior and to ensure that when a ship arrived from England to load with negroes or goods her cargo should be ready for collection at James Island. The second of these intentions was not, however, always fulfilled. Ninety days were thought necessary for a ship to load with goods and one hundred and twenty days for a slave cargo.[2] Ships from England had sometimes to seek their own cargo, so that in 1687 the company wrote to Agent Alexander Cleeve at James Fort: 'We cannot conceive what use you doe make of all those small vessells, pray informe us as soone as you can, and doe not put us upon unnecessary charge more than the trade can bare.'[3]

Comparing these two methods of trade, sloops appear to have been more economical, both of men and of goods, than factories. Such anyway was the opinion of Agent Thomas Thurloe in 1679:

for a factor once settled ashoare is absolutely under the command of the king of the country where he lives, and liable for the least displeasure to loose all the goods he hath in his possession with danger also of his life. Besides in case of mortallity it is very difficult to recover of the negroes any thing that was in the hands

[1] T. 70/1441.   [2] T. 70/1, fo. 19.   [3] T. 70/50, fo. 45d.

of the deceased. Whereas in a sloop if the factor die the vessell is soone brought down to the Island, and if he find no trade in one port may goe to another and not by lyable to sell their goods at the pleasure of the kings. Besides a sloop will be in the way of all canoes which come down to the river and they will rather sell what they have there than be at the trouble to come to the Island, when it may be they would passe by a factory, knowing that if they goe ashoare they must pay duties either to the master of the town or to the king or both; & there is likewise this convenience in buying goods of the canoes that are coming down, tho' it may be with an intent to come to the Island, yet if any interlopers happen to be in the river (which they will heare of before they can arrive here) perhaps wee shall never see them, so that buying their goods above prevents this going to interlopers.[1]

The factory method was never entirely given up, but sloops appear to have been preferred whenever they were available.

By no means the whole, and probably not the greater part, of the company's trade in the Gambia region was carried on directly with native merchants. Even at this date, north-west Africa attracted a few English settlers, mostly time-expired servants of the company, who were encouraged to live in the country. In war, it was hoped that they would help to defend English interests, and in peace they acted as intermediaries between the company and the natives.[2] The majority of European residents, however, were Portuguese or at least half-breeds of Portuguese origin. At Cacheu and the Bissaos Islands, official Portuguese settlements existed, while numbers of individuals lived amongst the natives and penetrated far inland. Cacheu was reckoned the chief place for trade in the whole region, and much of the company's ivory and wax was bought there from Portuguese middlemen.[3] Prices, however, were high, negroes in particular being dearly bought as a result of competition from Spaniards.[4] In order to promote trade at Cacheu, the English were obliged to extend credit to the Portuguese and a number of bad debts were contracted.[5] Trading through middlemen, though recognized to be a *pis aller*, was a generally accepted practice. In the Gambia ledgers sent back to England

[1] T. 70/10, fo. 2, 2d.   [2] T. 70/50, fo. 77d; T. 70/11, fo. 37.
[3] T. 70/10, fos. 1–2.   [4] *Ibid.*, fos. 1, 59.
[5] T. 70/11, fo. 34d; T. 70/51, pp. 165, 229.

names such as Anthony Diaz, Domingo Mora and Manuel Noonez figure prominently, and when Agent Alexander Cleeve falsified his accounts he chose a Portuguese name, Francis Lopuz, 'as a generall name to enter all the transactions of your factorie for the goods delivered out and received'.[1]

Apart from Cacheu and the Gambia itself, the principal places of trade within the orbit of James Fort lay in the north, along the coast to Cape Verde. Here quantities of slaves and hides could be obtained and, in the Senegal, gum. At Joal and Portudal on the coast, the company had temporary factories and drove some trade from sloops, but penetration into the Senegal was made increasingly difficult by the growth of French interests there.[2] The purchase of gum, never large, dwindled to nothing, and after 1692 none was imported.

In 1682 Agent Kastell, the company's chief at Gambia, estimated that in the whole region for which he was responsible he could dispose of £12,000 worth of trading goods,[3] but in no year was so much consigned there. Beads of all kinds, guns, gunpowder, brass and pewterware, amber, brandy and, above all, iron, were the staple needs. Neither English woollens nor East India textiles, which sold well in other parts of the Africa coast, were much in demand. From the Gambia ledgers a rough idea of the turnover can be obtained. Between November 1679 and April 1680, for example, takings amounted to 5 tons of ivory, 4 tons of wax, 13,000 hides and 106 slaves. The principal outgoings were 3,294 iron bars, 85 reams of paper, 3,587 lbs. beads, 89 guns, 4 barrels of gunpowder, 392 lb. of brassware and 284 lb. of pewter.[4]

Some four hundred miles south of the Gambia river lay Bence Island in Sierra Leone and, a hundred miles further on, York Island in the Sherbro river. In normal times, the two settlements were independent of each other. But in 1690 Bence Island was thought to be indefensible and was evacuated. A skeleton staff was left there under the orders of the agent at Sherbro,[5] and in 1700 settlement was re-established.[6]

[1] T. 70/50, fo. 107.
[2] T. 70/10, fo. 53; T. 70/50, fo. 36; T. 70/51, pp. 353–4.
[3] T. 70/10, fo. 60.   [4] T. 70/830.   [5] T. 70/50, fos. 106, 108–109d.
[6] T. 70/85, fo. 83; T. 70/51, pp. 75, 80.

The trade conducted from both these islands appears to have been chiefly coastal, rather than up-river, extending north into the orbit of James Fort and south-east as far as the Sestos river. Ivory, wax, gum and a few slaves were obtainable, but the principal product was a ligneous dye known as red-wood. Although costly to transport, excellent profits could be made from this commodity owing to the low price at which it was bought. When the competition of private traders was placed on a legal footing in 1698, the company was particularly anxious to retain control of the redwood trade, in which the separate traders were obliged to pay only five per cent. on imports to England instead of the ten per cent. payable on other African products.[1] Strict orders were sent to the agent at Sherbro to buy up all available supplies and thus discourage competitors.[2] Nevertheless, the separate traders possessed them-selves of part of the trade, one of the company's charges against them being that they had forced up the price of redwood.[3]

As in the Gambia, trade was carried on by out-factories and sloops, and much use was made of Portuguese and English middlemen. In 1692, for example, the company complained to Agent Corker at York Island that:

> we are fully assured that if our Agents and Factors did truly espouse & mind our interest as they ought to doe, we might have the choice of the commodities of those countries at the best hand & not be beholding to Robert Gun or any others who make great advantage by buying of the Natives at the best hand & selling to you at much higher prices, though (wee understand) they pur-chase them with the same goods wherewith you trust them.[4]

Three years later, however, the company was writing to Gunn, promising friendship and asking for favours. It is clear, there-fore, that though trading through middlemen was seen to be disadvantageous the company had no choice but to put up with it.

In an attempt to make the trade of this part of Africa more

---

[1] Above, p. 134.   [2] T. 70/51, pp. 1, 15, 60.

[3] About 1680 redwood could be bought for 11 or 12 bars a ton (about £3–£3 10s.) and sold in London for £35–£40 a ton. By 1700 and 1701 it was being invoiced from Africa at about £12 a ton.

[4] T. 70/50, fo. 137d.

profitable, the company launched schemes for the cultivation of indigo and the manufacture of potash. Indigo grew wild in several parts of West Africa, and in 1687 a trial consignment was sent over to the West Indies from Bence Island.[1] Four years later, the company's Court of Assistants set up a committee to promote the design, and several skilled men were sent to York Island.[2] Although hopes of success remained alive for ten years, heavy rain seems to have rotted the root and caused the leaf to fall before it was ripe.[3] Nevertheless, the experiment was taken seriously enough for the merchants and planters concerned in the Jamaican trade to petition against this competition from an unexpected quarter.[4] The potash project was no more successful. A potash maker was sent out in 1698 and another in 1699, but no evidence has been found of positive results.[5] Yet another scheme was for the development of a trade in locally made cotton cloths between Sierra Leone and the Gold Coast.[6] These experiments, though interesting, may probably be taken as evidence that the ordinary trade of this part of Africa was disappointing, at least as conducted by the company. Annual consignments to Bence and York Islands together never exceeded £5,000 and were generally no more than about £2,500.

From Sherbro the coastline falls south-east for 500 miles to Cape Palmas and then proceeds almost due east for a further 400 miles to Cape Three Points. Save for a few trading posts just to the west of Cape Three Points (of which Dutch Axim was the most important), the whole of this region in the later seventeenth century was devoid of European settlement and probably almost free of European residents. To the English, the eastern half of this, the second of the commercial regions of West Africa, was known as the Windward Coast. Its exact boundaries were undefined: for purposes of directing captains

---

[1] T. 70/11, fo. 72.
[2] T. 70/83, fos. 26, 29; T. 70/50, fos. 126d, 127, 132d, 133.
[3] T. 70/51, p. 128.
[4] *A.P.C.* (Colonial Series), 1680–1720, p. 217; *Cal. S.P. Col.*, 1689–92, No. 2546; T. 70/83, fo. 58; T. 70/169, fo. 95.
[5] T. 70/51, p. 10; T. 70/85, fo. 67.
[6] T. 70/51, p. 76.

where to dispose of their cargoes, Cape Mount and Cape Three Points were taken as the limits.[1]

By contrast with the sloop and factory trade of the Gambia, trade on the Windward Coast was entirely 'ship-trade', and was known as such. No factories were settled, other than huts borrowed for a day or two by passing vessels, and no permanent residents were stationed here by the company. The whole trade was at the discretion of the ship's captain who acted as consignee and generally as supercargo, selected the places at which he would do business and was responsible for barter with the natives. The trade of the Windward Coast had indeed changed little since the days of the voyages which Hakluyt chronicled. Natives signified their readiness to trade by smoke signals, and either came aboard in canoes or waited on shore for a party from the ship. Necessarily, therefore, the disposal of a cargo was uncertain and slow. Neither the gold and ivory which might be available nor the goods in demand could be accurately foreseen, and, even when trade was plentiful, much of it had to be carried on by the exchange of small quantities of goods here and there. Owing to the absence of settlements, records relating to the region are sparse. Only one ship's journal, that of the *James*, reports in detail the disposal of a Windward cargo: she arrived off Cape Mount in June 1675 and spent nearly three months on the Coast during which time quantities of gold and ivory were purchased.[2]

In the years immediately following the formation of the Royal African Company, few consignments to the Windward Coast can be traced, but by 1680 it had assumed a position of great importance. For the next decade, more goods were consigned from England to this region than to any other; between 1680 and 1687 cargoes to the value of nearly £150,000 were dispatched, more than a quarter of the company's total exports in that period. With the outbreak of war in 1689, however, the Windward trade was exposed to pirates and privateers who menaced all but the strongest ships edging slowly along an almost harbourless coast. Henceforth, few ships were sent out directly from England to this region; such trade as was carried on was at the discretion of the company's Agents at

[1] T. 70/61, fo. 3; T. 70/79, fo. 74d.   [2] T. 70/1211.

Cape Coast who, when it was safe to do so, sent ships on short voyages along the Windward Coast. This contraction was the result solely of war. As we shall see later, the company's trade here was thought to be more visibly and tangibly profitable than in many other parts of Africa. Nevertheless, when the Windward trade was at its height in the 'eighties, it was continually attacked and criticized by the company's Agents on the Gold Coast.[1] They alleged, first, that it drew off trade which would otherwise have come down to themselves. Though there may have been some truth in this, it was certainly not enough to justify the abandonment of the Windward trade for which some Agents pressed. Ships of other nations traded on the Windward Coast, and as long as they did so, goods would continue to be brought to them. Moreover, even if all Windward trade had entirely ceased, there was no guarantee that the English settlements on the Gold Coast would have been the beneficiaries. It was equally likely that the Dutch, Danish or Brandenburgher settlements would reap the advantage.

The Windward trade was disliked by the Gold Coast Agents for another and more substantial reason. Owing to the uncertainty that attended it, ships' captains frequently found themselves unable to dispose of the whole of their cargoes. Since the owners of these ships were generally allowed a share in the cargo,[2] it was essential that the accounts of each voyage should be wound up and profits distributed soon after the ship had returned to England. Unsold portions of Windward cargoes were accordingly dumped at Cape Coast, which became a graveyard for goods which were often unsuitable for trade, or damaged.[3] For these goods, the Agents at Cape Coast had to pay in gold according to their prime cost in England, with the result that remittances of gold to London from the castle were smaller than they would otherwise have been, and the efforts of the Agents were made to appear even feebler than they were. Discussions of the Windward trade in correspondence between London and Cape Coast tended, therefore, to resolve into wrangles between the Agents who demanded its

[1] T. 70/11, fos. 6, 9d; T. 70/50, fos. 12, 95, 95d.
[2] Above, p. 200.
[3] T. 70/16, fos. 40d, 61d; T. 70/50, fo. 7d.

curtailment and the company's directors who saw in it their 'cheife support' and source of visible profits.

East of the Windward Coast lay the Gold Coast, by which was understood in the seventeenth century roughly the limits of the modern British colony. This, the third of the commercial regions, was the main centre of European residence. In an earlier chapter, something has been said of the evolution of settlement in this territory.[1] No zones of influence existed, such as were beginning to emerge in the north-west. English and Dutch forts and factories were intermingled and sometimes adjacent to one another; the Danes still held Frederixborg and Christiansborg in 1672; and in 1685 the Brandenburghers built Gros Friedrichsburg. From their predecessors, the Royal African Company inherited Cape Coast castle, a substantial fort sited roughly in the centre of the settled portion of the Gold Coast, and probably also some smaller trading posts. Factories had been established by the Royal Adventurers at several places, but it is uncertain how many of them were resettled after De Ruyter's expedition in 1664.[2] Since 1672, both Cape Coast and Accra have been continuously occupied by the English, but the same cannot confidently be said of any other Gold Coast settlement. Most of them began as unfortified lodges inhabited by a factor and one or two soldiers; some were abandoned, while others grew into forts. In 1674, for example, the company possessed one fort, Cape Coast, and four factories, at Accra, Kommenda, Egya and Winnebah. At Egya there were two soldiers and one factor, at Accra and Winnebah three soldiers and one factor, and at Kommenda two soldiers and two factors.[3] Between this date and the end of the century, other settlements were made at Anomabu, Anashan, Dixcove and Sekondi.[4]

Trade on the Gold Coast was designated 'castle-trade', as opposed to the 'ship-trade' of the Windward Coast. Sloops and canoes were used, as in the north-west, but their main functions were collecting from and restocking out-factories. The company's ships from England sometimes traded along the coast, but this does not appear to have been common. In

---

[1] Above, p. 11.   [2] G. F. Zook, *op. cit.*, pp. 46, 68–9.
[3] T. 70/1440 fo. 2.   [4] Below, pp. 245–9.

principle, we may say, the African Company's trade in this region was in the hands of its permanent staff resident in forts or factories.

In the later seventeenth century, gold was still an important product of the region to which it had given its name.[1] Some gold was obtained from alluvial workings on or near the coast, but the greater part was brought down from the north. In the eleven years from 1682 to 1692, the company's imports (at £4 an ounce) were worth more than £250,000. Most of this went to the Mint, and in all, between 1672 and 1713, 548,327 guineas were coined from the company's gold.[2] A proportion of these aggregate imports derived from the Windward Coast, but it is probable that the bulk came from the Gold Coast. Thus a Cape Coast ledger for the twelve months from June 1687 to May 1688 shows that 517 marks of gold worth about £16,500 were taken by the castle and out-factories together.[3] The gold-trade, however, like all trade in this region, was subject to frequent interruptions, especially as a result of wars between African nations which closed the 'ways of trade' down from the north to the European settlements on the coast. The years 1697 to 1700, for example, when the company was struggling to re-establish itself, were largely wasted by the war between the Ashanti and Denkyera, and gold takings at the forts and factories fell away to very little.[4] Apart from the two years 1709 and 1710, when over 20,000 guineas were coined at the Mint from African gold, the company's gold-trade never recovered the position it had held in the 'seventies and 'eighties of the seventeenth century.

As well as being a major export, gold served as the currency of the region. The wages of the company's employees were paid in it, and occasionally factors, lacking appropriate trading goods, were obliged to use gold in order to buy slaves or corn. The company naturally objected to this practice, but there is no doubt that a significant fraction of the gold taken at the

---

[1] W. Bosman, *A New and Accurate Description of the Coast of Guinea*, second English edition, 1721, p. 77, gives estimates of annual takings.

[2] Appendix II.　　　　[3] T. 70/659, fo. 2d.

[4] T. 70/51, *passim*; W. W. Claridge, *A History of the Gold Coast and Ashanti*, 1915, I, pp. 194–5.

Q

company's settlements on the Gold Coast never reached England. In December 1706, for example, Sir Dalby Thomas, Agent-General at Cape Coast, wrote that he had purchased nearly nine hundred marks of gold since his arrival, but most of it seems to have been diverted to the payment of wages or other services.[1]

The slaves obtainable on the Gold Coast were much esteemed. This was partly because of their quality, and partly because both the company and the captains of its ships feared the delays which a visit to the alternative sources of supply might involve.[2] Supplies on the Gold Coast, however, were fluctuating and wayward, as the surviving ledgers clearly show. Thus in the seventeen months between June 1687 and November 1688 takings at Cape Coast, Accra, Sekondi, Kommenda and Egya totalled only 408 slaves.[3] This must have been an unusually low figure, for other years show better results. In eight months, April to December 1678, 1,854 slaves were brought to account at Cape Coast. Anomabu provided 366, Egya 330, Accra 166 and Winnebah 166: the remainder were either bought at Cape Coast or carried there from the Windward Coast. These were gross takings. In the same period 1,146 were shipped off the Coast, and 121 died or escaped.[4] In thirty-two months, September 1701 to April 1704, gross takings were about 3,000, including some slaves purchased by ships and delivered at Cape Coast; 2,320 were shipped off or put to work as castle-slaves, and 217 died or ran away, the remainder still awaiting shipment at the end of the period of account.[5] The main explanation of these fluctuations, as in the gold-trade, was war, but its effects on the slave-trade were quite different. As a general, though not universal rule, the gold-trade prospered in peace and languished in war, while the slave-trade thrived on war and declined in peace. In contrast to the Gambia region, where the slaves purchased had often travelled great distances, those bought on the Gold Coast seem to have come mostly from within three or four hundred miles of the sea. Though an African could be born in slavery or be enslaved either for debt or as punishment for a crime, there is little doubt that

[1] T. 70/5, fo. 27.   [2] T. 70/50, fo. 72.   [3] T. 70/659.
[4] T. 70/657.   [5] T. 70/662.

prisoners of war made up a large, if not the greater, part of the slaves sold to the Europeans. The connexion between the supply of slaves and the alternation of peace and war was certainly well appreciated by the servants of the Royal African Company. One wrote in 1682: 'Feare of a warr which will make gold scarce but negroes plenty.'[1] And in 1706 Josiah Pearson wrote from Anomabu that they 'were in daily expectation of the Arcanians coming to fight the Cabesterra People which, if they beat, there will be a glorious trade both for slaves & gold'.[2]

The company's aim was to get as many negroes as possible from the Gold Coast, falling back on other regions only to make up the required complements. But more often than not, the Gold Coast failed to provide the full cargo of a ship, and the captain's instructions were generally to take on what slaves he could get at Cape Coast, and then to proceed eastwards to Whydah for the remainder.[3] In 1687 the practice was begun of shipping Gold Coast negroes as 'guardians' of those bought at Whydah.[4] Anxious as the company was to obtain slaves from the Gold Coast, it nevertheless absolutely forbade the Agent at Cape Coast to use gold to buy negroes. 'If', runs a letter of 1686, 'the people will not take goods for their negro slaves, lett them keep them.'[5] This was written at one of the periods of acute scarcity of slaves on the Gold Coast which make it impossible to estimate with any accuracy what proportion of the company's negroes derived from this region. It does not seem likely to have been as much as a half, and must sometimes have been less than a quarter.

Although the Gold Coast is not one of the regions of West Africa traditionally associated with ivory, considerable quantities were bought there, especially in the early years of the eighteenth century. In February 1708, for example, Sir Dalby Thomas wrote that since the previous September he had dispatched 183 cwt., and in 1710 he loaded 226 cwt. on one ship.[6] Part of these consignments no doubt represent the takings of the Windward trade, but some ivory was purchased at the

---

[1] T. 70/10, fo. 51d.   [2] T. 70/5, fo. 18.
[3] T. 70/50, fo. 13; T. 70/61, fo. 3, etc.   [4] T. 70/61, fo. 38d.
[5] T. 70/50, fo. 8d.   [6] T. 70/5, fos. 38d, 66d.

Gold Coast forts and factories. Apart from gold, slaves and ivory, the only other product of the region of any importance was corn for the victualling of slave-ships on the Middle Passage. Some provisions were, as we have seen, brought out from England, but they needed to be supplemented by food to which the slaves were accustomed. Unfortunately for the company and for all European traders, the numerous wars of the coast and the interior which often produced gluts of cheap slaves resulted also in the burning and ravaging of crops.[1] Thus if corn was plentiful, slaves tended to be scarce; while slaves could be plentiful only as a result of the wars which destroyed the corn.

East of the Volta river the African trade changed its character. In the regions we have so far examined, slaves were one amongst several products; in the three remaining regions, they were virtually the only product. It is true that Calabar, Benin and Angola all yielded some ivory and corn, and on the Slave Coast a locally manufactured cloth known as 'Ardra cloth' could be bought for resale on the Gold Coast, but these were trifling subsidiaries. It is safe to say that, had it not been for the bountiful supplies of slaves, no European trader would have proceeded beyond the Gold Coast.

The greater part of the trade of the 'Slave Coast' (a term seldom used by the company's employees) was concentrated on two ports, Jaqueen in the kingdom of Ardra, and Whydah in the kingdom of the same name.[2] Offra or Ophra, close to Jaqueen, was chosen as the site for the African Company's first settlement in this region in 1674.[3] A post was established there soon afterwards, if not in the same year. In 1678 Thomas Clarke, the company's factor at Ophra, wrote that six or seven thousand slaves could be purchased annually,[4] and two years later John Mildmay reported that, given proper trading goods, he could dispatch a ship with five hundred negroes every five weeks.[5] Despite these claims, the company in 1683 moved its principal settlement to Whydah (otherwise known as Juda, Guydah and Fida), and it is probable that Ophra was abandoned. The explanation of this move is suggested in a letter written by the

[1] T. 70/10, fo. 45.   [2] H. A. Wyndham, *Atlantic and Slavery*, 1935, p. 34.
[3] T. 70/76, fo. 18d.   [4] T. 70/10, fo. 6.   [5] T. 70/1, fo. 47d.

company to the king of Whydah in 1701 asking for favourable treatment and mentioning that the reason for their coming to Whydah in the first place had been the bad treatment accorded to them by the natives of Ardra.[1] Supplies of slaves at Whydah appear to have been as good as or even better than at Ophra; indeed they were such that no major slaving power could afford to neglect it. The company, in a letter to Cape Coast in 1691, noted that the Dutch had been 'discouraged at Ophra and are setling at Whydah; that place is onely our remedie for want of Gold Coast negroes to fill up such ships who have beene with you'.[2] In 1704 the French likewise took up permanent residence there,[3] while the Portuguese became increasingly frequent visitors. Thus, by the early years of the eighteenth century, all four of the leading slaving nations had acknowledged the advantages of Whydah as a slave-mart.

The trade of the Royal African Company at Whydah cannot properly be designated either ship- or castle-trade, though it approximated more to the former than the latter. A factory was settled in 1683,[4] but cargoes destined for Whydah continued to be consigned to the captain of the ship that carried them. In 1687, the company appointed as its agent Captain Petley Weyborne, a former employee, who, having turned interloper, had lived at Whydah since 1684 despite all the company's efforts to dislodge him. Weyborne was now given a semi-independent status with freedom to trade on his own account, in return for supplying one hundred negroes at a fixed rate of £3 a head during every ten days that a company's ship was in port. Differences soon developed between him and the company, and when Weyborne died in 1690 the experiment was not repeated.[5] For the next nine years, the company kept an agent at Whydah but not for the purpose of carrying on castle-trade. He acted rather as a kind of consul, negotiating with the native authorities, and putting prospective sellers in touch with ships'

---

[1] T. 70/51, pp. 200–3.   [2] T. 70/50, fo. 122.

[3] S. Berbain, *Le Comptoir Français de Juda (Ouidah) au XVIIIe Siècle* (Memoires de L'Institut Français d'Afrique Nord, No. 3), Paris, 1942.

[4] T. 70/11.

[5] Above, p. 121n; T. 70/50, fos. 89, 89d, 103; T. 70/11 fo. 22; P.R.O., C.9/425/6.

captains to whom the actual buying and selling were left. 'We must', concluded the company in 1691, 'continue our interest amongst those people by having a factory, altho' the keeping thereof is all a losse; for, by experience, masters of ships buy their slaves as soone and as good as our factors can, and to be tied to receive them from our factors hath in Weyborne's time proved so fatall to the men & ships that none will goe unlesse they buy their owne negroes & thereby our factors are uselesse.'[1] By purchasing their own negroes, captains earned commissions of four in a hundred on those delivered alive in the Plantations, instead of two in a hundred on those put aboard by factors. In 1699 or 1700 a trading factor was again established at Whydah, and castle-trade seems to have prevailed there throughout the first decade of the eighteenth century.[2]

Beyond Whydah lay the Bight of Benin and New and Old Calabar, which furnished slaves, small quantities of ivory, and cotton cloths. No fort or factory was settled by the company in this region, and the absence of European residents may be attributed partly to the unhealthiness of the coast and partly to the safe refuges provided by river estuaries which made settlement a needless expense.[3] Records relating to the trade of this region are extremely scanty owing to the absence of settlement, but it is clear that commercially it was less developed than the great slave-markets of Whydah and Ophra. Something can be learned of trade in the New Calabar river from the journal of the *Arthur*, Captain Doegood, which sailed from London in 1677.[4] The *Arthur*, 64 days out from Gravesend, reached Calabar on 5 February 1678, and anchored three miles up the river. The king of New Calabar then came aboard and the prices to be paid for slaves were fixed at 36 copper bars for a man and 30 for a woman. None of the crew went ashore, slaves being brought for inspection in canoes. In the following five weeks, 352 negroes were bought, as many as 42 being

---

[1] T. 70/50, fo. 122.   [2] T. 70/85, fos. 58d; T. 70/51, pp. 26, 36.
[3] Sir A. Burns, *History of Nigeria*, third edition, p. 81.
[4] T. 70/1213. Cf. Barbot's voyage in 1699 in Churchill's *Voyages* (1746), V, p. 455. By this date New Calabar had become a place of much trade and some difficulty was experienced in settling satisfactory prices. Nevertheless six hundred negroes were bought in seven weeks (p. 460).

purchased in a single day. Without doubt the place was unhealthy. Many slaves fell sick immediately, and nineteen died
before the ship was clear of the river. Thirty-six more died
before the African coast was left behind, together with the
doctor, the doctor's mate and three seamen.

The last and most remote of the commercial regions of West
Africa was Angola, a designation which appears to have been
applied without discrimination to the coast both north and
south of the Congo. Angola proper, if such may be said to
exist, was a Portuguese sphere of influence being transformed
only slowly into a formal empire.[1] The Portuguese either did
not object to or were unable to prevent trading by other
nations even at places where they had settlements. The
English established no trading posts in this region and, as in the
Benin region, records of the company's trade are few; the
journal of the *Carlisle*, Captain Swan, which records a voyage to
Angola in 1680–1, gives almost the only account of the trade.[2]
As must have been easy enough to do, the *Carlisle* overshot her
mark and sailed too far to the south. She coasted north to São
Paulo de Luanda where four tons of ivory and 350 cannisters
of corn were purchased. Further north still, Swan set up temporary factories at Malimba, where 294 slaves were bought in
three months, and at Cabinda where 175 were bought in five
months. At both these places the Portuguese had mission
stations.[3] By comparison with the *Arthur's* experiences at
Calabar, this was very slow trading and the *Carlisle* was almost
twice as long in reaching the West Indies. After 1689, trade
with this region was much reduced; apart from the war, the
reason for this curtailment may be contained in a letter written
by the company to the king of Cacongo in February 1688: 'We
have frequent complaints by every shipp we send thither that
the slaves cost one third part more there than att all other places
in Guynie & that there trade canot be driven with that security
& faithfullness as we find in other places.'[4] It will be shown

---

[1] C. R. Boxer, *Salvador de Sá and the Struggle for Brazil and Angola*, Ch. vi.

[2] T. 70/1216. The establishment of a factory on the coast of Angola
was considered by the Court of Assistants in 1680, but not proceeded with.
T. 70/78, fo. 113.

[3] H. A. Wyndham, *op. cit.*, p. 95.   [4] T. 70/50, fo. 56d.

later that the company's complaint was justified, and it must be assumed that the extensive slave-buying of the Portuguese themselves was responsible for the high prices.

2. The Terms of Trade

The company's exports to Africa, as we have seen, averaged some £65,000 a year until 1689, £30,000 a year until 1705, and thereafter fell away to virtually nothing. Clearly, one of the most important problems which had to be solved was how to distribute these exports amongst the six commercial regions of West Africa to best advantage. The evidence upon which the solution had to be formulated was, to begin with, sketchy and confusing. In 1672 much less was known about West Africa than forty years later, and it is not surprising that the company made mistakes. Goods that were unwanted or unsaleable, or goods of the right kind but the wrong colour, were included in African cargoes, and had either to be sent home or left to rot in a Gold Coast warehouse. Correspondence between the company at home and its servants in Africa was commonly acrimonious, the latter complaining that they had no goods to sell, and the former that they got nothing in return for the goods which were sent. This bitterness should have diminished as knowledge and experience were accumulated, but relations became worse not better with the passage of time, due mainly to the exhausted condition in which the company found itself at the close of the seventeenth century.

While the supply of goods to the 'Northern parts of Guinea' appears from the accompanying table fairly constant, French depredations in the Gambia and assaults on Sierra Leone and Sherbro reduced consignments to almost nothing after 1705. The influence of European wars is indeed very marked in all regions. The Windward trade, so prominent in the 'eighties, was sharply contracted in the 'nineties, and the trades of Benin, Calabar and Angola were virtually abandoned. All these were ship-trades, and the explanation of their curtailment must lie in the activities of French privateers and warships. Conversely, the Gold Coast, which in the 'eighties received only a quarter

Distribution of Exports to Africa by Regions

Year	I	II	III	IV	V	VI	VII
			In £'s sterling				
1680	10,587	11,786	5,195	—	4,098	7,814	2,491
1681	6,499	20,650	19,616	8,275	6,691	7,633	3,627
1682	13,140	11,768	34,622	10,633	3,933	7,222	3,600
1683	10,767	22,212	13,187	14,097	1,752	10,063	2,541
1684	5,801	11,833	13,856	6,869	2,915	3,082	7,089
1685	11,211	20,832	14,451	16,974	4,937	7,901	440
1688	8,609	20,444	13,731	6,607	2,785	6,065	1,531
1689	1,693	17,022	1,650	1,266	538	1,736	1,793
1690	—	789	17,304	3,550	1,516	2,522	1,573
1691	8,746	1,551	8,262	—	—	—	—
1692	8,738	1,964	11,060	5,940	1,040	3,326	1,211
1693	8,205	9,440	21,270	9,414	903	4,388	377
1694	6,379	3,390	9,967	3,864	1,075	—	—
1695	6,943	2,163	10,575	2,303	—	—	—
1696	838	2,558	8,721	5,126	—	—	—
1697	1,292	—	10,707	1,979	—	1,820	—
1698	8,567	1,174	22,145	5,231	—	—	4,840
1701	4,709	1,110	10,463	14,878	2,601	3,982	—
1702	9,898	749	13,732	834	957	1,931	3,258
1703	3,029	772	14,834	10,915	—	—	—
1704	7,553	—	50,041	2,533	—	—	—

I	Gambia, Sierra Leone, Sherbro
II	Windward Coast
III	Gold Coast
IV	Ardra and Whydah
V	Benin, New and Old Calabar
VI	Angola
VII	Miscellaneous and unnamed destinations

of total exports, in the 'nineties received a half. Consignments to Whydah also increased proportionally to total exports, and there is no doubt that a large number of the company's slaves were purchased there after 1689.

The African trade, however, was a more complicated business than a simple alternation between a mixed castle- and ship-trade in peace and a predominantly castle-trade in war. There were other and more properly economic determinants which could be learned only by experience. There were, first, the questions of what to sell and where to buy. Bosman, at the end of the seventeenth century, calculated that 150 different commodities were required for the trade of the Gold Coast alone.[1] Including the many different varieties of English woollens and serges, East India cottons, metal goods, beads and so on, this may not have been an exaggeration. Statistics of twenty-seven commodities exported by the Royal African Company will be found in the Appendix,[2] and, in smaller quantities, swords, lead, tallow, writing paper, made-up clothes, trumpets, bells, mirrors, and spirits, were all regarded as important constituents of cargoes for the trade of one part of Africa or another. Certain regions had marked peculiarities. From a quarter to a half of all consignments to the Gambia, for instance, consisted of iron bars. Some iron was sold on the Windward and Gold Coasts, but very much less than in the Gambia, and none at all was sent to Angola. Essential for the trade of Angola were East Indian textiles, which also sold on the Gold Coast, but hardly at all in the Gambia; it may be that the difficulty of getting supplies after the outbreak of war in 1689 was a factor in the decline of the Angola trade. Cowries, also bought chiefly from the East India Company, were almost a *sine qua non* of trade at Whydah, Ardra and in the Bight of Benin; in the latter the brass half-rings known as manillas were also in demand. Neither of these commodities had much sale elsewhere on the West African coast.

Cargoes had therefore to be carefully selected and include a wide variety of goods. But even with goods that were well-established articles of trade it was easy to make a mistake.[3] Demand, especially on the Gold Coast, fluctuated, and a commodity much sought after in one year might be unsaleable the next. In June 1680, for example, Agent Bradley wrote from Cape Coast that the want of says and perpetuanas was driving away native traders; in March 1682 his successor reported that says were a drug on the market.[4] Four years later perpetuanas were again in brisk demand, but, wrote the company:

the Dutch had notice of it a month sooner than wee and bought

---

[1] W. Bosman, *op. cit.*, p. 79.   [2] Appendix I.
[3] T. 70/51, pp. 155–6, where ten items sent to Whydah in 1700 were said to be the sort that 'do never vend here'.
[4] T. 70/10, fos. 45d, 49d.

up greate quantitys of perpetuanos heare before wee knew anything of the reason of it, and made that commodity not to be gott
on the suddaine when wee came to heare they were in demand; soe
it must happen that the Dutch will have supplyed their Factoryes
before wee could.[1]

The commonest complaint from Africa, however, was not of the
wrong goods but of insufficient goods or no goods at all, a
situation which must have frequently arisen after 1689 and
which after 1705 was chronic.[2]

While the commodities appropriate to different regions could
be learned, changes in demand and the rapid glutting of the
market by traders of another nation remained natural hazards
of the African trade. Other problems, hardly less susceptible of
a ready solution, rose out of the differing standards of value held
by Europeans and Africans. When one civilization trades with
another, their values eventually become roughly assimilated,
but the process takes time, and it cannot be said to have been
completed in Africa by the end of the seventeenth century.
Bosman recognized this when he wrote that, while cowries (also
called boesies) were necessary for the trade of the Slave Coast,
care must be taken to mix them with other goods as 'slaves
paid for in Boesies cost the Company one half more than those
bought with other goods'.[3] The same appears to be true in the
gold-trade. In 1687, for example, we find gold being exchanged
for iron at Cape Coast at the rate of one ounce for thirteen or
fourteen bars. Iron was valued in the company's invoices at
about 4s. a bar, so that an ounce of gold bought with iron was
costing between 52s. and 56s. At the same time and place, gold
was being bought with gunpowder, one ounce exchanging for
one barrel. A barrel of gunpowder was rated at 46s., so that it
was more profitable to buy gold with gunpowder than with
iron.[4]

The impression left by the company's records is that the
pattern of trade was imposed by the African on the European
rather than *vice versa*. This is certainly true if we turn from
selling to buying. Slaves, as we have seen, could be obtained

[1] T. 70/50, fo. 40.
[2] T. 70/11, fos. 25d, 28d, 53d, 61d, 62d, 65; T. 70/5, *passim*.
[3] *Op. cit.*, p. 341.　　　　　[4] Details from T. 70/659.

in every commercial region of West Africa, including the Gambia river which in 1678 was thought to be capable of yielding between five and six hundred a year.[1] More were bought at Joal and Portudal, and consignments to the West Indies were normally made twice a year. Competition from French, Portuguese, Spanish and Dutch traders, and from English interlopers, however, forced up prices in north-west Africa,[2] and, after ten years of experience, the company came at last to realize that it was uneconomical to buy slaves in this region. In 1688 a letter to the Agent at James Fort stated that ivory and wax were the only commodities which 'turne to account', and orders were given that negroes should be re-exchanged for these goods.[3] Three years later, Agent John Booker reported that in accordance with his instructions he had refused to buy several hundred negroes, and as a result the African merchants had not come down the river with other goods. It was necessary, he wrote, to buy slaves in order 'to keep up the credit of the trade', even though they could be bought more cheaply elsewhere.[4]

Prices of slaves in other parts of Africa are not easily calculated, but they appear to have been lower on the Gold Coast than in the Gambia, and lower still at Whydah and Calabar. In 1685 Agent Nurse wrote from the Gold Coast that £3 would not purchase a negro.[5] In 1687, a man slave was bought at Cape Coast for one-and-a-half barrels of gunpowder which had cost the company £3 10s. in England; another was bought for 26 sheets, worth about the same.[6] At Whydah, in 1683, prices were stated to be 1½ longcloths or 3 fine sletias or 4 allejaes (East Indian textiles).[7] In terms of the valuations given in the company's invoices, the slave would cost 45s. 3d., 72s. or 74s. according to which of the three commodities was used, another example of how it could be much more profitable to trade with one article than another. In the 'seventies and 'eighties, the conventional price of an African slave was £3,[8] this being the

---

[1] T. 70/10, fo. 1.　　　　[2] T. 70/10, fo. 59; T. 70/15, fos. 23, 23d.

[3] T. 70/50, fo. 83.　　　　[4] T. 70/11, fo. 37; T.70/51, p. 145.

[5] T. 70/11, fo. 11d.　　[6] T. 70/659, fo. 71.　　　[7] T. 70/16, fo. 71d.

[8] So far as I have been able to discover, all prices of slaves quoted represent the invoice value of the goods with which they were purchased. In most cases this invoice value was the same as the price which the company had paid in England, with no allowance made for cost of transport.

rate at which Petley Weyborne contracted to supply negroes at Whydah in 1687. Twelve cargoes were made up in England in the years 1682 to 1685 for Calabar and Benin on the basis of goods to the value of £3 4s. for each negro to be purchased; twenty-nine cargoes for Whydah and Ardra in the same period assumed an average of £3 2s. Angola, however, shows markedly higher prices: thirteen cargoes valued at £19,802 were expected to buy 4,700 slaves, an average of £4 4s. each. These figures were, of course, only approximations; prices varied a good deal between regions, and also fluctuated within regions according to supply and demand. In a trade as international as the slave-trade had already become, the degree of control which the Royal African Company could exercise over these factors was very small. On the whole, slaves seem to have been most expensive in the 'northern parts of Guinea' and Angola, the two extremities of the company's trade, cheaper on the Gold Coast and in Benin, and cheapest of all at Whydah. After 1689 prices everywhere were much advanced, partly as a result of the increased cost in England of certain constituents of African cargoes, such as gunpowder; partly as a result of more open competition from interlopers, and from 1698 onwards, separate traders; and partly because of the growing interest of France in the slave-trade, culminating in the French settlement at Whydah in 1704. In 1693 the African Company's captains were instructed to buy what Gold Coast negroes they could at up to £5 a head.[1] After 1702, there were further increases, though possibly less marked at Whydah than elsewhere. Soon negroes on the Gold Coast were costing £10, £11 and £12 apiece, and in 1712 as much as £16 and £17 was being paid.[2] Thus in the course of little more than twenty years the price of a slave had risen almost five-fold. The African Company naturally blamed the competition of the separate traders for this increase, and there is no doubt that it played an important part, though probably the remarkable development of the French slave-trade had at least as great an effect.

The nature of the surviving records makes it difficult to form a clear picture of the profits or losses which the company made

[1] T. 70/84, fo. 11.
[2] B.O.T. Journal, 1704–9, p. 452; T. 70/5, fos. 48d, 67, 81.

in the different regions of Africa. Accounts in the Gambia, Sierra Leone, and Sherbro were kept in bars, shillings and pence, a currency of account. On the arrival of a cargo from England, its value was 'translated' from sterling into this currency and entered in the ledger. The value of the bar was generally 6s., though sometimes it was dropped to 4s.[1] It must be explained that, though iron bars played an essential part in the trade of this region, the bar of account and the iron bar were not necessarily or always the same. In the Gambia ledger for 1687, for example, we find a consignment of 2,000 bars of iron, rated in the invoice at £398 4s., 'translated' into 1,327 bars of account. Each iron bar was thus worth about two-thirds of a bar of account.[2] African commodities were also valued in bars: according to the Homeward Invoices, wax from Gambia cost 16–18 bars a cwt., rising to 20 after 1700; ivory 18 bars a cwt. for large tusks and 9 for small, rising to 20 and 10; hides three or four for a bar; slaves 20–30 bars according to age and sex. In 1700, for example, the Agent at James Fort was instructed to pay 30 bars for men and women, and 20 bars for boys and girls.[3] The bar then being at 4s., a man slave would cost £6 in English goods. All these prices were averages struck by the company's factors and concealed wide variations in the actual purchase price, as is shown by the journal of a voyage up the Gambia in 1704. Sample bargains show eight men slaves costing 156 bars of account, three costing 45 and four costing 64. In detail, we find a slave bought for five ounces of coral, four gallons of brandy and six pieces-of-eight.[4]

On the Gold Coast accounts were kept in marks, ounces and ackies of gold, the ounce bearing a nominal value of £4. The sterling value of goods from England was 'translated' into this currency in the same way as in the Gambia. It is clear, however, that the ledgers surviving from both regions give an incomplete and probably misleading picture of the profits and losses. The object of those who kept them was to achieve some kind of a balance rather than to record faithfully the transactions carried out. Accounts were cooked, and, even when they were

---

[1] J. M. Gray, op. cit., gives the conventional value of a bar in 1680 as 4s. For 6s. as the conventional value, see T. 70/108 inside front cover.

[2] T. 70/546. [3] T. 70/51, p. 111. [4] T. 70/834.

not falsified, they were badly kept, provoking complaints from the company in London.[1] To one such complaint the Agent at Cape Coast replied: 'Lament you may, without you send over people fitting to doe it, for what by sickness & mortallity in this damn'd cursed country we have hardly any People that are able to put penn to paper that understand anything.'[2]

Only in the trade of the Windward Coast is it possible to obtain an accurate statement of the profits made. Here, as we have already seen, the practice was to allow to owners of hired ships a share in the Windward cargo. The accounts of the sale of the cargo and the profits earned had therefore to be cast up soon after a ship returned to England, in order that the owners' share might be paid. Between 1680 and 1687 accounts have been preserved of ninety-five Windward cargoes from which the profit of each voyage, clear of incidental charges, can be calculated.[3] In these eight years, only three cargoes showed a nett loss; the largest profit recorded was 141 per cent. and the average 38 per cent. Some part of this profit was achieved, as we have seen, at the expense of Cape Coast castle where unsold goods were dumped at cost price. Nevertheless, there is every reason to regard these profits as satisfactory. They were probably greater than those accruing from any other region, and they fully confirm the wisdom of the company's decision to continue the Windward trade as long as it could and to ignore the criticisms levelled against it by the Gold Coast Agents. A ship-trade such as that of the Windward Coast could be begun and ended within a year. The castle-trades, on the other hand, were burdened with all sorts of charges which help to obscure the profits made or losses incurred. Before a general impression can be given of the company's successes and failures in castle-trade, therefore, it is necessary that an account should be given of these charges.

---

[1] E.g. T. 70/51, p. 249 et seq.   [2] T. 70/15, fo. 10.
[3] From the company's Freight Books, T. 70/962-7.

3. Forts, Factories and Men

Trade on the west coast of Africa, as we saw earlier in this chapter, may be roughly classified as either castle-trade or ship-trade, the former being practised entirely or in part on the Gold Coast, at Ophra and Whydah, and to some extent in north-west Africa, and the latter prevailing on the Windward Coast, in Benin and the Calabar rivers, and on the coast of Angola. At first sight, the regions where settlements existed might be thought to be economically more profitable to the company than those where a ship had to trust to the fortune of an almost entirely unorganized market. In theory the company, with its forts, its factories, its permanent staff, and its accumulated experience, should have had little difficulty in competing successfully with interlopers and separate traders who, to begin with, had none of these assets. In the following pages an attempt will be made to evaluate the economic and strategic advantages which the company derived from its permanent settlements; for it was upon the usefulness of the forts for trade and defence that the conflict between the company and the separate traders in Parliament, in the press and at the Board of Trade, largely turned.

Before these questions can be discussed, it is necessary to identify and describe the forts and factories established by the Royal African Company, and to explain the administrative arrangements devised for the government of the fifteen or twenty settlements and the two to three hundred men who lived in them. Although, as we have seen, forts and factories were occupied in north-west Africa and at Whydah, the Gold Coast remained, throughout, the chief region of settlement. Here the company was fortunate in inheriting from its predecessor the castle of Cape Coast (or Cabo Corso as it was still sometimes called), a fort built by the Swedes in 1652 which had passed into English hands in 1664. After Dutch Elmina, Cape Coast was the largest, strongest and best-garrisoned European fort in West Africa, the company's 'capital' from which its other settlements on the Gold Coast were ruled, and the seat of its Agent-General. The condition of the castle in 1672 is unknown; as a result of neglect in the later years of the Royal Adventurers it was certainly undermanned and probably dilapidated. The new company at once proceeded to strengthen the garrison and to enlarge the fortifications and amenities.[1] In 1710 the castle was described as being defended by out-works, platforms and bastions, with brick walls fourteen feet thick, and by seventy-four great guns, besides quantities of small-arms. There were living quarters for the Agent, factors, writers, artificers and soldiers, two large water-tanks, warehouses and granaries, rum-vaults, workshops, repositories for one thousand slaves, and a chapel.[2] Constant care was needed to maintain this fabric in a defensible condition. The great rains of 1694, for example, which washed away the fortifications of some of the smaller settlements on the Gold Coast, damaged the tower at Cape Coast.[3] ''Tis something strange', wrote the company in the following year, 'our severall forts should need so frequent and great repairs; wee doubt either skill or a due care has been wanting.'[4] Bricks and lime were made locally, but all other stores needed for building and maintenance, tools, timber, tar, nails and so on, had to be sent from England.[5] These, added to the wages of smiths, bricklayers, masons and carpenters, formed a permanent charge on the company's exiguous resources. After about 1706 evidence of dilapidation becomes common, and in 1708 a factor wrote that 'at Cape Coast there is never a dry room to lye in'.[6]

In 1673 the garrison of the castle was only thirty-eight, consisting of the Agent-General, Thomas Mellish, six merchants and factors, and thirty-one artificers and soldiers. The company took immediate steps to increase this number, and by September of the following year it had risen to fifty-three. Between 1683 and 1713, when records are available, the garrison never fell below fifty; commonly it was between sixty and ninety; and in 1688, 1689 and 1693 it exceeded a hundred.[7]

---

[1] Forty men were sent out at the end of 1673 or the beginning of 1674; *Cal. S.P. Col.*, 1669–74, No. 1176. Building was in progress in 1678 and 1679, T. 70/1, fos. 23d.–24.

[2] *House of Commons Journal*, XVI, pp. 317–19.   [3] T. 70/11, fo. 59d.

[4] T. 70/50, fo. 164.   [5] T. 70/1, fos. 23d–24; above, pp. 178–9.

[6] T. 70/5, fo. 41d.   [7] From T. 70/1440–5.

R

Even this number was not regarded as sufficient. In 1678, for instance, Agent Bradley estimated that a hundred soldiers were necessary to secure the castle, besides artificers and factors, and in 1698 the company itself, in a memorial to the Lord Chancellor, put the desired strength at 150.[1] Fluctuations in the strength of the garrison from year to year were very marked: in March 1693 there were 114 men at Cape Coast, and a year later only 75. Such changes were due partly to the incidence of mortality (which itself was far from being constant), partly to the regularity or otherwise with which reinforcements arrived from England, and partly to the requirements of other English forts and factories on the Gold Coast, to which men from Cape Coast had sometimes to be transferred.

The residents at Cape Coast, both civilian and military, may be divided into 'officers' and 'other ranks', though the gulf between them was not impassable. From 1672 to 1687, and from 1700 to 1711, the officers were headed by the company's Agent-General, assisted by two or more 'merchants', two, three or four 'factors' and the same number of 'writers', a chaplain, surveyor, bookkeeper, steward and surgeon. In command of the soldiers, though subordinate to the Agent, was either a lieutenant or one or two sergeants, with a corporal and a drummer. In all, the officers at Cape Coast numbered between ten and fifteen, the remainder of the garrison consisting of artificers and soldiers. Apart from the carpenters, smiths, bricklayers and masons employed in building and maintenance, coopers were needed for unpacking and packing goods in transit, armourers for repairing weapons, and gardeners for diversifying the diet. Whenever possible, soldiers were engaged who could also practise a trade. But those who claimed to be artisans did not always prove to be competent and, after the outbreak of war in 1689, the difficulty of recruiting skilled men obliged the company to train natives as artisans. In 1695 a carpenter and a bricklayer were sent to Cape Coast from England in order to instruct the Africans, each to have a bounty for every skilled man he trained up to his trade.[2] The experiment does not seem to have been wholly unsuccessful, for the names of 'Black Tom, the cooper' and several others are found

[1] T. 70/1, fo. 9; T. 70/101, fo. 67d.   [2] T. 70/50, fos. 166, 166d.

on the strength of Cape Coast in the ensuing years. In addition, the company employed here and elsewhere a number of castle-slaves, known as 'gromettos', generally brought from some other part of Africa. Unlike the free negro artisans, they did not figure in the company's establishment and received no pay.

Under the command of the Agent-General were not only the garrison of the castle, but the company's employees elsewhere on the Gold Coast and, except between 1687 and 1691 when Weyborne was factor, the officers and soldiers at Whydah, a total of 150 to 200 men and as many as fourteen or fifteen settlements. Some kind of regular constitution, both for the government of these communities and for the conduct of the company's business, was clearly necessary, and one was supplied in a document known as 'The Establishment', first drawn up by the Court of Assistants in January 1676.[1] It began with an injunction against profaneness, debauchery and blasphemy, which was probably little heeded, and instituted public prayers, 'as established by authority', to be read twice daily by the chaplain. Prayers and services may well have been observed, for more often than not there was a chaplain or minister on the strength of the garrison. Next, the powers of the Agent-General and chief officers were defined. 'The whole directive power in all matters either civill or military' was vested in a council of six, consisting of the Agent, the Chief Merchant, Second Merchant, and Third Merchant (all of whom were to reside at the castle), together with the Chiefs of Accra and Kommenda. Decisions at the Council were to be made by a simple majority and recorded with the signatures of those who assented to them. Dissenting opinions were also to be recorded, signed and sent home to England. 'The whole executive power in all matters', on the other hand, was vested in the Agent-General alone who also commanded the company's military forces. To give effect to these arrangements, extensive coercive powers were needed, as had been foreseen in the company's charter. Under the Establishment, the Agent and Council were empowered to demote, suspend, or send home factors, writers and other

[1] T. 70/76, fos. 67–9. Revised editions of 'The Establishment' were produced in 1678 (T.70/77, fos. 86–9) and in 1687.

civilians, to cashier soldiers, and to inflict imprisonment or other corporal punishment on both civil and military offenders.

Apart from the Agent-General and the merchants who formed the Council, the Establishment of 1676 envisaged a chaplain, five younger factors, a lieutenant, two sergeants, a surgeon and forty-seven soldiers 'of which as many to be coopers, smiths, carpenters, bricklayers, gardeners and masons as may be procured'. Sixty-one men were thus to reside at Cape Coast, assisted by thirty castle-slaves. At Accra, there were to be a Chief, second, third, four soldiers and four slaves; and at Kommenda a Chief, second, three soldiers and four slaves, giving a total strength for the Gold Coast of seventy-three whites. At this date, these appear to have been the only settlements occupied by the company in this region, but in the years immediately following there was much expansion, and in the period from 1683 to 1713 there were seldom fewer than twice as many white men in the company's Gold Coast service as the Establishment of 1676 laid down.

After prescribing salaries and allowances,[1] the Establishment concluded by defining the duties of the principal officers stationed at Cape Coast. The Chief Merchant was gold-taker; the Second warehouse-keeper; and the Third bookkeeper. But all were collectively to sign letters and accounts, and each was to have a key to the chest in which gold was stored. The out-factories were to correspond and account directly to London as well as to Cape Coast, and at least once every six months they were to be inspected by one of the senior officials.

The Establishment was subsequently varied in many respects, principally as regards salaries. A new version was issued in 1678,[2] which differed little, and another in 1687 which, although no copy appears to have survived, contained one radical constitutional change, the abolition of the office of Agent-General. Between 1672 and 1687 the company had been served by seven Agents-General, none of whom is known to have been conspicuous in either success or failure. Captain Abraham Holditch had been Agent at the time of the formation of the company in 1672; either in that or the following year her eturned to England, bought £400 of African stock, and was

---

[1] Below, pp. 252–3.   [2] T. 70/77, fos. 86–9.

elected to the Court of Assistants in 1675, 1676, and 1677. In November 1675 he was chosen to go out to Africa for a second term as Agent on terms highly favourable to himself.[1] He did not, however, proceed, and Captain Ralph Hodgkins was appointed instead.[2] Hodgkins succeeded Thomas Mellish, little record having survived of either of them. The next three Agents were Captain Bradley, Captain Henry Greenhill and Captain Henry Nurse, the first and last being former slave-captains. Greenhill, alone amongst the company's Agents, achieved a notable career on his return from Africa, rising to high rank in government service and standing (unsuccessfully) for Parliament in 1701.

Before Henry Nurse's term of office had expired, the company resolved that, in order to lessen expenditure, the name and office of Agent-General should be abolished, and the company's affairs on the Gold Coast remitted to a Council of three Chief Merchants, each of whom was to preside in turn for one month.[3] The new arrangement came into effect on 5 June 1687 and was not a success. There were many complaints from the company of failure to apply the new Establishment, the Cape Coast copy of which was kept with its face to the wall instead of being publicly displayed.[4] In 1691 oligarchical rule was modified by the appointment of one Merchant as perpetual chairman of the Council, and in 1700 the office of Agent-General was revived.[5] Captain Joseph Bagg was appointed to the position but died soon after arriving at Cape Coast. His successor, Colonel Spencer Boughton, 'a person well experienced in merchants and military affairs', died on the voyage out. Finally, in 1703, Dalby Thomas, well known for his interest in and writings upon the West Indies, was appointed Agent-General to preside over the foreign service of what was now almost a bankrupt company. Thomas, knighted before his departure, spent seven years at Cape Coast, dying there in 1711.

Although at different times the African Company had as many as seventeen settlements, designated either 'forts' or 'fac-

---

[1] T. 70/76, fo. 59.   [2] *Ibid.*, fo. 61.
[3] T. 70/50, fos. 27, 31, 33; T. 70/81, fos. 68, 72.
[4] T. 70/50, fos. 54d, 55, 74, 95d, 96, 123, 123d.
[5] T. 70/86, p. 65. No explanation of this decision is given.

tories', on the Gold Coast, only Accra and Cape Coast appear
to have been continuously occupied from 1672 to 1713. In principle and in intention, forts were permanent settlements,
defended by earth- and sometimes by stone-works, and gar-
risoned by between eight and twenty men. In fact, as we shall
see, the occupation of such forts as Kommenda and Sekondi
was not seldom interrupted. Factories, on the other hand, were

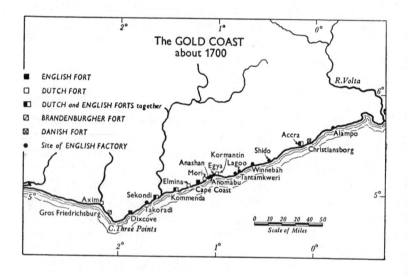

unfortified, consisting often of nothing more than a hut staffed
by one, two or three men; some of them subsequently developed
into forts, but in origin they were experimental and temporary,
being set up and withdrawn as circumstances suggested. The
chronology of English settlement on the Gold Coast in this important period of expansion being so imprecisely known, the
accompanying table has been compiled, showing the number of
men at each fort or factory between 1673 and 1713.[1]

Seven of these settlements ranked as forts. Accra was raised
from the status of factory in 1679 and given the name of James
Fort. Charles Fort at Anomabu was built at the same time.[2]

---

[1] From T. 70/1440–5.   [2] T. 70/1, fo. 24.

NUMBER OF MEN IN THE GOLD COAST FORTS AND FACTORIES, 1673–1713

	1673 Dec.	1674 Sept.	1683 Apr.	1684 July	1685 Apr.	1686 Jan.	1687 July	1688 May	1689 Jan.	1690 Nov.	1691 June	1693 Mar.	1694 Apr.	1695 Jan.
Cape Coast	39	53	64	80	55	73	105	115	102	84	97	114	75	80
In sloops attending	—	—	26	23	22	61¹	19	21	28	23	—	—	13	—
Accra	2	4	8	10	10	11	12	12	19	16	16	12	16	18
Alampo	—	—	—	—	—	—	—	—	—	—	—	—	—	—
Anashan	—	—	—	—	2	—	1	2	2	—	—	2	2	1
Anomabu	—	—	9	10	8	9	13	13	11	7	9	8	10	11
Dixcove	—	—	—	—	—	—	—	—	—	—	1	7	13	9
Egya (Agga)	—	3	2	2	2	3	2	3	3	—	—	2	2	2
Frederixborg (Ft. Royal)	—	—	—	—	7	4	15	11	18	12	8	9	9	4
Kommenda	2	4	1	1	1	2	2	—	—	—	—	—	—	8
Lagoo	—	—	—	—	—	—	—	—	—	—	—	—	—	—
Queen Anne's Point	—	—	—	—	—	—	—	—	—	—	—	—	—	—
Sekondi	—	—	2	2	3	6	9	13	7	6	7	5	—	—
Shido	—	—	—	—	—	—	—	—	—	—	—	—	—	—
Tantamkweri	—	—	—	—	—	—	—	—	—	—	—	2	—	—
Takoradi	2	—	—	—	—	—	—	—	—	—	—	—	—	—
Winnebah	2	4	—	—	—	—	—	—	—	—	—	—	2	9

¹ Includes some sailors temporarily on the Coast.

	1696 Aug.	1697 Apr.	1701	1702 Sept.	1703 Mar.	1704 Jan.	1705 Jan.	1706 Mar.	1707 Sept.	1708 Oct.	1710 Feb.	1711 Apr.	1712 Aug.	1713 June
Cape Coast	66	67	?	55	71	86	81	53	90	62	59	55	91	73
In sloops attending	—	—	13	7	—	—	—	—	—	—	—	—	—	—
Accra	17	16	17	12	17	16	21	11	17	19	13	14	18	20
Alampo	—	—	2	6	3	4	—	3	—	—	—	—	—	—
Anashan	1	1	—	—	—	2	—	—	—	—	—	—	—	—
Anomabu	12	10	16	14	13	8	11	6	7	7	7	7	9	9
Dixcove	12	13	12	10	8	9	9	6	7	9	8	12	13	13
Egya (Agga)	2	—	1	2	3	2	2	2	2	1	1	—	—	—
Frederixborg (Ft. Royal)	4	4	—	—	—	—	4	3	4	4	5	5	5	5
Kommenda	17	17	18	16	18	11	9	12	8	8	9	10	8	11
Lagoo	—	—	—	—	—	—	2	—	—	—	—	—	—	—
Queen Anne's Point	—	—	—	—	—	—	5	3	3	4	5	3	5	5
Sekondi	—	—	—	—	—	—	6	10	10	6	7	13	14	11
Shido	—	—	—	—	—	—	—	4	3	2	1	—	—	2
Tantamkweri	—	—	3	2	2	2	1	—	—	2	2	2	2	5
Takoradi	—	—	—	—	—	—	—	—	—	—	—	—	—	—
Winnebah	11	11	16	14	15	10	9	9	11	11	8	14	15	12

Kommenda, after being occupied as a factory since 1673, or earlier, was abandoned in 1687, the company's factor being 'forced from there by the blacks'.[1] It was resettled in 1694 and the construction of a fort begun which was still unfinished in 1698.[2] Sekondi likewise began as a factory. A fort was built there in 1685, but the fortifications collapsed in the following year as a result of heavy rain.[3] A small staff, however, remained until 1694 when the place was abandoned, to be resettled in 1704.[4] The only other forts built by the company on the Gold Coast in this period were Dixcove and Winnebah. An abortive attempt was made to settle the former in 1684, it being thought 'likely to be a place of trade', but building did not begin until 1692.[5]

Apart from these six forts built by the company, one, Frederixborg, was acquired by purchase from the Danes. The acquisition of this site, less than a mile from Cape Coast castle, was suggested by strategic, not economic, considerations.[6] Fortunately for the company, the Danes on the African coast were in a weak condition, and their commander was prevailed upon to sell Frederixborg to the English in 1685 for fourteen marks of gold.[7] The Danish government repudiated the bargain, but the African Company contrived to retain possession of the place, renamed it Fort Royal, and kept a sizeable garrison there until 1691. It was subsequently allowed to deteriorate into the condition in which Bosman saw it.[8] Another Danish fort, Christiansborg, was mortgaged to the English in 1685, but was redeemed four years later.[9]

The factories, as can be seen from the table, were settled and abandoned over and over again. Anashan, for example, in the thirty years between 1683 and 1713, underwent four periods of occupation and four of desertion, while Egya was three times settled and three times evacuated. Some factories, such as Tantamkweri and Lagoo in 1705, were withdrawn as unprofitable;[10] some such as Kommenda and Sekondi were abandoned as the

---

[1] T. 70/11, fo. 17d. [2] T. 70/50, fos. 164, 179d.
[3] T. 70/11, fos. 11d, 13, 15; T. 70/50, fo. 11. [4] Below, p. 268.
[5] T. 70/11, fos. 10, 25d. [6] *Cal. S.P. Col.*, 1675–6, No. 767.
[7] T. 70/11, fo. 11. [8] *Op. cit.*, pp. 45–6. [9] T. 70/11, fo. 20d.
[10] T. 70/5, fo. 4d.

result of hostility on the part of the natives or European rivals;[1] others may have been given up through a shortage of factors and soldiers to work them.[2] The abandonment of so many sites does not, however, reflect any discredit on the African Company; indeed, the company had little cause to be ashamed of its building record on the Gold Coast. Cape Coast was strengthened, six new forts built and one purchased, and several factories settled. The English interest in the Gold Coast was enlarged and consolidated in such a way that it is not fanciful to see in the company's activities in the last quarter of the seventeenth century a partial explanation for the eventual establishment of British rule in this region. British rule cannot and must not be regarded as having become at this early date the inevitable destiny of the Gold Coast; but we may conclude that, if the Gold Coast was to be subjected to a European power, it had already by 1700 become likely that either Britain or the United Provinces would be that power.

Despite the standing orders contained in the Establishment of 1676, the Chiefs of forts such as Accra and factories such as Anashan did not regularly correspond with London until the eighteenth century. They took their orders and received their goods from Cape Coast. Ophra and Whydah, however, corresponded with the company in London from the first, and consignments of goods were made directly to them. For certain administrative purposes such as staffing they were under the Agent-General. The chronology of English settlement in this region is even more obscure than on the Gold Coast. No settlement was inherited from the Royal Adventurers, and the factory at Ophra was probably first established in or soon after 1674.[3] Some years later, as we have seen, a new factory was set up at Whydah: correspondence from there began in 1683 when the factory was staffed by five men.[4] Captain Petley Weyborne, during his stay at Whydah, had factories at Popea and Appah, but these were short-lived and are not heard of again.[5] Whydah continued to rank as a factory until the beginning of the

---

[1] Below, pp. 267–8.

[2] T. 70/11, fo. 64d: 'Not enough men to send a factory to Alampo.'

[3] T. 70/76, fo. 18d.   [4] T. 70/1441. There were 9 men at Whydah in 1704, 11 in 1706 and 33 in 1713.   [5] T. 70/82, fo. 39; T. 70/61 fo. 77.

eighteenth century, when it began to be called William's Fort. The fortifications, however, were of earth not stone, and were liable to damage by rain.[1]

In addition to the forts and factories on the Gold Coast, the Agent-General usually had three or four small craft and twenty or thirty sailors at his disposal, as well as hired canoes with native crews. These were used chiefly for transportation and communication between settlements, rather than for trade, and the majority of the company's servants remained in or about their forts and factories conducting castle-trade. In the 'northern parts of Guinea', as we have seen, different methods of trading had to be adopted and the available men disposed accordingly. In 1684, for example, there were sixty-two men on the strength of James Fort in the Gambia. At the fort itself were the Second, a sergeant, corporal, gunner, steward, surgeon, smith, cooper, bricklayer, four carpenters and twelve soldiers, less than half the total strength. Five small vessels, with crews totalling twenty-nine, were trading on the coast and up-river, and eight more men were living at six out-factories.[2] The total strength of the Gambia establishment remained at between sixty and seventy until 1691, when the garrison was augmented by forty whites and seventy gromettos from Bence Island.[3] After the French assault on the fort in 1695, James Island was deserted, though it is probable that a few Englishmen continued to live in the region. Resettlement took place in 1699 and by 1705 there were fifty-five men on the strength. Thereafter numbers dwindled to thirty-four in 1708, and in the following year the fort was again deserted.[4] At Bence and York Islands, more men were employed at the main settlements and fewer in out-factories or ships. Until its evacuation in 1691, there were generally thirty or forty men at Bence Island. In 1704 after resettlement there were forty-six whites. At York Island there were forty-five in 1688 and about thirty in 1708.[5]

At its fullest extent, the company's African service employed well over three hundred white men besides castle-slaves. This point was reached just before the outbreak of war in 1689.

[1] T. 70/5, fos. 38, 60.   [2] T. 70/1441.   [3] T. 70/50, fo. 120.
[4] J. M. Gray, *op. cit.*, p. 148.   [5] T. 70/1445. Despite French attack, the garrison at York Island was kept up and in 1713 stood at 42.

There were then 188 men on the Gold Coast, 64 in the Gambia, 45 in the Sherbro, and 34 in Sierra Leone. The gromettos probably numbered about two hundred. In later years, numbers fell, as a result both of the company's poverty and of the difficulty of finding recruits in England, but as late as 1708–9 220 white men were on the establishment. Paying, feeding and housing these men involved an expenditure that went far towards offsetting any economic advantage which the possession of settled trading places might give.

Salaries, wages and allowances were first codified in the Establishment of 1676. The Agent-General received £400 a year, the three Merchants £200, £150 and £100 respectively, and all other officers £50. At Accra and Kommenda, the Chiefs were to have £150, the Second and Third £100 each. Soldiers were paid £12 a year, and the rates of pay for artisans were fixed by individual contracts, generally between £20 and £30. These were basic rates and were supplemented in all cases by allowances. The twelve officers at Cape Coast ate at the Agent's table, to which the company contributed £800 a year; the Agent himself received an entertainment allowance of £100; other ranks were given a weekly ration of bread and £13 a year to buy food. Even on the modest scale envisaged in 1676, therefore, salaries and allowances payable at Cape Coast alone cost nearly £3,500 a year. Later modifications were generally in an upward direction. The salaries of the Second and Third Merchants went up to £200 in 1677; living allowances were increased in 1678; and in 1680 the Agent-General was given a further £600 a year plus a gratuity of £200 at the end of three years' service in lieu of certain privileges of private trade which he had previously enjoyed.[1] The Agent's income thus exceeded £1,100, with free board and lodgings.

During the 'eighties the size and cost of the company's African establishment steadily mounted. The abolition of the Agency in 1687 did not lead to the expected saving, and by 1697 the cost of the officers' table at Cape Coast had reached £1,200 a year.[2] Economies effected by the reduction in the total number of men employed were largely offset by the high wages which in wartime had to be paid to skilled men to induce

[1] T. 70/77, fos. 61, 86–9; T. 70/78, fo. 100d.   [2] T. 70/50, fo. 174.

them to leave England. The revival of the Agency did nothing to lower costs, Sir Dalby Thomas drawing £1,000 a year, plus allowances, plus a commission of two per cent. on all returns from the Gold Coast.[1] By Thomas's time, the volume of the company's trade was much diminished, but the garrisons could not be correspondingly reduced, for the strategic value of the forts for the defence of English interests against the French was the company's strongest card and best hope for a favourable settlement of the trade. As late as April 1711, therefore, though the Agency was vacant through Thomas's death, there were still 135 men on the Gold Coast costing the company £3,076 a year in salaries and £2,281 in allowances for food.[2] Earlier the total cost had certainly been greater. Adding its expenditure in the northern region and at Whydah, the company's liabilities must have approached £10,000 a year.

Fortunately, both for the company's cash resources in London and for its employees, the greater part of these salaries was payable in Africa. Under the Establishment of 1676, officers were to receive two-thirds of their pay in gold on the Coast and the remaining one-third in England on the completion of service. Other ranks were paid entirely in Africa, though an optional scheme existed whereby allotments could be made to dependants in England. For paying these salaries and wages in Africa, gold was valued at £3 12s. an ounce. In the new Establishment issued in 1687, an attempt was made to depress wages by valuing gold at £4 an ounce. The soldiers at Cape Coast promptly mutinied, and a compromise settlement of £3 16s. an ounce was finally reached.[3] Under this arrangement the first 1,500 ounces of gold or thereabouts taken each year had to be appropriated to the payment of salaries and allowances of Gold Coast personnel, so that in several years after 1698, when the gold-trade was languishing, there was nothing left to remit to England.

Except for the emoluments of the Agent-General, the financial inducements which the African Company was able to offer

---

[1] T. 70/51, pp. 336–46.
[2] T. 70/1445. Of this total, Cape Coast castle accounted for £2,710, Accra Fort for £462 and Egya facory for £25.
[3] T. 70/11, fo. 17; T. 70/50, fo. 98.

cannot be regarded as particularly attractive, and recruiting was not always easy. Apart from the discomfort and danger of life in Africa, three deterrents were thought to be particularly important. In the first place, rumours reached England from time to time of arbitrary treatment of soldiers and civilians by officers of the company. Secondly, attempts were made to detain men beyond the terms of their agreement. And, thirdly, the arrangements for remitting home the effects of men who died on the Coast were seldom satisfactory. The company in London did its best to deal with all these abuses. The abolition of the Agency in 1687 was partly dictated by a desire to curb 'the exorbitant power which the former Agents practised', and instructions were sent to the Chief Merchants to avoid tyrannical actions.[1] After 1689 the temptation to retain time-expired men was great, but the company firmly resisted it. When two men wrote from the Gambia that they were being forcibly detained, the company informed its Agent there: 'Wee cannot retract our orders that you should permit any person out of their time to come away if desired, for the noise of any restraint . . . discourageth people to come into our service.'[2]   As for the remitting of dead men's effects, the company several times gave orders for the greatest care to be taken, and a large part of the correspondence between London and Africa deals with this subject.

To fill the gaps left by death, desertion (which was common), and retirement, many Irish, Dutch, French and Portuguese had to be recruited. In 1692 three-quarters of the men at Cape Coast were said to be foreigners.[3] The company's failure to send out adequate reinforcements forced its officers on the Coast to recruit from the human driftwood of many nationalities that found its way to West Africa. Commissioned officers, barring exceptional circumstances, were appointed only in England, but in the later years of the company's history wide discretion had to be left to senior officials who, subject to eventual confirmation from London, recruited writers and factors as well as other ranks, promoted soldiers to commissioned rank, appointed Chiefs of forts and nominated their own successors.

[1] T. 70/50, fos. 123, 123d, 129.   [2] T. 70/50, fo. 148.
[3] T. 70/11, fo. 25d.

Service in Africa gave scope for the highest qualities of skill, tact and intelligence. Ideally an officer needed to be versed in all the mercantile skills of accounting, to be familiar with the peculiar problems of a trade unlike any other, to be able to speak Dutch, French and Portuguese and to learn the languages of the natives, to be experienced in military engineering and siege-warfare, to know when to resent and when to accommodate disputes with traders of other nations, and finally to be able to conduct delicate negotiations in the complex inter-tribal politics of the African coast. And none of these qualities would be of much service to the company unless they were joined with the constitution of a horse and complete incorruptibility. Few, if any, approached this ideal. Some, like Booker of the Gambia, had a military flair; some like Thomas of Cape Coast were (seemingly) incorruptible; others were skilled in trade. But the general run of officers fell short not in one but in many of the qualities needed for success.

Complaints from London of the inefficiency and dishonesty of the company's employees begin in the earliest days and become more frequent; the replies are a blend of excuses and counter-accusations. Delation, especially after 1700, was common, so that it is difficult to know how seriously to take accusations of fraud or theft. Few officers completed their service without some recrimination. Private trade, dealing with interlopers or separate traders, and arbitrary conduct were the commonest charges. 'We have reason to complain', wrote the company in 1691, 'that our factors and some of the chiefs manage private trade, which is the way to encourage interlopers & ruine our stock by bearing the charge without having the advantage.'[1] A few years later: 'You have broak your trust by makeing private advantages upon our concernes and by assisting others in that trade.'[2] Such general denunciations were common. Particular charges of favouring or consorting with interlopers were made against Rogers at Sherbro, Bradley, Agent-General, and Ronan, a Chief Merchant. Accusations of private trade were made against Duffield at Whydah and Thurloe at Sekondi. Freeman and Hicks, Chief Merchants at Cape Coast, were dismissed for arbitrary conduct, a fault of

[1] T. 70/50, fo. 128d.   [2] T. 70/51, p. 87.

which Sir Dalby Thomas was frequently accused. Hanbury, who yielded James Fort to the French in 1695, was a coward; Chidley, one of his successors, a rogue; Freeman, who commanded at Sherbro when the French attacked in 1705, saved his own belongings and neglected the company's; and in 1707 Sir Dalby Thomas was obliged to dismiss the Chiefs of Sekondi, Dixcove and Anomabu for inefficiency and pusillanimity.

Instances of bad conduct are certain to be better documented than examples of good, but the former are too numerous to permit any conclusion other than that the company was, with a few exceptions, poorly served, and worse after about 1689 than before. Yet its officers were not all drawn from the dregs of Europe. To enter the company's service, they had to find securities who would enter into bonds for their good behaviour. Junior factors needed security for £400, merchants for £800–£1,500, the Agent-General for £2,000.[1] All securities were scrutinized by the Court of Assistants, and bad risks rejected. Over the years the sums required were increased, but, significantly, the company began to accept the officer's own bond. Few signs have been found of the company's recovering from these securities any substantial part of the damages it claimed to have suffered at the hands of its employees, and it is probable that in later years the bonds became little more than an elaborate formality.

Two principal reasons may be adduced for the shortcomings of the company's officers. In the first place, life in Africa was often miserable and uncomfortable, always precarious, and little conducive to hard work and application. A realistic appreciation of the chances of survival must have caused many men to live for the moment. Mortality rates were at times very high. In five months, for example, between November 1684 and April 1685, thirty-six men died on the Gold Coast and at Ardra, about one-quarter of the total strength.[2] Samples from the lists of dead suggest that one man died about every ten days, giving an average expectation of life on arrival of roughly four to five years.[3] Of sixty-four other ranks alive at Cape Coast in April 1685, eighteen were dead by the end of the following year. Drink, if it hastened death, made life more

[1] T. 70/1428.   [2] T. 70/1441.   [3] From T. 70/1440–5.

tolerable.[1] Morals were low; 'every man', wrote Henry Clarke from Bence Island, 'hath his whore for whom they steale'.[2] To the practice of bringing out wives from England the company offered no objection and even gave mild encouragement, but few availed themselves of the privilege.[3] For most men, West Africa was a place to get away from or to die in. While they lived, officers and men alike were at the pleasure of an arbitrary ruler. For the necessities and the comforts of life, they were largely dependent upon supplies from England retailed to them often at an exorbitant rate. The company, it is true, tried to check this abuse in 1688:

> We noe longer allow of a spunging house to make them pay extravagant rates for necessarys either for back or belly, but that att reasonable rates we will supply our warehouse with such clothes, hatts, shoes & stockings as you shall write for.[4]

That this instruction availed little is evident from Edward Kenyon's letter in 1703. Seeking support for his advancement either as 'seller' or factor, he wrote:

> without one of the two things, it is impossible to live here; all eatables and drinkables . . . being sold at least 200 *per cent.* above their prime cost in England. . . . To let you judge the whole by part:—English flower £1 10s. per hundred-weight; beere £1 10s. per dozen bottles. . . . From Gambia I writt to you; the conclusion of which was like most of my others, viz. begging. But least Mr. Frenchman has mett with it, it was for a few necessaries to wear, such as shoes, thread stockings, and a few callicoe shirts; but rather than by asking too much I lose all, pray doe not forget belly-timber and the maine supporter of life—good beere.[5]

In such fashion the servants of the African Company lived, and at death they rated no more notice than that given by Sir Dalby Thomas in 1708: 'Mr. Whitefield, chief at Annamaboe, lately dead; he purchased very ordinary slaves.'[6]

To live, work and die in such conditions, some incentive was

---

[1] Bosman, *op. cit.*, pp. 43–4. [2] T. 70/11, fo. 69d.
[3] T. 70/50, fo. 167d; T. 70/51, pp. 193, 236, 243. In 1702 some 'white women' were sent to Sierra Leone and Sherbro and allowed their keep.
[4] T. 70/50, fo. 59d.
[5] Historical Manuscripts Commission, *Kenyon MSS.*, No. 1083.
[6] T. 70/5, fo. 45.

S

needed beyond the reasonable but not over-generous salaries paid by the company. Service in the East Indies was made bearable, and indeed attractive, by the hope of a fortune at the end of it. In Africa fortunes were harder to come by. Unlike the East India Company, the Royal African Company was obliged, as we have seen, to place an absolute ban on private trading in 1680.[1] No doubt it was a necessary step; trade in Africa being so uncertain, the private interests of employees could be served only at the company's expense. But the prohibition removed for ever any chance that may have existed of honest service leading to a fortune. Thenceforth private trade could be carried on only by bad faith and fraud. That many did not scruple to break their oaths is clear. Contracts and promises were disregarded and the company's orders brought into contempt.

The directors of the company were not unaware of the need for incentives. In 1700, in an effort to stimulate activity, an elaborate commission scheme was introduced. At Sherbro, 20s. a ton on redwood, 5s. a cwt. on ivory, and 5s. a head on negroes was allowed, to be divided one-half to the Chief and one-quarter each to his Second and Third. At Gambia, the same scale, plus 10s. a hundred on hides and 4s. an ounce on gold, was put into operation. In 1702 the principle was extended to the Gold Coast.[2] On gold originating from the out-factories, a commission of £1 per mark was allowed, half to the factor responsible and half to the Chief Merchants at Cape Coast, who also received 10s. per mark on gold taken at the castle. On other goods, commissions were in proportion. But the innovation came too late. Increasingly factors at the company's African stations were finding themselves deprived of the trading goods without which returns could not be made or commissions earned. From 1705 to 1713 almost every letter from Africa contained a plea for goods. That of Joseph Holmes from the Gambia in 1707 is typical: it is 'a great pity that you should be at so great charge in maintaining a garrison there & ten per cent men & foreigners run away with the proffits—& your

---

[1] Above, p. 111. Occasional exceptions were made, but in principle the ban was maintained.

[2] T. 70/51, pp. 128, 172, 216.

servants can do nothing (but tell the sad truth) for want of proper goods'.[1]

We have estimated that the cost of salaries, wages and allowances of the company's African service was, at its greatest, of the order of £10,000. Building and maintenance, small craft for coastal communication and trade, and passages out and home may almost have doubled this charge. Thomas, in 1706, put 'coast charges' at £20,000,[2] and, though this may have been excessive for the Gold Coast alone, it cannot have been much of an exaggeration for the whole service. It remains to be seen what benefits accrued to the company from this heavy and recurring expenditure.

Three advantages were hoped for from permanent settlement. First, it was expected to facilitate trade by the presence of an experienced staff and a permanent stock of goods enabling barter to go on all the year round. Secondly, it was supposed to impress the African with the power or at least with the credit of those to whom it belonged. And, thirdly, it was designed as a defence against pirates and enemies. At certain times and in certain places, one or all of these functions were fulfilled by the company's settlements. But they were fulfilled much less often and much less completely than had been hoped. That the economic advantages of settlement, so clear and certain in theory, were in part illusions has already been indicated by the success of the interlopers and separate traders. There is ample evidence of a more particular kind to confirm this inference. Successive Agents at Cape Coast, as we have seen, advocated the discontinuation of ship-trade on the Windward Coast. The company refused to agree and in 1689 gave its reasons:

> Wee have often replyed to your opinion that wee should not send out Windward cargoes but leave all to your Factoryes, and as you putt it upon us wee have duely weighed our Intrest, and make it a great question whether wee had not better keepe our Castles only to protect our ships & trade in them than to sell any goods ashore, which requires such as extreame charge that our stock can scarse undergoe it, whereas what is sold aboard ship is without charge; & thereby a few soldiers & a cheife might be all our charge ashore, only to keepe an intrest with the country & to helpe

---

[1] T. 70/5, fo. 21 and *passim*.   [2] *Ibid.*, fo. 3d.

our shipps with fresh water. For by reasons of warrs or one thing or other you find to complaine on, wee can not have any dependance on a trade, nor know how to supply your occasions, but run on in a long account of remaines attended with many losses and casualties, wee know not how they happen; & what is done by shipping in a few months comes to some certaine end visible to us. Wee can not apprehend but that leaving the Windward Trade which sometimes hath been our cheife support (whilst the Castle hath not defrayed her owne expence) would be leaving the trade to other nations, especially the Dutch.[1]

One Agent-General admitted in 1682 that trading by ships was less costly than trading by factories.[2] 'It is unaccountable', wrote the company in 1699, 'that from all our out factories we should in so long time receive no gold, when at the same time the 10 per cent men make their voyages to satisfaction.'[3] At Whydah, in 1691, a factory was deemed necessary for preserving the company's interests, but 'the keeping thereof is all a loss'.[4] When Bence Island was evacuated in 1690, it was stated not to have defrayed its own charges.[5] As exports dwindled after 1700, the cost of maintaining the forts became greater proportionate to the trade they managed. In 1706 William Hicks reported from Kommenda that his takings did not meet a quarter of the charges of the place.[6] And at the last, in desperation, Sir Dalby Thomas was compelled in 1710 to free himself and his Chiefs from their obligations to the company on condition of themselves bearing the cost of the forts in their charge.[7]

One reason for the disappointments of castle-trade lies in the commercial characteristics of the Gold Coast. Trade, as we have seen, was subject to frequent interruptions by native wars; during such times the commerce of a fort or factory slowed down or ceased while the residents waited for the return of peace. A passing ship, meeting with no trade in one place, could sail to another where better luck might be found, but a permanent settlement was committed to sharing in the fortunes or misfortunes of the locality in which it was sited. Even in

---

[1] T. 70/50, fos. 95, 95d.   [2] T. 70/10, fo. 51.   [3] T. 70/51, p. 37.
[4] T. 70/50, fo. 122.   [5] Ibid., fo. 110.   [6] T. 70/5, fo. 9.
[7] T. 70/2, pp. 26–7.

peace local fluctuations in trade were marked, so that at one time or another almost every English settlement on the Gold Coast was described on the one hand as the greatest place for trade, and on the other hand as a burden to the company. The native traders, there is some reason to believe, preferred to deal with Europeans in ships rather than in castles: such anyway was the view of Agent-General Nurse in 1686 and Sir Dalby Thomas in 1707, and the reason is probably that suggested by Barbot, goods from settlements selling 25 per cent. dearer than goods from ships.[1] Certainly no evidence has been found to disprove the statement made by the company's adversaries in the House of Commons in 1691: 'that the English interlopers and other nations carry on their trade safer and as well on board their ships'.[2]

Settlement not only failed to yield the expected commercial advantages; it produced positive disadvantages and losses. Goods carried by interlopers or separate traders had, if unsold, to be brought back to England, where some part of their value might be recovered. Goods deposited in the company's warehouses, on the other hand, unless quickly disposed of, were almost certain to deteriorate. An inventory taken at Cape Coast in 1684 revealed goods that had lain in store for seven years. Damage and loss in this way must have been considerable, for in 1692 when the company in London was estimating that goods to the value of £60,000 or £70,000 were on the Gold Coast, the Chief Merchants were writing that they had nothing vendible left.[3] Fires, causing damage to stores and goods, were reported at Kommenda in 1686, at James Island in 1700 and 1704, at Whydah in 1706 and at York Island in 1710.[4] In war the forts were a temptation to the enemy, who systematically plundered James, York and Bence Islands, and in peace they invited and suffered from the embezzlements of the company's own employees.

To what extent European fortifications impressed and influenced the African must remain a subject for conjecture.

---

[1] T. 70/11, fo. 13; T. 70/5, fo. 34d; Barbot in Churchill's *Voyages* (1746), V, p. 274.
[2] Stock, II, p. 33. [3] T. 70/11, fos. 10, 25d.
[4] T. 70/5, fo. 13; T. 70/2, p. 22; T. 70/50, fo. 11, etc.

What is clear is that the establishment of a fort or factory drew the company into the expensive complexities of African politics. Ground-rents had to be paid for the sites of settlement, presents, bribes and loans distributed to the rulers and pretenders of many kingdoms. The full extent of this dabbling in African politics, which followed upon the establishment of a fort, will be examined later. For the present we may notice the pronouncement of John Snow in 1705: 'It is impossible to say what this concerning ourselves in the succession of their kings on suspicion they may be more inclined to the Dutch interest than ours hath cost both you and the Dutch, and I am very well sattisfyed nothing has been done to less purpose on either side.'[1]

Although the company itself was convinced that, as a means of carrying on trade with the natives, the forts cost more to maintain and staff than they earned, it clung to the belief that in the larger sense they were essential for the preservation of English interests in Africa. Its opponents, while challenging the capacity of the forts, in their existing state and under the company's management, to contribute to this end, did not seriously deny the principle: their proposals for settling the African trade invariably contained provisions for the upkeep of garrisons and strongholds. Parliament, too, though favouring now a joint stock and now a regulated company, never in the course of twenty years of discussion departed from the proposition that the forts must be preserved, and eventually, years after controversy had died down, came to their rescue with a subsidy. The question must remain a subject for speculation. On the one hand, the Spaniards, with every incentive to engage in the slave-trade, did not do so on any significant scale; they had no forts. The Portuguese, expelled from their forts on the Gold Coast in the first half of the seventeenth century, were obliged to trade in that region on terms less favourable than either English or Dutch.[2] On the other hand, Dutch and English interlopers appear to have managed well enough without benefit of settlement, while the separate traders, though entitled to use the Royal African Company's settlements as refuges, seldom did so.

---

[1] T. 70/102, pp. 47–50. Snow's letter is printed in Appendix V.
[2] Below, p. 276.

The capacity of the English forts to withstand assault by an enemy, when put to the test, proved wanting. Three, James, York and Bence Islands, were attacked by the French. All fell, through a combination of weakness and cowardice. None of the forts on the Gold Coast was directly attacked by another European power in this period, and their ability to resist must therefore remain in doubt. Cape Coast castle could probably have been defended against any assault that could reasonably have been expected to be launched against it, but it is extremely doubtful if any other fort could have withstood an expedition such as De Ruyter's in 1664. That no such expedition was launched must be attributed as much to a lack of interest on the part of the French as to the defence measures taken by the English. In the second phase of war, from 1702 to 1713, most of the English forts were in bad repair. Even Cape Coast was thought likely to be washed away by rain, and at Anomabu the fort was so ruinous that its occupants were 'afraid of being murdered by its fall'.[1] Although not subjected in this period to the ordeal of assault by Europeans, several forts on the Gold Coast belonging to the African Company and its rivals were attacked by natives. The results were scarcely encouraging. Cape Coast castle, as might be expected, withstood a siege engineered by the Fetuers in 1688, and Dixcove resisted attack in 1696. But Sekondi fell in 1694 and Anomabu in 1701; numerous other examples are recorded of African successes against European forts.[2] Indeed, Cape Coast and Elmina apart, the defence of the Gold Coast settlements against native attack depended less on fortification and more upon diplomacy and the dissensions amongst the African peoples of the region. At any time a concerted effort on their part could have driven the Europeans into the sea.

Nevertheless it remains true that the forts of the Royal African Company contributed something to the maintenance of a kind of balance of power on the African coast in which no single nation could easily achieve supremacy. Conceivably in 1700 France might have gained that supremacy; but the fact

[1] T. 70/5, fo. 42d.
[2] Churchill's *Voyages* (1746), V, p. 446; W. E. F. Ward, *History of the Gold Coast*, p. 87.

that England (and the United Provinces) possessed forts meant that the process would be difficult, expensive, possibly bloody, and probably not worth the effort. No nation was now willing to found its war-strategy upon the aim of winning West Africa; the forts, ruinous and undermanned as they were, were at least an insurance against the small-scale raids which were likely to be launched. In the broad sense they preserved English interests, the company carrying the national burden. The economic value was slight; the most obvious and immediate result of their existence was the creation, by the preservation of this balance of power, of the conditions in which interlopers and separate traders could flourish.

4. International Relations

In the train of settlement came problems of relations with other European powers established in West Africa giving rise to further expenditure by the company. To an extent greater than any other extra-European part of the seventeenth-century world, Africa was the resort of the ships and traders of many nations. English, French, Dutch, Portuguese, Germans, Scandinavians and Spaniards were to be met with; of the European nations, only the Italians and the Poles seem to be missing. Not all presented significant problems to the Royal African Company, and in certain parts of Africa, such as at Whydah, international relations seem to have been, if not harmonious, at least reasonably peaceful. In other parts, competition was keen, cold war endemic, and bloodshed never far away. That which gave an edge to the rivalry between nations was the possession of fortified settlements. To the aggressor, they presented a stationary target; to the defender, they were symbols of a hard-earned share in the trade. The effort and money lavished upon defending a nation's own forts and assaulting those of other countries were out of all proportion to the direct commercial advantages which, we have suggested, these permanent settlements conferred upon their owners.

In Africa, as in the Far East, the Dutch were our principal rivals. Their West India Company, impoverished after the conclusion of peace with Spain, had been in the course of the first fifty years of its existence deprived of the greater part of its monopolistic privileges. Only in West Africa did it cling to monopoly, and upon this trade, we may suppose, its main attentions were concentrated in the years following the reconstitution of 1674. Despite the loss of Goree to the French in 1677 and with it their footing in north-west Africa, the Dutch remained the strongest European power on the Gold Coast. In Elmina, a few miles west of Cape Coast, they had the largest and best-garrisoned fort in all West Africa. Axim, Kormantin, Accra and Mori, their principal settlements, were forts of a strength equal to or greater than their English counterparts. At the end of the seventeenth century, they were said to have 368 men on the Gold Coast, of whom nearly two hundred were at Elmina.[1] The total strength of the Royal African Company, as we have seen, fell only a little short of this figure, but was much more widely dispersed. While a statement by the Chief Merchants at Cape Coast that there were five Dutchmen for every Englishman can be accepted only as evidence of conscious inferiority, it is probable that on the Gold Coast the Dutch outnumbered the English by as many as two to one.[2]

By contrast to the Second Anglo-Dutch War, the war of 1672–4 produced no important repercussions in West Africa. The surviving records of the African Company at this date are extremely scanty, but it is likely that neither the English nor the Dutch were in a position to take the initiative. The English company had only just come into existence and did not wish to risk any part of its resources, while the West India Company was in the process of winding-up and refoundation. The interests of both appeared to call for a period of peace and consolidation, and to this end negotiations were set on foot in 1677 for the conclusion of a treaty between the two companies. The Dutch appear to have made the first approach, and on 31 January 1677 the Royal African Company obtained a licence to treat from the King.[3] Two commissioners, a director and a doctor of law, came over from Holland in August with a letter

[1] Sir M. Nathan, 'The Gold Coast at the End of the Seventeenth Century', in *Journal of the African Society*, IV, p. 3.
[2] T. 70/11, fo. 64d.   [3] *Cal. S.P. Col.*, 1677–80, No. 31.

from the West India Company expressing its hope of a friendly understanding.[1] The object which both companies particularly desired was a reciprocal agreement for action against interlopers: the encouragement given by one to those who infringed the monopoly of the other was seen to be disastrous to both. The English company, always a little uncertain of its power to mount effective action against interlopers, took counsel's opinion,[2] and, evidently satisfied, authorized commissioners of its own to treat with the Dutch. The text of the treaty finally agreed upon does not appear to have survived in the company's archives, but the Sub-Governor and some of the Assistants waited on the Duke of York in January 1678 to get approval of its articles.[3]

It remained to be seen whether this accommodation, concluded so easily and quickly in London, could be enforced in Africa. Again, records are scarce, but it is clear that Anglo-Dutch relations on the Gold Coast were little improved as a result of the treaty. As early as August 1679 the company was considering whether to continue the agreement or not;[4] in 1680 Agent-General Greenhill requested a man-of-war to defend English rights against 'the insolence of the Dutch and the frequency of interlopers';[5] and in 1683 he wrote that the differences with the Dutch on the coast would not be ended in his time.[6] By now the African Company had shed any illusions it may have had. 'It is our intrest', runs a letter of 1685, 'as much as wee can to obviate the incroachments of the Dutch for, if wee doe not, their good nature is to graspe all into their owne hands.'[7] For the next two or three years, relations appear to have been a little better,[8] but throughout the 'eighties grievances were accumulating on both sides. There were four main sources of friction: the encouragement of interlopers belonging to the other nation, the harbouring of deserters who fled from the forts of one to seek refuge in those of the other, the ceaseless intrigues in which the Agents of both companies bribed or incited native tribes to attack the other, and the siting of cer-

---

[1] *Cal. S.P. Col.*, 1677–80, No. 394; T. 70/77, fos. 47, 48.
[2] T. 70/77, fo. 48d.   [3] *Ibid.*, fo. 67.   [4] T. 70/78, fo. 65.
[5] T. 70/1, fo. 54d.   [6] T. 70/11, fos. 4d, 5.   [7] T. 70/50, fo. 3.
[8] T. 70/11, fo. 17; T. 70/50, fo. 33.

tain settlements, notably Kommenda and Sekondi, to which both companies laid claims.

Anglo-Dutch relations on the Gold Coast between 1691 and 1698 show clearly how little European alliances were regarded in Africa. The accession of William III might have been expected to bring about some relaxation of the tension. The Royal African Company itself believed that this would be the case, and wrote in June 1689 that 'as affaires now are, wee need not much feare the Dutch; their Prince of Orange being now our King, our alliances are very close & such as that wee now beleive none of their servants abroad dare violate', but added 'yet you must not trust them'.[1] A move was made for a new understanding in 1691,[2] but, before any progress could be made, events at Kommenda touched off the worst period in Anglo-Dutch relations in Africa since 1667. The situation at Kommenda was such that neither side had a legal title recognized by the other, while both were possessed of enough power to do harm, but not sufficient to force a conclusion. As in all disputes about European occupation, the English claimed to have been 'anciently settled' there. The Royal Adventurers had placed a factory there,[3] and the Royal African Company had been in occupation in 1673 and 1674. In 1681 the English had made an agreement with the king of Eguafo for the building of a fort; none was built, and the factory was destroyed by fire in 1686.[4] In the following year the English returned, only to have their representative evicted by the natives.

As the English moved out, the Dutch moved in. Their claim to the place was grounded on a right of conquest from the Portuguese, and on a deed of assignment from the king of Eguafo dated 8 September 1659.[5] Legal technicalities, however, mattered little; more important was that, when the English were ready to return, they were prevented from doing so by the fort which the Dutch had now built. In 1691 the English flag was pulled down, at Dutch instigation the English alleged, by the natives according to the Dutch themselves. Diplomatic action in Europe failed to produce any noticeable result and, when another English attempt at settlement was

---

[1] T. 70/50, fo. 97d.   [2] T. 70/169, fo. 83.   [3] G. F. Zook, *op. cit.*, p. 46.
[4] T. 70/50, fo. 11.   [5] T. 70/169, fos. 96–98d.

made in 1692, it was driven off by gunfire. At last in 1694 a foothold was gained, and the building of the fort begun. According to the English version, the Dutch did everything to hinder the operation, short of killing. Shots were fired at, but not into, the fort and over the heads of workmen in order to frighten them; a blockade was enforced; and. the king of Eguafo was incited to attack the English.[1] Nevertheless the fort was eventually completed, the Dutch being left, as Bosman put it, with 'a nice bone to pick'.[2]

Meanwhile disputes at Sekondi and Dixcove, though less well-documented, were reaching the stage of bloodshed. The English fort at Sekondi had been begun in 1685, chiefly because the Dutch were also building there.[3] In 1694 the natives of the place, set on by the Dutch, attacked the fort, plundered its contents, and massacred the men there. Bosman, who tells the story, does not mention Dutch participation, but the English were fully satisfied that their rivals were responsible.[4] Twelve years later the 'massacre of Sekondi' was still a bitter memory, and one Englishman, enraged by Bosman's 'Disingenuity, Partiality and Malice', undertook to write the true history of the affair, but does not appear to have completed the task.[5] At Dixcove, the English were more fortunate. This fort was begun in 1692[6] and on 6 August 1696, when still unfinished, was attacked by the natives. As at Sekondi, the Dutch were accused of having engineered the assault, but no supporting evidence has been found. This attack was beaten off, and the fort eventually completed.

Not surprisingly the acts of provocation and hostility directed against the Royal African Company are better-documented in its archives than those of which itself was the author. Neither company had much reason to be proud of its record. Bosman says nothing of the Dutch aggressions that have just been described; but the English archives are silent on his allegation that the African Company stirred up the king of Kommenda to fight the Dutch.[7] The English at Cape Coast had indeed explicit instructions 'diligently to countermine the designs of the

[1] T. 70/169, fos. 120–133d.   [2] Op. cit., p. 27.
[3] T. 70/11, fo. 11d; T. 70/50, fo. 3.   [4] T. 70/169, fos. 125–6.
[5] T. 70/5, fo. 11d.   [6] T. 70/11, fo. 25d.   [7] Bosman, op. cit., p. 30.

Dutch',[1] and there can be no doubt that both sides were guilty of concealed aggression on a number of occasions.

In 1698 relations began to improve. An agreement for the use of the landing-stage at Kommenda was patched up,[2] and some kind of understanding appears to have been reached by the companies in Europe. In 1700 and 1701 they were in friendly correspondence,[3] and, though no formal treaty was concluded, instructions were sent to Cape Coast not to countenance Dutch interlopers.[4] In 1702 the company wrote to its Chief Merchants: 'Wee have a very good understanding with the Dutch Guiney company, & they with us; they have sent to their Agents upon the coast to consult and agree with you in what shall be most advisable to promote trade.'[5]

As in 1678, however, friendly agreement in Europe did not mean harmony in Africa. Sir Dalby Thomas, the next Agent-General, though protesting his anxiety for an accommodation with the Dutch, was himself freely accused of promoting misunderstandings.[6] To him the Dutch remained 'the greatest Amboina rogues in the world'.[7] Nevertheless, an agreement of some kind between the African representatives of the two nations was reached, and no incidents comparable to those of the 'nineties were reported.[8]

Next to the Dutch, the most serious menace to the Royal African Company was provided by the growth of French power and influence in north-west Africa. It was an intermittent rather than a steady growth, periodically speeded up by the formation of a new French company to handle the African trade and lapsing into stagnation as the inevitable bankruptcy approached. Nevertheless, the years between the treaties of Nymwegen and Utrecht saw an impressive consolidation of the French hold on the Senegal river; the strengthening of Goree, captured from the Dutch in 1677; and the beginnings of penetration into the north-western interior. A French attempt to gain a foothold on the Gold Coast in 1688 was repelled by the

---

[1] T. 70/50, fo. 169d.   [2] T. 70/51, p. 7.
[3] T. 70/51, pp. 111–13; T. 70/170, fos. 23, 23d.
[4] T. 70/51, p. 38.   [5] Ibid., p. 254; cf. p. 322.
[6] T. 70/5, fos. 6, 7d, 37, 37d.   [7] Ibid., fo. 17.
[8] Ibid., fo. 47; H. A. Wyndham, op. cit., pp. 27–8.

Dutch, but in 1704 they achieved permanent settlement at Whydah and entry into the great slave-trade of that port. For most of the period, however, the main French effort was still in the north, just as the activity of the Dutch was concentrated on the Gold Coast. Of the three most active African powers in the last quarter of the seventeenth century, England alone attempted to spread her inadequate resources over both regions.

Anglo-French relations in north-west Africa in the later seventeenth and early eighteenth centuries revolved round two disputed issues. The French, in virtue of their long-standing interest in the Senegal river, claimed to exclude ships of other nations from its trade. At moments when their power was great and that of their competitors weak, they sought also to monopolize the trade of the coast between Cape Verde and the Gambia, including Rufisque, Joal and Portudal. The English, by the same token of long occupation, claimed the trade of the Gambia as their own. Neither side was as yet prepared to recognize the title of the other, and enforcement depended entirely upon which nation happened at any time to be the stronger. From 1679 to 1689 the French undoubtedly had the advantage. Their claim to the trade of the coast north of Gambia was, it is true, scarcely vindicated. In 1680 and 1681 two English vessels were seized for trading there, but in both instances the Royal African Company obtained full restitution or satisfaction.[1] Until 1688 English ships traded there without further interruption. But the Senegal itself and the gum-trade remained French preserves. In 1687 the English company discovered that African gum was a commodity suitable for use in the making of hats and reckoned that a hundred tons a year could be sold in London at £30 a ton.[2] In reply to orders from England, Agent Cleeve at Gambia promised to send a ship into the Senegal, the first evidence of an attempt on the part of the company to challenge the French position.[3] It failed, and furthermore led to an incident which embittered Anglo-French relations for many years to come. The English ship was intercepted and fired on by a French vessel at Portudal, and on a second voyage the English commander, James Jobson, seized

---

[1] Gray, *op. cit.*, pp. 103–4.   [2] T. 70/50, fo. 36.   [3] T. 70/11, fo. 34.

four Frenchmen and carried them to James Island.[1] The reprisals for this act were the beginnings of hostilities which were soon merged in the European war between France and England.

If the English failure to penetrate the Senegal is suggestive of their inferior strength, French success in trading in the Gambia amply confirms it. Between 1678 and 1681 several French factories were established in the river itself and territorial concessions secured from the natives.[2] The French remained there until 1687, trading above James Island and creating new demands amongst the natives for brandy and silver which the English could not easily meet.[3] The problem of how to deal with such competition was in some ways similar to the problem created by the interlopers. For, even when the company's agents had the necessary force, they were frightened of the consequences of using it. 'I am apt to beleive', wrote John Kastell in 1681, 'that in a shortt time the French will presume to goe up the river; now I only want your order signed to bear me harmless for preventing them, and you shall find I will keep them in subjection.'[4] Cleeve, in 1684, asked for similar instructions, but the company's answers, had any been preserved, would probably have been as guarded as those concerning interlopers. In 1686, following an incident in which an English ship was fired on in sight of James Fort, the company sought, but does not appear to have obtained, guidance from the King.[5]

The position in the years before the outbreak of war, therefore, was that the French, holding firmly to the Senegal as their own, had successfully challenged the English monopoly of the Gambia. In 1688 came evidence of the extension of their influence south of the Gambia. A French man-of-war sailed into the river 'spreading vague reports that it had orders to seize all vessels trading on the coast, that English influence was waning, that the English would have to give way to the French, and that if they met the English agent they would have his life'.[6] Sailing from there to Bissao in Portuguese Guinea, the

[1] *Ibid.*, fo. 34d; T. 70/169, fos. 51–2. [2] Gray, *op. cit.*, pp. 99–101.
[3] T. 70/11, fo. 28d. [4] T. 70/1, fo. 63d.
[5] Gray, *op. cit.*, pp. 104–5; T. 70/169, fos. 45d, 46.
[6] *Cal. S.P. Col.*, 1685–8, No. 1803.

Frenchman seized the English company's ship, *Lady Mary*, and a valuable cargo, killing one man and wounding another.[1] Though the English company continued for many years to reckon amongst its assets the damages thereby sustained and to press for satisfaction, no compensation was ever obtained.[2]

The war of 1689–97 was fought with great bitterness in northwest Africa and, though the French were ultimately left as the masters, the initial successes went chiefly to the English. John Booker, appointed Agent at James Fort in 1688, revealed unusual qualities of energy, resource and generalship, and, until his death in 1693, the French cause was a declining one. It is true that the English lost five ships in this region in 1689 and 1690, but Booker was successful in capturing three or four French vessels.[3] In 1692, reinforced by the arrival of forty men from Bence Island, Booker was able to put into effect his long-cherished plan of an attack on the French settlements in the Senegal and at Goree. His success was complete.[4] On 1 January 1693 the French governor of the Senegal surrendered, and on 8 February the campaign was completed by the capture of Goree.

For the moment French power in Africa had been broken, but the resurgence was swift and far more damaging to the English than their own efforts had been to the enemy. Through lack of men, Booker had been obliged to leave Goree deserted, and the French reoccupied it in the following summer, the inadequate garrison left in the Senegal surrendering at the same time.[5] Worse was to come. In December 1694 the African Company advised Booker's successor, Hanbury, of an impending French assault on James Island,[6] and in the following July six enemy ships appeared in the Gambia. Hanbury offered no resistance, the English garrison was forcibly evacuated, and the fort plundered and left deserted. Anglo-French rivalry in north-west Africa for the time being was over.

With the coming of peace in 1697, both sides attempted to re-establish themselves. In that year Brue was sent to the Senegal to begin his long and successful career in Africa, and in 1699

---

[1] T. 70/11, fo. 35; T. 70/169, fos. 55–7.   [2] T. 70/169, fos. 58, 58d.
[3] T. 70/11, fos. 36, 38d, 39; T. 70/50, fo. 134d.
[4] Gray, *op. cit.*, pp. 111–12.   [5] *Ibid.*, p. 114.   [6] T. 70/50, fo. 161.

the English resettled James Island. Neither company was anxious for a repetition of the events just described, and between 1699 and 1701 negotiations were begun in Europe for an agreement. There were many points of difference, principally French rights in the Gambia and English rights on the coast up to Cape Verde.[1] In 1700 the French company wrote asserting its claim to trade in the Gambia, but promising to instruct its agents to arrange with the English that prices of European goods and African products should be agreed upon, that the native chiefs of the region should be obliged to trade only with the companies, and that all interlopers should be discouraged.[2] The English company likewise instructed its agent at Gambia to settle the trade in amity with the French.[3] In 1701, though war was apprehended, orders were given for consultations with the French 'wherein we may at least have the equall advantages either for settling a peace on the coast or methodizing the trade with the natives'.[4] Even after war had begun the company approved of a correspondence being kept up with the French.[5]

These arrangements proved no more effective than the Anglo-Dutch agreement of 1678. In November 1702 James Island surrendered to a French force and was ransomed for £6,000 payable in bills of exchange drawn upon the Royal African Company. In 1704 it was again taken by a French privateer, and again ransomed.[6] The English were by now incapable of aggression, and their only satisfaction was that the unpaid bills continued to provide a fruitful subject for international discussions until at least 1727. In 1704 a fresh attempt was made to secure agreement between the two companies, and in the following year articles of neutrality were signed.[7] The French could not, however, control the activities of privateers of their own nation, even had they wished to do so. Both Bence and York Islands were attacked and plundered, and in 1708 James Island had to be ransomed for the third time, the French privateer on this occasion taking slaves, ivory

[1] T. 70/170, fos. 12d, 14d, 15, 22d.; *Cal. S.P. Col*, 1700, No. 536.
[2] T. 70/51, pp. 113–15.   [3] *Ibid.*, pp. 162–3.
[4] *Ibid.*, p. 194; Gray, *op. cit.*, pp. 125–30.   [5] T. 70/51, p. 298.
[6] Gray, *op. cit.*, pp. 133, 142.   [7] *Ibid.*, p. 144.

T

and gold. In the following year the Royal African Company abandoned Gambia, and, since the French company was also in a weak condition, the river was left to the separate traders.

Although the French had traded on the Gold and Slave Coasts for many years, it was not until the closing years of the seventeenth century that they became important commercial rivals of the English and Dutch in those regions. As early as 1670 there was a French factory at Ophra and, some time later, a lodge was occupied in the kingdom of Whydah. Continuous settlement at Whydah, however, did not begin until 1704.[1] Thereafter the development of the French slave-trade was rapid. Sir Dalby Thomas, alarmed by French success, wrote in September 1705 that the Whydah trade would be lost if a stop was not put to the new settlement.[2] In 1711 the English factor there reported that in the previous twenty-two months the French had carried away nine thousand slaves.[3] Despite this competition, Whydah in the war of 1702–13 had the appearance of a free port. Exactly what agreement was made between the English, Dutch, and French who traded there has not been discovered from the African Company's archives, but in 1706 Richard Willis, the English factor, wrote of his intention to enter into articles with the French, and in 1708 that he was renewing these articles, the Dutch having already done so.[4] The truce did not, of course, extend beyond Whydah; ships of the French company bombarded Cape Coast in 1703 and privateers were active all along the southern coast of West Africa, taking several of the English company's ships.

French plans to settle on the Gold Coast during this period came to very little. In 1686, according to French sources, an attempt was made at Kommenda which was repulsed by the Dutch.[5] In 1688 a settlement was actually made there, but the French were obliged to withdraw almost at once, again as a result of Dutch contrivance.[6] Fresh efforts were made at the beginning of the eighteenth century, but the French factory at

---

[1] Berbain, *op. cit.*   [2] T. 70/5, fo. 3d.   [3] *Ibid.*, fo. 77d.
[4] *Ibid.*, fos. 13, 55.   [5] Berbain, *op. cit.*, p. 39.
[6] T. 70/11, fo. 18; T. 70/50, fos. 71d, 91d; W. W. Claridge, *op. cit.*, I, pp. 125–6.

Assini was abandoned in 1705 and no further settlements made on the Gold Coast.

No European power, other than the Dutch and French, was of sufficient strength to disturb the trade of the Royal African Company, and its relations with Denmark, Portugal and Brandenburgh can be summarized briefly. Anglo-Danish relations in West Africa in this period were concerned entirely with the forts of Frederixborg and Christiansborg to which reference has already been made. In 1675 letters from Cape Coast suggested to the English company that the Dutch had a design to seize Frederixborg, a small fortified settlement close to and overlooking Cape Coast castle; the condition of the place was said to be such that they would certainly succeed.[1] The Dutch plan, if such existed, came to nothing, but in the following years the possibility of acquiring the Danish settlement was frequently discussed by the Court of Assistants. In 1676 a Dane, and in 1678 'a person', offered to put the English in possession, but, though the company was willing to listen to these proposals, nothing came of them.[2] The Danes in Africa, however, were at a low ebb, living precariously by trade with interlopers, and in 1684 or earlier their governor was obliged to mortgage Frederixborg to the English.[3] In 1685 the mortgage was converted into a sale by the payment of fourteen marks of gold, and the place (it could scarcely be described as a fort) passed into English hands. At the same time the other Danish settlement on the Gold Coast, Christiansborg at Accra, was mortgaged to the African Company.[4]

As soon as the news reached Europe, the conveyance was repudiated by the Danish authorities.[5] Negotiations proceeded throughout 1686 and 1687, in the course of which the English asserted the usual claim, based on assignments made by the natives in 1650, to prior occupation of the ground. The Danish king offered to repay the purchase price with interest, and for a time the company was uncertain how the dispute would end.[6] In 1688, however, an agreement was concluded and ratified whereby, in return for the renunciation of all claim to Chris-

---

[1] P.R.O., C.O. 1/31, No. 39.   [2] T. 70/76, fos. 81d, 84; T. 70/77, fo. 71.
[3] T. 70/80, fo. 81d.   [4] T. 70/11, fo. 11.   [5] T. 70/169, fo. 40.
[6] *Ibid.*, fos. 37d–38d; T. 70/50, fo. 16.

tiansborg and the payment of another £900, the English company was given an absolute title to Frederixborg.[1]

The African Company's reasons for wishing to gain possession of Frederixborg had more to do with defence than trade. Its relations with Portugal on the other hand were purely commercial. As we have seen, many of the middlemen upon whom the company leaned so heavily in the trade of north-western Africa were Portuguese or half-breeds of Portuguese origin. On the Gold Coast and at Whydah in the early years of the eighteenth century there are signs that the functions were sometimes reversed, the English playing the part of middlemen and supplying the Portuguese with slaves. The failure of the latter to win back settlements on the Gold Coast did not apparently deter them from trading there, for in 1690 or 1691 the African Company's Chief Merchants at Cape Coast, for no ascertainable reason, seized three Portuguese ships.[2] The company ordered immediate restitution, but it was not until 1697 that the dispute was concluded.[3] The obvious anxiety on the part of the English for an amicable settlement may have been caused by their recognition of the possibility of profitable commerce between the two nations. Certainly the period of Sir Dalby Thomas' Agency from 1703 to 1711, though one of decline and stagnation in most respects, saw some development of Anglo-Portuguese trade in Africa. In 1706 Thomas struck up relations with a partnership of two Englishmen and a Portuguese in Brazil and expressed himself very hopeful of the outcome.[4] In the same year Richard Willis at Whydah reported that he had sold ninety-four negroes to the Portuguese for thirty-five marks of gold.[5] The Portuguese were still anxious to gain a settlement on the coast, and in 1708 it was rumoured that the king of Portugal had offered the king of Prussia £50,000 for Gros Friedrichsburg.[6] In the meantime, the English company was drawing profits from the one branch of trade in which they appear to have had some advantage over the separate traders.

Welcome as they were, these benefits were insignificant com-

[1] T. 70/169, fos. 52–3; T. 70/50, fos. 63, 71d; T. 70/11, fo. 20d.
[2] T. 70/50, fos. 123–125d.   [3] Ibid., fo. 179d.   [4] T. 70/5, fos. 27, 34d.
[5] Ibid., fo. 29d.   [6] Ibid., fo. 45.

pared to the losses suffered and the expenditure incurred by the Royal African Company as a result of the activities of French and Dutch. In 1697 at the conclusion of the first phase of the war, the company estimated that it had lost £12,000 by French depredations before hostilities had begun, £10,000 by the French recapture of Senegal, £25,000 by the capture of James Fort in 1695 and £2,500 by the plunder of Sierra Leone.[1] All these items, especially the second, were probably exaggerated, but it is nevertheless clear that the company had suffered heavy blows. Between 1702 and 1708 further losses totalling £22,000 were claimed for the plunder of James Fort in 1702 and 1704, of Bence Island in 1704 and of York Island in 1705.[2] The value of the trade lost, as opposed to the material damage inflicted by the French, is incalculable, as are the expenses of 'countermining' Dutch intrigues on the Gold Coast. Very little of this expenditure was of the nature of positive investment. The advantage accruing to the company by the triumphant capture of Senegal in 1693 was negligible; forts such as Kommenda and Dixcove, after years of effort to get them established, benefited the company economically but little. Although it is possible to point to military operations in West Africa, such as the expulsion of the Portuguese by the Dutch or the French capture of Goree, that were both conclusive and profitable, the wars and intrigues of one European nation against another in the West Africa of the later seventeenth century were mostly of a kind in which the victors suffered only a little less than the vanquished.

5. Native Relations

The occupation of forts and factories must not, of course, be held solely responsible for the fierce rivalry of European nations engaged in the African trade. The root causes of that rivalry were the fluctuating and often inadequate supplies of African products and the absolute necessity that nations with West Indian possessions should obtain slaves. Settlement greatly magnified and intensified competition, but it cannot be said to have created it. When, however, we turn to the complex

---

[1] T. 70/169, fo. 118d.   [2] T. 70/175, reverse, pp. 34–7.

problems of the relations between European traders and the natives of Africa, we find that they were much more directly and clearly the consequences of settlements. On the Windward Coast and in Nigeria, for example, where no settlement was made, European contacts with native merchants and rulers were simple. Customs were paid and might be a source of friction. But with no permanent 'interest in the country' the Europeans could switch from one place to another, and, because there was no settlement to attract it, trade remained dispersed rather than concentrated at a few known markets. Where settlement took place, permanent relations with rulers had to be established and some kind of *modus vivendi* reached.

The Europeans themselves might well have preferred, once it had become clear that conquest and occupation were out of the question, that this *modus* should be as simple as possible and that contacts should be restricted to purely mercantile transactions. Over a large part of the West African coast this was roughly the situation. On the Gold Coast, however, the English, like the Dutch, were unable to avoid, even had they wished, closer relations with the African nations. Few of these nations were large or homogeneous; those of the coastal region, Kommenda, Fetu and Saboe, with which the English had most to do, were quite small. But each appears to have had connexions, or been able to make alliances, with other and more powerful states inland. Thus wars begun upon some trifling pretext spread easily and far, and armies of several thousand men, equipped with firearms, took the field. From the European standpoint, this situation had one great merit and many drawbacks. The almost incessant wars between kings who could seldom entirely destroy one another were immensely productive of slaves. This was the advantage. But while the Europeans reaped this harvest, they suffered, as we have seen, from the interruptions to trade which war entailed and which could bring the business of a fort or factory almost to a standstill. Trade could rarely be guaranteed: 'I must confess this trade to be a lottery', wrote Josiah Pearson from Whydah, and his remark applies to the trade of the greater part of West Africa.[1] And because no single native ruler had the power to

[1] T. 70/51, pp. 155–6.

impose his will, the Europeans were fatally tempted to meddle in the tangled quarrels of Gold Coast politics in an effort to secure advantages which in a country with a centralized government could have been obtained by negotiation.

The problems of native relations at the end of the seventeenth century may be considered as having their roots in three sets of circumstances. In the first place, the forts which the Europeans built in Africa, like the castles of the Middle Ages, attracted natives who settled under their walls. They came possibly for protection, but also no doubt to make a living out of the needs of the white men. Fishermen, salt-makers, the crews of the canoes extensively used for coastal communication, poultry-farmers and market-gardeners found employment in this way. Here also native brokers and merchants and the agents of up-country traders and rulers resided either temporarily or permanently.

The populations of these towns seem to have fluctuated a good deal. Elmina, according to Barbot, had 1,200 houses in 1678, but was later much reduced by war and disease.[1] Tylleman in the last decade of the seventeenth century gave some indication of the size of the coastal towns in his day, though his accuracy is unchecked.[2] At Accra, for example, he thought that sixty men with guns could be raised from the negro settlement about Fort James, and five hundred from about the Dutch Fort Crevecœur. From Cape Coast town the English could call on four hundred armed men, while the native settlements at Fort Nassau could supply the Dutch with one hundred. Elmina, according to Tylleman, yielded several thousand men, all with guns and well-trained, a very different report from Bosman's of the same date. Cape Coast, like Elmina, was smaller about 1700 than it had been twenty years earlier. Barbot described it as containing 'above five hundred houses',[3] but in 1707 an English factor wrote to the company: 'that in his 13 years being there he never did see Cape Coast town in so despicable a condition, that there is no person of note or reputation & but few free people live there'.[4]

Over these negro towns the Dutch appear to have exercised a

[1] H. A. Wyndham, *op. cit.*, p. 16.   [2] Sir M. Nathan, *op. cit.*
[3] Barbot in Churchill's *Voyages* (1746), V, p. 168.   [4] T. 70/5, fo. 46.

fairly strict supervision, raising taxes and administering justice. In the early history of the English Royal African Company, there is no evidence of the same being attempted. By 1691, however, the company was alive to the advantages that might thereby be gained and wrote to its Chief Merchants at Cape Coast: 'Wee hereby require you to insist upon as good termes with the natives where wee have fortifications as the Dutch makes with their neighbours.'[1] In 1702 the company ordered that:

> the natives, traders and inhabiting in our negro town under our protection & cheif castle should signe a palavara or obligation not to dispose of any gold but for goods out of our store, provided we have the goods they want . . . wee order that you encourage such Capasheers or chief traders as will begin and promote this design, and to make the most considerable of them cheif Capasheers of the negro town under our castle.[2]

In the following year taxation of town-dwellers was proposed 'for the benefitts they enjoy'.[3] No regular system of taxation appears to have been established at this date, though Sir Dalby Thomas thought that it might be done.[4] The company was not entirely without a sense of responsibility towards the inhabitants of its towns and, apart from providing them with protection, sent out John Chiltman in 1694 to be schoolmaster to the children living near Cape Coast castle.[5]

Whether the government of these towns was carried on by regular courts or merely by occasional interventions does not appear. At Cape Coast in Bosman's time, all power was in the hands of a mulatto called Edward Barter. Bosman thought little of him, and his career was more harmful than serviceable to the company. In July 1702 the company wrote to Cape Coast:

> We find you are sensible how much wee have suffered in our trade by Ned Barter's promoting his own private interest before our common good, his dealing with & giving encouragement to

---

[1] T. 70/50, fo. 123.   [2] T. 70/51, p. 214.
[3] *Ibid.*, p. 322.   [4] T. 70/5, fo. 50.
[5] T. 70/50, fo. 139. This is probably the earliest example of English education in Africa. The schoolmaster was to teach the children of Africans, not only half-breeds.

other traders, which gives us good assureance you will not only use all endeavours to seize his person & estate in order to make satisfaction for the murther he has committed and the damage he has done, but will be very carefull that none of our servants under your care shall practise the like for the future.[1]

Barter thereupon fled to the Dutch for protection, got it, and died at Elmina in 1703.[2] No more profitable to the African company was the career of John Kabes, a Kommenda negro. He began as a friend to the Dutch but, according to Bosman, was responsible for inviting the English to build their fort at Kommenda.[3] For twenty years or more, Kabes served one side or the other, and quarrelled with both.[4] In the diary of William Baillie, from 1714 to 1716, he appears as the chief man in the English town of Kommenda and is described as the 'company's servant'.[5] His main functions were to ensure that his people traded only with the English and to influence up-country nations to do the same. But he discharged neither to the satisfaction of the company's Chief. Baillie did not believe in his boasted influence with the King of Ashanti and noted several instances of the 'ways of trade' from the north being stopped by Kabes' disputes with inland peoples. At the same time, while owing money to the English, Kabes intrigued and traded with the Dutch. The value set upon this puppet ruler is shown by an entry in the diary which follows one of the numerous quarrels: Kabes threatened 'he'll stay no longer at this place to be constantly troubled but go live in the bush; whereupon I told him he might live where he wou'd for any good he does the company'.

Although, as we have seen, the English at Cape Coast, Kommenda, and probably at other places, were coming to exercise authority over the towns beneath their walls, their legal standing on the Gold Coast approximated more to that of tenants than sovereigns. The circumstances under which settlement was originally made varied no doubt from place to place, but it is probable that most forts and factories were established by invitation, or at least with the consent of the

---

[1] Bosman, *op. cit.*, pp. 44–5; T. 70/51, p. 253.
[2] T. 70/13, fo. 47.   [3] Bosman, *op. cit.*, pp. 26–7.
[4] W. W. Claridge, *op. cit.*, I, pp. 164–5.   [5] T. 70/1464.

local king or magnates. Settlement on any other terms would have been difficult. Some kind of bargain would normally be struck between African and European whereby the latter received permission to build and trade. This bargain might include a contract to pay rent for the ground to be occupied, in which case something like the relations of landlord and tenant would come into existence. The sites of certain European forts were sometimes claimed to have been acquired as freeholds: Thomas Crispe, for example, deposed that he bought the land on which Cape Coast was built in 1650 for goods to the value of £64, and the Dutch, in their disputes with the English over Kommenda, produced a copy of a deed of sale from the king of Eguafo.[1] It is, however, likely that the native parties to such transactions would have put a different construction upon them.

Ground-rents were certainly paid in respect of many forts and factories, and they proved important as a means of embroiling the Europeans in African affairs. It is well-known that the capture by the Ashantis of the Note of the lease of Elmina marks their first formal contact with the European settlements on the coast.[2] The relations of the English with the ground landlords of Cape Coast are less well-known but illustrate the same process. The castle lay in the small coastal kingdom of Fetu, and it was from this king that Crispe had obtained his concession in 1650. In 1696 the rent paid was nine marks of gold (or £288, valuing the gold at £4 an ounce), and the same king received a further six ounces for the company's factory at Anashan.[3] The early history of the relations between the company's Agents and this kingdom is obscure, but according to Barbot English influence extended to sending two representatives to the supreme court of Fetu held at Abramboe, twenty-seven miles inland.[4] Relations were not, however, always as harmonious as this might suggest. In September 1688 the king, for reasons that have not been ascertained, marched on Cape Coast with 4,000 men, laid siege to it, and demanded a ransom of 120 bendas of gold. According to the English account, this attack was concerted by the king with the Dutch at Elmina and

[1] T. 70/169, fos. 35–36d.   [2] W. E. F. Ward, *op. cit.*, pp. 115–16.
[3] T. 70/661.   [4] Barbot in Churchill's *Voyages* (1746), V, p. 172.

one of its objectives was the seizure of Fort Royal, the former Danish settlement, overlooking the castle.[1] The attack failed, but relations with Fetu were bad for many years. Doubtless the king exploited differences between Dutch and English; in 1694 he was reported to be a friend to the former while his dey or vizier was said to favour the latter.[2] The Fetu people were of course well-placed to interfere with trade coming down from the north, and to channel it either to Cape Coast or to Elmina as their advantage went. In 1706 Sir Dalby Thomas was moved to write that if he had 150 well-chosen soldiers at Cape Coast he could and would destroy Fetu and 'foarse an inland trade'.[3] He thought that a settlement in that country might have the same effect, and in 1708 he reported that he had given leave for 'Cimbio, a town belonging to the Fetue country to be settled'. The connotation to be put upon this statement is uncertain, but the terms were that the inhabitants of the place were to pay one-fifth of their crops, corn and yams, to the company. Thomas believed that he could make similar arrangements all over Fetu, and also oblige the fishermen to pay a quint.[4] It is clear, therefore, that just as Dutch influence extended beyond their towns over the country of Axim,[5] so English authority was moving inland, though much more slowly. The rulers of a small kingdom such as Fetu, though determined to extract every advantage both from their own geographical position and from Anglo-Dutch dissensions, were probably not entirely unwilling to accept a measure of protection. For their own purposes they could involve the Europeans in war, and, as a last resort, could shelter around the castle. Thus in January 1711 the Fanti invaded Fetu, partly in order to capture slaves and partly because the Fetuers were then regarded as Anglophile, while the Fanti were notoriously in the Dutch interest. On this occasion most of the Fetu women and children were killed or taken, but the men escaped to Cape Coast.[6]

Through the Fetuers, the company was brought into touch not only with the Fanti but with the Saboes and many other

[1] T. 70/11, fo. 20.   [2] *Ibid.*, fo. 59.   [3] T. 70/5, fo. 6.
[4] *Ibid.*, fo. 50.   [5] H. A. Wyndham, *op. cit.*, p. 17.
[6] T. 70/5, fo. 74; cf. Barbot in Churchill's *Voyages* (1746), V, p. 294.

peoples of the Gold Coast. But even more effective than the ground-leases in embroiling the English in native affairs was the fierce international rivalry described in the previous section. Just as the Africans themselves exploited European rivalries for thier own purposes, so English and Dutch intrigued to set tribe against tribe. We have already noticed accusations by the English that the Dutch incited the natives to attack Sekondi in 1694. The Dutch themselves in the same year were involved in war with the Kommendas, another coastal people. The English were not slow to make the most of the situation and encouraged the king of the Kommendas in his efforts. The Dutch, seeking allies, engaged the Fanti as mercenaries and paid them £900, whereupon the English are said to have paid them a further £900 to remain neutral.[1] Similarly, in 1694 the Assims and Saboes were encouraged by the English to attack the king of Fetu, then in the Dutch interest.[2] Intrigues of this kind are common in Gold Coast history, and these examples are sufficient to show how the competition between Europeans both promoted and was served by the rivalries of the warring kingdoms and peoples of the coast.

The position of the English, and indeed of all Europeans on the Gold Coast, was extremely difficult. Partly because they hoped to gain advantages over their rivals, partly because they were unable to avoid doing so, they were drawn into quarrels which they had not sufficient force to conclude. No English 'army' appears to have taken the field, for the men available were too few. The use of forces of native auxiliaries under European command might have provided a solution, and Dalby Thomas was of the opinion 'that there ought to be a force to keep the blacks in subjection & 1000 negroes in arms would effectually secure the trade to you'.[3] In default of such troops, the only tools that could be used were bribery and diplomacy, terms that were almost synonymous. From the 'trifle of a dashee' (gift or bribe) to persuade the small trader to come to Cape Coast instead of to Elmina to the subsidies paid by Dutch and English to the Fanti and Denkyera, bribery was a normal condition of the transaction of almost every kind of

---

[1] Claridge, *op. cit.*, I, pp. 147–51.   [2] *Ibid.*, I, p. 144.
[3] T. 70/5, fo. 64d.

business. Sometimes it took the form of a loan. Between 1692 and 1698 the accounts of the king of Fetu in the Cape Coast ledgers show him to have owed the company well over £1,000. The 'king of the Arckanyes' owed £1,100 and the king of Saboe £250. In 1699 twenty-one Gold Coast notables owed the company about £4,000: they include the king of Eguafo (£2,000), Little Taggee (£400), the Braffo of Fantyn (£250), and John Kabes, Cabbasheer of Kommenda (£250).[1] The ledgers contain many other entries, 'to sundry accounts trusted him' or 'to gold lent him'.

The impression left by both correspondence and accounts is that few of these loans were repaid in full. In 1690 for example the Chief Merchants reported that the wars on the coast had been concluded but that the company was 'like to loose the mony lent'.[2] Four years later, after the defeat of Fetu, they wrote that the conquerors (presumably the Saboes) required a loan, adding that what had hitherto been lent 'hath been a charge without profit to the company'.[3] John Snow, whose balanced appreciation of the European position on the Gold Coast is printed as an Appendix, thought not only that long-standing debts could not be collected but that any attempt to do so would have disastrous political consequences. He preferred to make small gifts instead of granting large loans, and he was probably right. His own views have already been quoted;[4] Bosman, recording that both English and Dutch paid large sums in bribes and subsidies, believed that they enjoyed an equal power, 'that is none at all'.[5] It is possible, however, that the Dutch enjoyed more success with the natives than the English. This at least was the belief of the African Company which wrote in 1691 to the Chief Merchants at Cape Coast:

We understand the Dutch are by capitulation with the Kings of the Countries impowered to seize such natives and their goods who trade with any other European native but they of their nation, that they have authority to seize & confiscate the canoes, goods & persons of such natives who they shall take goeing aboard or comeing from any interloper of theirs or of any other nation, or seeking to trade with any but their companies servants, as also to

---

[1] T. 70/661. [2] T. 70/11, fo. 22. [3] *Ibid.*, fos. 58d, 59.
[4] Above, p. 262. [5] Bosman, *op. cit.*, p. 52.

lay a duty or port charge on any Porteguez who shall desire to come ashore or seeke protection; but such advantage as our factors make hitherto hath prevailed against our interest, & none espouses our advantage with regard to the great charge wee are at. What can be done with your neighbouring governments, put in execution; it may be of service to prevent interlopers carrying the trade from us & make us more vigourously to prosecute the trade.[1]

Intervention in native affairs was not only costly, but almost always failed to achieve the desired result and sometimes initiated wars which ruined trade. The murder of the king of the Kommendas in Cape Coast castle, for example, began a war in which the company's ally was the king of Saboe.[2] This event proved very unfortunate, as the company pointed out in a letter of 1700:

> You have, by suffering the king to be murdered in our castle brought an odium upon all our managers and our whole affaires, encreased the debt you pretended to lessen, and entailed a charg which to us has no prospect of an end, and by this means given all our compettitors in the trade an advantage over us.[3]

Other instances of the futility of intervention can be adduced. In 1709 Sir Dalby Thomas reported that the Queen and Cabbasheers of Fetu, though supported by the English, were 'very villainous in turning the trade from us underhand'.[4] In the same year he wrote that the king of Eguafo who had received many favours from the company now stopped the trade.[5]

For an explanation of the failure of bribery and diplomacy, the Europeans found a ready answer in the character of the African. Permanent understandings were thought by some to be impossible. 'A blackman', wrote Snow, 'forgetts all obligations but the present; those are his friends & his masters that dashee him offenest & allways (in negroes English) does him well.' He added that the trusting of a negro was a sin against the company hardly to be forgiven.[6] Bosman concurred: 'The negroes are all, without exception, crafty, villainous and fraudulent, and very seldom if ever to be trusted; being sure to slip no opportunity of cheating an European nor indeed one another.

---

[1] T. 70/50, fo. 123.   [2] Claridge, *op. cit.*, I, p. 153.   [3] T. 70/51, p. 87.
[4] T. 70/5, fo. 58.   [5] *Ibid.*, fo. 64d.   [6] Appendix V.

A man of integrity is as rare amongst them as a white falcon!'[1]
There is no need to quarrel with these sweeping judgments. No
doubt those made by the Africans upon the European, had
they been preserved, would have been substantially the same.
Relations developed in an atmosphere of mutual suspicion in
which both sides felt free to break promises.

The most complete statement by an Englishman upon the
subject of native relations in this period is contained in John
Snow's letter to the company in 1705.[2] The policies there suggested were unorthodox and were never adopted, but they
give an interesting indication of the kind of problems with
which the company had to deal. In explaining the company's
many failures, Snow believed that 'that which challenges the
first place is the perpetuall force and constraints put on the
blacks to trade nowhere but with the forts'. Snow proposed
that no violence of any kind should be offered. Treat the
negroes, he advised, 'with a kindness very dunstable[3] . . . there
being no people on earth that you can gaine a point sooner of
than the blacks, if soft & easy methods are used'. 'All other
methods of violence', he continued, 'served only to raise devills
that none as yett have had the good fortune to lay.' Ground-
rents and customs should be punctually paid, old debts forgiven, and no new ones contracted; instead presents must be
given 'to spirit trade downe'. Next to violence as a cause of the
company's misfortunes, Snow placed 'the concerning our selves
in the succession of their kings on suspicion they may be more
inclined to the Dutch interest than ours'. He concluded with
proposals for an agreement with the Dutch to preserve the
status quo and make no new settlements.

Sir Dalby Thomas, Agent-General when Snow was on the
Gold Coast, acted, or was accused of acting, contrary to every
one of these proposals. He stopped payment of the ground-
rent of Winnebah as a punishment to the natives for allowing the Dutch to settle at Beraku, and in 1708 he refused
the Braffo of Fantyn the rents for Anomabu and Egya on the
excuse that there was no trade.[4] He dabbled in African politics
continuously, and, as Snow forecast, to little effect. In 1706,

---

[1] Bosman, *op. cit.*, p. 100. [2] Appendix V.
[3] Dunstable = Straightforward. [4] T. 70/5, fos. 28, 49.

for instance, Pearson, the company's Chief at Anomabu, wrote that Thomas was 'mightily imbroiled with palavers in the country particularly about Cape Coast, the Saboes, Fetues, the Aquaffo country, besides John Cabess, all being utter enemyes to Sir Dalby'.[1] Finally, he obstructed, or was alleged to have obstructed, an understanding with the Dutch, though an agreement of sorts was eventually reached.[2]

Whatever his shortcomings in other directions, however, Sir Dalby Thomas must be credited with shrewdness and perspicacity in recognizing in the Ashanti a new and formidable power on the Gold Coast and in seeking their alliance. In the first thirty years of the company's history, no trace has been found of the Ashanti, either as traders or warriors. They were consolidating their northern kingdom and preparing for the series of conquests which in the eighteenth and nineteenth centuries were to raise them to the position of the greatest power in West Africa. In or about 1700 they fought the Denkyeras and won victories which established them as a first-class power.[3] To support this position and to strengthen it still further, guns and gunpowder were essential, and from soon after 1700 Ashanti traders began to appear at the coastal forts. Thomas saw in them the counterweight which he needed against the Fanti who acted, if in anyone's interest but their own, on behalf of the Dutch. He was, too, the first of a long line of Englishmen, soldiers, writers and administrators, to discover in the Ashanti qualities which were thought to be lacking in other African peoples. In 1706, for instance, the king of Ashanti sent his cousin to Dixcove with a present of rock gold for the English; Thomas' admiring comment was 'that this king is the best of them, for he returns dashee for dashee'.[4] Relations being thus established, trade went well. In 1709 there was 'great trade from the Ashantees'; the trade, Thomas concluded, was so important and Ashanti friendship so valuable that 'you can't be to generous to the king'.[5] The Fanti, as might be expected, resented the English connexion with Ashanti and threatened to attack Fetu in 1709; as we have seen,

[1] T. 70/5, fo. 9.   [2] *Ibid.*, fos. 37, 37d, 47d.
[3] Claridge, *op. cit.*, I, pp. 197–200.   [4] T. 70/5, fo. 11.
[3] *Ibid.*, fos. 56–7.

they did so in 1711.[1] In securing the Ashanti alliance, however, the English had won an important diplomatic victory over the Dutch, and it was unfortunate for the company that bankruptcy and the virtual cessation of exports prevented the exploitation of this opportunity. In 1710 three hundred Ashanti traders intending to trade at Cape Coast found it lacking the goods they required, and were obliged to go instead to Elmina.[2]

By 1714–16, the period of William Baillie's diary, the Ashanti trade had become the chief concern of Kommenda.[3] The arrival of parties of merchants from Ashanti was frequently recorded; they brought chiefly gold and slaves, and their requirements were 'guns, sheets, pewter, brass, large perpetts, tallow & powder'. From the palavers and incidents related by Baillie it is clear that, although Ashanti power was growing rapidly, it was still incapable of keeping the 'ways of trade' down to the coast free from interruption. The chief agents of dislocation were a people called the 'Cuifferoes', whom Baillie described as 'at present onely a scatterd nation harrassing their neighbours whenever they have opportunity, onely liveing by plunder & roguery'. Several times in 1715 the course of trade with Ashanti was stopped by these people. An entry in the diary for 9 July well illustrates the complexities of Gold Coast politics, rendered even more intractable by the existence of such semi-nomadic nations:

> the Dutch had hired a private warr, vizt. the Fanteens against the Commenda or Aqwaffoe people for 40 bendys—in order to reinstate Tagee Cooma in that kingdom, and those Fanteens have agreed with the Cuifferoes, if they will first help them in their design against Aquaffoe, they will afterwards assist them against John Cabess.

But even when quarrels and wars were not spoiling the trade, the lack of proper goods prevented the consolidation of Anglo-Ashanti commercial relations. The Asantahene exchanged friendly messages with Baillie, but he could promise no more than that his traders should first come to the English fort at Kommenda. This they did, but, failing to find what they wanted, were often obliged to buy elsewhere.

[1] *Ibid.*, fos. 64d, 74.   [2] *Ibid.*, fo. 67d.   [3] T. 70/1464.

U

Fast as the Ashanti power was growing its appearance was too late to be of any real service to the Royal African Company. Had the Ashanti succeeded in conquering the coastal lands and imposing peace on them, the slave-trade might perhaps have languished, but the gold-trade would have flourished. But while they were still only beginning their two centuries of growth, the company had already passed into that condition of commercial paralysis in which it was to linger until 1750.

7

THE COMPANY IN THE WEST INDIES

1. Deliveries and Prices

For the master and crew of a slaving-ship, the last sight of the African coast must have been an occasion for relief and congratulation. Two-thirds of their voyage, it is true, still lay before them, and for the next few weeks they would have beneath their feet a cargo as difficult to handle as any on the seven seas. But to be clear of West Africa and its deadly diseases was enough to brighten the mariner's hopes of survival. Nor should the danger of violence from the slaves be exaggerated. Mutinies or revolts were not unknown, but they seem generally to have occurred before a ship was out of sight of land. Once the African coast dropped below the horizon, the negro, knowing nothing of ships or how to work them, was at the mercy of his owners. If he rebelled, it was probably from hopeless despair rather than with any plan of escape. Such despair might as easily take the form of suicide, as in the case reported by Captain Blake of the *James* on 17 April 1676: 'This afternoon I had a stout man slave leaped overboard and I hoysted out my pinnace and sent her after him, and just as they came upp with him hee sunke downe. Alsoe my cockswaine runn downe his oare betweene his armes, but hee would not take hould of it, and soe drowned.'[1] Little evidence has been found at this time of violence directed against the master or crew after a ship was clear of Africa; only once do we find in the accounts of the disposal of slaves the item 'Condemned & burnt for killing a seaman'.[2]

But if the master's problems were eased, the company's were

[1] T. 70/1211.   [2] T. 70/937, 20 February 1677.

not. Its record in West Africa, we have seen, was not a happy one. Profits could not easily be extorted from the trade of that region, and the charges which they had to cover were very great. Turning to the third and last sphere of the company's operations, the West Indies, we might expect to find more favourable conditions. If the profits in Africa were small, could they not be augmented in the colonies? If one 'leg' of the trade was unrewarding, might not another provide compensation? These are the assumptions with which many historians of the slave-trade have approached their subject. For certain periods they are probably valid assumptions. But the suggestion of this chapter will be that the years of the company's monopoly were not one of those periods. On the contrary, it will be shown that almost every stage in the trade from Africa to London was marked by losses which whittled down and often extinguished such profits as had been wrested from Africa. The West Indies, far from enlarging the company's profits, were their graveyard.

Losses began at once with the mortality of slaves on the Middle Passage, a subject which has (properly) been chiefly considered in terms other than economic. The death-rate varied enormously from ship to ship, and from voyage to voyage. Few ships can have come through with a mortality of less than five per cent. and few can have had the terrible experience of the *Francis* which, in her voyage from Calabar to Nevis, lost 199 of 267 negroes taken aboard.[1] The incidence of mortality for the later seventeenth century established by the Committee of the Privy Council which investigated the slave-trade in 1789 almost certainly derives from the company's own records and is confirmed by independent enquiry.[2] This committee found the average death-rate on the Middle Passage for the years 1680 to 1688 to be 23½ per cent. Early in the eighteenth century this rate was much reduced, so that by 1734 the company had come to assume an average of only 10 per cent.[3] Exactly how the responsibility for this appalling incidence of mortality should be apportioned is not and probably never will

[1] T. 70/169, fo. 42d.
[2] *Report of the Privy Council Committee on the Trade to Africa* (1789), Part IV, No. 5.
[3] T. 70/93, pp. 228–9.

be completely clear. The guilt of the white purchaser is documented; that of the black vender is not. Given a slave-trade, some deaths were unavoidable, for seafaring was a hazardous trade and a slaving voyage claimed European as well as African victims. What is uncertain is the physical condition of the negroes at the time of purchase and the treatment to which they had been subjected on their (often long) marches to the sea. Buyers naturally rejected slaves in obviously poor condition, but it must have needed a practised eye to discover maladies which may have been partly psychological. In default of a body of evidence for this period sufficient to permit generalization, it is worth recalling the history of the *Arthur*.[1] Nineteen of her slaves died within a few days of purchase, before the ship was clear of the Calabar river, and before overcrowding or brutal treatment could have taken effect, and thirty-six more before the African coast was left behind. In all, this cargo suffered eighty-four casualties, of which only twenty-nine occurred in the Middle Passage proper between Anomabu and Barbados.

Nevertheless the fact that the incidence of mortality could be and was lowered in the early eighteenth century can be taken as evidence that the chief, if not the sole, responsibility for the death-rate of the Middle Passage rests with the captains of slaving-ships and those who gave them their orders. Overcrowding was the most obvious fault, and in the years before 1689 it was encouraged by the low price of slaves in Africa. Calculations of profit, when a negro cost only £3, did not point so clearly towards a reduction in the number carried as they did in later years when the price was £10 or more. Though they did not tackle the basic problem of overcrowding, both the company and individual masters did something to mitigate conditions. All parties, company, owners and captains, had a direct pecuniary interest in the number of negroes alive at the end of a voyage.[2] All the company's ships carried a quota of negro-provisions from England which was supplemented by corn collected in Africa. Failure to obtain an adequate supply could be disastrous: the *St. George*, for example, lost 132 negroes through 'smallpox and want of corn'.[3] The tradition that on

[1] Above, p. 231.   [2] Above, p. 199.   [3] T. 70/10, fo. 14d.

unexpectedly long passages food supplies were conserved by throwing slaves into the sea may be founded in fact, but an entry in the journal of Captain Doegood shows that this did not always happen. Five days before sighting Barbados he wrote: 'God continue the gale, otherwise wee doubt itt will be hard for us all, intendinge to give our negroes white men's provisions if theres should fall shortt.'[1] Such freedom and diversion aboard ship as it was felt safe to give the slaves, the company's captains were ordered to provide: 'To prevent the mortality of negroes you must observe frequently to wash the decks [with] vinegar and divert them as much as you can with some sorts of musick & play.'[2] The outrage to morality which the Middle Passage must always be should not obscure the fact that it was also an outrage to sound economics. Had the company contrived to keep alive the victims of the Middle Passage, the history of its monopoly and its finances might have been different.

The majority of the slaves delivered alive by the company in the colonies were consigned to its agents and sold by them as quickly as possible. But some, the exact proportion is uncertain, were delivered to 'contractors'. The practice of contracting for negroes was well established: merchants in London, generally syndicates, agreed in advance with the company to buy cargoes or fractions of cargoes at a fixed price payable in London. They or their representatives were the consignees of such slaves and had the disposal of them. Prior to 1672 this seems to have been a normal way of supplying the colonies.[3] For the slave-trader it had obvious merits, a guaranteed market and price, few or no agency costs, no debts, no lawsuits for the recovery of debts, and no problem of how to remit effects from the West Indies to London. The company accordingly encouraged contractors, and soon after its formation announced its readiness to consider tenders for fractions as small as one-twentieth of a cargo.[4]

Contract-negroes were supplied by the company only

---

[1] T. 70/1213, 16 May 1678.

[2] E.g. T. 70/61, fo. 159d. Compulsory dancing is often represented as one of the brutalities inflicted upon slaves. This may be true in the eighteenth century: but I have found no evidence to suggest that it is true of this period.

[3] T. 70/76, fos. 8–9.   [4] *Ibid.*

between 1672 and 1689; normally they were delivered in the colonies, though on occasions off the coast of Africa, in which case the contractor bore the cost of freight and the hazard of mortality. The prices of those to be delivered at the Plantations were proclaimed by the company in 1672: £15 a head at Barbados, £16 in the Leewards, £17 in Jamaica, and £18 in Virginia.[1] Those sold off the African coast were priced at £8 a head for Gambia negroes and £6 for an Ardra cargo.[2] How many were brought to the colonies under contract it is impossible to say, no record having been kept of sales. All the slaves delivered to Virginia were supplied on contract, the business being chiefly in the hands of two prominent merchants, Jeffrey Jeffreys and Micajah Perry. References in the minutes of Courts of Assistants to negotiations with them are plentiful, but the number of negroes reaching Virginia cannot now be established from the company's records.[3] Contracts were also made for the supply of the West Indian colonies, but again it is difficult to measure how extensively. At certain times there seem to have been almost as many contracted as uncontracted negroes arriving in the West Indies: between August 1681 and May 1682, for example, nearly 1,600 were delivered.[4] But, while the material for counting arrivals is sketchy and inadequate, the probability is that the annual average was at nothing like so high a figure. After 1689 when monopoly ceased to be enforceable, the contract system fell into disuse; merchants such as Jeffreys who had formerly been contractors now became separate traders.

At Barbados and Jamaica the company kept two or three permanent agents, at the smaller islands one or two, into whose hands all slaves, other than those contracted for, were delivered. Their duties were various. They had to be at the quay-side to board a ship newly arrived from Africa before the master or

[1] *Cal. S.P. Col.*, 1669–74, No. 985.

[2] T. 70/80, fo. 85; T. 70/81, fo. 35; T. 70/82, fo. 8d.

[3] The following are references to negotiations for the supply of slaves to Virginia which I have noticed: T. 70/76, fos. 46d, 56d, 90d; T. 70/77, fo. 45; T. 70/78, fos. 17, 27d, 32d; T. 70/80, fos. 46d, 85; T. 70/81, fos. 35, 66d, 75d, 78d; T. 70/82, fos. 8d, 25d, 59; T. 70/50, fo. 4d; T. 70/57, fo. 38; T. 70/61, fos. 4, 6, 6d. This does not purport to be a complete list.

[4] T. 70/1, 10, 11, 15, 16.

crew could spirit negroes ashore by illicit means. Having checked the captain's journal and accounts, they mustered the negroes and lotted them in preparation for the sale which normally took place within two or three days of arrival. For purposes of calculating freight and certain other charges, a negro was alive if he could 'go over the side', that is, walk off the ship. Sales were by 'inch of candle'. The resultant debts had to be collected by the agents, and debtors prosecuted. Takings were remitted to London in specie or bills of exchange, or laid out in sugar and other goods; for the latter the agents had to find shipping and see to the formalities of loading. At the same time they managed the company's property in the colony, kept watch for infringements of the monopoly, and in every way represented the company in the Plantations. Clearly much depended on them. Unlike the company's servants in Africa they were well-paid, sharing a basic commission of 7 per cent. on all returns sent to England. The same rate was earned on remittances made in bills (which were far less troublesome to the agents) as in goods, and on all money disbursed in the colony. For the small part they played in the disposal of contract-negroes they received a commission of $1\frac{1}{2}$ per cent. on gross takings.[1] The annual value of remittances from Jamaica or Barbados might be as much as £40,000, so that a 7 per cent. commission even when divided amongst two or three amounted to a considerable sum. Later the rates were raised. In 1692 when William Beeston, the Governor of Jamaica, was appointed agent he was given $3\frac{1}{2}$ per cent. for himself, the aggregate commission paid to the agency being increased from 7 to $9\frac{1}{3}$ per cent.[2] Five years later, in an effort to reduce the debts owed to it by the planters of the West Indies, the company introduced a comprehensive revision of the terms of its agencies. Agents were made personally responsible for all credit given to planters and were obliged to undertake to remit to the company the entire proceeds of a cargo of slaves within twelve months of sale; in return their commission was raised to 10 per cent.[3]

An agency for the Royal African Company must, therefore,

[1] T. 70/16, fo. 17.   [2] T. 70/83, fo. 55d; T. 70/57, fo. 118d.
[3] T. 70/85, fo. 11; T. 70/57, fos. 133d–134, 135d, 137d, 138d.

have been amongst the best remunerated private employments in the English colonies, particularly since it was normally combined with some form of public service or private trade or both. Competition for the posts, especially in the early years, was keen. Stephen Gascoigne was chosen agent in Barbados in 1674 'by ballett among eight competitors', and the short-list of candidates for the Jamaican agency in the following year was at least as large.[1] On these terms, the company could expect to attract more talent to its West Indian than to its African service, and it was not always disappointed. Edwin Stede, agent at Barbados for more than twenty years, held office in the colony as Provost Marshal, Deputy Secretary, Collector of Customs, Councillor and Secretary; between 1685 and 1690 he was Lieutenant-Governor, acting Governor, of what was still one of the most prized possessions of the English Crown.[2] Hender Molesworth, appointed agent at Jamaica in 1677, became Lieutenant-Governor in 1683 and was acting Governor from 1684 to the end of 1687. For nearly three years, therefore, the two most important English West Indian islands were under the government of the African Company's agents. In 1692 William Beeston was simultaneously appointed Governor of Jamaica and agent of the company, continuing in both offices until disqualified by the Act of 1698.[3] Other agents held official positions in their colonies: John Balle, Charles Penhallow, and Walter Ruding, Councillors of Jamaica, Rowland Powell, Secretary of the same colony, Benjamin Skutt and Stephen Gascoigne, Councillors of Barbados, Thomas Belchamber, Councillor of Antigua and St. Christopher's.[4]

The benefits which the company drew from the official standing of its agents were, however, partly offset by the handle thereby given to the opponents of monopoly. The economic authority which they wielded was in any case great, and open to misuse;[5] with office added to this power, the agents held,

---

[1] T. 70/76, fos. 24, 42d.

[2] *Cal. S.P. Col.*, 1675–6, Nos. 387, 485, 670; 1677–80, No. 889.

[3] T. 70/83, fo. 55d.

[4] T. 70/77, fo. 32; T. 70/78, fo. 47d; T. 70/169, fo. 45; *A.P.C.* (Colonial Series), 1680–1720, Appendix II.

[5] Below, pp. 322–3.

wrote Governor Russell of Barbados in 1695: 'such a sway here as almost to stop any proceeding, for if a man does not vote as they would wish for a vestryman or assemblyman they proceed against him for what he owes them for negroes (most of the planters being in their debt), thus ruining him and his family'.[1]

In 1698, when the trade to Africa was thrown open to all who paid the ten per cent. duty, a clause was inserted in the Act debarring Governors, Deputy-Governors and Judges in the Plantations from serving as agents for the sale of negroes on behalf of either the company or the separate traders. Governor Beeston of Jamaica was forced to resign his agency, foreseeing ill-consequences from the Act, for many office-holders in the colonies were *ex-officio* justices, and thus disqualified. Councillors, for example, sat as justices of appeal, and a case is on record where an appeal to the Council of Jamaica could not be heard, three members being disqualified by the Act of 1698.[2]

Although the profits of an agency were such as to give the company the choice of men of greater ability and probity than it could reasonably hope to attract to Africa, the history of the West Indian agents is not a particularly happy one. In the end the company contrived to quarrel with most of them. Skutt was dismissed in 1691 for his 'uneasie carriage to the planters, as also to us';[3] Stede, after retirement, was accused of changing a '1' into a '3' by 'legerdemain';[4] Walter Ruding, killed in the Jamaican earthquake of 1692, left his affairs in a tangle and his securities were sued for reparation to the company;[5] under different circumstances the securities of Charles Penhallow, Edward Belchamber and Giles Heysham were similarly prosecuted.[6] That the last chapter in the relations between the company and so many of its West Indian agents should have been written in the law-courts does not necessarily betoken excessive severity on one side or excessive negligence and dishonesty on the other. Agents, by definition, were indebted to the company at all times, and untimely death was bound to leave their

[1] *Cal. S.P. Col.*, 1693–6, No. 1930.
[2] *A.P.C.* (Colonial Series), 1680–1720, pp. 564, 570.
[3] T. 70/57, fo. 66d.   [4] *Ibid.*, fo. 90.   [5] T. 70/85, fo. 44d.
[6] *Ibid.*, fos. 50d, 66; T. 70/86, p. 100.

accounts in disorder. Many disputes originated in the accounting methods characteristic of the time, in poor communications,
and in misunderstandings. These were common to all forms of
business, but in a large-scale enterprise they were accentuated.

The precise number of negroes passing through the hands of
the company's agents in the West Indies cannot now be discovered. Reasonable approximations can, however, be made.
Records of sales by auction have been preserved for all years
but four between 1672 and 1711, and the missing evidence can
to some extent be made good from other sources. Reliable
records of negroes supplied on contract between 1672 and 1689
have not survived; as we have already seen, the number
delivered in this way was at times large and must be taken into
account when estimating the grand total of slaves brought by
the company to the Plantations. The number sold by auction
in each colony, year by year, will be found in Appendix III,
together with a further discussion of the sources from which the
statistics have been collected.

It will be seen that between 1672 and 1711 the company sold
by auction in the West Indies some 90,000 slaves, of whom
nearly a half were delivered at Barbados and more than a
third at Jamaica. The largest number known to have been
sold in any single year was about 5,000, though this figure may
have been exceeded in 1686 or 1687. Barbados, absolutely
in proportion to size, was best served, and in several years
and deliveries there exceeded 2,000. Nearly two-thirds of
the grand total arrived in the sixteen years from 1674 to 1689.
To these figures must be added cargoes sold in bulk to contractors, and it is not unreasonable to suppose that about
10,000 were disposed in this way. We may conclude that
between 1672 and 1713 the company delivered alive approximately 100,000 negroes in the colonies, which (assuming an
average mortality of 20 per cent. over the whole period)
would suggest 120,000–125,000 shipped from Africa.

Of those delivered alive, the majority were adult males. An
analysis of 60,000 slaves delivered between 1673 and 1711
shows that 51 per cent. were men and 35 per cent. women;
of the remainder 9 per cent. were boys and 4 per cent.
girls. Men naturally commanded the best prices, though their

value declined swiftly over the age of forty. The company's ordinary requirements are shown in the following typical instruction:

> In slaving our ships alwayes observe that the negroes be well-liking and healthy from the age of 15 years not exceeding 40; and at least two 3rds. men slaves, in which be as exact as you possibly can; 8 or 10 boyes & girles in a ship's complement you may take tho' they be under the age of 15 & that you have them cheap & find your advantage in getting others with them, but children & old people you must by no means buy.[1]

Further experience showed that this age-range was set too high, and in 1701 the Agent-General at Cape Coast was ordered to buy boys and girls of twelve to fifteen years in preference to adults over thirty.[2]

The critical questions in the history of both the Royal African Company and the English West Indian colonies are whether these were adequate supplies, and whether the company's monopoly contributed to or retarded the growth of the Plantations. Before answering them, the economic state of the colonies in 1672 must be briefly considered. With the introduction of sugar-making into Barbados in 1640, the economies of the English West Indies began to undergo a transformation. From the first the new crop was based upon slavery, and in the eleven years following its introduction the slave-population of Barbados appears to have risen from 1,000 to 20,000; twenty years later, by the time of the formation of the African company, it was believed to be 40,000.[3] Barbados was a small island and economically it matured rapidly: within twenty years sugar had given it a value out of all proportion to its size. For many years, wrote Governor Dutton in 1681, Barbados had been fully settled, and well before that date the colony had supplied emigrants for new Plantations.[4] From about 1680

---

[1] T. 70/51, p. 50.   [2] *Ibid.*, pp. 159–60.

[3] C. Y. Shephard, 'British West Indian Economic History in Imperial Perspective', in *Tropical Agriculture*, XVI, Nos. 7 and 8; in 1673 Sir Peter Colleton reported 33,184 slaves and suggested that one-third should be added for concealments; *Cal. S.P. Col.*, 1669–74, No. 1101. In 1680 the total was put at 37,315; *Cal. S.P. Col.*, 1677–80, No. 1336 xxiv.

[4] *Cal. S.P. Col.*, 1681–5, No. 136; O. P. Starkey, *Economic Geography of Barbados*, New York, 1939, p. 77.

to the middle of the eighteenth century, the slave-population (a true index of productive capacity and intensity of cultivation) seems to have remained more or less stationary at between forty and fifty thousand. The Royal African Company, therefore, entered the history of Barbados at a moment when that colony had already passed the 'frontier-stage', and indeed had gone far towards maturity. Its role was to be the maintenance of the slave-population at the level which had already been achieved rather than the promotion of further expansion. This did not prevent Barbados from demanding more negroes than were really needed, in order to get them as cheaply as possible. But the early attainment of something very much like economic maturity meant that opposition to monopoly lacked the urgency it might otherwise have had.

Barbados had a start of nearly twenty years in sugar-production over the other English colonies, the significance of which cannot be measured only in time. They were years in which the policy of the Old Colonial System had not yet reached full flower, and in which the English Government was distracted from colonial affairs by events at home and in Europe. At this critical stage of her growth, from 1640 to 1660, Barbados had enjoyed, not free trade, but something much nearer to it than she was to see again for many years. Of all the liberties which the mother-country through neglect or preoccupation permitted, none was more precious than the freedom to buy slaves from merchants of all nations. Barbados, wrote Sir Thomas Modyford from a quarter of a century's experience in the West Indies, 'had never risen to its late perfection, had it not been lawful for Dutch, Hamburghers, our own whole nation, and any other, to bring and sell them blacks or any other servants'.[1] Other colonies were less fortunate. The Spaniards had made little of Jamaica, and when the island came into English hands its economic significance was not immediately perceived. Sugar-cultivation there did not begin in earnest until 1664, nine years after the capture of the island.[2] In 1658 there were but 1,400 negroes in the colony, and in 1673 there were fewer

[1] *Cal. S.P. Col.*, 1669–74, No. 264 iii.
[2] E. E. Cheesman, 'History of the Introduction of Some Well-known West Indian Staples', in *Tropical Agriculture*, XVI, No. 5.

than ten thousand.[1] When the Royal African Company was founded, therefore, the development and exploitation of Jamaica had scarcely begun; twenty times the size of Barbados, she had barely a quarter as many slaves. Her potentialities were enormous, as can be seen from the growth that took place in the next eighty years. While, as we have seen, the slave-population of Barbados changed little between 1670 and 1750, Jamaica's was thought to have quadrupled to 'nearly 40,000' by 1700, doubled again to 80,000 by 1722, and advanced to 130,000 by 1754.[2]

Of the smaller English colonies, Nevis alone resembled Barbados in having approached full development by the time of the company's formation. Between 1678 and 1744 her slave-population increased only from 3,860 to 6,511, while those of Antigua and St. Christopher's increased eightfold, and that of Montserrat fivefold.[3] Nevis in 1672 was economically the most important of the four; by the middle of the eighteenth century she had become the least. Antigua, the largest in area, did not receive sugar until two years after the formation of the Royal African Company. Her position was similar to that of Jamaica, except that the critical period in her development came some years later, after the monopoly of the African Company had been broken.

Although these six colonies were at different stages of growth, their aggregate need for labour was such that in 1672 demand appeared to constitute no problem for the company. Jamaica's demands were virtually unlimited, though Jamaica's capacity to pay was another matter. Antigua, Montserrat and St. Christopher's were similarly placed. All were ripe for development, and all, in the twentieth century, would have been good candidates for the investment of public and private capital. Barbados and Nevis, though much nearer to saturation, needed replacements in order to keep up the numbers of their slaves. Exactly what was the natural decrease in the slave-

---

[1] F. W. Pitman, *The Development of the British West Indies, 1700–63*, New Haven, 1917, Appendix I.

[2] *Ibid.*, and *Cal. S.P. Col.*, 1700, No. 565.

[3] C. S. S. Higham, *The Development of the Leeward Islands under the Restoration*, 1921, p. 145, and Pitman, *op. cit.*

populations of the West Indies at this date is uncertain: Edward Lyttelton estimated that the owner of one hundred slaves must expect to buy six a year in order to maintain that total.[1] This may be an exaggeration; Lyttelton was campaigning for a free labour-supply and trying to discredit monopoly. But some replacements were undoubtedly necessary.

Since the needs of the colonies differed, their reactions to the supplies provided by the company also differed, and it will be convenient to consider them separately. At Barbados, agitation for free trade stretched back beyond the formation of the Royal African Company; the Royal Adventurers had had to face their share of complaints until the early liquidation of monopoly by the Second Dutch War. With the revival of monopoly in 1672, the new company did not have to wait long for the renewal of a struggle which at times seems to have been carried on as much for principles as for interest. The company's activities were, as we have seen, restricted by war in 1672 and 1673, and only 220 slaves were supplied to Barbados in those years. In the following year more than a thousand were sold, but at an average price of £17 which the planters thought excessive. In February 1675, therefore, the Council and Assembly began their agitation against the new monopoly with an address to the Governor on the 'insupportable injuries' done to Barbados by the Royal African Company, and a petition in the same terms was forwarded to the King. They complained that the supply of slaves had been totally inadequate to meet the needs of the island and that those that had been delivered had been sold at £20 and £22 a head.[2] The company firmly denied both charges. It claimed to have 'appointed' eight ships with 3,000 negroes for Barbados in 1675; in fact only 838 were sold by auction in that year, but it is possible that others were delivered to contractors. By reference to its books, the company had no difficulty in showing that the average price of slaves in 1675 had been little more than £15. It was not until October 1676, more than eighteen months after the original complaint of the planters, that the Lords of Trade and Plantations investigated the charges; by this time the supply of

[1] *Groans of the Plantations*, 1689, p. 18.
[2] *Cal. S.P. Col.*, 1675–6, Nos. 438, 485, 714 ii.

slaves to the colonies was running much more smoothly, and the company was able to rout its opponents. Col. Thornburgh, agent for Barbados in London, was forced to admit that the island was now well supplied, and that the shortages of 1673 and 1674 had been occasioned by war.[1] According to one authority, 1,372 negroes had been sold in Barbados between March and June 1676, and another 424 forwarded to other colonies in default of buyers.[2]

The company's victory was complete; and it was rubbed in by an official rebuke sent to Governor Atkins for sponsoring a complaint proved to be frivolous.[3] No further official complaint emanated from Barbados until 1690, from which it is not unreasonable to infer that the colony received in these years supplies equal or almost equal to its needs. Exactly what those needs were it is difficult to say. Governor Atkins, who was no friend to the company, estimated annual requirements at between two and three thousand.[4] Between 1676 and 1689 there were sold by auction an average of about 1,675 negroes a year. In addition there were contract-negroes and those delivered by interlopers, so that if Atkins' figure was correct, the colony's needs were probably met. There were years of shortage, such as 1679, but from 1681 to 1687 supplies were generally good and average prices well below £15. There remained nevertheless an undercurrent of dissatisfaction with monopoly that found expression in private complaints,[5] in writings,[6] and in the warm support accorded to interlopers.

After 1689 war caused a serious contraction in the supply of negroes to Barbados. The annual average sold by auction fell by more than a half, and sales on contract ceased altogether. Prices rose sharply. It is true that the price of sugar in London also rose, but it is unlikely that the planter was the chief beneficiary. The number of ships engaged in the carrying of West Indian commodities to England diminished; the cost of cargo-space soared; many cargoes were lost; and the credit-system

---

[1] *Cal. S.P. Col.*, 1675–6, No. 911; *A.P.C.* (Colonial Series), 1613–80, pp. 676–7.

[2] *Cal. S.P. Col.*, 1675–6, No. 1102.   [3] *Ibid.*, No. 1190.

[4] *Cal. S.P. Col.*, 1677–80, No. 11.   [5] *Ibid.*, No. 969.

[6] E.g. Lyttelton's *Groans of the Plantations*, 1689, pp. 5–8.

linking the planter to his agent in London was much impaired.[1]
Barbados' reaction was to join the mounting number of vocal
critics of monopoly. Twice in 1690, and again in 1694, the
'merchants and planters trading to and interested in' the
colony petitioned Parliament against the confirmation of the
company's charter.[2] In 1693 the Assembly of Barbados drew
up a remonstrance in which it was claimed that monopoly:

> is always an evil, and the warm trade driven in Africa by foreign
> nations, despite the pretensions of the Company, threatens to
> drive the English out. Moreover it is a fact that the Colonies have
> not been so well or cheaply furnished with slaves as before the
> establishment of the Company; and the consequence is injury to
> the sugar industry which will thus fall into the hands of the
> French.[3]

Towards the close of the war the situation further deteriorated. In 1695 the company sold no negroes in Barbados, and
the few delivered in the following year were sold at an average
price of £27 10s. a head. In July 1696 the Council and
Assembly drew up another representation of grievances against
the company: supplies were only half what were needed and
prices exorbitant.[4] For this situation the system of monopoly
was not entirely to blame. The trade of the company was confined not only by its own lack of money, but also by governmental embargoes and restrictions. As for prices, negroes which
before the war could be bought for £3 in Africa now cost £5
or more, while freight-charges for slaves transported to the
West Indies had doubled.[5] High as the price of negroes had
risen in the colonies, the company was nevertheless upbraiding
its agents for selling cheaper than the interlopers who 'far
outdo us and trade to great gain whilst we must do it to little
or loss'.[6] The planters were not much interested in these explanations of restricted supplies and high prices; monopoly
they felt was the basic cause, and Barbados joined the agitation
of 1697–8 which resulted in the ten per cent. Act.[7]

---

[1] *T.R.H.S.*, Fifth Series, II, p. 98.   [2] Stock, II, pp. 21, 29, 102.
[3] *Cal. S.P. Col.*, 1693–6, No. 655, 677.   [4] *Cal. S.P. Col.*, 1696–7, No. 125.
[5] Above, p. 199.   [6] T. 70/57, fos. 83d, 116d, 117.
[7] *Cal. S.P. Col.*, 1697–8, Nos. 272, 481.

X

The Act, however, was little more to the liking of some of those who claimed to represent Barbados than it was to the separate traders, and the 'merchants and planters' petitioned against it in February and May 1698.[1] On the same day that the second of these representations was presented to the House of Lords, however, a third petition was heard, this time in favour of the bill, from persons calling themselves the 'planters and merchants' of Barbados.[2] The split in Barbadian opinion thus revealed is probably, at this stage, more apparent than real. It is highly likely that the separate traders had been lobbying extensively; the company certainly had, having sent to its agents in each colony instructions to obtain the signatures of 'our debtors and others' to a petition on behalf of monopoly.[3] Pressure of this kind was unlikely to effect a conversion amongst convinced opponents of monopoly, but the company's record in Barbados was better than elsewhere, and the planters were possibly a little more responsive. Official opinion in the colony, as expressed by the Assembly, remained hostile to the company.[4]

Subsequent events produced a truer division of opinion. We have already seen that the introduction of paper money in the colony and the ensuing inflation promoted a certain reaction in favour of the company.[5] For a time the separate traders delivered virtually no slaves, while the company contrived to deliver more between 1702 and 1710 than it had done between 1689 and 1697. The reaction cannot, however, be said to have gone very far. In a petition to the House of Commons in 1709, the 'planters and inhabitants' of Barbados complained impartially of both the company and the separate traders. Later in the same year, two petitions were heard from persons claiming to represent the interest of Barbados, one in favour of monopoly and the other for free trade.[6] Only one other petition appears to have been presented in the name of Barbados, in February 1712, against the company.[7] While the significance of this split in Barbadian opinion should not be exaggerated, the African Company can on the whole be acquitted of having

---

[1] Stock, II, pp. 218, 240.   [2] Ibid., p. 241.   [3] T. 70/57, fos. 127d–129d.
[4] Cal. S.P. Col., 1699, No. 954 iii.   [5] Above, pp. 146–7.
[6] Stock, III, pp. 202–3, 223–4.   [7] Ibid., p. 276.

seriously retarded the development of Barbados. The colony may even be said to have drawn certain benefits from the hated monopoly. That the price of negroes under monopoly was lower than under a system of free trade was due partly, though not entirely, to the exclusion of English private traders from the slave-markets of Africa. This exclusion meant that the English colonies in general were starved of labour; but Barbados received more than her fair share and at the same time enjoyed the advantage of low prices. Her experience under monopoly, though not uniformly happy, was certainly more fortunate than that of any other English colony.[1]

The record of the African Company in Jamaica is quite different. The need for negroes was, or could be represented as, much greater than at Barbados; yet, except for isolated years, the company sent fewer and charged more for them. There

[1] Edwin Stede, the company's chief agent in Barbados, compiled the following memorial in 1694:

'During the time of my being in Barbados, which wanted but few weeks of twenty yeares in all which time I was one of the agents for the said Company, there was for the most part of the time a very considerable number of negros yearly imported by the said Company to that island & some times such numbers more then that island then seamed to want that though they were sold by the agents & factors att moderatt rates with long day for payment, yett sometimes the agents have been ten daies or more in selling & disposing two hundred & fifty or three hundred negros, though good able people, & have been forced to retaile them to the Marchants & others that sold them againe or shiped them to forraigne parts; & att one time the agents not finding vent in the said island for about 300 negros & upwards imported into the said island in the ship John & Allexander who lay there many daies with designe to sell the negros att moderate prises with long time of pay, yett the Company's agents could not dispose of them there but were forced to send them to a remoater markett. . . . Soe great creditt was given to the inhabitants of that island that generally att the yeares end in making up the Company's accounts the people of that island were found to be in debt to the Company some times forty to fifty & sixty thousand pounds sterling, as appeared by the books of accounts and the account current yearly sent home to the Company; & I have heard many considerable gentlemen, planters, marchants & others of that island who have dealt with the Company's agents & with privat traders for negros, say that they were furnished by the company with better negros on more moderate tearmes & greater conveniences in point of time for payment then from the interloopers, & for that reason would & did for the future deale only with the Company.' Brit. Mus., Harleian MSS, 7310, No. 17.

were, of course, peculiar difficulties in Jamaica that did not
exist at Barbados. The real need was for long-term credit for
the development of an island of immense possibilities. Short-
term credit, however, was the most that could be hoped for,
and in a time of falling prices such as 1660–88 planters must
have been able to extricate themselves from debt only by great
exertions or good luck.

The Royal Adventurers had sent no slaves to Jamaica after
1665,[1] though the island was doubtless supplied by private
traders under licence. The first consignment delivered by the
new company did not arrive until November 1674, and by that
time the first protests of the colony had begun to come in.[2] In
the following May a contest began that was to last, with brief
intermissions, until 1712. The Council of Jamaica led off with
a petition to the Duke of York asking him to order a plentiful
supply of negroes for the island.[3] Supplies certainly did improve in the next few months, and in September 1675 the
Governor reported that they were adequate.[4] But, he added,
prices were excessive, and this continued to be the burden of
complaint in the following year. It was easier to attack high
prices than inadequate supplies, for, while everyone agreed in
wanting labour as cheaply as possible, no one was sure how
many slaves the island needed or could afford to pay for.
Governor Vaughan thought the number delivered in 1675
(about two thousand) a good supply; five years later the
planters put their needs at three to four thousand a year.[5]
Prices fell steadily from 1674 to 1680, and between 1681 and
1683 no consignment fetched an average price as high as £17
a head.

The planters were far from satisfied with these improvements,
and in 1680 they stated their demands to the Lords of Trade as
three to four thousand slaves a year 'and every year more and
more', to be sold at £16–£17 a head.[6] The company's reply
was that Jamaica either could not or would not pay for the
slaves that had already been sent her, let alone for additional

[1] *Cal. S.P. Col.*, 1669–74, No. 277.   [2] *Ibid.*, Nos. 1062, 1389.
[3] *Cal. S.P. Col.*, 1675–6, No. 554.   [4] *Ibid.*, No. 673.
[5] *Ibid.*; *Cal. S.P. Col.*, 1677–80, No. 1575.
[6] *Cal. S.P. Col.*, 1677–80, No. 1575.

supplies.[1] It claimed that the total debt then owing in Jamaica was £60,000.[2] The settlement propounded by the Lords of Trade was that the company should deliver to Jamaica each year three thousand 'merchantable negroes', to be sold at six months' credit for £18 a head.[3] In no year had the company hitherto sold by auction much more than half this number, though more may have been delivered on contract. The settlement must, therefore, be regarded as a victory for the colonists, and they proceeded to enlarge upon it by embodying the conclusions of the Lords of Trade in an Act of the Jamaican legislature.[4] This Act made the planters themselves judges of what were or were not merchantable negroes, and absolutely forbade the company to sell at prices exceeding £18. The company had for some time been selling at *average* prices well below this figure, though slaves of a particularly good quality had fetched more. Now it was prohibited from recovering losses on some cargoes by charging more for others.

Free trade in negroes was Jamaica's aim. While these discussions were in progress, some of the planters petitioned the King for permission to send a ship to Angola to buy slaves. The request was refused; and the planters were told that if they really wanted to participate in the trade to Africa they were at liberty to subscribe £60,000 to the capital of the Royal African Company.[5] Free trade for the time being, then, was unobtainable; it was essential first to smash the company, the Negro Act being a step in the right direction. In January 1683 the company petitioned for the disallowance of the Act, pointing to the great and increasing debts owed in Jamaica, and blaming high prices on the competition of interlopers in Africa and the clipped money current in the colonies.[6] The planters replied with the usual catalogue of grievances and, under cover of concessions, raised their demands yet higher. They asked that, if the maximum price was to be abandoned, the company should be obliged to supply them with 5,000 slaves in the first year and 3,000 a year thereafter.[7] On this occasion the company carried its point and the offending Act was disallowed.

[1] *Ibid.*, No. 1574.   [2] Below, p. 319.   [3] *Cal. S.P. Col.*, 1677–80, No. 1583.
[4] T. 70/169, fos. 5d–6d.   [5] *A.P.C.* (Colonial Series), 1680–1720, p. 20.
[6] *Cal. S.P. Col.*, 1681–5, No. 891.   [7] *Ibid.*, No. 1293.

After further negotiations a fresh compromise was reached in 1683–4 more favourable to the company. Three thousand slaves were to be delivered to Jamaica annually; price-control was to be abandoned; and an Act to be passed by the Jamaican legislature (conditional on the fulfilment by the company of its undertaking to deliver the agreed number of slaves) imposing a fine of £5 on the purchaser of each illicitly imported negro.[1] In the short while remaining before the outbreak of war in 1689, deliveries at Jamaica increased, some thirteen or fourteen thousand being sold by auction between 1682 and 1687. Jamaica, however, remained a strong opponent of monopoly, exploiting every argument which could possibly be turned against the company. Until 1686 some of the best negroes brought by the company were sold not to the planters but to the Spanish agents of the *Asiento*. Although this trade did not involve very large numbers, it provided the planters with another useful stick with which to beat the company.[2]

Grievances were thus very much alive when the opportunity for redress came. From 1690, in Parliament and out, the Jamaican interest presented a solid front in opposition to the company.[3] A comparison between this colony's experiences under monopoly and competition provides an illuminating demonstration of the merits and demerits of the two systems. Between 1698 and 1708 the company brought fewer than 7,000 slaves to Jamaica, while the separate traders succeeded in delivering five times as many.[4] And, to make a more legitimate comparison, monopoly in fifteen years of peace brought the island 25,000 slaves at most compared to 42,000 delivered in eleven years of free trade, of which seven were war-years. No other conclusion is possible than that the existence of monopolistic control of the labour-supply was bad for Jamaica and its overthrow a necessary preliminary to the full realization of the island's possibilities.

Of the remaining English West Indian colonies, Nevis, pro-

---

[1] *Cal. S.P. Col.*, 1681–5, Nos. 1349, 1385, 1512, 1563–4, 1570–1, 1616–17, 1656, 1678, 1687.

[2] Below, p. 333.

[3] Stock, II, pp. 20, 29, 103, 161, 183, 217, 237; III, pp. 191, 204–5, 248.

[4] Above, p. 143.

portionately to her size, was well supplied with negroes by the company. In fifteen years, from 1674 to 1688, more than six thousand slaves were sold there by auction. Some of them were probably re-exported to adjacent islands, but there is no reason to suppose that Nevis needed more slaves than she was allotted. The colony indeed stands alone as the one English West Indian island which, until 1689, recorded no official protest against the company's monopoly. Elsewhere in the smaller islands, the company's record is less impressive. Only a few hundred slaves were delivered direct to St. Christopher's and Montserrat, while Antigua received no more than eight hundred in twenty years.[1] In 1680 the Councils of St. Christopher's and Montserrat complained (though politely) to the Lords of Trade of the inadequacy of their supplies,[2] and as a result more attention was paid to them. A separate agency for Antigua and Montserrat was opened in 1685,[3] and the number of negroes consigned there was increased. Antigua, however, remained dissatisfied and her resentment found expression in the imposition of vexatious restraints upon creditors, of whom the company was of course one of the greatest.[4]

The company itself estimated that the Leeward Islands could absorb annually 3,200 negroes, but it is unlikely that as many as half that number was delivered in any year.[5] These colonies appear, however, to have contributed little to the controversies about the future of monopoly that began in 1689. Not until the ten per cent. bill was before the House of Commons, was any intervention made; then the 'planters' of the Leewards twice petitioned in favour of the bill, and the 'inhabitants of Montserrat' put in a petition of their own to the same effect.[6] Since Jamaican opinion was so generally opposed to the bill as putting too heavy burdens on the separate traders, support for it may be taken to indicate a viewpoint less hostile to the company. It is extremely probable that all these petitions were stimulated by the company's agents, who would have had little difficulty in obtaining signatures in small debtor-colonies. As in Barbados, the reaction in favour of the company, if such it

---

[1] Plus any delivered on contract.
[2] *Cal. S.P. Col.*, 1677–80, p. 573, Nos. 1442, 1583.   [3] T. 70/81, fo. 34d.
[4] Below, p. 320.   [5] T. 70/107, p. 11.   [6] Stock, II, pp. 222–3.

may be called, swung further in the early years of the eighteenth century. Nevis fared worse under the Act of 1698 than under the pre-war monopoly, especially during the aftermath of the French invasion of 1706.[1] Antigua was better treated, as befitted a colony of growing importance, but neither St. Christopher's nor Montserrat was well supplied. In 1709 the 'planters and inhabitants' of Montserrat and Nevis petitioned Parliament for relief from an arrangement whereby the company and the separate traders alike had failed to bring them the labour they needed; those of Nevis petitioned in the same terms in 1710 and 1712.[2] The issue between the company and the separate traders, however, was clearly going to be decided by the weightier voices of Jamaica and Barbados. And, since Jamaica had never wavered in opposition to monopoly, while Barbados had at best given equivocal support, the balance of colonial opinion was for the separate trader.

It could scarcely have been otherwise, for, broadly speaking, and with the exceptions noted, the Royal African Company had failed to meet the needs of the colonies for slaves. By putting forth its maximum effort, it had more or less satisfied Barbados and Nevis for fifteen years; but even in peacetime Jamaica had been ill-served. And war so dislocated the company's trade that the credit of monopoly, never good, was fatally impaired. For the company's failure there were explanations and even extenuating circumstances; but failure it was. The success of the separate traders on the other hand cannot be regarded as entirely convincing; they neglected small colonies, starved Barbados, and by competition in Africa helped to force up prices. But they did bring more negroes to the West Indies in war than the company had in peace.

The merits of the rival systems of monopoly and free trade and large- and small-scale enterprise should not, however, be judged simply on the number of negroes delivered to the colonies. The prices at which these negroes were sold are also a relevant consideration, and here the company's shortcomings are less obvious. Average prices of slaves sold at Jamaica and Barbados will be found in Appendix III. It must of course be remembered that an average price for slaves is somewhat mean-

---

[1] Above, pp. 145-6.   [2] Stock, III, pp. 205, 207, 225, 284.

ingless. An adult male in first-class condition could always fetch a good deal more than the average price obtained for an ordinary cargo. Most ship-loads included some 'refuse' negroes sold very cheaply; a few slaves arrived in such poor condition that they were 'delivered to Dr. Neale on condition that he is to have half of as many as he recovers'.[1] In the Spanish slave-trade a standard *pieza d'India* was recognized: it equalled one first-class slave or two, three or more slaves of inferior quality. Price-fixing was thus simplified, though room was left for disagreement about the equivalent of a *pieza*. In the English trade no such standard existed, and the price-figures have to be accepted with this qualification. They are useful, however, for establishing general trends.

The first parcel of negroes delivered to Barbados in 1673 fetched £18 a head: this was regarded as high and helped to produce the reactions noted above. But in the next four years the average price in this colony sank to £14 and did not rise again above £15 until the outbreak of war. At Jamaica prices were bound to be higher, partly through the demands of an expanding economy, partly because the cost of shipping to and from Jamaica was greater. Not until 1677 did the average price there fall below £20. Thereafter it fell until in 1681–3 it was between £15 and £16. It rose again in 1684–6, possibly as a result of purchases by the agents of the *Asiento*,[2] but appears to have dropped again in 1687 and 1688. Such prices whatever the planters alleged, must be regarded as 'reasonable', and the company had no reason to be ashamed of its record in this respect.

The outbreak of war in 1689 was accompanied by an immediate upswing in Jamaica and a slower one in Barbados. Originally this must be ascribed to the increased costs of freight, but as the war continued, other and more permanent factors began to take effect, ensuring that prices would never return to their pre-war level. Notably the cost of negroes in Africa was advanced, partly as a result of open competition from interlopers and separate traders, and partly because of the increasing participation of the French in the slave-trade. Negroes costing about £3 before 1688 were being bought in 1710 for

[1] T. 70/937, Barbados, 25 May 1676.   [2] Below, p. 330.

£10 or £12 a head, and even higher prices were known.[1] This rise or a large part of it proved permanent, and slaves were never sold as cheaply by the separate traders as they had been by the company.

It is tempting to see in this contrast between prices under the company and prices under the separate traders the greater efficiency of the larger enterprise. That this would be far from the truth can be seen by a comparison of costs and prices before and after 1688. Before that date negroes were bought for £3 and the cost of transporting them to Barbados was £5; they were sold for £13 or £14. Between 1702 and 1712 the purchase-price trebled or quadrupled and the transport-cost doubled; the selling-price in the Plantations, on the other hand, rose by less than one hundred per cent. From this it will be seen that the wartime price of £25 betokens at least as much efficiency (and perhaps more) as the peacetime price of £13 to £15. The portion of the selling price set aside to cover costs other than purchase and transport was no greater, and may well have been smaller, under competition than under monopoly. Nor is this all that can be urged on behalf of the separate trader. In the period of monopoly the company failed in the first duty of a commercial enterprise, the making of a profit. Whether consciously or not, it passed on to the buyers the profits that by rights belonged to the shareholders. Selling at £13–£15 a head between 1678 and 1688 meant that only £5–£7 remained on each negro to cover the heavy costs of the African establishment, mortality on the Middle Passage, agency costs in the colonies, bad debts, the losses frequently incurred in remitting effects from the West Indies to London, and all the other charges that have been mentioned. An examination of the finances of the company has suggested that this margin was not enough. There was no profiteering by the company; there were scarcely any profits. If profits are the criterion by which the efficiency of a business is to be judged, the Royal African Company must certainly fail the test. Unfortunately we do not know and are never likely to know the order of profits made by the separate traders in the early eighteenth century. They were probably smaller than expected. Some merchants in-

[1] Above, p. 139.

deed must have made losses, and dropped out of the trade. But others remained, and we have to assume that they were rational creatures who traded only because they found it profitable to do so. In this they differed from the company. It traded partly in hopes, partly in ignorance, and partly because, being invested by public authority with a monopoly of an essential service, it had no alternative but to make the best of a bad job.

The separate traders, it seems, could sell level with or only a little above the company at this date and make a profit where the company made none. The supposed inefficiency of the small business appears, therefore, to be reducible to one particular: instead of a single buyer in Africa, there were now many, who competed with one another for the available supplies and forced up the prime cost of negroes. This rise in prices, however, was, as has already been suggested, a complex phenomenon. In part it must be attributed to increasing French participation in the trade, especially after 1704. In part it was due to the fact that the English, company and separate traders together, were taking many more negroes from Africa in the eighteenth century than in the seventeenth. The wasteful buying methods of private individuals is only one among several factors.

The termination of monopoly in the English slave-trade thus contributed something (though precisely how much we cannot say) to the transformation of slave-labour in the course of the eighteenth century into a less economical method of cultivation than it had once been. But it also made possible the spectacular growth of Jamaica and the southern colonies of North America. Under monopoly, prices had been reasonably low, but supplies inadequate. Given that the slaves supplied by the company were insufficient, monopoly had to go; given the abolition of monopoly, the cost of labour was likely to increase. The planter had to balance the merits of the two systems; the evidence of this book is that, if free trade did not give him all he expected, he nevertheless chose rightly.

2. The Planters' Debts

The negroes sold by the Royal African Company in the West
Indies might be paid for in coin, in kind, or in paper. Coin was
probably the least common. None of the colonies issued coins
of their own in the seventeenth century; in the larger islands
foreign coins of various kinds had some circulation, but in the
smaller colonies there were few coins of any description.
Pounds, shillings and pence had not yet been universally
established even as the currency of account: in Nevis, for
example, the company's accounts were kept in pounds of sugar
throughout the period, and, even in the accounts of Barbados,
sugar was not finally displaced until 1685. After this date all
Barbadian accounts were kept in pounds, shillings and pence
as had been the practice at Jamaica from the beginning. The
pound, however, remained an accounting unit only. Debts
might be contracted in pounds, but were discharged in Spanish
silver pieces-of-eight, or in sugar valued at the current prices.
These Spanish coins bore values determined from time to time
by colonial legislatures; but as a result of clipping and wear
there was much 'light' money in circulation, the intrinsic value
of which might be well below that fixed by the legislature. For
assemblies of debtors, such as many colonial legislatures must
have been, it was a standing temptation to overvalue foreign
coins, and early in the eighteenth century the English Government was obliged to seek powers from Parliament to check
abuses.[1] For the period of the company's monopoly, and for
long after, chaotic monetary conditions and the ever-present
threat to the creditor of legislation in favour of debtors be-
devilled the economic development of the colonies.

It was not until the eighteenth century that the American
and West Indian colonies began their experiments with paper-
·money. But in Barbados, even at the beginning of the company's history, the bill of exchange was a common method of
paying debts. Instead of selling their produce locally, some
planters sent sugar to factors or agents in England who under-

[1] 6 Ann. c. 30.

took the marketing functions. The proceeds of the sale were then held by the agent as a credit upon which the planter could draw bills either for goods ordered out from England or for slaves purchased in the colonies. The bill soon established itself as a means of settling any kind of debt in the colony, and served as a useful medium for remitting effects to Europe.[1] In the course of the next century, the relations thus initiated between the planter and his agent in England became of critical importance in the organization of the sugar-trade.[2] In the company's time bills were not unknown in other colonies, but it was in Barbados that they were in commonest use.

In Barbados, therefore, all three methods of payment for slaves, bills, coin and kind, are to be found; in Jamaica, coin and kind predominated; and in the Leewards, kind only. Despite these differences, the selling of slaves in the English West Indies had everywhere one common characteristic: virtually all buyers, whatever form their eventual payment might take, demanded and got credit. There were it is true a few 'ready-money buyers', but they were not numerous enough to affect the general picture. Throughout the later seventeenth and eighteenth centuries, the economies of the English West Indies were debtor-economies. They could scarcely have been otherwise. Early in the seventeenth century they had been little more than desert islands; fifty years later in the case of Barbados, somewhat longer in the others, they had been made fertile and productive. This transformation, especially the changeover from small farms producing a variety of crops to large estates producing a single cash-crop, could not have been achieved without credit. Here, as elsewhere, reliance on one crop meant that the whole of the grower's annual produce matured at about the same time. Between the last sugar-crop in early summer and the first crop of the following spring, the plantation produced nothing and consumed much. Access to credit, therefore, was essential. Until about 1660, the Dutch appear to have played an important role in the development of Barbados by extending

[1] *T.R.H.S.*, Fifth Series, II, pp. 89 ff.
[2] R. Pares, *A West-India Fortune*, 1950.

necessary credit in goods and services.[1] Jamaica and the Leewards were less fortunate; their needs were greatest at a time
when the English Government had severely restricted the part
the Dutch were permitted to play. English merchants no
doubt contributed something to the capitalization of the West
Indies: as early as Cromwell's time, they claimed that, while
the planters had dug the land, 'it had not yielded so much
wealth if the merchants had not sowed it (as it were) with their
gold'.[2] But the elimination of the Dutch left a gap. Barbados,
deprived of Dutch credit, Jamaica and the Leewards, which
had scarcely known it, were obliged to turn elsewhere for a
service with which they could not dispense.

They turned to the dealers in slaves. In 1672, as part of the
assets of its defunct predecessor, the Royal African Company
inherited a substantial debt owed by planters in the West
Indies for negroes supplied but not paid for. Part of this may
eventually have been recovered, but twenty years later efforts
were still being made to get in debts contracted to the Royal
Adventurers.[3] And from the first, the new company was obliged to accumulate debts of its own. These debts were of two
kinds. On the one hand, there was and must always have been
a large floating debt owed by planters for slaves sold on four or
six months' credit or longer. The existence of this debt need not
necessarily have been fatal to the company, though it placed a
heavy strain on its capital resources. But at the same time,
there can be discerned a growing core of permanent debtors,
who were either unwilling or unable to pay when their time
arrived. In 1676, for example, the company stated that its
total debt owing in Barbados alone might be as much as
£70,000, the equivalent of two-thirds of its share-capital. The
greater part of this formed a floating debt, but there was
believed to be a core of £25,000 of debts of longer standing.[4]
By the same year, the Jamaican debt had reached £25,000, and

[1] G. L. Beer, *The Origins of the British Colonial System*, New York, 1908, pp.
355–9; Dalby Thomas, *An Historical Account of the Rise and Growth of the West-
India Collonies*, 1690, pp. 36–7.

[2] 'The State of the Difference . . . between the Merchants and the
Planters in relation to free trade att the Charibee Islands' (undated),
Brit. Mus., Add. MSS. No. 11411, fos. 3d–4d.

[3] T. 70/57, fos. 65, 65d.   [4] *Cal. S.P. Col.*, 1675–6, No. 911.

four years later it had swollen to £60,000.[1] In 1680 the total debt owing to the company in the West Indies was put at £120,000; in 1684 at £136,000; in 1690 at £170,000.[2] This seems to have been the limit. In the last decade of the seventeenth century the figure was quoted as between £120,000 and £140,000, of which Jamaica owed £50,000 to £60,000, Barbados £40,000 and the Leewards £30,000.[3] In 1708 the Plantation Debt, as the company called it, was given as £160,000, of which only half was reckoned fit to rank among the company's assets.[4] The company could, therefore, claim (and often did) that for almost the whole of its history the equivalent of its share-capital, and more, was locked up in debts in the colonies.[5]

The floating debt was inevitable: a planter who bought slaves in September could scarcely be expected to pay before April. The company's misfortune was that a minority of planters failed to pay at the agreed time, and that the machinery for coercing them was exceedingly defective. In contracting a debt, the company did not of course rely merely on the planter's word. Robert Helmes, agent at Nevis, described the terms upon which credit was extended as follows:

> The factors att Nevis take bonds or penall bills of all persons who buy the companies negroes of them, to pay att six or nine monthes or att some shorter time according as they cann agree with the planters. Att the expiration of the said respective time, according as the bill or bond is taken, if not then paid, the bonds or bills are putt in suite and runn up to a judgement, by which their land may be extended and their goods and chattells sold. Butt no interest is allowed by the law of that island. They doe endeavour to take the planters' bonds or bills without any time, by which meanes they cann gett the debt sooner paid.[6]

This account gives little indication of the vexatious difficulties under which the creditor was obliged to labour in the West Indies. Authority, both legislative and judicial, was mobilized on the side of the debtor, and the victimization of creditors is a perennial theme in colonial history. The Royal Adventurers

---

[1] *Cal. S.P. Col.*, 1677–80, No. 1574.
[2] From Annual Reports to General Courts, T. 70/100–1.
[3] T. 70/101, fos. 38d, 43, 50d, 55, etc.   [4] *Ibid.*, fo. 100.
[5] T. 70/57, fo. 38d.   [6] T. 70/107, p. 24.

were not the last to discover this, complaining to the Privy
Council in 1664 that judicial proceedings at Barbados 'afford
no remedy but what is worse than the disease'.[1] In 1671 they
again carried their case to the Council, and obtained an order
that planters who did not pay their debts should be incapable
of holding offices of profit or places of honour in the colonies.[2]
No improvement was noticeable, and during the monopoly of
the African Company the lot of the creditor worsened in some
particulars. Jamaica proposed, though the Lords of Trade for-
bad, that her Chancellor should be empowered to stay execution of judgments obtained by creditors.[3] In the Leewards,
there were peculiar difficulties. As we have already seen, the
creditor at Nevis could not charge interest for his forbearance.
In that island and at St. Christopher's, a creditor who obtained
judgment and distrained upon the debtor's estate was obliged
to accept goods at a valuation set upon them by the debtor's
neighbours: if their valuation exceeded the debt the creditor
was obliged to refund the overplus.[4] In Antigua, under a law
of 1669, a creditor who obtained judgment could distrain only
upon goods and chattels. If these were not sufficient, the
debtor's lands could be extended and appraised by four of his
neighbours; so long as the debtor paid a sum equal to the
annual 'profit' of the estate established by this appraisal, the
creditor could take no further action. If the debtor defaulted
on this payment, the creditor could obtain possession of the
estate, first giving security for double his debt against any
damages he might do. The debtor could appoint a spy or
'person of trust' to live on the estate in order that the creditor
might be obliged to pay treble value for any damages occasioned
by his negligence or misusage. A clause in the Act permitted
creditors to recover negroes unpaid for, but the African Company nevertheless felt its interests to be prejudiced: the Act
was repealed by the home government in 1685.[5] Such in an
exaggerated form were the restrictions which the colonists
sought to impose on those who had lent them money.

[1] *A.P.C.* (Colonial Series), 1613–80, pp. 381–3.
[2] *Ibid.*, p. 573.   [3] *Cal. S.P. Col.*, 1677–80, No. 1622.
[4] T. 70/16, fo. 55d; *Cal. S.P. Col.*, 1681–5, No. 1363.
[5] *C.O.* 1/23, fos. 233–7.

The case of Charles Atkinson of Jamaica shows how the chances of recovery were affected by the death of the debtor. He died in 1678, owing the company £700. His heirs, to escape payment of this debt, refused to take out letters of administration. In order to recover their debt, therefore, the company's agents, as principal creditors, were obliged to take out letters themselves and begin proceedings against Atkinson's own debtors. The business would not be completed, they wrote, 'without many a suit at law both as plaintiff & defendant'.[1] In practice, the company did sometimes obtain favourable judgments and enter into possession of the estate of a debtor. This did not, however, necessarily afford full satisfaction. The company's great need was for liquid assets: it had more than enough 'dead stock' in Africa. And a plantation, when in possession of the company, could not always be sold for cash, at least in the smaller islands. In 1682, for example, the agents at Nevis obtained possession of the estate of a debtor: but to sell it, they wrote, 'must be to make a new debt, there being noe person that will or can lay downe ready pay for it'.[2] In this vicious circle, years of costly litigation and forbearance might result only in the exchange of one debt for another.

In some islands the charging of interest on unpaid debts was permitted, and the company was able to obtain greater satisfaction. Rates certainly were high, ten per cent. being regarded as usual in Barbados.[3] But the income which the company drew from the Plantation Debt was a poor compensation for the withholding of principal. Between February 1692 and August 1693, for example, the sums paid in interest on the Barbadian debt amounted to £4,238. This was a useful income, but not nearly so useful, for a company starved of liquid capital, as the repayment of the principal.

The legal defences surrounding the debtor were permanent features of the colonial economies of the seventeenth and eighteenth centuries. From time to time, resourceful Assemblies intervened on the same side in another and more spectacular fashion. The promotion of inflation by tinkering with

[1] T. 70/15, fo. 8d.　　　　[2] T. 70/16, fo. 32d.
[3] T. 70/57, fo. 65d; T. 70/81, fo. 92.

Y

the value of money may indeed be regarded as the classic strategy of the colonial debtor; two examples of it occurred in the West Indies between 1672 and 1713, and particularly affected the Royal African Company. In 1688, the Assembly of Jamaica struck a mighty blow on behalf of debtors by enacting that Spanish pieces-of-eight weighing more than 16 dwt. should pass for 6s. and those of between 13½ and 16 dwt. for 5s.[1] The company objected to the Act, calling its framers 'an Assembly of unqualified persons of ill-repute and indigent fortunes', upwards of twenty of whom were debtors for slaves.[2] It claimed that the Act would at one stroke deprive it of sixteen per cent. of the debt of £90,000 owing in Jamaica. As in the case of the Antiguan debt law, the English Government came to the rescue and disallowed the Act.[3] But even without legislation of this kind monetary conditions in the colonies were unfavourable to the company. In 1683, for example, the company opened its dispute with Jamaica by complaining to the Lords of Trade that the clipped pieces-of-eight circulating there caused sugar-prices to be higher than in other colonies.[4] Already a disparity existed between the £ sterling and the £ Jamaican, partly if not entirely the result of 'light money'. Thus one thousand pieces-of-eight, selected for their heaviness, were worth £250 in Jamaica, but could be sold in London for no more than £190 or £200. The other example of currency manipulation in favour of debtors was the Barbadian paper-money Act of 1706, some of the effects of which have already been noticed.[5]

It must be admitted that the company derived certain benefits from its status as the greatest common creditor. Its agents were freely accused of abusing their position, and the charge may not be without foundation. In 1681, for example, the agents at Jamaica reported to the company:

A person of quallity that is your debtor in noe inconsiderable summe, living neer the place where Daniell the interloper landed

---

[1] T. 70/169, fos. 53d, 63d–64d, 71, 71d; T. 70/82, fo. 34; Cal. S.P. Col., 1689–92, Nos. 59, 259, 374.
[2] T. 70/169, fos. 63d–64d.   [3] Ibid., fos. 71–71d.
[4] Cal. S.P. Col., 1681–5, No. 891.
[5] T. 70/170, fo. 63d; Journal of B.O.T., 1704–9, passim; above, pp. 146–7.

his negroes, having (as wee are informed) showen them more countenance then suites with our intrest, wee have declared our resentments against him in such a manner as by due course of law must very much endamage him or reduce him to such termes as wee desire for the future, soe as to bind him to us, which will be a president of noe small advantage.[1]

Such advantages, however, were not nearly as great as they would have been under laws which gave the creditor a fair chance of recovering his due, and they were probably offset by the sympathy which colonial officials, judges and assemblymen must have felt for their fellow-debtors.

Chief amongst the company's West Indian problems, then, was how to recover its capital, and failure to solve it put serious restrictions on the capacity to trade. This failure was not for want of trying. Exhortations to the colonists from the English Government were secured; slight modifications in debt procedure, such as the prohibition in 1700 upon long adjournments of the Courts, were obtained;[2] debtors were encouraged to make the company their selling-agent in London and could do so free of charge instead of paying the usual rate of three per cent. for commission and brokerage;[3] supernumerary agents were appointed to act as debt-collectors;[4] and in 1697, as we have seen, the company's agents were made fully responsible for all credit extended to planters.[5] None of these devices proved fully effective: in 1701 we find the Committee of Eight resolving to offer the debts in Barbados and Jamaica for sale to the highest bidder, with what result we do not know.[6] Two other expedients were open to the company but, as far as has been discovered, were never adopted. It could, in the first place, have refused to sell slaves to those who already owed money. This policy does not seem ever to have been officially countenanced, though some agents may have followed it on their own initiative. There were obvious difficulties. Negroes were a necessity, and credit was regarded by the planters as a right not a privilege. To cut off supply of the one for over-indulgence in the other would have resulted in uproar and

[1] T. 70/15, fo. 49.   [2] *Cal. S.P. Col.*, 1700, Nos. 257, 257 i; 280, 280 ii.
[3] T. 70/57, fo. 26.   [4] *Ibid.*, fo. 65.   [5] Above, p. 296.
[6] T. 70/86, pp. 146–7.

added fuel to anti-monopolist propaganda. Here, as in all its dealings with the Plantations, the company was obliged to make concessions for the sake of public relations. In a more practical sense, to deny labour to a debtor might seriously affect his capacity ever to pay the debt. 'Would you but trust Moone', wrote the agents at Jamaica in 1682, 'with £500 more in negroes he may very well pay you the one half the first yeare & £500 a yeare afterwards untill your whole debt be extinguished.'[1] It was hard to resist such arguments, for often there must have been no alternative. If debtors were excluded to whom was the company to sell? As early as 1675, there were 144 debtors at Jamaica alone.[2] All planters needed labour; the company was the only lawful supplier; all planters were potential or actual debtors. From this logic there was no escape.

The other possibility was to reduce the number of slaves brought to the colonies in order to lessen the debt. This the company more than once resolved to do. In 1689, for example, the agents at Jamaica were told:

> The patiance we must exercise must exceed our reason to followe such a trade; & it seemes we have not yett given soe much creditt as your island requires, notwithstanding our capitall stocke is nere all amongst you, & we cannot see a likelyhood of saveing our stocke from ruine better than by slackeing our future supplyes.[3]

It is very doubtful if such threats were ever implemented. A deliberate reduction in the number of slaves supplied would not necessarily have produced a reduction of the debts, but it would certainly have made the company even more vulnerable to attack by discontented planters. The Plantation debts certainly contributed to the curtailment of supplies of negroes, but the company's action was involuntary, resulting from a shortage of funds. It transported all the slaves it had the resources to supply; in this as in other branches of its commerce, it traded to capacity or even beyond what might reasonably be regarded as its capacity.

---

[1] T. 70/16, fo. 31d.
[2] T. 70/936, 31 July 1675. The total sum then owed was £17,840.
[3] T. 70/57, fo. 38d; cf. T. 70/78, fo. 16.

Why did these debts accumulate to a point where they undermined the company's financial stability? It is tempting to regard the planters as more unwilling than unable to meet their obligations. The company was after all in a class of its own, a target for any abuse and hostile action. Such an interpretation may contain a little truth. Certainly the company believed that slaves delivered by interlopers and separate traders were not sold on such long credit. 'Wee are satisfied', runs a letter of 1691, 'that private persons get quick pay for negroes & doe not run out their estates in debts.'[1] And in 1700 Governor Beeston of Jamaica wrote: 'The Royal Company usually supplied negroes at £22 and £24 per head and gave 6, 8 and 12 months' credit, now the merchants sell for £34 per head and give no credit at all.'[2] Beeston had been the company's chief agent, and his statement may be exaggerated. But it may not be entirely devoid of truth: the planters of Montserrat, for example, petitioning Parliament in 1698, had put their names to a complaint of 'credit very much lessened since private merchants have had admittance to trade to Africa'.[3] The hatred of the planters for the company is, however, only a partial explanation of their indebtedness to it. The truth is that from the beginning of their history the planters had always been indebted to someone, and would continue to be long after the African Company had disappeared. In the first half of the seventeenth century they owed money to the Dutch; in the second half to the African Company. In the eighteenth century they were indebted on bills and mortgages to their agents in England, the great commission houses of London and other cities.[4] In the company's time, the commission system was only just beginning, and the planters had not yet learned its full potentialities. It was natural, therefore, that they should look for, and indeed demand, the credit which they had to have from the company on which they depended so much.

[1] T. 70/57, fo. 65.   [2] *Cal. S.P. Col.*, 1700, p. 19.
[3] Stock, II, pp. 222–3.   [4] R. Pares, *op. cit.*

3. The Company and the 'Asiento'

The story of the commerce in slaves between the Royal African Company and the Spanish-American colonies is largely one of unfulfilled promise and frustrated expectations. Twice at least this trade seemed about to burgeon into one of great advantage, only to fall away as the result of circumstances beyond the company's control. But the hopes and fears which it aroused figure prominently in the company's relations with the English West Indian colonies, and some account of them must therefore be given.

In prospect, the trade looked to be good business from the point of view of both the company and the Spaniards. After the revolt of Portugal in 1640, Spain could meet the needs of her colonies for labour only by the sacrifice of what was regarded as a cardinal principle of Spanish imperialism, the Seville monopoly. It was of course open to Spanish merchants to go themselves to the sources of supply in Africa. This they sometimes did,[1] but never it seems in large numbers. In default of direct commerce with Africa, it was inevitable that Spain should depend for her negroes on either rebels (the Portuguese), heretics (the English), rebels and heretics (the Dutch), or enemies (the French), for no other nation had a sufficient interest in the slave-trade. From 1640 to 1662 the Spanish Government buried its head in the sand and made no provision of any kind for the supply of negroes, tenders from English, Dutch and Portuguese merchants being rejected.[2] This ostrich-like neglect served the Spanish colonists well, for in default of an official supply they were allowed to help themselves to negroes illicitly imported by the Dutch. 'C'est lorsque la métropole cessa de leur en envoyer que les colons furent le mieux fournis d'esclaves', writes M. Scelle.[3] Clearly, Spain would not permit this to continue indefinitely: if heretics were to supply slaves, it was better that they should be supervised

---

[1] Above, p. 218.

[2] G. Scelle, *La Traite Négrière aux Indes de Castille*, the standard work on the *Asiento* and the Spanish slave-trade in general.

[3] Scelle, I, p. 490.

than unsupervised. The occasion of the revival of the *Asiento* in 1662, it should be noted, was not concern for the economic well-being of the colonies. Chiefly it was fiscal: Spain wished to build ships, and hoped to finance her programme from the revenue of licences to deliver slaves. The history of the *Asiento*, littered as it is with broken contracts and bankrupt contractors, cannot be understood unless it is realized that to the Spanish Government the slave-trade was first and foremost a source of revenue, and only secondarily a method of supplying the colonies with labour.

Tender consciences were satisfied in 1662 by the grant of the *Asiento* to two Genoese, Grillo and Lomelin. They were given permission to make sub-contracts with any nation in amity with Spain, and immediately opened negotiations with the Dutch West India Company and the English company of Royal Adventurers. From this it will be seen that the revival of the *Asiento* gave to England her first real chance of competing with the Dutch in the Spanish colonial trade. The prospect was altogether too exciting for the Adventurers, and in 1663 they concluded an agreement with Grillo for the supply of 3,500 slaves a year, to be delivered at Jamaica and Barbados.[1] This absurd contract, to sell as many negroes to Spain as the company could reasonably hope to transport to the West Indies, may well reflect the ignorance of elementary mercantile realities that characterized the Royal Adventurers in its early years. It was never fulfilled, and the collapse of monopoly in the English slave-trade as a result of the Second Dutch War put an end to the first challenge to Dutch supremacy. The Grillo *Asiento* was terminated in 1671, and for the next decade the supply of slaves to the Spanish colony was formally vested in Garcia, a Madrid businessman, the *Consulado* of Seville, and a sub-contractor, Don Juan Barrosso, all of whom were obliged to lean heavily upon the Dutch.

During the 'seventies, therefore, little was achieved by England; but Englishmen remained optimistic about securing a share in the Spanish trade. Jamaica was their trump card. The Dutch possessed no more suitable commercial base in the

[1] G. F. Zook, *Company of Royal Adventurers Trading to Africa*, p. 93; Scelle gives 5,000 as the figure.

West Indies than Curaçao, and, as an anonymous memorialist wrote in 1675, 'negroes will come att lower rates, it being near 20 ps. 8 cheaper to give 110 ps. 8 per head att Jamaica then att Curosao'.[1] The Royal African Company gave this paper its attention and concluded that the trade was feasible and indeed desirable, provided the Spaniards could be permitted, and induced, to come to the English colonies for their supplies.[2] The company at this date was clearly interested in the possibilities of the *Asiento*, but careful not to commit itself to an agreement such as that of 1663. In 1674 Francis Millington, and in 1676 Peter Proby, both shareholders, put forward proposals, the latter for 250 negroes to be delivered at Cadiz.[3] Nothing seems to have come of these moves, but in 1677 two members of the Court of Assistants were desired: 'to endeavour an agreement with the Spaniards at Sivill to take off negroes from this company to be delivered at the Plantations if possible, if not to drive it as farre as they can & informe the Court their proceedings therein'.[4]

No connexion has been established between this approach and the arrival in Barbados in the same year of a Spanish ship, the *Santo Domingo*. The destination and intentions of this vessel, however, were known in England beforehand, and instructions were sent by the Government to the Governors of Jamaica and Barbados to provide all protection consistent with the Navigation Acts and the laws of the colonies.[5] Governor Atkins, reporting the arrival of the ship, wrote that the company had made a contract with the Crown of Spain to furnish negroes,[6] and it may be that some kind of limited agreement had been made. What the company would not do at this date was to bind itself to supply large numbers of negroes to Spain. Thus in 1681 when Richard (or Ricardo) White, former agent of the Grillo *Asiento*, proposed the renewal of the contract of 1663, he was told that there were 'severall covenants soe disadvantagious to this company's intrest as they doe not think fitt to medle therein'.[7] It was a wise decision.

---

[1] Brit. Mus., Egerton MS. 2395, fo. 501.
[3] *Ibid.*, fos. 19d, 90d.
[5] *Cal. S.P. Col.*, 1677–80, Nos. 234–6.
[7] T. 70/78, fo. 178.

[2] T. 70/76, fos. 45, 45d.
[4] T. 70/77, fo. 63d.
[6] *Ibid.*, No. 241.

No attempt seems to have been made by either side to follow up the trade initiated by the *Santo Domingo*, and it is not until 1681 that there is evidence of further activity at Barbados. In a letter of 14 March of that year, Stede and Gascoigne, the company's agents, reported that a Spaniard from Vera Cruz had bought 600 negroes.[1] Three days later, they referred to another, Thomas Croaker, lately arrived from Cadiz to buy 200 slaves. Again, there is a hint that some kind of previous arrangement had been made, for Croaker refused to avail himself of the credit the company had provided for him, preferring to spend the money he had brought with him.[2] About this time, Spanish trade at Barbados was evidently considerable: in January of the following year, the company's agents wrote that 'Cosker the Spaniard' had purchased 870 negroes and intended to come again.[3] At this point, however, Barbados drops out of the story, and interest switches to Jamaica. This change was probably at Spanish instigation: the African Company would no doubt have preferred to deal at Barbados, where it had less difficulty in satisfying the needs of the English planters, and where the presence of competitive buyers would be correspondingly less unpopular.

The Spaniards had traded at Jamaica sporadically for a number of years past.[4] But it was not until about 1680 that evidence begins to multiply of continuous activity in which the African Company had any share.[5] From this time until 1686, the Spaniards were frequently at Jamaica and indeed for some years had a buyer permanently stationed there. There is evidence of a non-statistical nature to suggest trade on a considerable scale.[6] Unfortunately it is difficult to form an accurate impression of the African Company's share in this trade. It laid no claim to a monopoly of re-exporting negroes, and for the first two or three years the trade seems to have been mainly in other hands. In February 1683, for example, the agents at Jamaica explained that they had sold some slaves to

[1] T. 70/10, fo. 17.   [2] T. 70/15, fo. 51.   [3] T. 70/10, fo. 20.

[4] *Cal. S.P. Col.*, 1669–74, pp. 316–17; *Cal. S.P. Col.*, 1677–80, No. 446.

[5] C. Nettels, 'England and the Spanish-American Trade', in *Journal of Modern History*, III.

[6] Part of it has been assembled by Nettels, *op. cit.*, note 4.

the Spaniards 'that others might not ingrosse unto themselves all the advantages that are to be hoped for from that trade'.[1] In a memorial to the Committee of Trade and Plantations in the same year, the company claimed to have refused several pressing invitations to sell to the Spaniards, preferring to leave to the Jamaicans the disposal of unwanted slaves.[2] This statement had, however, ceased to be true by the end of that year. The period is one when the records of sales of slaves are defective, owing to the loss of some invoice books, but we know that in the twelve months beginning October 1683, 336 negroes were sold to Abraham Gill, agent of the *Asientist* Porcio, to 'Don Juan Genes & Co.' and to 'Don Juan Espino'.[3] The record for the next twelve months has perished, but between November 1685 and March 1686 there is evidence of brisk trade: in five months, 857 negroes were sold to 'Don Alexander Oliver', representative of the Coymans *Asiento*.[4] This was probably the apogee of the company's trade with Spanish-America. Already there were indications of decline; in January 1686, Lieutenant-Governor Molesworth wrote that a large ship of the *Asiento* had been obliged to wait fourteen months for a cargo, and in August of the following year he was writing of the Spanish trade as a thing of the past.[5] No more sales by the company are recorded after March 1686.

In volume, therefore, the Spanish trade of the Royal African Company, except perhaps in 1685 and 1686, was disproportionate to the noise and passion it engendered. Though the company was slow to seize the opportunity offered at Jamaica, the potential benefits appeared to be great. The prices the Spaniards were prepared to offer were undoubtedly higher than those which at this date the English planters could be brought to pay. It is true that they insisted on value for money so far as concerned the physical condition of a slave; top prices were paid only for the best quality. Nevertheless the gain to the company was considerable. From the cargo of the *Robert*, for example, in December 1685, 113 slaves were sold to Olivero at £23 10s. apiece and 26 at £13 10s. No doubt they were the pick of the consignment, but the higher average prices ob-

---

[1] T. 70/16, fo. 43.   [2] T. 70/169, fo. 14d.   [3] T. 70/941.
[4] T. 70/942.   [5] *Cal. S.P. Col.*, 1685–8, Nos. 548, 1374.

tained in the disposal of the company's cargoes in Jamaica in 1684–6 show that the presence of Spanish buyers was profitable.[1]

Even more important than these high prices, the Spaniards, under pressure, could be brought to pay for their negroes in hard cash. In October 1683, the Jamaican agents wrote:

> The Spaniard (or Mr. Gill for him) hath bin with us not lesse then half a dozen times with severall proposalls for this shipp of negroes or such of them as may proove for his turne. At last wee brought him to acknowledge that he had some peeces of 8/8 aboard but he expected to pay us with money he was to have upon creditt; but wee plainly told him that if he had these he must give us the hard peeces of 8/8 for them.[2]

Later, the danger from privateers and pirates in the Caribbean made the transport of silver dangerous and caused the trade to be conducted on a credit basis: in the disturbed state of both the *Asiento* and international relations in the Caribbean this was disadvantageous to the suppliers, and a number of Jamaican merchants, though not the company, eventually burned their fingers.[3] So long as it was a cash-trade, however, there were good hopes of profit, and we may assume that the falling-off of sales to Spanish agents in 1686–7 was not at the company's instigation.

Nor was the English Government responsible. Its attitude towards the trade was generally favourable, and on a number of occasions between 1660 and 1690 instructions were sent to Governors of West Indian colonies to favour it. No Government indeed was likely to neglect a trade productive of bullion. The trade in negroes had the further merit of inserting an English foot into the door of the Spanish-American colonies, and thus promising fulfilment of a dream cherished for more than a century. Once the sale of negroes had been put upon a regular footing, it was hoped, trade in other commodities would follow. Legally, negroes were goods or commodities, and their export from English colonies in Spanish ships was therefore a breach of the Navigation Act. Such anyway was the opinion of the Solicitor-General in 1677, whereupon the Lords of Trade

---

[1] Appendix III.   [2] T. 70/16, fos. 68d, 69.   [3] Below, p. 334.

resolved to advise that the trade should be discontinued.[1] Their
advice, however, was not acted upon by the English Government; on the contrary, when the question was discussed again
in 1684, orders were issued to the Governor of Jamaica to
cause visiting Spanish ships to be civilly treated.[2] The following year, a circular was sent to Governors of all colonies
specifically excepting Spanish ships seeking negroes from the
general instructions to seize foreign ships trading to the English
Plantations.[3] Doubts about the legality of this trade arose from
time to time, as in 1689 and 1708; in 1690 there was talk of a
special Act of Parliament to deal with the matter.[4] But material
expectations overbore the rigours of the law.

This favourable attitude was shared by certain elements in
Jamaica. Of the four Governors in the 'eighties, two, Lynch
and Molesworth, especially the latter, did much to encourage
the trade. In 1688, when it was at a low ebb, Molesworth and
seventy-six 'planters' of Jamaica signed a certificate in which
the benefits to the colony resulting from the trade were enu-
merated. Much silver, they claimed, had been brought to the
island; customs had been increased; the Spaniards had been
supplied with victuals, rum, sugar and cattle; the planters had
'turned into ready mony all their rogues, rebellious and run-
away negroes'; and the commerce of the Dutch had been impaired.[5] These views were not, however, universal amongst
the planters, and for obvious reasons. The best negroes went
to the buyers with the 'hard peeces of 8/8'; the general level of
prices was forced up; and the planter was left with the refuse.[6]
When possible, the company's agents sought to minimize the
dissatisfaction of the planters by allocating to the Spaniards
negroes of a type unpopular in Jamaica; in 1684, for instance,
they reported the sale of a consignment from Gambia whereby
'wee shall not much dissatisfye the countrey who have noe
esteeme for those sort of negroes who are used to eat soe much
flesh in theire owne countrey that they seldome proove well

[1] *Cal. S.P. Col.*, 1677–80, Nos. 346, 584.
[2] *Cal. S.P. Col.*, 1681–5, Nos. 1840, 1928, 1930, 1948, 1974, 2026.
[3] *Cal. S.P. Col.*, 1685–8, No. 120.   [4] T. 70/57, fos. 45, 45d.
[5] T. 70/169, fos. 65d.–66d.
[6] *Cal. S.P. Col.*, 1689–92, No. 295.

under our dyet, except it be for house negroes'.[1] But this could not always be conveniently arranged, and it was inevitable that, with aggregate supplies so restricted, the sale of even a few negroes outside the island should give a useful argument to the company's enemies.

The resentment of the planters found expression in duties laid by the Assembly on the export of negroes;[2] in attempted seizures of Spanish vessels for breaches of the Navigation Act;[3] in attacks upon the expensive provision of royal ships for convoying vessels trading between Jamaica and the Spanish colonies;[4] and in criticisms of the perquisites and *premios* paid by the Spaniard to Governor Molesworth.[5] But the decline of the trade in 1686–7 does not seem to have been principally due to this hostility. The lawlessness of the Caribbean was one cause: twice in 1686 Molesworth referred to the ruin of the trade by the 'South Sea pirates'.[6] The effect of this was to make the Spaniards hesitant about transporting bullion, and to necessitate the extension of credit to them by Jamaican merchants. The African Company may perhaps have decided that it had debts enough already. Another explanation of the falling-off of the trade can be found in the internal history of the *Asiento*, which in 1685 was split from top to bottom by the rival factions of Nicholas Porcio and the Dutch firm of Coymans. How this complicated situation arose it is not necessary here to enquire; its detrimental effects on Anglo-Spanish trade, however, are clear. For a time there were representatives of both factions in Jamaica, pursuing one another through the island's law-courts, and embarrassing the Governor with their importunities.[7]

All through the 'eighties the African Company had wisely avoided concluding any large-scale agreement with the *Asientists*. In trading with the Spaniards, long-term contracts were to be avoided; those who observed that rule might prosper, as the Dutch seem to have done between 1640 and 1662.

---

[1] T. 70/16, fo. 79d.

[2] *Journal of Modern History*, III, pp. 11–12; T. 70/10, fo. 26d; *Cal. S.P. Col.*, 1693–6, No. 635.

[3] *Cal. S.P. Col.*, 1681–5, No. 1673; *Cal. S.P. Col.*, 1685–8, No. 85.

[4] *Journal of Modern History*, III, p. 13.   [5] *Cal. S.P. Col.*, 1685–8, No. 643.

[6] *Ibid.*, Nos. 778, 971.   [7] *Ibid.*, Nos. 193, 193 i, 378, 548.

The temptation to enter into an agreement, however, proved in the end to be too much for the African Company. The motive for so doing was probably the hope of reviving a trade that had become moribund; the opportunity was the visit to England in June 1689 of Santiago Castillo (Anglicized as Sir James Castille), formerly Porcio's agent in Jamaica. Terms were quickly arranged, and on 17 September the contract was sealed. The company was to furnish 2,000 negroes at Jamaica in twenty months, the price to be 80 pieces-of-eight of $17\frac{1}{2}$ dwt. each.[1] The conclusion of this agreement once again called into question the legality of a trade that contravened the Navigation •Acts; once again the law-officers declared against it; and again the English Government chose to override or ignore the law.[2] The contract could hardly have been made at a worse time, for the war destroyed any hope there may have been of fulfilling it. By July 1690, Castillo was back in Jamaica and clamouring for negroes; supplies, however, were too short to allocate more than a few to a buyer whose price was not now as attractive as it had been in peace.[3] In mitigation of its breach of contract, the company claimed 'restraint of princes',[4] but this did not stop Castillo from beginning a lawsuit, with what result we do not know.[5] The company was indeed lucky to have come off as lightly as it apparently did; few *Asientists* were so fortunate. As it was, the fate that would have befallen the company was reserved for a group of Jamaican merchants who made some kind of agreement with Castillo in 1693. Fifteen years later, they were still seeking payment of 86,014 pieces-of-eight due to them.[6]

This seems to have been the end of direct participation by the Royal African Company in the Spanish slave-trade. Trade at Jamaica continued on and off, even during the war of 1702–13, but the company does not appear to have taken any considerable share in it. The profits, if there were any, went to the

---

[1] T. 70/82, fos. 61, 62, 66d.
[2] *Cal. S.P. Col.*, 1689–92, Nos. 368–9, 371, 398, 423–4, 477, 500–1, 528–9, 538, 542, 610, 760; *A.P.C.* (Colonial Series), 1680–1720, p. 153.
[3] T. 70/17, fo. 10d.   [4] T. 70/57, fo. 55.
[5] *Ibid.*, fos. 64, 68, 68d, 70, 72, 80d; T. 70/83, fo. 47d.
[6] *Cal. S.P. Col.*, 1708–9, No. 525.

separate traders. With the conclusion of peace in 1713 and the formal vesting of the *Asiento* in English hands, the company sent out half a dozen ships to Africa to buy slaves on behalf of the South Sea Company, but that revival was short-lived and is, in any case, another story.

4. The Final 'Profit'

In the slave-trade, as it is commonly understood, there were three distinct transactions. Manufactured goods of European or Indian origin were exchanged for slaves in Africa; slaves were exchanged in the colonies for goods, chiefly sugar; and sugar was sold in England for cash. The assumption is that at each stage the trader made a profit. 'Chaque transaction', writes M. Gaston-Martin, 'doit s'accompagner d'un bénéfice.'[1] In the eighteenth century, or at least in certain years of the eighteenth century, this assumption may well be valid. But the history of the Royal African Company suggests that the concept of the third or final 'profit' in the slave-trade is worth re-examining. It is not in the eighteenth century, but in the years between 1674 and 1689, that the true explanations of the company's failure have to be sought, and there are grounds for believing that during that period there was little or no final 'profit' in the slave-trade; on the contrary, there were at times losses serious enough to affect the company's position as a profit-making enterprise.

With the slaves sold and the resultant debts (or some of them) collected, it remained only to remit to England the effects thus acquired. At first sight this would seem a straightforward task; we should have expected the company or any other slave-trader to invest all West Indian assets in goods and consign them to London. It is true that some planters chose to pay for their slaves, not in commodities, but in coin or bills of exchange. But it was perfectly feasible for the company to invest its coin in sugar and to buy staple products locally with its bills of exchange. The choice of the medium in which remittances were made was the company's, and there was nothing to

[1] Gaston-Martin, *Nantes au XVIIIe Siècle*, p. 13.

prevent it from remitting all its assets in sugar, had it wished to do so. In Appendix II will be found the total annual remittances in sugar and other commodities, in bills and in coin, and it will be immediately apparent from these figures that the company did not choose to make the whole, or even always the greater part, of its remittances in goods on which it might be supposed the final profit would be earned. On the contrary, in a number of years, remittances in bills and coin, on which no profit could be earned, exceeded in value remittances in goods.

Why did the company thus voluntarily abdicate the final 'profit'? The answer to this question is to be found in the behaviour of sugar-prices in London, and indeed in Europe at large, during the critical period from the foundation of the Royal African Company to the outbreak of war in 1689. World-supply in these years, it can hardly be doubted, was outstripping world-demand. In the early seventeenth century, a large part of the requirements of Europe had been met from a single producing region, Brazil, which had prospered exceedingly. But there were other places in the New World where sugar could be profitably cultivated, and it was only a question of time before the Brazilian hegemony was challenged. That challenge began in or before 1640, developed rapidly, and in a few years had undermined the prosperity of the older-established producer.[1] Dutch, English and French rivals were in the field, competing for a market which was still a limited one. Sugar in the mid-seventeenth century was poised between the status of the luxury it had been and the necessity it was to become. Falling prices no doubt contributed something to the spreading of sugar consumption amongst new classes, but the adjustment cannot easily have been made. Over-production is a relative term, but the history of the English West Indian colonies between the Restoration and the Revolution and the experience of the Royal African Company suggest its presence. In order to establish this point, it is not necessary to rely on the evidence of the complaints of the colonists themselves; neither in the seventeenth nor in the eighteenth centuries were they backward in voicing their grievances, real or imaginary. In

---

[1] V. M. Godinho, 'Le Portugal, Les Flottes du Sucre et Les Flottes de l'Or', in *Annales-Economies-Sociétés-Civilisations* (1950).

this period, however, the history of sugar-prices, as far as it can be established, confirms the plight in which both planters and merchants found themselves. In 1657 Richard Ligon gave 25*s.* per 100 lb. as an ordinary price for unrefined sugar in Barbados, and showed how at this rate a fortune could be made.[1] Such a price in the colonies must have been the equivalent of at least 35*s.* in Europe. Yet, when the Royal African Company sold its first consignment of sugar in 1674, the ruling price for muscovado in London was no more than 25*s.* Worse was to follow, as the figures quoted in Appendix IV show. For the next twelve years, prices fell until in 1686 they reached their lowest point. In that year, average Barbados muscovado was sold in London as low as 15*s.* 9*d.* a 100 lb.; Nevis sugars at 14*s.* 6*d.*; Jamaican at 18*s.* These were prices not only lower than any previously recorded, but lower than the ruling price in all but a few years until 1884.[2] And these low levels, it should be remembered, were achieved at a time when, of all the English sugar-colonies, only Barbados and Nevis were producing at anything like full capacity. Had Jamaica and the others been intensively exploited and given over entirely, as Barbados was, to sugar cultivation, the fall in price would have been even more catastrophic. It was bad enough for planters and merchants alike. Small wonder that the former had difficulty in paying their debts to the company, or that the latter sought ways to escape from a trade that left little or no room for profit. This year, 1686, however, was the nadir; in 1687 and 1688 there was some slight improvement. Then, with the outbreak of war and the disruption of the West Indian trade, prices were caught by scarcity and tossed up to nearly four times the level that had ruled in the depression. Twice they fell and rose again, before settling down to a more normal course in 1714; but neither in the wild fluctuations of war nor in the steadier levels of the post-war period did they go as low as in 1685 and 1686.

The years that were decisive in the history of monopoly in the slave-trade, therefore, were years of depression in sugar. There

[1] *True and Exact History of Barbados,* 1673, p. 95.

[2] Appendix IV and tables of prices in N. Deerr, *History of Sugar,* 1950, II, 530–1.

Z

was nothing that the African Company could do to mitigate circumstances beyond the control of itself, the planters and the English Government. Of the English merchants engaged in the sugar-trade, the company (involuntarily as we shall see) must have been the greatest. In ordinary years, its imports averaged about one thousand tons. We do not know the aggregate of imports into England at this date: in 1668–9 between eight and nine thousand tons were brought to London alone.[1] The company's share between 1674 and 1689 can, therefore, scarcely have exceeded ten per cent. of the total, and may well have been less. This was by no means a large enough fraction to enable the company to exercise any important influence on sugar-prices in London. Once the negroes were sold the monopoly ceased, and on the final stage of the slave-trade the company had to compete with other merchants. And, since part of the produce of the English West Indies was destined for re-export, prices in London were also determined by supplies entering Europe from other regions. Sugar-prices even in the seventeenth century were world-prices, sensitive to changes outside as well as inside the protected economy of England and her colonies. How sensitive they were is suggested by the following passage from a letter written by the company to its agents at Barbados in 1699:

> Here is in town a short account of some damage done at your island by a tornado, but find none that have the particulars. Sugars began to advance upon it at first, but since that we have had the account of the arrivall of the Brazil Fleet at Lisbon with an extraordinary quantity, which makes it stand or rather decline; and so soon as the Forreign Marketts are supplyed from thence sugars will fall here very considerably. And should your next crop prove plentifull the price must come very low or otherwise the importers of sugars must lose at least one half their returns.[2]

Against a background of falling prices the company's policy with regard to remittances becomes more intelligible. The problem was not so much how to maximize as how to minimize

[1] In the year Mich. 1668–Mich. 1669, 190,496 short cwt. were imported into London, Brit. Mus., Add MSS., No. 36,785. This equals 8,500 tons.

[2] T. 70/57, fo. 150.

imports of sugar, not how to seek the final profit but how to keep down the final loss. Each island offered different solutions to this problem and will be briefly considered. From Barbados, as we have seen, remittances could be made in coin or bills as well as in goods: this may partly explain why more negroes were delivered there than at the other colonies. Nevertheless, the company's agents had no easy task. From 1677, the quantity of sugar remitted fell steadily; in 1684 only twenty-five tons were imported, and the problem of how to find an alternative medium had become acute. Despite the urgent need for cash in London, large balances accumulated in the hands of Stede and Gascoigne, the company's agents in Barbados, for which no satisfactory means of repatriation could be found. In 1681, for example, they had £7,000 in cash lying idle.[1] In that and the following year, they laid out part of this money in the purchase of bills of exchange.[2] They were not, however, alone in seeking this escape from sugar, and bills quickly went to a premium. 'Unles', they wrote in 1683, 'money should grow very scarce here that soe bills of Exchange may be had again at par wee shall not find it very easy to make returnes.'[3] In 1684 and 1686, they again reported large sums of money in hand, 'a grate cash which they must lay out in goods, being noe bills'.[4] One device adopted to lessen these balances was to advance 'a pretty quantity' of money to planters who undertook to repay the company in London out of the proceeds of consignments of sugar.[5] Resort to expedients like this and the purchase of bills that could never be completely creditworthy should be enough to indicate the company's anxiety to forgo the final 'profit' on remittances in sugar.

In Jamaica the problem was even more serious, for the bill of exchange was less common than in Barbados. Here, too, balances accumulated which could be remitted to England only on unfavourable terms. In 1683, for example, the Jamaican agents informed the company: 'Wee never yet had a greater cash then now wee have or lesse encouragement to lay it out. But returnes you must have, and wee shall endeavour to order it soe as may be done to your least disadvantage.'[6]

---

[1] T. 70/16, fos. 13, 13d.   [2] T. 70/15, fo. 53d.   [3] T. 70/16, fo. 50.
[4] *Ibid.*, fo. 68d; T. 70/12, fo. 9.   [5] T. 70/16, fo. 50.   [6] *Ibid.*, fo. 56.

'To your least advantage' not 'to your utmost profit'; the choice of words is significant. Far from there being expectations of gain, the most that is promised is that losses will be as small as possible. In the following year, in reply to complaints from the company, there came an even more explicit statement:

> The complaint you are pleased to make of your losse upon returnes is what wee cannot remedy. 'Tis the common fate of the place; & wee are apt to beleive that (the quantity considered) noe traders here have better successe than yourselves. . . . As sugar is the staple commodity of the island & our dealing with the planters soe very considerable, it is not to be supposed but that the maine part of our returnes must be made in that commodity.[1]

From Jamaica, and to some extent from Barbados, remittances could be made in specie. On this of course there was no profit to be made; indeed the company made a loss by carriage costs and by the difference between the official value of a coin in the Plantations and its intrinsic value in England. The fact that remittances were made in this medium is some measure of the flight from sugar.

In the Leewards, the problem of remittances was incapable of any satisfactory solution at all, for assets could be repatriated only in goods. This was explained to the Committee of Trade and Plantations by the company in 1687. In the trade of Barbados and Jamaica, it was said, a 'losing trade in sugars' could be partly remedied by bills and silver. But in the trade of the Leewards there was no such escape. On this occasion, the company offered to supply these islands with negroes at a lower price if payment could be made in London.[2] It is no wonder that here and indeed everywhere the company encouraged contractors who paid for their slaves in England; thereby it avoided not only debts but losses on the final stage of the triangular trade. It is true that sugar was not the only West Indian commodity available; but it does not seem that indigo, ginger, logwood or cotton turned to much better account. In most years only small quantities were imported. As for

---

[1] T. 70/16, fo. 71d.   [2] T. 70/169, fos. 46d–47d.

tobacco, still grown in some of the islands, the company wrote
to Antigua in 1687: 'Though we loose much by sugers, yett the
tobacco turnes much worse to account.'[1]

It is not suggested that in every year between 1672 and 1689
the sugar-trade was a losing one, though this would be compatible with its continuance. Provided sufficient profit could be
made on the outward trade, supplying the colonies with food,
wine, clothes, cask or slaves, some loss could be sustained on
returns and the merchant still left the gainer. For the company
and probably for other importers, the sugar-trade in this period
has the appearance of an unfortunate necessity, undertaken in
order that capital might be repatriated. Some indication of
how and where losses were incurred is given in a letter from the
company to its agents at Barbados in 1687:

> Our markett here doth nott give encouragement to any to raise
> the prices of goods there [in Barbados]; for 14s. per centum lbs.
> on suger there, considering the wast & diffarence in weight, is as
> much as itt will yield here, for which deduct for caske, your com-
> mission, freight and custome & you may soone make up the
> account of what will be remaining.[2]

In 1686, the lowest point in sugar-prices, average muscovado
was being invoiced from Barbados at 9s. 3d. a 100 lb. The miscellaneous charges for packing, lighterage and carriage in the
colony and in England totalled 1s. 9d. a 100; the agent's commission 9d.; freight 4s. or 4s. 6d.; and duty (following the
additional impost placed on sugar in 1685) 3s. 11d.; total
charges 10s. 11d.[3] A good price in London that year was 17s. and
much lower prices were recorded: so that, even allowing for
some discrepancy between Barbadian currency and sterling,
the company probably stood to lose on every consignment

---

[1] T. 70/57, fo. 16d.   [2] *Ibid.*, fo. 14.

[3] Miscellaneous charges: packing and unpacking, storage, lighterage,
pilotage, lodminage, etc. at both ends. An examination of a number of consignments suggests that these averaged 10 per cent. in the colonies and 6d.
a 100 lb. in England. Commission, 7 per cent. on prime cost and incidentals
in the colonies. Duties: on Jamaican sugar, 1s. 5d. per 100 lb. until 1685,
addition of 2s. 1d. in 1685, taken off in 1693; on Barbadian sugar, the same
plus the 4½ per cent. duty payable in the island. Deerr, *History of Sugar*, II,
pp. 427–30.

imported. This is the blackest period, but it is clear, both from the course of prices and from the correspondence between company and agents already cited, that 1686 was only the climax of a depression that had long been threatening.

The war that began in 1689 changed everything. Its immediate effects were to shatter the bill-mechanism between Barbados and London, bill after bill being protested.[1] After 1692 the number of bills received by the company diminished, and for the time being this method of remittance was almost abandoned. Initially, this flight from bills may have been due to the circumstances of war, for the goods consigned to England to meet bills already drawn went to the bottom of the sea. But the flight would have occurred in any case, for the soaring price of sugar in London, even when allowance is made for losses at sea, reinstated the final profit. 'Wee should be glad', wrote the company in 1692, 'that you could get in our debts to make us large returns while the freight may be had there for 8 l. per tun, beleiving that sugar, indico or any other commoditie will turne better to account than to give 25% on bills.'[2] In 1695 the company could pay the planter 20s. a 100 in Barbados and, by selling in London at 52s., could make a profit, clear of charges, of 13s. or 14s.[3] Of course the artificial scarcity of war could not last, and in February 1697 the company told its agents not to pay more than 12s. 6d. a 100 for sugar or 10l. a ton for freight, 'sugars sell here so badly'. Nevertheless there was some permanent gain for the merchants. Sugar did not fall to the pre-war price. While in 1698 the company was asking only for the cheapest and coarsest varieties, by 1700, being informed that 'sugars will come pritty reasonable about 20s. per cwt', it was writing for 'large returns & upon as good terms as any others can procure'.[4]

In the war of 1702–13 (though the London prices deriving from the company's records for most of the period are corrupt) the price of sugar again climbed to famine levels. Apart from some large consignments of silver in 1706 (a year when London

---

[1] *T.R.H.S.*, Fifth Series, II, p. 98. [2] T. 70/57, fo. 78.
[3] Charges for Barbados being as follows: Incidentals 2s. 6d., Commission 1s. 9d., Freight 12s., Duty 2s. 2d., total 18s. 5d.
[4] T. 70/57, fos. 136, 159d.

prices were, for wartime, abnormally low), virtually the whole of the company's effects in the West Indies was remitted in sugar. Hence the phenomenon that in years in which, as we have seen, the activity of the company was severely restricted in all directions, its imports of sugar were almost as large as they had ever been. Exports to Africa dwindled; far fewer slaves were delivered than before; yet nearly as much sugar was brought to England. The planters, we might infer, could now afford to pay their debts; but, more important, the final profit had reappeared.

It came too late to be of service to a company that had already lost its grip on solvency. Once again the explanation for the failures of 1689–1713 is found in the 'good years' of 1672–89. The harvest which the company reaped from the West Indian trade in the days of its monopoly scarcely provided enough seed for the next crop. The final profit materialized at a moment when the company ceased to be able to take advantage of it. The separate traders were the beneficiaries, and it was their good fortune to go into business in 1698 and not in 1672.

8

CONCLUSION

THE history of the Royal African Company from the reconstruction of 1712–13 to the final dissolution in 1752 will here be only briefly outlined. It is, on the whole, a record of decay and inactivity, punctuated by attempts at revival all of which proved fruitless. In the years 1713 to 1715, under the stimulus of peace, fresh funds, and a share in the business of the *Asiento*, a total of forty ships was dispatched from England.[1] This effort was not sustained, and in the following years the company was once again in a moribund condition: between 1715 and 1721, only 1743 slaves were delivered in the Plantations.[2] Another and more notable revival occurred between 1720 and 1724. In the year of the South Sea Bubble, investors were prepared to support projects with far less chance of success than the African Company, and fresh capital was obtained. New spirit, as well as money, seems to have been put into the company by the Duke of Chandos.[3] In many ways this attempt at resuscitation was the most pathetic in the whole history of the company. The following figures of the company's exports tell their own story:

1720 (from July)	£53,093
1721	£69,449
1722	£75,040
1723	£102,560
1725	£3,917
1726	£2,943[4]

[1] T. 70/63.　　　[2] T. 70/956–7.
[3] A. B. Dubois, *The English Business Company after the Bubble Act*, p. 394; Donnan, II, pp. 249, 250, etc.
[4] T. 70/922–4.

In 1723, therefore, the company for the first and only time in its history exported goods to the value of more than £100,000. To some extent, this burst of activity was mirrored in a temporary revival of the company's fortunes: in 1723 2,284 slaves were delivered to the colonies, and in 1724 1,212. From 1721 to 1724 9,801 ounces of gold and 1,486 cwt. of ivory were brought home from Africa. Yet the effort, impressive as it was, came to nothing. The exports of 1720-4 did not earn enough even to carry on the trade in the following years, let alone to enable profits to be distributed. Between 1725 and 1729 only 563 slaves were delivered in the colonies. About 1730, yet another revival took place, on a smaller scale but equally sterile.

This seems to have been virtually the end of the company as an active trading corporation. It continued to own and administer the forts in West Africa, but was clearly incapable of preserving them in a defensible condition out of its own resources. In 1730 a subsidy of £10,000 was given to the company by the Government to aid in this work, and until 1743 the same sum was granted annually. In 1744 it was increased to £20,000, but in the following year reduced to the original figure; after 1746 it was withheld entirely.[1] Without a subsidy the company could not continue for long, and the end came in 1750. In that year an Act was passed creating a regulated company, in which both the general management of the African trade and the forts were vested.[2] Two years later, the old company's affairs were formally wound up by another Act, the proprietors of its stock being recompensed to the extent of about £25,000.[3]

After a life of exactly eighty years the Royal African Company finally disappeared. By how much it had diminished the fortunes of individual shareholders and creditors in that time has already been suggested. Yet its achievements were not negligible. This book has been concerned only with the first forty-one years of the company's history: in that time it exported goods to the value of £1½ million, dispatched 500 ships to Africa, delivered 100,000 slaves to the Plantations, imported

---

[1] Donnan, II, p. xxxii.   [2] 23 Geo. II c. 31.
[3] 25 Geo. II c. 40; Dubois, *op. cit.*, p. 123.

30,000 tons of sugar, coined more than half a million guineas, and built or rebuilt eight forts on the African coast. These are the achievements which entitle the company to a place in history. No other company associated with the slave-trade, with the exception of the Dutch West India Company, came near to equalling them. Yet this study of the African Company has proceeded on the assumption that it was a failure, and for this reason. It was a capitalist organization, created in a world which, if not yet capitalistic, already acknowledged the criteria of the capitalist; and it is by these criteria that success and failure must be principally determined. The men and women who invested in the African Company did not do so in pursuit of an ideal of imperialism; their aim was to make money. They were interested in exports and imports, shipping and slaves, forts and factories, only in so far as they contributed to the making of profits. Historically important as they may be, the achievements of the company do not entitle it to be called a success, for it failed in the primary duty of a joint-stock company, the making of profits in a form in which they could be distributed to shareholders.

The problem that survives this inquiry is not why the company failed, but rather the selection amongst a variety of causes of the weightiest and most effective. There is, indeed, an embarrassing number of explanations. In part this embarrassment derives from examining a trade which was spread over three continents; the emphasis given to one explanation or another is likely to vary according to the point of view from which the subject is approached. In England, the accident of political change and a financial policy that was, to say the least, unwise, appear to loom largest. In West Africa, on the other hand, we are introduced to international competition, and the shortcomings of the company's servants. And in the West Indies, the Plantation Debt and the losses of the sugar-trade seem to be decisive. Over all hangs the toll of losses in war.

Neither the Revolution of 1688 nor the wars that followed were fundamental explanations of failure. They were tremendous blows which greatly hastened the process of decay. But the argument of this book has been that the company ought to be judged on its performance in the years before the

Revolution. Evidence has been brought to suggest that already in this period the failure to earn satisfactory profits can be established. But for the events of 1688 and the war, the process of dissolution might have taken much longer; but it is unlikely that it could have been arrested.

It is therefore in the 'good' years, from 1672 to 1689, that the causes of failure have to be sought. Responsibility has to be divided between the company itself and the trade upon which it was engaged, in proportions which it would be unwise to guess. The large-scale enterprise (and the African Company was this) seems to have made its appearance in history before the time was fully ripe for it. Especially in the case of a commercial corporation, there were structural defects which were hard to eradicate. In particular the exercise of effective control over employees thousands of miles away proved difficult. In the twentieth century such control is facilitated by devices which were wholly lacking 250 years ago. Modern accounting methods also play a part in the promotion of standards of efficiency in large businesses that was then unknown. In the seventeenth century the basic principles of accounting were well understood and, in the case of the Royal African Company, faithfully followed; but the interpretation of these accounts and the uses to which they were put were limited. The directors of a large enterprise, no matter how industrious they might be, were forced to leave more to the honesty and discretion of the men on the spot than was compatible with efficiency, and the enterprise was likely to suffer in consequence.

Nor does it seem to be only the telegraph, the fast steamship, the railway, and other effective means of control available in modern times, which explain why the large corporation can succeed in business where 250 years ago it contained structural defects. The servants of the African Company, for all their oaths of fidelity, did not identify their own interests with those of their employer to the same extent that occurs in the modern world. This is especially true of the company's African service, and it may well be an important reason for the success of the East India Company and the failure of the Royal African that in the one the interests of employer and employee proved compatible and in the other they did not. In neither do these interests appear to have been fully identified in the seventeenth and early eighteenth centuries. The servants of both went out to make private fortunes; those who went to the East could do so and were content, those who went to West Africa could not, and sought recompense in idleness, negligence or fraud.

It is true that there are notable exceptions to the generally dismal record of joint-stock enterprise in the sixteenth and seventeenth centuries. But they are few. Of all the prominent English companies, only the East India and Hudson's Bay can be regarded as successful in the sense in which hundreds of large businesses are successful today: they lasted, and they made profits. These examples suggest that the large business could succeed in the seventeenth century only under circumstances that were especially favourable. Of the remainder, some were short-lived; others, like the Royal African Company, had a long life but earned small profits or none; others were both short-lived and unprofitable. To the political historian, familiar with the structural defects of the greatest corporation of all, the state, it should cause little surprise that the record of big business is no better.

That the nature of the slave-trade goes some way to explaining the fate of the African Company is easier to appreciate now than twenty or thirty years ago when this branch of English commerce was seldom referred to without the epithet 'lucrative'. Historians dredging amongst the scattered papers of private merchants in the eighteenth century have modified the African trade's reputation for huge profits and shown that some voyages were attended with losses.[1] Profits there must have been, but they do not seem to have been easily earned. The truth is that the trade was a gamble: profits might be made, but the risk of loss was always present. All trade in the eighteenth century contained an element of risk; but the slave-trade must have been amongst the riskiest. Success depended not only upon the personal qualities of trader and captain, but

---

[1] S. Dumbell, 'The Profits of the Guinea Trade', in *Economic History* Supplement to *Economic Journal* (1931); T. S. Ashton (editor), *Letters of a West African Trader*, C.P.B.A., 1950; F. E. Hyde, B. B. Parkinson, S. Marriner, 'The Nature and Profitability of the Liverpool Slave Trade', in *Ec.H.R.*, Second Series, V (1953).

upon a range of variable factors beyond the control of either. The alternations of war and peace in the remote African interior could determine scarcity or glut of negroes; an outbreak of disease on the Middle Passage could wipe out profits in a few days; and the fluctuations of the colonial economies and the world-prices of colonial products could make or mar the whole voyage. Such risks might theoretically be best met by a large capital able to withstand the buffets of fortune. But the history of the Royal African Company showed that such a capital would need to be not only large, but very large, and probably far larger than was ever likely to be made available. And even if a giant corporation with a capital sufficient to cover all risks could have been devised, its structural weaknesses would almost certainly have offset the gain.

Yet when due consideration has been given to all these factors, it remains true that the African Company had to battle with difficulties that were peculiar to its own time. On the one hand, its monopoly coincided with a severe depression in the sugar-trade. And on the other hand, the company was made to carry a burden which in later years was borne wholly or partly by the state, the burden of defence. Until 1730, the British Government refused to accept responsibility for the preservation of English interests in Africa beyond the dispatch of an occasional man-of-war. The granting of a subsidy in that year was a step towards the assumption of greater responsibility. Fifty years earlier, no such step had been even contemplated. The Government's policy then had been to develop the colonies by an assured labour-supply. But being totally unable itself to provide this supply, it had struck a bargain. The African Company was created in order to assume responsibility for an essential link in the imperial economy, and in exchange was granted a monopoly. The attempted fusion of public responsibility and private interest which this bargain implied was characteristic of the seventeenth century. In the crude form in which such bargains had to be struck, the interests of the contracting parties were often irreconcilable: either the state had to lose or the businessmen become altruists.

APPENDIX I

EXPORTS

A. TOTAL EXPORTS

FIGURES of annual exports for most years between 1672 and 1712 have been obtained from the company's Invoice Books, Outward (T. 70/910–920). This series is incomplete, and in the following table has been supplemented by figures compiled by the company itself. These are shown in italics. The company appears to have produced other sets of figures, especially for the years 1698–1708, which differ somewhat from these.

In the company's Invoice Books the value placed upon an article appears to be the cost of purchase plus an allowance, where appropriate, for any processing paid for by the company, e.g. dyeing, packaging, pressing.

1673 from 15 Nov.	£19,257	1694	£27,987
1674	£40,040	1695	£24,710
1675	£36,262	1696	£19,040
1676 to 15 Nov.	£19,701	1697	£17,936
		1698	£45,567
1680	£44,574	1699	*£44,603*
1681	£76,885	1700	*£26,686*
1682	£88,467	1701	£45,322
1683	£78,006	1702	£35,794
1684	£54,542	1703	£33,591
1685	£82,550	1704	£66,072
1686	*£66,129*	1705	*£16,838*
1687	*£77,696*	1706	*£14,802*
1688	£65,612	1707	*£23,121*
1689	£28,465	1708	*£5,386*
1690	£29,738	1709	*£4,139*
1691	£20,678	1710	—
1692	£36,882	1711	—
1693	£58,170	1712	—

B. INDIVIDUAL COMMODITIES compiled from Invoice Books, Outward, T. 70/910–920.

(1) Metal and Metalware

	Iron Bars		Copper Bars		Brassware		Pewterware	
	Weight tons cwt.	Value £	Weight tons cwt.	Value £	Weight cwt.	Value £	Weight cwt.	Value £
1673 from 15 Nov.	40 3	642	1 0	132	6	36	24	137
1674	170 17	2705	23 16	3251	216	986	53	380
1675	216 17	3469	26 0	3890	179	1860	24	161
1676 to 15 Nov.	162 14	2529	11 14	1733	89	465	30	211
1680	491 17	7646	12 7	1553	377	2952	73	502
1681	493 9	6916	20 6	2704	443	2900	186	1254
1682	361 3	4740	27 4	3595	404	2578	252	1569
1683	288 6	3945	10 5	1346	423	2722	294	1718
1684	210 2	2850	12 16	1661	143	1019	335	1807
1685	516 6	7954	17 16	2349	533	3242	454	2383
1688	285 6	3488	8 5	1054	217	1431	370	1969
1689	103 17	1457	1 12	197	71	485	208	1049
1690	93 0	1276	4 0	477	86	686	73	352
1691	97 2	1431	1 10	214	90	634	54	346
1692	299 8	4366	1 12	218	278	1913	128	768
1693	280 16	3840	3 6	455	263	1929	291	1404
1694	219 7	3161	4 19	675	123	769	90	466
1695	114 5	1985	— —	—	100	892	170	944
1696	60 17	1084	— —	—	113	985	152	737
1697	92 5	1614	— —	—	89	754	84	477
1698	225 17	3354	0 11	100	295	2473	271	1433
1701	111 13	1566	3 18	652	351	2944	349	1765
1702	66 5	861	3 12	534	465	3762	84	420
1703	74 7	1002	0 12	96	69	533	15	67
1704	325 1	5156	— —	—	298	2508	2	12

(2) British Woollens

	Perpetuanas		Says		Welsh Plains	
	Pieces	Value in £s.	Pieces	Value in £s.	Pieces	Value in £s.
1673 from 15 Nov.	1975	2875	2110	5892	37	55
1674	3025	4835	2020	5656	236	354
1675	2435	3986	2020	5656	229	343
1676 to 15 Nov.	958	1405	1012	2587	168	228
1680	2197	3243	1880	4262	363	466
1681	7281	10622	4760	11319	341	416
1682	7514	10354	3217	7512	499	609
1683	4840	6982	2995	6985	462	563
1684	4755	6382	2440	5171	430	531
1685	3940	5144	2019	3855	596	745
1688	9348	10937	1375	2632	115	144
1689	5164	6037	1515	3008	102	122
1690	4690	5452	1370	2740	200	240
1691	1500	1744	600	1200	300	372
1692	4350	5111	1300	2547	133	177
1693	13250	15569	1180	2389	428	527
1694	3850	4524	100	200	310	377
1695	4120	4967	160	325	285	358
1696	2600	3180	190	380	340	425
1697	3939	4727	—	—	24	31
1698	9386	10364	320	673	753	945
1701	8655	6767	200	400	108	147
1702	6757	4707	—	—	160	208
1703	9660	6400	—	—	60	82
1704	18490	14387	225	394	70	97

(3) East India Textiles

	Allejaes		Baftes		Brawles		Guinea Stuffs		Long Cloths	
	Pieces	Value in £s.	Pieces	Value in £s.	Pieces	Value in £s.	Pieces	Value in £s.	Pieces	Value in £s.
1673 from 15 Nov.	140	115	—	—	2100	525	3840	448	400	600
1674	300	239	1456	1835	4762	1190	4548	653	1054	1513
1675	345	263	1932	1214	2950	860	4784	767	1526	2321
1676 to 15 Nov.	40	36	1030	709	3258	865	680	96	156	219
1680	30	35	1114	897	2708	689	2586	353	91	148
1681	712	634	929	740	5206	1641	7202	1599	595	947
1682	1263	1109	1794	865	5682	2055	6227	1342	3020	3698
1683	1336	1166	2295	1272	4550	1874	3850	1024	2230	2403
1684	600	464	2428	1474	2260	756	1430	257	430	522
1685	2571	1974	2330	1184	2630	564	3731	498	1270	1354
1688	396	331	3055	1736	6355	1398	11000	1689	635	840
1689	293	254	520	398	1155	262	2320	363	332	450
1690	—	—	405	392	2388	520	2895	434	760	1587
1691	—	—	1050	1187	20	5	300	52	240	588
1692	280	336	1533	947	2463	591	2670	445	21	58
1693	75	90	779	769	887	242	1928	515	—	—
1694	—	—	—	—	720	207	440	125	210	392
1695	—	—	—	—	33	13	200	55	246	406
1696	—	—	60	30	450	146	—	—	—	—
1697	—	—	191	216	230	66	210	45	14	21
1698	—	—	203	174	600	193	850	335	510	1163
1701	120	201	770	1011	900	320	1046	251	1020	2521
1702	60	100	497	628	150	54	520	135	65	153
1703	18	30	—	—	190	68	248	99	1115	2315
1704	—	—	20	15	1054	259	—	—	445	1011

2A

East India Textiles (continued)

	Longees		Nicconees		Pautkes		Tapseels	
	Pieces	Value in £s.	Pieces	Value in £s.	Pieces	Value in £s.	Pieces	Value in £s.
1673 from 15 Nov.	168	57	1760	688	—	—	936	725
1674	—	—	1106	537	440	80	1890	1429
1675	6	3	3599	1906	1923	352	1521	1131
1676 to 15 Nov.	—	—	2294	1207	106	20	2051	1320
1680	1046	379	2050	793	2120	380	910	720
1681	2318	926	2368	1237	2203	457	1692	1415
1682	2185	808	4060	1941	9661	1930	5329	4169
1683	3260	928	6390	3736	1502	284	1058	996
1684	1664	484	2530	1154	5820	962	1830	1472
1685	1265	390	2796	1210	3310	430	2793	1687
1688	2164	720	3563	2389	3990	657	1545	1345
1689	750	319	570	389	340	56	410	351
1690	1235	824	436	306	3100	646	221	199
1691	—	—	—	—	120	25	—	—
1692	379	122	532	367	1013	279	445	400
1693	81	73	384	287	—	—	361	284
1694	—	—	70	59	600	157	170	149
1695	—	—	30	25	—	—	70	66
1696	—	—	—	—	—	—	—	—
1697	—	—	227	214	40	11	25	22
1698	—	—	100	62	300	79	206	176
1701	—	—	460	417	—	—	498	664
1702	20	6	109	130	—	—	72	63
1703	—	—	330	282	—	—	80	66
1704	—	—	360	162	—	—	—	—

(4) Miscellaneous Textiles

	Annabasses		Carpets		Sletias		Sheets		Boysados	
	Pieces	Value in £s.	Num.	Value in £s.	Num.	Value in £s.	Num.	Value in £s.	Num.	Value in £s.
1673 from 15 Nov.	—	—	83	40	2004	2209	7277	1001	45	124
1674	—	—	301	120	4666	4563	23400	3802	50	137
1675	—	—	—	—	2685	2694	9750	1584	50	137
1676 to 15 Nov.	3000	382	—	—	472	308	5670	871	40	107
1680	20670	2156	—	—	1107	827	13780	1837	50	119
1681	20504	2136	413	103	3972	3826	25220	3372	123	295
1682	16182	1791	102	28	4657	3517	28600	4098	366	887
1683	18376	1966	434	100	4771	3949	28470	4952	757	1777
1684	7200	743	2931	1082	1369	1474	17095	2833	1145	2462
1685	21804	2195	3420	1171	3150	1774	29900	4734	581	1162
1688	16900	1562	2255	674	1385	607	32565	4799	735	1458
1689	4110	388	2026	577	757	381	15925	2466	283	560
1690	4243	534	2422	698	254	95	16250	2437	576	1137
1691	—	—	500	144	—	—	10855	1628	210	415
1692	12603	1315	2139	612	700	264	14040	2106	21	42
1693	8350	933	5550	1603	2228	851	25090	3763	500	1000
1694	100	12	500	144	520	187	22945	3442	60	118
1695	100	12	200	60	—	—	13000	2112	49	98
1696	—	—	1900	570	—	—	9750	1517	182	364
1697	3210	336	600	180	126	195	9750	1544	—	—
1698	140	32	2500	739	1437	609	32500	4796	200	396
1701	6800	609	2150	618	2794	1142	10075	1389	60	117
1702	2890	254	108	31	1630	642	9685	1312	20	39
1703	140	31	300	86	3778	1513	18850	2610	20	39
1704	50	11	1259	363	4370	1737	77367	11556	—	—

(5) Gunpowder, firearms, knives

	Gunpowder		Firearms		Knives	
	No. of barrels	Value in £s.	No. of Pieces	Value in £s.	No. of dozen	Value in £s.
1673 from 15 Nov.	300	900	2200	870	668	67
1674	50	150	2100	951	4755	397
1675	60	180	1038	504	2371	199
1676 to 15 Nov.	122	342	943	429	4096	354
1680	875	2283	3111	1691	2182	311
1681	479	1194	2505	1222	2894	354
1682	832	1864	3357	1746	3089	427
1683	769	1766	3170	1540	2798	386
1684	1092	2818	1849	859	2929	374
1685	1810	3958	1695	958	9424	1193
1688	838	1849	890	587	6067	749
1689	426	1226	210	138	5881	701
1690	525	1733	386	270	2889	337
1691	185	694	272	237	1992	239
1692	197	911	787	647	5212	619
1693	204	1018	548	454	6729	839
1694	120	363	270	217	6872	856
1695	175	729	—	—	7908	999
1696	285	1410	200	140	4978	652
1697	322	1419	244	197	5861	760
1698	598	1300	867	596	18212	2249
1701	202	580	8068	4782	1898	221
1702	142	593	7921	5222	1351	158
1703	208	1212	4520	3599	1980	221
1704	279	1659	12445	9272	6535	710

(b) Miscellaneous

	Cowries		Beads		Coral	
	Cwt.	Value in £s.	Cwt.	Value in £s.	Oz.	Value in £s.
1673 from 15 Nov.	—	—	19	89	—	—
1674	239	918	69	542	—	—
1675	182	729	84	548	—	—
1676 to 15 Nov.	128	509	26	180	194	48
1680	148	502	107	807	1542	372
1681	1225	5078	118	915	2056	587
1682	1309	6946	199	1439	6354	1308
1683	1624	8747	267	1686	3129	591
1684	1036	4196	230	1403	2624	497
1685	2260	9670	418	2615	1802	373
1688	573	2592	285	1631	1907	314
1689	328	1479	56	321	1243	245
1690	325	1480	34	216	1682	279
1691	148	704	173	1539	1908	354
1692	473	2367	153	1209	3009	543
1693	750	3329	137	845	5141	1121
1694	574	2102	118	835	2768	583
1695	372	1679	17	154	1406	347
1696	429	3003	12	88	2178	443
1697	79	596	4	39	512	115
1698	104	1482	111	924	7943	1639
1701	319	2976	186	1184	3061	860
1702	306	3376	248	1671	1790	515
1703	321	2174	88	721	636	167
1704	399	2063	163	1499	2744	676

APPENDIX II

IMPORTS

A. From West Indies

(i) Sugar, 1673–1711, compiled from Invoice Books, Homeward, T. 70/936–956.

Year	Barbados	Jamaica In Tons	Leewards	Total
1673	90·8	39·9	—	130·7
1674	520·6	34·3	43	597·9
1675	280·3	299·8	421·4	1001·5
1676	132·6	269·2	233·8	635·6
1677	648·9	315·9	398·2	1360
1678	615·4	317·5	523·6	1456·5
1679	472·1	624·2	470	1566·3
1680	280·6	318·5	393·2	992·3
1681	186	689·8	329	1204·8
1682	164	433·9	428·8	1026·7
1683		no record available		
1684	25·8	641·2	422·2	1089·2
1685		no record available		
1686	181·5	732	342·3	1255·8
1687		no record available		
1688	243·8	338	292·8	874·6
1689	353·7	276	135	764·7
1690	288·6	458·8	—	747·4
1691	299·7	297·9	162·5	760·1
1692	375·9	390·8	360·2	1136·9
1693	154·1	91·2	136·7	382
1694	235·9	363·7	207·4	906
1695	735·2	147·8	55	938
1696	529·2	241	28·4	798·6
1697	147·2	98·8	404·2	650·2
1698	683·5	99·5	129·2	912·2
1699	466·4	157·9	356·9	979·2
1700	578·3	271·2	466·1	1315·6
1701	387·4	185·6	432·2	1005·2
1702	127·1	314·3	275·8	717·2

Year	Barbados	Jamaica	Leewards	Total
		In Tons		
1703		no record available		
1704	511	79·6	854·7	1445·3
1705	513·8	113	269·6	896·4
1706	443·2	546·6	325·2	1315
1707	443·4	92	204·6	740
1708	353·2	457	181·8	992
1709	253·1	19·2	114·9	387·2
1710	248·6	—	160	408·6
1711	178·7	—	60	238·7

Aggregate Total (35 years) 31,628·6 tons

(ii) Bills of Exchange, 1673–94, compiled from Bill Books, T. 70/269–277, 1695–1707 compiled from Cash Books, T. 70/225–234.

Year	Barbados	Jamaica	Leewards	Virginia	Total
		In £s.			
1673	1994	—	—	—	1994
1674	9532	—	—	—	9532
1675	5603	2184	418	—	8205
1676	8183	140	546	4608	13477
1677	20039	731	—	—	20870
1678	11962	145	2240	1476	15823
1679		no record available			
1680 (incomplete)	8204	144	—	—	8348
1681	18459	6048	20	—	24527
1682	26372	198	9548	—	36118
1683	21598	—	—	—	21598
1684	23828	70	241	—	24139
1685	19610	2368	—	—	21978
1686	13605	—	—	—	13605
1687	17009	1315	—	1003	19327
1688	8378	130	—	—	8508
1689	6181	500	164	40	6885
1690	4666	1100	—	21	5786
1691	12839	—	—	100	12939
1692	16532	308	—	—	16840
1693	11874	—	—	—	11874
1694	11675	—	—	—	11675
1695 (incomplete)	1815	—	—	—	1815
1696	464	150	—	—	614
1697	1441	—	—	—	1441
1698	1361	—	1801	—	3162
1699	1048	—	—	—	1048
1700	559	—	—	—	559

Year	Barbados	Jamaica	Leewards	Virginia	Total
			In £s.		
1701	1346	—	720	—	2066
1702	555	—	1283	—	1838
1703	100	—	690	597	1387
1704	—	—	220	632	852
1705	—	—	—	1145	1145
1706	—	—	—	548	548
1707	—	200	—	728	928

(iii) Other Commodities, 1673–1711, totals only, compiled from T. 70/936–956.

Aggregate Totals (35 years)	Ginger:	7,311 cwt.
	Indigo:	1,581 cwt.
	Cotton:	297,837 lb.
	Silver:	£66,308 sterling

B. From West Africa.

(i) Gold, 1673–1711, the number of guineas coined for the company at the Mint, from T. 70/216 and T. 70/1186, p. 144.

Year	No. of Guineas	Year	No. of Guineas	Year	No. of Guineas
1673	2208	1687	32440	1701	4984
1674	7933	1688	39371	1702	—
1675	12271	1689	25493	1703	897
1676	15278	1690	1562	1704	1836
1677	33871	1691	26700	1705	1358
1678	5005	1692	19036	1706	—
1679	25277	1693	7506	1707	5568
1680	17147	1694	15801	1708	2918
1681	24852	1695	21504	1709	11155
1682	23235	1696	2410	1710	10382
1683	25589	1697	11443	1711	—
1684	20684	1698	17828	1712	2925
1685	46066	1699	2214	1713	146
1686	23434	1700	—		

Aggregate Total (41 years): 548,327 guineas

(ii) Other Commodities, 1674–1713, totals only, compiled from T. 70/1513, supplemented by Minutes of Courts of Sales.

Aggregate Totals:	Ivory (40 years)	17,113 cwt.
	Wax (40 years)	6,662 cwt.
	Redwood (32 years)	2,313 cwt.

APPENDIX III

DELIVERIES AND PRICES OF SLAVES IN ENGLISH WEST INDIES 1672–1711

THE exact number of slaves delivered to the English West Indies can never be established. Records of those sold by auction in the colonies were kept in the company's Invoice Books, Homeward (T. 70/936–956). From this source the totals of slaves delivered to ships' captains both on account of commission and in part-payment of freight can also be devised; they are included in the aggregates given below. The books for 1683, 1685, 1687 and 1703 are missing. No record was normally kept in these books of negroes delivered on contract and no entirely satisfactory way of remedying this defect has been found. Professor V. T. Harlow in his *History of Barbados* and Mr. C. S. S. Higham in his *The Leeward Islands under the Restoration* supplemented the aggregates of auction-sales by references in the surviving correspondence to arrivals of contract-cargoes. The letters from the West Indies for the period 1672–89 are, however, extremely defective, surviving if at all chiefly in abstracts. There can, therefore, be no certainty that a note of every contract-cargo has been preserved. I have, accordingly, preferred to present only the series which I can be reasonably sure is complete. For contract-negroes I have (pp. 295, 299 above) estimated roughly what I believe the total to be.

To some extent I have been able to remedy the loss of the four missing Invoice Books from the series of Freight Books surviving for 1678–1713 (T. 70/962–972). From this can be devised the number of slaves delivered in *hired* ships. I have suggested above (p. 195) that until the outbreak of war in 1689 the company used almost exclusively hired ships in the West Indian trade. I believe, therefore, that the Freight Books are a nearly complete substitute though they may be less useful for 1703 than for the three missing years in the 'eighties.

Most of the Invoice Books, Homeward, cover complete years, one or more. But the year which they cover is the 'London year' not the 'West Indian year'; that is to say, the first entry in a new book

361

will record a transaction (either the consignment of sugar or the sale of slaves) that took place in the West Indies in the previous October or November but which has only in January been brought to account in London. This would be of no consequence if the series was unbroken. As it is, in supplying the deficiencies, I have been obliged to run together pairs of years, as 1682–83, 1684–85, etc. This arrangement of the Invoice Books, Homeward, also explains why it is possible to devise average prices of a sort (unreliable because generally based on one cargo only) for years in which a book is missing. One further point about prices should be observed. Until 1685 at Barbados the price at which some of the slaves were sold is recorded in pounds of sugar. These have been ignored and averages made only from those sold for pounds, shillings and pence.

Of the various other series of statistics of slave-deliveries, two may be mentioned. One, that collected by colonial governors in 1707 on the instructions of the Commissioners of Trade and Plantations and discussed above (pp. 142–3), is usually regarded as defective, and may well be so. There are certainly some curious discrepancies between this series and the figures obtained from the Invoice Books, but the totals over a period do not seem to be very different. The other series is in the *Report of the Privy Council on the Trade to Africa* (1789), Part IV, No. 5, Appendix B. This almost certainly derives from the company's own records which must have been fuller then than they now are. Unfortunately figures were collected only for nine years, 1680–88, when the company is shown to have delivered an aggregate of 46,396 slaves 'to America', including presumably Virginia. My own figures give an aggregate for these years of 40,371. Since the trade in contract-negroes was then at its height, my assumption of about 10,000 slaves delivered on contract between 1672 and 1689 would not seem unreasonable.

Clearly any set of statistics that necessitates as much preliminary explanation as this must be regarded as subjective. As the matter is not without importance, I have felt it desirable to give some account of the sources and meaning of my figures in order to facilitate any further work that may be undertaken.

A. *Deliveries*

Year	Barbados	Jamaica	Nevis	Antigua	St. Chr.	Monts.	Total
1673	220	—	—	—	—	—	220
1674	1066	410	469	—	—	—	1945
1675	1512	1269	502	—	—	—	3283
1676	1836	1188	571	—	—	—	3595
1677	940	1156	495	—	—	—	2591
1678	2392	990	627	—	—	—	4009
1679	676	464	495	210	201	152	2198
1680	1673	1623	819	—	214	—	4329
1681	2404	1150	738	—	91	—	4383
1682–83	3676	3483	626	—	118	21	7924
1684–85	3630	3841	151	104	—	—	7726
1686–87	3585	6223	678	170	—	159	10815
1688	1516	447	363	80	—	93	2499
1689	1119	682	368	282	—	244	2695
1690	520	359	—	—	—	—	879
1691	1175	579	—	—	—	—	1754
1692	645	583	—	—	—	—	1228
1693	282	1332	—	84	—	—	1698
1694	2130	369	—	—	—	—	2499
1695	—	1129	296	—	—	—	1425
1696	491	113	—	—	—	—	604
1697	997	—	—	—	—	—	997
1698	469	313	312	—	—	—	1094
1699	961	161	125	—	—	—	1247
1700	1123	897	490	211	—	171	2892
1701	—	1071	161	—	—	—	1232
1702–3	1726	558	216	677	—	—	3177
1704	1215	801	484	—	—	52	2552
1705	685	1384	157	—	—	98	2324
1706	759	—	—	—	—	281	1040
1707	544	196	—	472	—	—	1212
1708	782	1709	51	110	—	—	2652
1709	578	—	51	587	—	—	1216
1710	439	—	—	—	—	—	439
1711	345	—	—	—	—	50	395
Totals	42,111	34,480	9,245	2,987	624	1,321	
					Grand Total		90,768

B. *Prices* (These prices are in colonial currency, not sterling. In the course of the eighteenth century, very large discrepancies appeared between the colonial £ and sterling, due to the issue of paper-money. In these years, however, except during the period of the Barbadian paper-money experiment (above, pp. 146–7), the discrepancies were much smaller, deriving chiefly from the over-valuation of silver coins (above, p. 316).)

Year	Barbados		Jamaica	
		to nearest 5s.		
1673	£18		—	
1674	£17		£22	10s.
1675	£15	10s.	£22	
1676	£15	5s.	£21	5s.
1677	£14		£19	15s.
1678	£14	15s.	£17	15s.
1679	£13	10s	£17	10s.
1680	£14		£17	
1681	£13	5s.	£15	5s.
1682	£14	15s.	£15	15s.
1683	£12	10s.	£15	10s.
1684	£13	5s.	£17	10s.
1685	—		£17	15s.
1686	£14	5s.	£18	5s.
1687	£13	10s.	£14	10s.
1688	£14	5s.	£14	15s.
1689	£16		£20	10s.
1690	£17	15s.	£24	10s.
1691	£17	5s.	£23	5s.
1692	£18		£17	15s.
1693	£20		£20	
1694	£21	5s.	£22	
1695	—		£20	
1696	£27	10s.	—	
1697	£21		—	
1698	£16	10s.	£23	
1699	£19	10s.	£20	5s.
1700	£21	15s.	£23	15s.
1701	—		£16	15s.
1702	£20		£21	
1703	—		—	
1704	£27	15s.	£27	5s.
1705	£35	15s.	£25	
1706	£28	10s.	—	
1707	£25	15s.	£22	5s.
1708	£26	10s.	£25	15s.
1709	£24	10s.	—	
1710	£26	15s.	—	
1711	£24	5s.	—	

APPENDIX IV

THE PRICE OF SUGAR, 1674–1713

THIS table shows the price of sugar sold by the Royal African Company in London according to the colony of origin. It has been compiled from the records of the company's sales, preserved in the Minute Books of the Court of Assistants. In any interpretation of these figures, the following facts should be kept in mind:

(1) Sugars varied a good deal in quality. Two or more qualities might be put up for sale at the same time and very different prices obtained. In this table I have selected the quality that seems average, and taken the price at which the largest quantity of this average sugar was sold.

(2) Sales were held as often as six times a year in ordinary times; in wartime, convoy arrangements made for fewer and larger consignments and therefore fewer sales. Sales might be in any month of the year but the summer months were commonest. The greater part of the annual crop normally reached London between June and September. The prices recorded here (except where otherwise noted) are all taken from sales held in those months. July was the month in which sales were most often held and the majority of these prices are for that month.

(3) The prices for 1697–1710 (with the exception of 1699) are corrupt. As already explained (above, p. 183), the company adopted the practice of accepting its own bonds in payment for goods sold, sometimes as to one-quarter, sometimes as to one-half, and occasionally as to the whole of the purchase price. Since these bonds changed hands at a discount, the prices recorded here must have been inflated above their true level. They are, therefore, printed in italics.

Prices in shillings, per 100 lb. of muscovado sugar.

Year	Barbados	Jamaica	Nevis
1674	$23\frac{1}{2}$	30	$26\frac{3}{4}$
1675	$20\frac{1}{2}$	$25\frac{1}{2}$	23
1676	23	28	25
1677	$20\frac{3}{4}$	$24\frac{1}{4}$	23
1678	$23\frac{1}{4}$	$26\frac{1}{2}$	$24\frac{1}{2}$
1679	$21\frac{1}{4}$	24	$22\frac{3}{4}$
1680	$22\frac{1}{4}$	25	$24\frac{3}{4}$
1681	$21\frac{1}{2}$	$24\frac{1}{2}$	23
1682	$17\frac{1}{4}$	$22\frac{3}{4}$	$18\frac{1}{4}$
1683	$21\frac{3}{4}$	$22\frac{1}{2}$	$23\frac{1}{2}$
1684	19	$23\frac{1}{2}$	$21\frac{1}{2}$
1685	$20\frac{1}{4}$	$21\frac{3}{4}$	$19\frac{1}{4}$
1686	$16\frac{3}{4}$	$19\frac{3}{4}$	$14\frac{1}{2}$
1687	18	20	$16\frac{1}{2}$
1688	Oct. 25	$27\frac{1}{4}$	$23\frac{3}{4}$
1689	$27\frac{1}{2}$	$33\frac{1}{2}$	$28\frac{3}{4}$
1690	$32\frac{1}{2}$	Nov. 40	—
1691	Oct. $34\frac{1}{2}$	May $34\frac{1}{4}$	May 30
1692	$29\frac{1}{4}$	$33\frac{1}{2}$	$28\frac{1}{2}$
1693	37	Oct. $41\frac{1}{4}$	$32\frac{1}{2}$
1694	43	May $43\frac{3}{4}$	—
1695	52	$65\frac{1}{4}$	Mar. $48\frac{1}{2}$
1696	$54\frac{3}{4}$	$62\frac{1}{2}$	—
1697	*31*	$44\frac{1}{4}$	*30*
1698	*25¼*	35	*32½*
1699	*34¾*	$40\frac{1}{2}$	—
1700	$38\frac{3}{4}$	$45\frac{1}{2}$	$36\frac{3}{4}$
1701	*48*	$56\frac{3}{4}$	$45\frac{1}{2}$
1702	$42\frac{3}{4}$	$55\frac{3}{4}$	Oct. *43*
1703	$45\frac{1}{4}$	56	Nov. *38*
1704	$41\frac{1}{2}$	*50*	*39*
1705	$27\frac{1}{4}$	$35\frac{1}{2}$	$28\frac{1}{2}$
1706	Apr. $29\frac{1}{2}$	Nov. $30\frac{1}{4}$	Apr. $26\frac{3}{4}$
1707	$32\frac{3}{4}$	*36*	—
1708	Nov. $33\frac{1}{4}$	Oct. $43\frac{1}{2}$	—
1709	Mar. *45*	Mar. $52\frac{1}{4}$	—
1710	75	—	—
1711	—	—	—
1712	—	—	Nov. $29\frac{1}{4}$
1713	$30\frac{1}{4}$	35	$23\frac{1}{4}$

APPENDIX V

JOHN SNOW'S LETTER TO THE ROYAL AFRICAN COMPANY
31 July 1705
[T. 70/102, pp. 47–50.]

HONOURED GENTLEMEN,

I have in obedience to your commands sett downe what appeares to me to be the great causes of the decay of your trade to Africa & have undertooke to give my thoughts how so many misfortunes may be prevented & a trade after so many losses carryed on that might indeed be benificiall to your Honours.

That which challenges the first place is the perpetuall force and constraints put on the blacks to trade no where but with the forts, & this prosecuted to such a height as panjarding[1] of their goods, killing people from the forts, & brandering their persons.

To remedy these evills it may be thought necessary to order that no manner of violence should be offered the blacks, but that they may be left free as to our molesting them to goe as they would themselves; but then, not to seem supinely to neglect the trade, that propper methods should be taken with the kings & cabbashiers[2] of the country that they might oblige their people to come first to the forts with their slaves, & that what should be refused there the black should be left to his liberty to seeke his markett.

The advantages that would arise to your servants by this method are first a handle to remove all the odium and aversion that the blacks have contracted to your trade by being ill used by your servants & what they now will complaine of from their masters.

Besides you will become more masters of them than ever . . .[3] make you, since they regard none of your threats while out of the . . .[3] these; when on the other hand the interest you have with their cabbashiers shall make them submitt to whatsoever terms you yourselves will propose, which would be two great points gained; & in order to have them fairly continued great care should be taken

---

[1] Confiscating, forcibly detaining. [2] Chief men.
[3] Document illegible.

367

here at home what persons are entertained into your service that they should have an experience of mankind as well by their yeares as their conversation, such qualityes being extreamly wanting on the Coast to gaine the affection of the negroes; and in a country where so great mortallity happens a ladd has oftentimes the directing men who wants sense to governe himselfe & receives a charge that serves only to give him an oppertunity to doe more mischiefe than ever he could have thought in his power, such was Coleback & abundance more.

The experience that I mean is that the party should have good sence & good nature enough as will teach him how to manage people that are not so nice but would be glad to be courted with a kindness very dunstable.[1] The last of the two qualetyes tho' something of the other be abated is sure to gaine all the points your interest requires, there being no people on earth that you can gaine a point sooner of than the blacks if soft & easy methods are used and their understandings but brib'd by a trifle of a dashee[2] into an apprehension that what is desired of them is reasonable.

All other methods of violence & force however just the reasons are have served only to raise devills that none as yett have had the good fortune to lay.

What may pass for a second reason is the not paying customes (whether wisely at first begun is not now the question) but are reckon'd rights, the deniall of their ground rents or skotching of old debts contracted by their predecessors & the haveing no silkes & fine scarlett cloths to send sometimes to a king or cabasheer to spirit the trade downe.

It is easy to see by this article how much ill blood must be created among the great ones & how disadvantagious that must be to your interests, & in points where the blacks thinke they have the right on their side as they are extreamly tenacious of anything that has been a custome, it must still be indulged them.

And oftentimes a complying with them in one point has proved a gaineing five in other things.

Thus denying the cabasheers of Anamaboe their customes, the first time your factor there went to Agga the cabasheers arm'd their people & would not admitt his returne till paid.

Thus was refuseing the rent to the queen of Enguina a downright hindrance to your trade, nor did any come to Winnebah but from a straine I tooke of being particularly kind to the cabasheers of Enguina who tould the queen while I was there they would permitt the trade.

[1] Straightforward.   [2] Gratuity, bribe.

Nor are the setting of old debts less injurious to your interests. The quarrells your former managers weakely fell into against the Dutch gave a handle for them by carrying on the warr; & to gett them paid now by deductions occasions only ill natured disputes for it is not harde to thinke that those who have not honesty enough to pay their owne debts should be brought very willingly to pay debts contracted by others.

The Dutch was under this very dilemma once but they struck the talleys cleare & made little Taggee, late King of Aquaffoe, their friend by it who was made king at your charge but never durst trust himselfe with us lest he should be detained for the debt; & by that means ruined the trade of Commenda.

The trusting of blacks I take to be soe great a sin against your interests that I thinke it hardly to be forgiven, & I cant helpe thinking it next to that of useing them ill. The remedy I would humbly propose against so mischievous a practice should be that whosoever should trust a blackman should be liable for the summ, which would render the chiefs at Cape Coast Castle allwayes so cautious as never to trust but on gold pawns, which would have no consequence in the world on your trade.

The last thing is that there should be allwayes silke or very fine scarlett cloth in your factoryes that when trade is dull a piece might be sent for the quickening of it.

I have seen this succeed so wonderfully with the Dutch & by my owne experience at Winnebah that I can nott but assure your Honours that this is a point of as much importance to your interest as possible. By these methods it is whenever the upcountry blacks come downe they goe allwayes first to the Dutch &, lett us have never such a stock of goods, the Dutch catch the gold, & slaves being little of their trade they then dismiss them to us. And this will appeare with a very little reflection to be the true reason why the Dutch can send a ship home with 15 or 20,000 *l.* worth of dust & you in the best times of late with scarce 4.

Another reason for your misfortunes is the concerning our selves in the succession of their kings on suspicion they may be more inclined to the Dutch interest than ours.

It is impossible to say what this article hath cost both you and the Dutch & I am very well sattisfyed that nothing has been done to less purpose on either side. A blackman forgetts all obligations but the present; those are his friends & his masters that dashee[1] him offenest & allways (in negroes English) does him well; & lett this

---

[1] Gratuity, bribe.

only be the practice of your agents or chiefs there never will be a reason to be jealous of any of the advantages the Dutch would gaine by their nominations.

The last reason is a new errour that under the collour of enlargeing trade it should be thought necessary to send people to the up countryes to give notice how goods are sold, what prices are given for slaves, & by what weights gold is taken.

As this is a new thought it has proved like a thousand other things whose speculation would admitt of being no otherwise confuted than by experience. The misfortune of it is that it had not only no success but did a great deale of harme; for the waterside blacks tooke it presently as a designe to hinder their tradeing, & therefore to be even with the project fell directly into the tenn per cent trade and would not sell their slaves till the shipps arrived.

Nor is it easy to shew what disputes it occations on the borders of each countrey since every kingdome makes a trade on the goods & every one is fond to have them at the cheapest rates, that in the place of trade nothing but dispute has been the consequence & it is well if nothing worse succeed.

So farr as to the blacks. As to the Europeans it is certaine that the perpetuall difference between the Dutch & us on points that it's impossible to decide on whose side the right belongs since both make settlements by invitations from the natives, have been one of the great stepps to the ruine of trade.

To make a constant peace on this side I can thinke of nothing else but that to end the present difference the Dutch should quitt Barracoe never to resettle there againe, & wee Secondee on the same conditions; & if your Honours dare believe me you have the advantage in this article.

That between Cape Tres Puntas & the River Vulter no new settlements should be made on any pretences & whatsoever are made since January 1704 be removed, never to be resettled againe.

That no desertour on any pretence should be received on either side. In such a case the party shall be delivered up to either agent as he shall be taken.

That whosoever of the agents should breake articles so agreed on by both companyes should be recalled home.

It will appeare by all that's said that the same good sense, the same usage, the same cautions, the same harmony with your neighbours in trade, are as necessary for carrying it on in Africa as in Europe.

And all this is easy to be done where humour & passion & opinion don't prevaile, where people are content to sacrifice those for the interest of them that employ them.

It's hard for me to guess how this essay may be accepted. What I mean by it is to shew your Honours I as heartily now wish your success as I have in my poore station endeavoured it. Should it be thought either troublesome or impertinent the best reason & the best apology I know for it is that it is owing to commands I did not know how to disobey. I am, Honourable Gentlemen, your Honours' most obedient humble servant: JON: SNOW.

APPENDIX VI

THE SEPARATE TRADERS, 1702–1712

A VOLUME amongst the African company's records (T. 70/1199) supplies the material from which the following list has been compiled. It records the sworn value of consignments of goods to Africa by separate traders between 1702 and the expiry of the Act of 1698 in July 1712. I believe that only names of separate traders of London are given. In the following list only the names of the principal traders are given; those who made consignments in only one year are not included.

Name	No. of Years in which Consignments were made	Aggregate Sworn Value of these Consignments to nearest £
Robert Atkins & Co.	5	6643
James Berdoe	8	1848
Peregrine Browne	6	5060
John Burridge	3	902
Joseph Caine	2	740
Alexander Cleeve	3	10471
Thomas Coalshurst	7	3117
Anthony Forty	3	3161
Lawrence Galdry & Co.	3	3895
William Gardner	3	1756
Stephen Godin & Co.	2	1189
Richard Harris	9	25121
Robert Heysham	9	33920
Melitia Holder	2	695
Holditch & Brooke	9	20336
Peter Hollander	3	3163
Joseph Jackson	2	708
Daniel Jamineau	9	6637
Sir Jeffrey Jeffreys	3	3231
Lewis Johnson	3	1170
Charles Kent	3	5036
Edward Lascelles	3	2998
William Love	3	672
Joseph Martin	8	19359

Name	No. of Years in which Consignments were made	Aggregate Sworn Value of these Consignments to nearest £
Mayhew & Co.	3	980
Thomas Merrett	7	476
John Mills	2	880
Isaac Milner	10	21475
Humphry Morice	4	5720
John Norton	3	1194
Peter Paggen	3	11636
Christopher Prissick	2	931
Edward Searle	10	3310
Henry Smith	3	1267
Robert Smith	2	1432
John Taylor	6	4625
Anthony Tourney	9	3912
John Travers	2	1256
James Waite	10	14455
Benjamin Way	5	6730
William Wood	3	699

Total Consignments by Separate Traders (presumably of London) including the above:

Year	Sworn Value in £s.
1702	34,332
1703	38,777
1704	28,448
1705	24,138
1706	16,721
1707	28,797
1708	16,101
1709	36,698
1710	31,497
1711	29,221
1712 to July only	10,414

APPENDIX VII

THE RECORDS OF THE ROYAL AFRICAN COMPANY

THE archives of the Royal African company are preserved at the Public Record Office, amongst the records of the Treasury (T. 70). A full account of them has been given by a former Deputy Keeper of the Records in *T.R.H.S.*, Third Series, vi (1912) (H. Jenkinson, 'Records of the English African Companies'). It is to the author of this article that we owe the arrangement of the records in their present form.

The company's archives may be regarded as falling into three main classes:

(1) Minute Books and Letter Books. The Minutes of the General Court are T. 70/100–101, and of the Court of Assistants T.70/76–88. There are also minutes of some of the important sub-committees of the Court of Assistants, notably the Committee of Accounts (T. 70/107–111), Committee of Goods (T. 70/128–130), and Committee of Eight (T. 70/102).

The Letter Books are less complete. Until about 1700, few complete letters inward have survived. Instead, we have fragments or abstracts made from the original letters for one committee or another. Thus a letter from Africa might be abstracted by the Committee of Correspondence, Shipping or Goods, each recording only that part which was of immediate concern to it. This accounts for the telegrammatic character of several of the quotations given in the preceding pages, e.g. 'About the charge of the place & the small returnes. The retournes he hath made not despicable. How he employeth the shipping. . . . A discouragement that their endeavours should be slighted & not to be supplied as desired.' This reduces considerably the value of the records. Among the letter books which I have found most informative are T. 70/1, 2, 5, 10–13, 15–17 for letters received, and T. 70/50, 51, 57, 61–63 for letters sent.

(2) Account Books. These are numerous. I have relied principally on the Invoice Books, Outward (T. 70/910–920) for export

figures; Invoice Books, Homeward (T. 70/936–956) for imports and records of sales of slaves; entry books of Bills of Exchange (T. 70/269–283); and Freight Books (T. 70/962–972). I have used the General Ledgers (T. 70/601–608) and Cash Books (T. 70/216–235) only for reference. A few ledgers recording transactions in Africa have survived for this period, notably T. 70/657, 659, 662 for Cape Coast, and T. 70/830 for Gambia.

For the accounts of shareholders and transfers of stock, I have employed T. 70/185–188.

(3) Miscellaneous Books. Amongst the most valuable have been the following ships' journals, T. 70/1210–1213, 1215, 1216. The Kommenda Diary of 1714–16 is T. 70/1464. Particularly valuable for the African establishment are the Lists of the Living and the Dead (T. 70/1440–1445).

INDEX

The names of all Governors, Sub-Governors, Deputy Governors and members of the Court of Assistants of the Royal African Company elected between 1672 and 1712 are included in this index, whether mentioned in the text or not. The following abbreviations are used: A. (Assistant), D.G. (Deputy Governor), S.G. (Sub-Governor), G. (Governor). The years of election are also given: thus A.1673-5 denotes election as an Assistant for three consecutive years. In this example the period of office would be January 1673 to January 1676. The principal entries in the index (e.g. Gambia, Sugar, etc.) are in capitals, with tabulated sub-headings.

Abramboe, 282

Accra, 224, 243, 246, 250, 252, 265; James Ft., 246; garrison, 247-8; population, 279; slaves, 226

Acton, Richard (A.1701)

Admiralty, Court of, interlopers in, 117

Africa, West, climate, 4-5; commerce, 2, 4, 214-32; Europeans in, 2, 6, 6n.; exploration, 5; international rivalry, 7-10, 12-13, 15-16, 264-77; politics, 5-6

African House, Throckmorton-st., 164; Leadenhall-st., 164

Akwamu, 6n.

Alampo, 190; factory, 247-8, 250n.

Albemarle, see Monck

Albert, Fletcher, 93

Albert, Thomas, 93-4

Aldworth, Thomas, 69

Allejaes in Af. trade, 353

Allington, William (A.1675-7)

Amber, in Af. trade, 172, 219

Amsterdam, 24n.,172-6, 179

Anashan, factory, 224, 247-8, 249, 250; ground-rent, 282

Andrewes, Sir Jonathan (A.1701-10, D.G.1711, S.G.1712)

Andros, Sir Edmund, 65

Anglo-Dutch wars (1664-7), 12, 42-3, 57, 59, 61-2, 327; (1672-4), 59, 60, 63, 265

Anglo-French wars (1689-97, 1702-13), 79, 192-3, 201-3, 205-12, 272, 277, 342-3

Angola, 1, 8, 10, 186; corn, 228; Dutch attack on, 8, 12; ivory, 214, 228; slaves, 188, 237; trade, 45, 231, 231n., 232-3, 234

Annabasses, in Af. trade, 175, 355

Anne, Queen of England (G.1709-12), 156

Anomabu, 224, 227, 256, 257, 288, 293, 368; Charles Ft., 246, 263; garrison, 247-8; ground-rent, 287; slaves, 226

Antigua, 14; African trade, 191; debt laws, 320; freight from, 203; interlopers at, 113; slave population, 302; supply of slaves, 45, 143, 143n., 190, 311-12, 363; tobacco, 341

Appah, 250

Ardra, 190, 214; mortality at, 256; slaves, 121n., 228, 237; trade, 234, 240; see Ophra

Arguim, 20

Arlington, see Bennet

Ashanti, 139, 225, 281, 288-90

Ashburnham, William, 66

Ashby, John (A.1679-81, 1686-7, 1689-90)

Ashley, see Cooper

Asiento, 13-14, 60, 151, 152, 310, 313, 344; Eng. govt. and, 331-2; R. Adventurers and, 43, 44; Af. Co. and, 326-35

Assada Adventurers, 29n.

Assim, 284

Assini, 275

Atkins, Sir Jonathan, Govr. of Barbados, 118, 304, 328

Atkins, Robert, & Co., sep. traders, 372

Atkinson, Charles, 321

Avery, pirate, 211

Axim, 221, 265, 283

Backwell, Edward, 56, 64

Baftes, in Af. trade, 353

Bagg, Capt. Joseph, Agent-General at C. Coast, 245

377

Baillie, William, factor at Kommenda, 281, 289
Baily, Arthur (A.1695-7)
Balle, Charles (A.1694-1702)
Balle, John, agent for Af. Co. in Jamaica, 297
Baltic trade, 67, 193
Bancks, James, 171n.
Bancks, John (A.1676-7), 171n.
Bank of England, 32, 37
Banks, bankers, banking, 47, 48, 49, 50, 52-3, 56, 66, 67
Banks, Sir John (A.1672-3, 1676-8, S.G. 1674-5), 68, 68n., 71n., 72n.
Banner, Samuel, 178
Bantam, 186
BARBADOS, 14, 293, 294
    African trade, 126, 138n., 190-1
    agency of Af. Co., 295-8
    Asiento and, 327, 328-9
    bills of exchange, 359-60
    currency, 316, 322, 341
    debt laws, 320
    debt to Af. Co., 318-19, 320, 323
    freight from, 201-3
    freight to, 198-9
    interlopers at, 113, 118
    need for credit, 317-18
    opposition to Af. Co., 126, 127, 133, 149, 303-7
    Paper Act, 146-7, 150
    remittances from, 339, 340
    slave-population, 300-1, 300n., 302
    slave-prices, 143-4, 199, 295, 303-7, 312-15, 364
    slave sales, 200, 317
    sugar, 358-9
    sugar prices, 337, 341, 366
    supply of slaves, 45, 143, 143n., 146-147, 190, 201, 299, 300-1, 303-7, 307n., 339, 363
    support for monopoly, 143-5, 306-7
Barbot, John, 230n., 261, 279, 282
Barra Kunda, 215, 216
Barrosso, Juan, and Asiento, 327
Barter, Edward, mulatto, 280-1
Bath, see Granville
Bathurst, Sir Benjamin (A.1677-9, 1684, 1687-8, 1690-5, 1700, D.G. 1680-1, S.G.1682-3, 1685-6, 1689), 157, 162n.
Bathurst, Benjamin (A.1703-4)
Bays, in Af. trade, 176
Beads, in Af. trade, 172, 173, 174, 177, 219, 234, 357
Bedford, Robert (A.1712)
Beeston, Sir William, Govr. of Jamaica, agent for Af. Co., 296, 297, 325

Belasyse, Thomas, Visc. Falconberg (A. 1677-9, 1682-3, 1689-91), 65, 163
Belchamber, Thomas, agent for Af. Co. at Nevis, 297, 298
Bell, Capt. Robert, 201
Bellamy, John (A.1703)
Bells, in Af. trade, 234
Bence Island, see Sierra Leone
Bence, John (A.1672-3, 1675-7, 1680-2, 1685-7)
Bendall, Capt. Hopefor (A.1682-3)
Benin, 205; corn, 228; ivory, 228; slaves, 121, 237; trade, 45, 230, 232-3, 234, 240
Bennet, Henry, Earl of Arlington, 62, 64, 65, 65n., 68
Bennet, John (A.1700-2)
Bennett, Capt., 110
Benson, Samuel (A.1707)
Beraku, 287, 370
Berdoe, James, sep. trader, 372
Berkeley, Lord George, of Berkeley (A.1674-6, 1679-81, 1684-6), 50n., 65, 65n., 72, 163, 163n.
Betts, William (A.1704, 1706)
Beuzelin, Francis (A.1712)
Bills of Exchange, in W. India trade, 187, 189, 195, 200, 296, 317-18, 335-6, 339, 342, 359-60
Birmingham, goods for Africa, 178; opposition to Af. Co., 149
Bissagos (Bissaos), Islands, 216, 218, 271
Blacksmiths, Company of, 51n.
Black Tom, 242
Blake, James (A.1709-12)
Blake, Capt. Peter, 291
Bludworth, Sir Thomas (A.1675-6, 1678), 159n.
Boesies, see Cowries
Bonnell, Capt. John (A.1695-6)
Booker, John, agent in Gambia, 128, 236, 255, 272
Bosman, William, 233-4, 235, 268, 285, 286
Bottomry, see Royal Af. Co., debts
Boughton, Col. Spencer, Agent-General at C. Coast, 245
Boun, George (A.1684-6, 1689-92, 1695-7, D.G.1687-8, S.G.1693-4)
Bovery or Bouverie, William (A.1686-1688, 1691-2)
Boynton, Francis, 171n.
Boysadoes, in Af. trade, 175, 176, 355
Bradley, Capt. Nathaniel, Agent-General at C. Coast, 120, 178-9, 234, 242, 245, 255
Bradyll, Roger (A.1684)

Brandenburgh, Af. trade, 1, 2, 6n., 12; see Gros Friedrichsburg
Brandy, in Af. trade, 45, 173, 219, 238, 271
Brassware, in Af. trade, 177, 178, 219, 351
Brawles, in Af. trade, 353
Brazil, 12, 15, 21, 23, 276, 336, 338
Brazil Company, 18
Brewers, Company of, 51n.
Bristol, 189, 207; Af. trade, 126, 137n., 152; opposition to Af. Co., 132, 133
Bristow, Robert (A. 1695-6)
Broadcloth, in Af. trade, 176
Brooke, Joshua, 107n.
Browne, Peregrine, sep. trader, 372
Brue, Sieur de, 272
Brydges, James, Duke of Chandos, 344
Bubble Act, 38, 80
Buckingham, see Villiers
Buckworth, Sir John (A.1674-5, D.G. 1672-3), 69
Bull, James (A.1698-9, 1701)
Bull, John (A.1673-4, 1680, 1682-4), 72
Bulmer, Bevis, 35n.
Burridge, John, sep. trader, 372
Burton, John (A.1702-3, 1705-7)
Buruko, 216
Butler, Thomas, Earl of Ossory, 64

Cabinda, 231
Cacheu, 216, 217, 218, 219
Cacongo, 231
Cadiz, 328, 329
Caine, Joseph, sep. trader, 372
Calabar, 6, 10, 19; corn, 228; ivory, 228; slaves, 188, 236-7, 292, 293; trade, 230-1, 230n., 232-3, 240
Campbell, John (A.1709-12)
Canada, 2, 32, 35
Canaries, 186
CAPE COAST, 40-1, 41n., 42, 43, 138, 190, 191, 198, 200, 201, 223, 224, 236, 239, 246, 250, 252-3, 255, 258, 259, 261, 268, 280, 286, 288, 369
  Ashanti trade, 289
  bombardment, 274
  castle, 240-1, 263
  chaplain at, 242, 243
  foreigners at, 254
  garrison, 241-3, 244, 247-8
  gold trade, 235
  ground-rent, 282
  interlopers at, 113, 114, 120
  mortality at, 256
  mutiny at, 253
  plundered, 129
  population, 279
  schoolmaster at, 280, 280n.
  siege, 263, 282
  slave-trade, 226
Cape Lopez, 188
Cape Mount, 214, 222
Cape Palmas, 207, 221
Cape Three Points, 221, 222, 370
Cape Verde, 42, 216, 219, 270, 273
Caribs, 3
Carloff, Hendrik, 41, 41n.
Carpets, in Af. trade, 178, 355
Carteret, Sir George, 62, 65, 65n.
Cartwright, Jarvis (A.1672-3)
Cass, Col. John (A.1705-8)
Castile, Af. trade, 7
Castillo, Santiago, agent of Asiento, 334
Cater, John (A.1693-4)
Chandos, see Brydges
Chappell, Roger (A.1673-5, 1678-9)
Charles I, King of England, 27, 102
Charles II, King of England, 61-2, 63; R. Adventurers and, 42, 64, 103; Af. Co. and, 99, 115; R. Fishery Co. and, 22n.; monopolies of, 60, 102-3, 102n., 180
Chidley, John, agent in Gambia, 256
Childe, Sir Josiah (A.1675), 68, 68n., 156n.
Chiltman, John, schoolmaster at C. Coast, 280
Christiansborg, 6n., 8, 224; mortgaged to Af. Co., 249, 275-6
Cimbio, 283
Clarke, Henry, factor at Sierra Leone, 257
Clarke, Thomas, factor at Ophra, 228
Clayton, Sir Robert (A.1681), 68, 68n.
Cleeve, Alexander (A.1696-8, 1700-7), agent in Gambia, 69, 217, 219, 270, 271; sep. trader, 372
Clifford, Thomas, Lord, 62, 62n.
Clothing, in Af. trade, 178, 234
Coalshurst, Thomas, sep. trader, 372
Codrington, Christopher, 116-17
Colbert, J. B., 9, 19, 21, 22
Colleton, Sir Peter (A.1677-9, 1683-1685, 1688-90), 62, 65, 65n., 300n.
Colston, Edward (A.1681-3, 1686-8, 1691, D.G.1689-90)
Commissioners of Trade and Plantations, 175; consideration of Af. trade by, 136, 141-51; enquiry into slave-trade, 142-9; reports on slave-trade, 142, 149, 150, 151
Compagnie du Guinée, see France

Compagnie des Indes Occidentales, see France

Compagnie du Sénégal, see France

Companies, in African trade, 17–24; see Joint-stock companies, Regulated companies

Comport, Robert (A.1706, 1708)

Congo, 121, 231

Convoy, 186, 208, 210

Cooke, John (A.1680–2, 1687–9, 1692)

Cooke, John (A.1703–12)

Cooke, Nicholas (A.1706)

Cooke, Sir Thomas (A.1690–2, 1701–2, 1705–9, S.G.1703–4), 160n.

Cooper, Anthony Ashley, Earl of Shaftesbury (A.1674, S.G.1672–3), 58n., 62, 64, 65, 65n., 68, 107n., 163

Copper bars, in Af. trade, 170–2, 177, 230, 351

Copperware, in Af. trade, 172

Coral, in Af. trade, 172, 238, 357

Corker, Thomas, agent at Sherbro, 220

Corn, in Af. trade, 228

Cotton, 179, 180, 182, 187, 190, 340, 360

Cotton cloth, Af. manufacture, 221, 228

Courland, Duchy of, Af. trade, 11, 42, 215

Coventry, Sir William, 62, 65

Cowries, in Af. trade, 170, 173, 234, 235, 357

Coymans, Balthasar, and *Asiento*, 330, 333

Craddock, Richard (A.1684–6, 1689–1695)

Craven, Sir Anthony, 66

Craven, William, Earl of (A.1673–4, 1677–9, 1682–4, 1687–9), 62, 65, 65n., 163

Crediton, opposition to Af. Co., 130

Crispe, Thomas, factor on Gold Coast (1649), 40–1, 282

Crispe, Thomas (A.1673–4, 1676–7)

Croaker, Thomas, agent of *Asiento*, 329

Cudworth, John, 72

Curaçao, 14, 23, 328

Curson *v.* R. Af. Co., 97n.

Cutting, John (A.1705, 1707–12)

Daems, Henry, agent in Amsterdam, 172n., 175

Dandridge, Francis (A.1710)

Daniel, an interloper, 322

Darcy *v.* Allen, 101n.

Darien Company of Scotland, 130–1, 134

Darnall, John (A.1702–5)

Dashwood, Francis (A.1675–6)

Dashwood, Sir Francis (another) (A. 1693–5, 1697–1700, 1704, 1706–7, 1709–12)

Dashwood, Sir Samuel (A.1672–4, 1677–9, 1682–4, 1687–9, 1692–3, 1698–9, 1701–3, 1705), 68, 68n.

Davenant, Charles, 142n., 148, 160

Davenant, Rowland (A.1708)

Dawes, Sir Jonathan (A.1672)

Delmé, Sir Peter (A.1706)

Denkyera, 225, 284, 288

Denmark, Af. trade, 1, 12, 19–20; relations with Af. Co., 40–1, 275–6; settlements in W. Africa, 6n., 249; W. India Co., 11

De Ruyter, Admiral, 13, 42, 215n., 224, 263

Des Bouverie, see Bovery

Deutry, Dennis (A.1698)

Diaz, Anthony, 218

Dickinson, Capt. Richard, 106, 106n.

Dixcove, 139, 224, 256, 263, 288; Anglo-Dutch rivalry, 268, 277; fort, 249, 268; garrison, 247–8

Dockwra, William, 106, 129, 129n.

Doegood, Capt. Robert, 230, 294

Dover, Treaty of, 61, 62

Downing, Sir George, 62

Drainage, companies in, 35

Drapers, Company of, 51

Du Bois or Duboys, John (A.1693–4)

Ducke, Thomas, 67

Duffield, Peter, factor at Whydah, 255

Duncombe, John (A.1709–10)

Du Puy, Lawrence (A.1676–8), 62, 66, 163

Dutch, see United Provinces

Dutton, Sir Richard, Govr. of Barbados, 118, 300

Dyewood, 45, 132, 183, 185, 197, 198, 207, 215; see Logwood, Redwood

EAST INDIA COMPANY, 24, 27, 32, 33, 38, 163n., 347–8

Assada Adventurers and, 29n.

capital, 32, 37, 54

charter, 28

country trade, 169

debts, 52, 54, 76

formation, 67

freedom of, 28

goods bought from, 161, 234

interlopers, 99, 101, 101n., 108

James II and, 103

Madagascar, 100

opposition to, 105

private trade in, 29, 29n., 109, 110, 258
sales, 179
shareholders, 68, 68n., 103
shipping, 192
stock, 27, 42, 70, 80–1, 83
voting rights, 156
East India Co. *v.* Sandys, 101, 101n., 108
East India Company (New), 37
East India Company (United), 37
East India goods, in Af. trade, 45, 161, 170, 205, 219, 234, 236, 353–4
Eastland Company, 123
Edwards, Francis (A.1698)
Edwards, Sir James (A.1676), 159n.
Edwin, Sir Humphrey, 69
Eguafo, 267, 268, 282, 285, 286, 288, 289, 369
Eguina, 368
Egya, factory, 224, 226, 247–8, 249, 287, 368
Elizabeth I, Queen of England, 22, 28, 39
Elliott, William (A.1709–12)
Elmina, 8, 12, 240, 263, 265, 279, 282
England, early Af. trade, 1, 7, 9, 10–11, 14, 15, 38–41
Espino, Juan, agent of *Asiento*, 330
Essex, clothiers of, opposition to Af. Co., 126, 127
Evance, Sir Stephen (A.1692–3, 1696, 1703, 1707, 1710)
Evans, John (A.1696–8, 1703–5, D.G. 1699–1700, S.G.1701–2)
Exchequer, Cursitor Baron of, 135
Exeter, goods for Africa, 177; opposition to Af. Co., 128

Falconberg, see Belasyse
Fanti, 283, 284, 285, 287, 288, 289
Farnaby, Francis, 66
Farrington, Thomas (A.1672–3)
Fawkener, William (A.1679–81)
Fazakerley, Sir William (A.1693–1703, 1706–9, 1711–12)
Fellow, John (A.1693–7)
Fetu, 41, 263, 278, 282, 283, 285, 286, 288
Fida, see Whydah
Fisheries, companies in, 35; see Royal Fishery Co.
Fishmongers, Company of, 51n.
Fleete, Sir John (A.1693–4, 1699–1702, 1704, S.G.1697–8), 160n.
Foley, Edward (A.1704–5)
Ford, Sir Richard (A.1672)
Fort Royal, 247–8, 283

Forty, Anthony, sep. trader, 372
France and French, Af. trade, 1, 2, 7, 9, 10, 11, 15, 18–21, 22, 144n., 176n., 214, 219, 229, 236, 237, 264, 269–70, 274, 313–14, 315; *Asiento* and, 326; *Comp. du Guinée*, 20; *Comp. des Indes Occ.*, 19–21, 22; *Comp. du Sénégal*, 19–20; *Nouvelle Comp. du Sénégal*, 20; privateers, 186, 190, 203, 205–12, 232–3, 273, 274; Rouen Comp., 18; relations with Af. Co., 269–75; serve in Af. Co., 254
Frederick, Elector of Brandenburgh, 11
Frederixborg, 40, 224, 249; sold to Af. Co., 275–6
Freeman, Howsely, Chief Merchant at C. Coast, 255
Freeman, John, agent at Sherbro, 256
Frowd, Sir Philip, 64
Furbroh, 216
Fustians, in Af. trade, 176

Galdry, Lawrence, & Co., sep. traders, 372
GAMBIA (James Fort and Island), 1, 39, 41, 43, 185, 186, 197, 214, 258
abandoned by Af. Co., 274
Anglo-French rivalry, 270–3
English settlement, 9, 12, 42, 218
exploration, 5, 15
fire at, 261
French attacks on, 131, 232, 251, 256, 261, 263, 272, 273, 277
garrison, 251–2
ivory, 182, 214; see Ivory
James Fort, 9, 42, 215, 216, 220
products, 215
resettlement, 273
slaves, 121, 187–8, 214, 226, 236–7, 238, 332–3
trade, 44, 215–19, 233, 234, 238
Gambia Adventurers, Company of, 30, 43, 99, 100, 214–15, 215n.
Garcia, and *Asiento*, 327
Gardner or Gardiner, John (A.1675), 67, 67n., 129, 129n.
Gardner, William, sep. trader, 372
Garth, George, 66
Gascoigne, Stephen, Af. Co.'s agent in Barbados, 279, 329, 339
Gefferyes, Sir Robert (A.1691)
Genes, Juan, agent of *Asiento*, 330
George I, King of England, Governor of Af. Co., 156
George of Denmark, Prince (G.1703–8), 156
Germain, Sir John (A.1709, 1711–12)

Gilbert, Nicholas, cashier of Af. Co., 165

Gilds, 24-5

Gill, Abraham, agent of *Asiento*, 330, 331

Ginger, 14, 179, 180, 182, 187, 340, 360

Girdlers, Company of, 51n.

Godin, Stephen & Co., sep traders, 372

Godolphin, Charles (A.1690-1)

Gohier, James (A.1709-10)

Gold, 60, 98, 134, 166, 207, 215, 216; as currency in W. Africa, 225-6; imports by Af. Co., 45, 179, 181, 225, 345; of Gambia, 258; of Gold Coast, 225, 228, 258; of Windward Coast, 222; trade, 4, 5, 7, 38, 40, 41; value in W. Africa, 235, 253; see Guineas

Gold Coast, 6n., 10, 190, 213, 214; corn, 228; Dutch, 12, 265-9; early English settlements, 9, 12, 42; French, 269-270, 274; mortality on, 256; politics, 278-9; Portuguese, 8, 276; slaves, 121, 226-8, 236-7; trade, 45, 188, 224-8, 234, 238-9, 240, 260-1

Goldsmiths, Company of, 51

Goree, 6n., 8, 12, 20, 128, 206, 214, 269, 272, 277

Gorges, Ferdinando (A.1672-4), 65, 65n.

Gould, Sir Edward, 92

Gourney, John, 69

Graham, Col. William (A.1710-12)

Grain Coast, 213

Granville, John, Earl of Bath, 64, 65

Gray, Sir James (A.1702-5, 1707-9 1711-12)

Greenhill, Henry, Agent-General at C. Coast, 245, 266

Grey, Baron Ralph of Warke (A.1674-1675)

Grey, Thomas (A.1672)

Grillo, and *Asiento*, 14, 327, 328

Gromettos, 243

Gros Friedrichsburg, 11, 224, 276

Guadeloupe, 14, 206

Guiana, 23

Guinea, North parts of, 214-21

Guinea Company (1618), 39-41

Guinea Stuffs, in Af. trade, 353

Guineas, coined for Af. Co., 181, 225, 346, 360; price, 73n., 183

Gum, 179, 182, 185, 197, 207, 215, 219, 220, 270

Gum Coast, 213

Gunn, Robert, trader at Sherboro, 220

Gunpowder, in Af. trade, 173, 177, 178, 205, 219, 235, 236, 288, 356

Guns (carbines, fowling-pieces, fusees, muskets, pistols, snaphances) in Af. trade, 45, 173, 174, 175, 176, 177, 219, 288, 356

Guydah, see Whydah

Hakluyt, Richard, 168

Hall, Thomas (A.1696, 1700), 72

Hall, Urban (A.1693-6, 1703-9, D.G. 1697-8, 1701-2, S.G.1699-1700)

Hallamshire, Cutlers of, oppose Af. Co., 127

Hamburg, 171, 172

Hamond, William (A.1696-8)

Hanbury, John, agent in Gambia, 256, 272

Hanger, John (A.1692, 1694-5)

Harris, Sir Arthur, 50n.

Harvests, effects of, 55-6

Hatsell, Lawrence (A.1693-4)

Hawkins, Sir John, 15, 39

Hawley, Francis, Baron, 62, 65

Hayes, Daniel (A.1706, 1708, 1710-12)

Hayes, Frances (A.1697-1701)

Hayward, Nicholas, 72

Heatley, Thomas (A.1683-5, 1688-90)

Hedges, Sir William (A.1689-91, 1694, 1696)

Helmes, Robert, Af. Co.'s agent at Nevis, 319

Henrietta, Princess, 64

Henry the Navigator, Prince, 2

Herbert, Philip, Earl of Pembroke, 64

Herbert, William, Earl of Powis, 65, 65n.

Herne, Frederick (A.1698-9)

Herne, Sir Nathaniel (A.1701-2)

Heron, Samuel, secretary of Af. Co., 164-5

Hethcot, Mr., 129

Heysham, Giles, Af. Co.'s agent in Barbados, 298

Heysham, Robert, sep. trader, 372

Heywood, Capt. Peter, 107n.

Hickman, Nathaniel (A.1712)

Hicks, William, Chief Merchant, at C. Coast, 255

Hicks, William (? another), factor at Kommenda, 260

Hides, 45, 132, 179, 182, 197, 215, 217, 219, 238, 258

Hill, Abraham (A.1683-5, 1688-90, D.G.1691-2)

Hill, John, 67

Hodges, Cornelius, 5, 215-16

Hodgkins, Capt. Ralph, Agent-General at C. Coast, 245
Holder, Melitia or Melisha, 129, sep. trader, 372
Holditch, Capt. Abraham (A.1675–7), 69, 70, 109n.; Agent-General at C. Coast, 244–5
Holditch & Brooke, sep. traders, 372
Hollander, Peter, sep. trader, 372
Hollands (cloth), in Af. trade, 176
Holmes, Joseph, factor in Gambia, 258–9
Holmes, Robert, 12, 42
Holt, Sir John J., 117
Hopegood, Sir Edward (A.1672–3, 1676–8, D.G.1674–5)
Hopegood, Francis (A.1685–7, 1690–3, 1695, 1697–1700)
Hopkins, John (A.1700–1)
Horne, John (A.1698–9)
Houghton's *Collections*, 80
Hounslow, gunpowder mills at, 178
Hudson's Bay Company, 32, 33, 163n., 348; capital, 32, 36, 54; monopoly, 36–7, 105, 125; Prince Rupert and, 103; stock, 80–2, 83
Humphreys, Sir William (A.1706–9, 1712, S.G.1710–11)
Hussey, Sir William (A.1683–5, 1688–1690)

Indigo, 14, 187, 340, 342, 360; cultivated in W. Africa, 221
Ingram, Sir Arthur (A. 1673–5, 1679), 159n.
Insurance, 52, 208–9; companies in, 35
Interest, Rate of, 50, 51–2, 53, 56, 76–7, 205
INTERLOPERS in African trade, 11, 188, 261, 262, 266, 305, 325
    frauds of, 124–5
    in W. Africa, 108, 113, 114, 120, 121n., 229
    in W. Indies, 113, 114
    lawsuits against Af. C., 124
    legal position of, 99, 116, 118–19
    problems of, 115–16
    R. Navy used against, 106–7, 107n. 115
    rum trade of, 115
    seizure of, 106–7, 113, 115n., 117, 118, 119, 123, 125
    success of, 114, 115n., 117, 259
    support for, 116–20
Investments, in 17th century, 48–54
Ireland, Afr. trade, 136; Irish in Af. Co., 254
Iron, in Af. trade, 45, 170–2, 174, 177, 219, 234, 235, 238, 351

Isinghams (cloths), in Af. trade, 176
Ivatt, William (A.1685–7, 1690–4, D.G.1695–6)
Ivory, 4, 7, 38, 45, 60, 98, 114, 127, 132, 185, 197, 198, 207, 214, 215, 216, 217, 218, 219, 220, 222, 227–8, 236, 238, 258, 345, 360
Ivory Coast, 213, 214

Jackson, Joseph, sep. trader, 372
JAMAICA, 14
    Act against interlopers, 118
    Af. Co's agency, 295–8
    Af. trade of, 138n., 191
    Asiento and, 327–8, 329–34
    bills of exchange, 359–60
    currency, 316, 322
    debt laws, 320, 321
    debt to Af. Co., 309, 318–19, 322–3, 324, 325, 333
    freight from 201–3
    freight to, 198–9
    French attack, 208
    interlopers at, 113, 117, 118
    need for credit, 308, 318
    opposition to Af. Co., 126, 127, 130, 131, 133, 144, 145, 149, 221, 308–310, 311, 332–3
    remittances from, 339–40
    sales of slaves, 317
    slave population, 301–2
    slave prices, 199, 295, 308–10, 312–15, 330–1, 332, 364
    slaves supplied to, 45, 143, 143n., 145, 146, 190, 299, 301–2, 307–10, 324, 363
    sugar, 358–9
    sugar prices, 366
James I, King of England, 28
James II, King of England (Duke of York) (G.1672–88), 22, 117, 123, 163; and East India Co., 103; and R. Adventurers, 64, 156; and Royal Af. Co., 60, 62, 65, 65n., 71, 74, 103, 104, 106, 156, 266; and monopolies, 103, 180
Jamineau, Daniel, sep. trader, 372
Jaqueen, 228
Jarret, William (A.1683–5)
Jeffreys, Edward (A.1702)
Jeffreys, Sir Jeffrey (A.1684–6, 1692–8), 295; sep. trader, 372
Jeffreys, John (A.1672–3, 1675)
Jeffreys, John (another) (A.1690–1, 1693)
Jeffreys, L. C. J., 108
Jermyn, Henry, Earl of St. Alban's, 64
Jermyn, Stephen (A.1697)

Joal, 216, 217, 219, 236, 270
Jobson, James, 270–1
Jobson, Richard, 5, 9n., 15, 215
John II, King of Portugal, 7
Johnson, Sir Henry, 34n., 196
Johnson, Sir John (A.1695–6)
Johnson, Lewis, sep. trader, 372
Johnson, William (A.1687–9)
Joint-stock companies, 24–38, 347–9
Jollife, William (A.1699–1706)
Jorey, Col. Joseph (A.1696–7, 1699–
     1712)
Joye, Peter (A.1678–80, 1683–5, 1688–
     1689, 1691–2, 1695), 67, 171–2
Juda, see Whydah

Kabes, John, of Kommenda, 281, 285,
     288, 289
Kastell, John, agent in Gambia, 219,
     271
Katherine, wife of Charles II, 64
Kent, Charles, sep. trader, 372
Kenyon, Edward, 257
Kersies, in Af. trade, 176
Kidderminster, support for Af. Co.,
     131
King, Sir Andrew (A.1672–4, 1678–9,
     S.G.1676–7)
Kingsbridge, opposition to Af. Co.,
     130
Knives, in Af. trade, 172, 174, 175, 176,
     177, 178, 356
Kommenda, 139, 224, 243, 252, 260,
     278, 281, 284, 285, 286, 369; Anglo-
     Dutch rivalry at, 267–8, 269, 277;
     Ashanti trade, 289; fire at, 261; fort,
     249; French at, 274; garrison, 247–8;
     interlopers at, 113; king of, 268;
     slaves, 226
Kormantin, 9, 40, 42, 265

Lade, John (A.1712)
Lagoo, factory, 247–8
Lake, Thomas (A.1694–8, 1704–11)
Lancashire, Col. Robert (A.1692,
     1701–4)
Lancaster, William (A.1705–12)
Land, as investment, 49–50, 53
Langhorne, Sir William (A.1684–6), 69
Lascelles, Edward, sep. trader, 372
Lawrence, Sir John (A.1672)
Lead, in Af. trade, 234
Lee, Godfrey, 171, 171n.
Lee, Ralph (A.1674)
Lee, Ralph (? another) (A.1700–1)
Leeward Islands, 14, 311–12; bills of
     exchange, 359–60; debt to Af. Co.,
     319; freight to, 198; need for credit,

318; remittances from, 340–1; sale of
     slaves, 317; slave prices, 199, 295;
     sugar, 358–9; supply of slaves, 340;
     support for Af. Co., 133. See Antigua,
     Montserrat, Nevis, St. Christopher's
Lethuillier, Sir John (A.1681–3), 159n.,
     171n.
Levant Company, 32, 33, 67, 123, 163n
Ligon, Richard, 337
Lisbon, 338
Little Taggee, see Taggee
Liverpool, 137n., 149, 152
Loans on bond, 49, 50–1, 53. See East
     India Co., debts; Royal Af. Co.,
     debts
Locke, John, 58n., 62, 65, 65n.
Logwood, 179, 183, 340
Lomelin, and Asiento, 14, 327
London, aldermen in Af. Co., 67–8,
     104; artisans support Af. Co., 149;
     borrowing by, 51; dyers oppose Af.
     Co., 133; Fire of, 55; Lord Mayors in
     Af. Co., 67; M.P.s in Af. Co., 104;
     sep. traders to Africa, 137n., 372–3;
     sheriffs in Af. Co., 67; shipwrights,
     for and against Af. Co., 191
Long Cloths, in Af. trade, 353
Longees, in Af. trade, 354
Lopuz, Francis, 219
Love, William, sep. trader, 372
Lowther, Sir John, of Lowther, 66
Lowther, Sir John, of Whitehaven, 66
Lucy, Jacob (A.1680–2, 1686–8, D.G.
     1684–5), 67
Lynch, Sir Thomas, Govr. of Jamaica,
     332
Lyttelton, Edward, 129, 129n., 303

Madagascar, slaves from, 100
Madeira, 186
Madrid, 327
Malaguetta, 39, 179, 182
Malimba, 231
Manillas, in Af. trade, 178, 234
Maria, Princess, 64
Martin, Joseph, sep. trader, 372
Martinique, 14, 206
Maryland, 136; opposition to Af. Co.,
     131, 133, 143, 145, 149; supply of
     slaves to, 143, 143n.
Mason, William (A.1707–9)
Master, Streynsham, 69
Mathews, Eusebius, 66
Mathews, Sir John (A.1678–80, 1683)
Mayhew & Co., sep. traders, 373
Mead, John (A.1676–8, 1681–3)
Mead, John (another) (A.1707)
Mead, Nicholas (A.1678–80)

Mead, William (A.1710–12)
Mediterranean trade, 169, 193, 209
Mellish, Thomas, Agent-General at C. Coast, 241, 245
Mercers, Company of, 51n.
Merchant Adventurers, Company of, 25, 67, 171, 171n.
Merchant Taylors, Company of, 51n.
Merrett, Thomas, sep. trader, 373
Merry, Capt. John (A.1704–7)
Metallurgical industries, companies in, 35
Meulenaer & Magnus, Af. Co.'s agents in Amsterdam, 172n.
Middle Passage, mortality in, 198, 231, 292–4, 299, 349; mutinies on, 291; ships in, 194; suicides on, 291
Mildmay, John, factor at Ophra, 228
Millington, Francis, 328
Mills, John, sep. trader, 373
Milner, Benjamin (A.1699)
Milner, Isaac, sep. trader, 373
Minehead, opposition to Af. Co., 130
Mineral and Battery Company, 32
Mines Royal, Company of, 30, 32
Mining, companies in, 34, 35, 35n.
Mirrors, in Af. trade, 178, 234
Modbury, opposition to Af. Co., 130
Modyford, Charles (A.1672).
Modyford, Sir Thomas, Govr. of Jamaica, 301
Molesworth, Hender, Lt.-Govr. of Jamaica, Af. Co.'s agent, 297, 330, 332–3
Monck, George, Duke of Albemarle, 64
Monmouth, Duke of, 103
Monopolies Act, 26–7, 36
Monopoly, 27, 102–5; as constitutional issue, 101–2, 107, 108–9
Montagu, Edward, Earl of Sandwich, 64
Montserrat, debt to Af. Co., 325; freight from, 203; opposition to Af. Co., 149; opposition to sep. traders, 149; slave population, 302; supply of slaves, 45, 190, 363; support for Af. Co., 133
Moone, Mr., planter in Jamaica, 324
Moore, Arthur (A.1709–10)
Moore, Sir John (A.1687–9, 1700)
Mora, Domingo, 218
Morea Company, 25n.
Morgan, John (A.1675, 1680–2, 1685–7, 1690–1711)
Mori, 265, 279
Morice, Humphrey, sep. trader, 373
Morice, John (A.1674–6, 1679–81, 1684–6, 1689–93, S.G.1695–6), 67

Morocco trade, 38
Mortimer, Mark, 67
Mostyn, Richard (A.1711–12)
Mounteney, Nathaniel (A.1687–9, 1694)
Mounteney, Richard (A.1679–81)
Mounteney, Richard (another) (A.1699)
Moyer, Samuel (A.1672–3, 1680–1)
Moyer, William (A.1680–2)
Mun, Thomas, 170
Murthwaite, Thomas (A.1674–6)
Muscovy Company, 28, 29, 32, 33, 123

Nash, Samuel, 107n.
Navigation Acts, 331–2, 333, 334
Neale, Dr., 313
Nevis, 292; currency, 316; debt to Af. Co., 319, 321; debt laws, 319–20, 321; freight from, 203; French attack on, 145–6, 205, 208, 312; interlopers at, 113; opposition to Af. Co., 149; opposition to sep. traders, 149; slave population, 302; supply of slaves, 45, 145–6, 310–12, 363; sugar prices, 337, 366
New England, 3–4, 136, 143n.
Newland, Sir Benjamin (A.1675–7, 1682–4, D.G.1678–9, S.G.1680–1), 69,162n.
New Netherlands, 23
New River Company, 22n., 32
Nicconees, in Af. trade, 354
Nicholls, Richard (A.1675)
Nichols or Niccolls, Thomas (A.1677–9, 1682–4, 1687–9, 1692), 69
Nicholson, Capt. John (A. 1698–1704, 1707–10, D.G.1705–6)
Niger, 4, 5
Noonez, Manuel, 218–19
North, Sir Dudley (A.1681, 1685–6, D.G.1682–3, S.G.1684), 162, 162n.
North, Capt. John (A.1686–8)
Norton, John, sep. trader, 373
Nouvelle Comp. du Sénégal, see France
Nurse, Capt. Henry (A.1689–90, 1693) Agent-General at C. Coast, 69, 111, 236, 245, 261

Oliver, Alexander, agent of Asiento, 330
Ophra, 250, 274, see Ardra
Ossory, Earl of, see Butler

Paggen, Peter, sep. trader, 373
Palm Oil, 179, 182
Paper, in Af. trade, 219, 234

Paravicini or Paravisin, Sir Peter (A.1683–5, 1694)
Park, Mungo, 5
Parliament, Af. trade considered by, 94, 96, 136, 262; (1671) 123–4; (1679–81) 106–7, 107n.; (1690) 126–8; (1694) 128–9; (1695) 130–1; (1696) 131–2; (1697) 132; (1708) 142; (1709) 149–50; (1710) 150–1; Act concerning trade to Africa (1698), 46, 133–7, 140, 141–2, 151, 298, 305–6; Act of Union, 149; bills concerning Af. trade, 128, 132, 133, 150, 151; reports concerning Af. trade, 127–8, 128–9, 130–1, 131–2
Partnership, 27, 30–1, 34, 39
Pautkes, in Af. trade, 354
Pearson, Josiah, factor at Anomabu, 227, 228; factor at Whydah, 278
Pembroke, Earl of, see Herbert
Pendarves, Stephen (A.1703–12)
Penhallow, Charles, Af. Co.'s agent in Jamaica, 297, 298
Pepper, 7
Pepys, Samuel, cited, 61
Perpetuanas, in Af. trade, 176, 176n., 177, 234–5, 352
Perry, Micajah, 295
Pery, Col. John (A.1686–8, 1683–4, 1698–9), Secretary of Af. Co., 164–5
Pewterware, in Af. trade, 177–8, 219, 351
Philip IV, King of Spain
Pierce, Edmund, agent in Sierra Leone, 116n.
Pindar, Thomas (A. 1698–1702, 1711, D.G.1703–4, 1707–10, 1712, S.G. 1705–6)
Piracy, 116, 211
Pitts, Stephen (A.1683–5)
Plains, Welsh, in Af. trade, 177, 352
Plantation Debts, see under Royal Af. Co. and under Barbados, Jamaica, etc.
Popea, 250
Porcio, Nicholas, and Asiento, 330, 333, 334
Portudal, 216, 217, 219, 236, 270
Portugal and Portuguese, African settlements, 6, 6n., 8, 21, 267; Af. trade, 1, 2, 4, 5, 6–9, 10, 13, 17–18, 39, 128–9, 150, 214, 229, 231, 236, 262, 264, 276, 286; Asiento and, 326; as middlemen, 218–19, 220, 276; relations with Af. Co., 276; serve in Af. Co., 254; war with Dutch, 12
Portuguese Guinea, 1, 216
Potash, made in Sherbro, 221

Povey, Thomas, 62, 65
Powell, Rowland, Af. Co.'s agent in Jamaica, 297
Powis, see Herbert
Powis, Richard (A.1708)
Prichard, Sir William (A.1699–1700, 1704), 68, 68n.
Prissick, Christopher, sep. trader, 373
Privateers, see France
Proby, Sir Peter (A.1672, 1674, 1676–8), 69, 328

Queen Anne's Point, 247–8

Raper, Henry (A.1711)
Recoinage of 1696, 183
Redwood, 40, 98, 134, 179, 180–1, 220, 258, 360
Regulated Companies, 25–8, 36; proposed in Af. trade, 127, 150, 152
Revolution of 1688, 46, 104, 122–3, 146–7
Reynolds, Anthony (A.1708, 1711)
Riccard, Sir Andrew, 64
Richards, Henry (A.1674)
Richardson & Co., gunpowder makers, 178
Richelieu, Cardinal, 9, 18
Rickard, Capt. Samuel, 123
Roberts, Sir Gabriel (A.1672–4, 1680–1682, 1685, 1689, D.G.1676–7, 1686, S.G.1678–9, 1687–8, 1690–2), 68, 68n., 158, 162n.
Roberts, Gabriel (A.1695–1701)
Roberts, Lewes, 36
Roberts, William (A.1673–5, 1678)
Robinson, Sir John (A.1673–5), 64, 159n.
Rogers, Zachary, agent at Sherbro, 215n., 255
Ronan, William, Chief Merchant at C. Coast, 255
ROYAL ADVENTURERS TRADING TO AFRICA
Company of, 32
Charles II and, 42, 103
charter, 41, 97, 97n., 98, 123
contract with Asiento, 60, 327
Court of Assistants, 154, 163
debts, 57–8, 91
debts owed to, in W. Indies, 318, 319–20
failure, 97, 163
finances, 41–2, 43–4
licences granted by, 43, 44, 106
settlements in W. Africa, 42–3, 224, 267
shareholders, 63–4

slave-trade, 43
stock, 42, 57, 59
winding up, 44, 57–8, 74, 91
ROYAL AFRICAN COMPANY OF
ENGLAND
African establishment, 242–5, 253,
259
Agent-General in Africa, 242, 243,
244–5, 252–3, 254
agents in Europe, 171, 172, 175
agents in W. Indies, 295–9, 322–3
Asiento and, 327–35, 344
by-laws, 154, 155, 179
charter, 58, 97–100
Committee of Eight, 154, 160, 323
contracts for goods, 171–2, 177–8
Court of Assistants, 154–64, 201
creditors, 90–6
debts, 52, 56, 76–9, 87–90, 91, 183–4
dissolution, 345
dividends, 72–3, 73n., 78–9, 155, 160
employees in Africa, 111, 119–20,
125, 138n., 252–3, 254–9, 261,
347–8
employees in England, 163–5
exports, 45, 74–5, 85, 88, 127, 137,
151–2, 161–2, 165–6, 170, 179,
209, 232–3, 258–9, 344–5, 350–7;
see under various commodities
failure, 346–9
forts, 78, 121–2, 127, 129, 132, 134,
141–2, 151, 152, 178–9, 240–50,
259–64, 281–2, 345, 346
General Court, 98, 155
Government subsidy, 345, 349
imports, 179–83, 358–60; see under
various commodities
James II and, 60, 62, 65, 65n., 71,
74, 103, 104, 106, 156, 266
licences granted by, 112–13, 125–6,
127, 128n., 129
monopoly, 45–6, 60, 79, 98, 103, 104,
122–3, 151
Plantation Debt, 75, 78, 90, 309, 318–
325
private trade in, 109–11, 258
records, 155–6, 374–5
relations with Africans, 277–90,
367–70
relations with Denmark, 40–1
relations with Dutch, 264–9, 283,
284, 289, 369
relations with French, 269–75
relations with Portuguese, 276
sales, 179, 181, 182–4
share capital, 74–6
shareholders, 59, 60, 62, 63–70, 103,
104

shipping, 112, 162, 162n., 192,
194–205
shipping costs, 204–5, 75, 211
ships dispatched, 191–2, 195, 206–7,
344, 345
ships in W. India trade, 191
slave contracts, 294–5
stock, 69, 70–1, 81–3, 84–5, 85–7,
90, 91–6
stock, price of, 72–4, 72n., 80, 82,
84, 85, 96, 160
stock, transfers, 70–2, 81–3, 86–7
subscription, 58–9, 62–3
voting rights, 58–9, 62–3
war losses, 132, 186, 203, 205–10,
272, 273–4, 277, 346. See Interlopers, Separate Traders, etc.
Royal Af. Co. *v.* Dockwra, 106n., 124n.
Royal Af. Co *v.* Doegood, 110n.
Royal Af. Co. *v.* Gowing, 110n.
Royal Fishery Company, 22n., 32, 54,
57, 103
Royal Mint, 181, 225, 360
Royal Navy, 203, 209; assists Af.
Co. 106–7, 107n., 115, 119, 210, 211,
349
Rudge, Edward (A.1673–5, 1678–80,
1690–5)
Rudge, John (A.1697–1701)
Ruding, Walter, Af. Co.'s agent in
Jamaica, 297, 298
Rufisque, 216, 270
Rum trade, from W. Indies to W.
Africa, 45, 115–16, 173, 190–1
Rupert, Prince, 41, 62, 64, 65, 103
Russell, Francis, Govr. of Barbados,
298
Rustat, Tobias, (A.1676, 1679–80),
66, 66n., 163, 163n.

Saboe, 278, 283, 284, 285, 286, 288
Sahara, 4
St. Albans, Earl of, see Jermyn
St. André (St. Andrew's) island, 42,
215
St. Christopher's, debt laws, 320; slave
population, 302; supply of slaves, 45,
311–12, 363
St. Eustatius, 14
St. Malo, 205
Sambrooke, Sir Jeremy (A.1685–7,
S.G. Jan.-Feb. 1689), 69
Sambrooke, Samuel, 70
Sandwich, Earl of, see Montagu
Sangrigoe, 216
São Paulo de Luanda, 231
São Thomé, 7
Says, in Af. trade, 176, 177, 234, 352

Scarlet cloths, in Af. trade, 175, 176, 369
Scissors, in Af. trade, 178
Scotland, Af. trade, 1, 19–20; opposition to Af. Co., 149; see Darien Co.
Scott, W. R., 35, 40
Scriveners, see Banks
Searle, Edward, sep. trader, 373
Searle, John (A.1676–8, 1681–2)
Sedgwick, William (A.1688–90)
Sekondi, 139, 224, 256, 263, 370; Anglo-Dutch rivalry at, 267, 268, 284; fort, 249; garrison, 247–8; slaves, 226
Senegal, 2, 5, 6, 6n., 9, 10, 39, 128, 178, 206, 214, 216, 219, 269, 270, 271, 272, 277
Senegal Adventurers, Company of, 39
SEPARATE TRADERS TO AFRICA, under Act of 1698, 46, 135–51, 207, 212, 240, 261, 262, 276, 306, 325, 370
exports, 137n., 147n., 148, 372–3
frauds, 140
kidnapping of slaves, 142
profits, 314–15
raise price of slaves, 139, 140, 144, 315
redwood trade, 220
success of, 138–40, 147–9, 259
supply of slaves by, 143–4, 143n., 310, 312
war losses, 139, 148
Serges, in Af. trade, 234; see Perpetuanas and Says
Seville, 327, 328
Shaftesbury, see Cooper
Shaw, Sir John (A.1672–3)
Sheets, in Af. trade, 172–3, 236, 355
Shephard, Philip (A.1704–6, 1708–9, 1712)
Shepheard, Samuel (A.1695–8)
Sheppard, William, 83
Sherard, Sir John (A.1708, 1712)
SHERBRO (York Island), 10, 40, 43, 45, 185, 186, 198, 215n., 216, 258
English settlement, 6n., 9, 42
French attack on, 205, 208, 232, 256, 261, 263, 273, 277
garrison, 251, 252
indigo cultivation, 221
interlopers at, 255
trade, 181, 188, 220–1, 233, 238
white women at, 257n.
York Fort, 215, 219. See Redwood
Shido, 139, 247–8
Shipping, 34; investment in, 49, 52, 53, 196; see Chapter 5

SHIPS, Africa, 136; Alexander, 123; Alexandre, 34n.; Angola, 207; Ann, 207; Anne, 106n.; Arcana Merchant, 197n.; Arthur, 188, 293; Averilla, 193, 203; Barbados Merchant, 207; Carlisle, 186; H.M.S. Constant Warwick, 107; Davers, 190; Delight, 186; Dolphin, 186; Dorothy, 120; Falconbergh, 189–190; Francis, 292; Freizland, 196; Golden Fleece, 34n.; Guinea Hen, 142n.; H.M.S. Hunter, 106–7, 115, 124; James, 186, 188, 196, 291; James (another), 211; John & Alexander, 307n.; John & Mathew, 106n.; Katherine, 188; Lady Mary, 272; Lisbon Merchant, 211; Lucitania, 110; Margaret, 186; Maurice & George, 207; Mayflower, 115n.; H.M.S. Mordaunt, 115; H.M.S. Norwich, 107, 115; H.M.S. Orange Tree, 115, 189; H.M.S. Phoenix, 115; Robert, 201; St. George, 117; St. George (another), 293; St. Paul, 118; Santo Domingo, 328, 329; Society, 34n.; Thomas & Elizabeth, 197–8; Three Brothers, 193
Short, John (A. 1685–7)
Sibley, John & Co., gunsmiths, 175
SIERRA LEONE (Bence Island), 1, 9, 40, 43, 45, 185, 186, 197, 215, 257
English settlement, 6n., 42, 215
evacuation, 219, 260, 272
French attack, 205, 208, 232, 261, 263, 273, 277
garrison, 251, 252
indigo cultivation at, 221
interlopers at, 108, 116
trade, 220–1, 233, 238
white women at, 257n. See Redwood
Silver, in Af. trade, 271; in Span. American trade, 331, 332, 333; imported by Af. Co., 179, 181–2, 360; see Specie
Skutt, Benjamin (A.1672–4, 1677–9, 1682–4), Af. Co.'s agent in Barbados, 297, 298
SLAVES,
age and sex, 299–300
bought at Ardra, 228
bought at Cacheu, 218
bought at Calabar, 230–1, 230n.
bought at Cape Verde, 219
bought in Gambia, 215–17, 219
bought in Gold Coast, 226–8
bought in Sherbro and Sierra Leone, 220, 258
bought in W. Africa, 213–14, 215, 216
bought at Whydah, 229–30

price in W. Africa, 139, 140, 144, 144n., 200, 236–7, 238, 293, 295, 313–14
price in W. Indies, 143–5, 199, 211, 295, 303–5, 308–9, 312–15, 330–1, 332, 364
trade in, 4, 7, 13–14, 15, 60, 126, 133, 166, 179–80, 214, 348–9
Slave Coast, 121, 213, 228, 235
Sletias (silesias), in Af. trade, 172, 335
Smith, Adam, 152, 153, 158, 184
Smith, Henry, sep. trader, 373
Smith, Sir James (A.1702)
Smith, John (A.1694–7)
Smith, Robert, sep. trader, 373
Snow, John, 262, 285, 286, 287, 367–71
Somerset, clothiers of, oppose Af. Co., 133
South Sea Bubble, 37, 38, 344
South Sea Company, 37, 152, 344
Spain, Af. trade, 218, 236, 262, 264; empire in America, 2, 3, 4, 5, 6, 13–14; slaves for, 13, and see *Asiento*
Specie, remittances from W. Indies in, 195, 296, 336, 339, 340, 342–3
Spirits, in Af. trade, 177, 178, 234
Stamper, Robert (A.1702–4)
Stanier, Sir Samuel (A.1686–8, 1691–2, 1695–9, 1702–6, 1708, 1710–11, D.G.1693–4), 160n.
Staplers, Company of, 25
Stapleton, Sir William, Governor of Leeward Islands, 118
Stede, Sir Edwin, Govr. of Barbados, Af. Co.'s agent, 297, 298, 307n., 329, 339
Stevens, William (A.1675, 1680, 1682–1684, 1690–1)
Stockjobbing, 83
Stop of the Exchequer, 52, 60–1
SUGAR, 7, 14–15, 15n., 16, 60, 166, 199, 200, 317–18
duties on, 341, 341n.
freight of, from W. Indies, 202–3, 342
imports, 179, 180, 182, 187, 188, 189, 190, 338, 338n., 346, 358–9
price, 60n., 187, 189, 195, 211, 304, 336–8, 341–3, 349, 365–6
re-exports, 338
remittances from W. Indies, 296, 335–43
Sugar trade, losses in, 335, 338, 340–2, 346
Swan, Capt. Charles, 231
Sweden, 45, 170–2; Af. trade, 1, 2, 11, 12, 41
Swords, in Af. trade, 174, 177, 178, 234

Tagee, Cooma, 289
Tagee, Little, 285, 369
Takoradi, 247–8
Tallow, in Af. trade, 177–8, 234
Tantamkweri, 247–8, 249
Tapseels, in Af. trade, 354
Tasso Island, see Sierra Leone
Taylor, John, sep. trader, 373
Taylor of Ipswich, Case of, 101n.
Temple, Sir William, 62
Tench, Fisher (A.1711–12)
Thomas, Sir Dalby (A.1699–1703), Agent-General at C. Coast, 139–40, 190, 226, 227, 245, 255, 257, 259, 260, 274, 276; accused of arbitrary conduct, 256; hostility to Dutch, 269; relations with Africans, 280, 283, 284, 286, 287–8; salary, 253; views on castle-trade, 261
Thompson, Maurice, trader to Africa (1649), 40
Thornburgh, Col. Edward, 304
Thurloe, John, factor at Sekondi, 255
Thurloe, Thomas, agent in Gambia, 217
Timbuktu, 215
Tobacco, 14, 179, 180, 182, 341
Tourney, Anthony, sep. trader, 373
Travers, John, sep. trader, 373
Treby, Sir George, 101n.
Trumpets, in Af. trade, 172, 178, 234
Tulse, Sir Henry (A.1675–7, 1680–2, 1685–7, S.G. Feb.-Oct. 1689), 159n.
Turner, Sir William (A.1676–8, 1681–3, 1686–8, 1691), 34n., 50n., 51n., 52n., 68, 159, 159n.
Tylleman, Eric, 279
Tyssen, Francis (A.1693–4)

Ulster, colonization of, companies in, 35
UNITED PROVINCES and Dutch, Af. trade, 1, 2, 7, 10–11, 15, 18, 19–24, 61, 234–5, 264–5, 369
Asiento and, 13, 14, 15, 326, 327–8, 333
East India Company, 21, 174
goods bought in, 172–6
relations with Africans, 279–80, 285
relations with Af. Co., 264–9, 283, 284, 289, 369–71
serve in Af. Co., 254
shipping, 194
wars, 12, 15, 21; see Anglo-Dutch wars
West India Company, 21–4, 174, 264–6, 269, 346

Upton, John (A.1699–1701)
Utber, Capt. John, 109n.

Vansittart, Robert (A.1705, 1707, 1710–11)
Vaughan, John, Lord, Govr. of Jamaica, 308
Velvets, in Af. trade, 176
Venice, 136, 173, 175
Vera Cruz, 329
Vere, Charles (A.1710)
Vernatti, Constantine (A.1690–2)
Verney, Sir John (A.1679–81, 1686–8, 1691–2, 1696–7)
Vernon, Thomas (A.1672–4, 1677–9, 1682–4), 67, 171
Villiers, George, Duke of Buckingham, 64, 65, 65n.
Virginia, 136; bills of exchange, 359–360; opposition to Af. Co., 131, 133, 143, 145, 149; price of slaves, 143, 295; supply of slaves, 45, 141, 143, 143n., 295
Virginia Company, 35n.
Volta River, 121, 370
Vyner, Sir Robert (A.1672–4), 56, 62, 64, 159, 159n.

Waite, James, sep. trader, 373
Walker, William, 70, 109n.
Walter, Thomas, trader to Africa (1649), 40–1
Ward, James (A.1679–80)
Warren, Nicholas (A.1672)
Warren, William (A. 1676–8, 1681–3, 1690–3), 177
Waterman, Sir George, 69
Wax, 45, 132, 179, 182, 185, 197, 207, 215, 217, 218, 219, 220, 236, 238, 360
Way, Bejamin, sep. trader, 373
Westerne, Robert (A.1697)
Westerne, Thomas, 67, 171
West Indies, 3, 14–16; debts of, 75, 78, 90, 316–25; freight rates to, 305; opposition to R. Adventurers, 43; opposition to Af. Co., 45–6; rum-trade, 115–16; shipping, 188–9, 201–203; support for interlopers, 116–17; supply of slaves, 144, 145, 295, 299–312; see Antigua, Barbados, Jamaica, Montserrat, Nevis, St. Christopher's
Weyborne, Capt. Petley, 121n., 229–230, 237, 243, 250
Whale fishing, companies in, 34
Whitcombe, Peter (A.1700, 1702–3)

White, Richard, agent of *Asiento*, 328
Whitehaven, opposition to Af. Co., 130
Whitfield, John, factor at Anomabu, 257
Whorwood, Broom, 66
WHYDAH, 119, 190, 206, 214, 243, 253, 255, 264
  Dutch at, 6n., 121, 229
  English at, 6n., 121, 228–9, 250–1, 260, 261
  free port, 274
  French at, 121, 144n., 229, 237, 270, 274
  interlopers at, 121n.
  Portuguese at, 229, 276
  trade, 227, 229, 233, 234, 234n., 236–7, 240, 278
William III, King of England, (G.1689–1702), 156
Williams, Lady, 50n.
Williamson, Sir Joseph (A.1673, 1675–1677), 62, 65, 65n., 163
Williamson, Robert (A.1680–2, 1685–6, 1688–9, 1691)
Williamson, Robert (? another), Treasurer of Af. Co., 165
Willis, Richard, factor at Whydah, 274, 276
Wilshaw, Benoni (A.1694–5)
Wilshaw, Capt. Francis (A.1679–81)
Wilson, Rowland, trader to Africa (1649), 40
Wiltshire, clothiers of, oppose Af. Co., 133
Windham, Wadham (A.1703, 1705)
Windward Coast, 278; gold, 225; profits, 239; trade, 112, 182, 188, 200–1, 221–4, 227, 232–3, 234, 240, 259–60
Winnebah, 139, 224, 368; fort, 249; garrison, 247–8; rent, 287; slaves, 226
Withers, Sir William (A.1697–8, 1706, S.G.1707–9), 160n.
Witney, support for Af. Co., 128
Wood, John, trader to Africa (1649), 40
Wood, William, sep. trader, 373
Woolf, Sir Joseph (A.1688–90, 1692)
Woollens, in Af. trade, 176–7, 219, 234, 352
Woolley, Robert, 183
Worcestershire, Receiver-General of, see Albert, Thomas
Wren, Mathew (A.1672), 62, 66

York, Duke of, see James II
York Island, see Sherbro
Young, Richard (A.1672)